Imaginary Communities

Imaginary Communities

Utopia, the Nation, and the
Spatial Histories of Modernity

Phillip E. Wegner

UNIVERSITY OF CALIFORNIA PRESS
Berkeley · Los Angeles · London

University of California Press
Berkeley and Los Angeles, California

University of California Press, Ltd.
London, England

© 2002 by the Regents of the University of
California

Library of Congress Cataloging-in-Publication Data

Wegner, Phillip E., 1964–
    Imaginary communities : utopia, the nation,
and the spatial histories of modernity / Phillip E.
Wegner.
        p.   cm.
    Includes bibliographical references and index.
    ISBN 978-0-520-22829-0 (paper : alk. paper)
    1. American fiction—History and criticism.
2. Utopias in literature.   3. Orwell, George,
1903–1950—Criticism and interpretation.
4. More, Thomas, Sir, Saint, 1478–1535. Utopia.
5. Literature, Comparative—American and Russian.   6. Literature, Comparative—Russian and
American.   7. Russian fiction—History and criticism.   8. Space and time in literature.   9. Nationalism in literature.   10. Community in literature.   11. Modernism (Literature)   I. Title.
    PS374.U8 W44 2002
    809′.93372—dc21   2001008657

Manufactured in the United States of America
12   11   10   09   08   07   06
10   9   8   7   6   5   4   3   2

To my parents—
Nancy Wegner Hanson
and
in memory of
Kenneth James Wegner
(December 25, 1938–January 15, 1989)

You . . . remain.

Every social community reproduced by the functioning of institutions is imaginary; that is to say, it is based on the projection of individual existence into the weft of a collective narrative, on the recognition of a common name, and on traditions lived as the trace of an immemorial past (even when they have been fabricated and inculcated in the recent past). But this comes down to accepting that, under certain conditions, *only* imaginary communities are real.

Etienne Balibar, "The Nation Form: History and Ideology"

Contents

Acknowledgments

Although this is a book about the power of imaginary communities, in writing it I have incurred a tremendous debt of gratitude to a number of very real ones. I want to begin by expressing my thanks to my teachers. Fredric Jameson served as the director of the dissertation out of which this book grew, and his scholarly presence, commitment, and example of "deep listening" (*l'écoute*) shape this work throughout. The other members of my dissertation committee, Frank Lentricchia, Toril Moi, Michael Moses, and, especially, Barbara Herrnstein Smith, have all taught me different lessons about what it means to be an intellectual and a teacher that extend beyond these pages. Darko Suvin deserves special thanks for his heroic contributions as an outside reader, and for the energetic support and insight he has provided in the years since. And finally, I want to thank my first mentor, John Hartzog, without whose wisdom and vision none of the rest would have been possible.

I would like to express my gratitude to the readers of the entire manuscript, Peter Fitting and Dan Cottom for the press and, later, Don Ault, Jim Epstein, Peter Hitchcock, Brandy Kershner, and Evan Watkins: they have all provided inestimable support, encouragement, and friendship over the years in many other ways as well. Tom Moylan, who also read the whole manuscript, has offered an inspiring and ongoing exchange of words and ideas. Expertise, insight, and advice in a diverse range of fields have come from readers of various chapters, and for this I would like to thank Raina Joines, Rick Joines, David Leverenz, Jack Perlette, Robert Philmus, Kenneth Roemer, and the unnamed readers at *Utopian Studies*. John Evelev, Andy Neather, and Rob Seguin also commented astutely on various portions of the manuscript, as well as sharing superb meals, conversation, and much else.

I have been especially fortunate to have been part of outstanding intellectual communities at Duke University, the University of Florida, and other happy places, and I would like to acknowledge the camaraderie and exchanges of ideas over the last few years of Alvaro Áleman, Bryan Alexander, Nora Alter, Bill Beverly, Marsha Bryant, John Cech, Kim Emery, Pamela Gilbert, Christian Gregory, Dorothy Hale, Tace Hedrick, Maude Hines, Anne Jones, Rebecca Karl, Kenneth Kidd, Jeff Knapp, Sheryl Kroen, Elizabeth Langland, John Murchek, Scott Nygren, Min-Seok Oh, Jim Paxson, Jan Radway, Robert Ray, Malini Schueller, Dina Smith, Stephanie Smith, Csaba Toth, Maureen Turim, Greg Ulmer, Trish Ventura, and Mark Wollaeger. Caren Irr, Amitava Kumar, Carolyn Lesjak, Michael Liu, Chris Pavsek, and Michael Rothberg have shared their wisdom and friendship for many years. Ira Clark, my first chair at the University of Florida, contributed to my professional growth, as did John Leavey, who, in addition, offered a great deal of support in the last year of work on the manuscript. It has been an immense pleasure to have worked through many of these ideas with the energetic students in undergraduate and graduate courses at the University of Florida. The Society for Utopian Studies has also provided an ideal interdisciplinary forum for both the study and experience of utopia, and I want especially to acknowledge Lyman Tower Sargent for his indefatigable work as editor. Much appreciated material support was provided, first, by the Mellon Fellowship in the Humanities and, later, by two summer research grants from the University of Florida.

At the University of California Press, I wish to thank Linda Norton for her reception of this project, her aid in moving it efficaciously through the editorial process, and, most of all, for being an exemplary figure in a rapidly changing field. Thanks also to Mary Koon and Mary Severance for their help in bringing the manuscript to completion; the unnamed press reader for an enthusiastic letter of support; and my friend Eric Smoodin, for beginning the process in the first place.

My brothers and sisters—Paul, Cynthia, Christine, David, Stephen, and Daniel (and Eric and Adrian)—first taught me much about the power of communities, as did the members of my extended families,

Toms and Wegner, Sally and George Hegeman, Ed Hanson, my grand-parents, and, especially, my parents, to whom this book is dedicated. And finally, I can never truly express the depth of my gratitude to Susan Hegeman—gifted scholar, ideal colleague, patient reader, best friend, and the one who makes each day's journey utopian.

An earlier version of the first part Chapter 5 appeared in *Utopian Studies* 4, no. 2 (1993); and portions of Chapters 1 and 2, in a different form, in *Utopian Studies* 9, no. 2 (1998). I am grateful to the Society for Utopian Studies for the permission to reprint.

Introduction

The Reality of Imaginary Communities

> It seems to me that we are living through a long revolution,
> which our best descriptions only in part interpret. It is a
> genuine revolution, transforming men and institutions;
> continually extended and deepened by the actions of millions,
> continually and variously opposed by explicit reaction and by
> the pressure of habitual forms and ideas. Yet it is a difficult
> revolution to define, and its uneven action is taking place
> over so long a period that it is almost impossible not to get
> lost in its exceptionally complicated process.
>
> > *Raymond Williams,* The Long Revolution

Taking up the critical project Raymond Williams announced in the early
1960s of reinterpreting and extending the ideas and values of the past
"in terms of a still changing society and my own experience of it," this
book examines some important dimensions of the changing relationship
between space and community during the "long revolution" of Western
modernity.[1] In addition to contributing to a reconsideration of modernity in terms of its "spatial histories," this book also does a number of
other things: most important, it looks at the origins and subsequent adventures of the singularly modern construct of the nation-state; it inves-
tigates some of the difficulties that arise for those in the twentieth century who attempt to imagine new spaces, communities, and histories; it
reflects on the potentialities of different kinds of representational and
narrative practices, questions made especially important for us today in
the light of new electronic literacies and information technologies; and,
finally, it explores some alternatives to contemporary methods of studying modern literature and culture.

Drawing together these various agendas is the particularly rich and,
as I will show in the following pages, uniquely modern literary genre of
the narrative utopia. There has been a surge of interest in the question

of utopia lately, signaled by a number of important new studies, the publication of a major new narrative utopia in Kim Stanley Robinson's *Mars Trilogy* (1993–96), and the staging of an international exhibition in Paris and New York in the year 2000.[2] I believe all this interest points toward a recognition of the deep relationship between utopia and the experience of a modernity now widely understood to be in the midst of a thoroughgoing transformation. While the story that unfolds in the following pages centers on the institutional and formal development of the genre of the utopia, this generic history is understood to be inseparable from a history of modernity in which the works comprising this important genre play such a significant role. Throughout this book then, I argue for the "reality" of the imaginary communities realized within these earlier texts. They are not real in that they portray actual places in the world; rather, they are real, in the sense suggested by Etienne Balibar in the epigraph to this book, in that they have material, pedagogical, and ultimately political effects, shaping the ways people understand and, as a consequence, act in their worlds.[3] In short, narrative utopias serve as a way both of telling and of making modern history, and in this lies their continued importance for us today.

As many readers will recognize, the title of this book also recalls that of Benedict Anderson's influential study of the rise of the "imagined communities" of the modern nation-state.[4] Anderson too describes such communities as "imagined" precisely because while most of their members will never encounter one other, each believes they all share some deep, transhistorical bond. Such a belief has had tremendous consequences for the history of the modern world, a fact made evident almost daily in newspaper headlines. Liah Greenfeld has called this imagined community the "constitutive element of modernity," and much of the story I tell in the following pages focuses on the formation and the subsequent history of this construct.[5] I argue that the narrative utopia plays a crucial role in the constitution of the nation-state as an original spatial, social, and cultural form. Beginning with the work that founds the genre, Thomas More's *Utopia* (1516), there has been a continuous exchange of energies between the imaginary communities of the narrative utopia and the imagined communities of the nation-state, the former providing one of the first spaces for working out the particular shapes and boundaries of the latter. These imaginary communities are "nowhere," as the etymological root of the term *utopia* bears out, precisely to the degree that they make *somewhere* possible, offering a mechanism by which people will invent anew the communities as well as the places they inhabit. The utopia's imaginary community is thus not only a way of imagining subjectivity, but also a way of imagining space, thereby helping the nation-state to become both the agent and locus of much of modernity's histories.

If the particular social and cultural institution known as the nation-state has a history, then like any other history, it will be marked by intense moments of upheaval, contradiction, and change. The dawn of the twentieth century witnessed one such moment, in which, beginning in the early decades of this century, the narrative utopia became one of the places where a crisis in this conception of the subject and object of modernity was first registered, a crisis that has taken on a new significance and intensity in our own present. The second half of this book explores the ways some of the most influential narrative utopias of the twentieth century navigate this new social and cultural terrain, as modernity enters into a new phase, marked by a growing consciousness of the place of the nation-state in a global cultural and social space (although, as I argue, the spatial histories of modernity, from their very beginnings, always already take shape on a world stage). The questions these works address are crucial ones: If our social and cultural space is now global, what will be the nature of the communities, the subjects of history, that will operate within it? How do we imagine such a space? And how might we speak its history? A discussion of the formal evolution of the narrative utopia thus also offers a way of bringing into focus some of the monumental changes that occurred earlier in this century in both the practice and representation of space.

In addition to offering new ways to read the histories of modernity, my study of narrative utopias also aims to alter our understanding of how we use diverse narrative forms to make sense of—indeed, to make —our world. Such a reconsideration becomes especially important as we attempt in the new millennium both to imagine innovative forms of political activity and to come to grips with the immense possibilities made available by emergent information technologies. At the heart of this book lies my contention that the narrative utopia is a specific kind of representational act, and also a particular way of conceptualizing the world. I use the term *re-presentation* here in the sense given by the German word, *Darstellung,* with its double implication of representation *and* presentation, encompassing both practices of reproduction and those of a much more active performance of the world. The specificity of the narrative utopia's representational and cognitive practices is too often overlooked in many other discussions of the form that tend to see it either as a lesser kind of literature or a branch of social theory, and thus relegate it, on the one hand, to the specialized domains of the literary critic or, on the other, to those of the intellectual historian or political scientist.[6]

Neither characterization adequately grasps the nature of the work performed by the utopia. The representational practices of literature give expression to the unique and concrete lived experiences of collective or, in the case of most modern texts, individual ways of being in the world—that is, of particular phenomenological inhabitations of its spaces. The representational practices of theory, on the other hand—or what Louis Althusser calls "science"—attempt to perceive in a coherent and systematic fashion the abstract principles organizing the totalities in which these experiences take place. And never, apparently, do these two meet. However, the narrative utopia, along with the larger class of representational practices of which it is a part, occupies a middle ground between the phenomenological concreteness of the literary aesthetic and the abstract systematicity of the theoretical, working instead to develop a conception or, to use a term whose significance will emerge later in my discussion of the groundbreaking work of Louis Marin, a *figuration* of a space whose lived experience and theoretical perception only later become possible. Thus, in a very real way, first mapping the terrain that will be inhabited by literary art and theory, the narrative utopia serves as an in-between form that mediates and binds together these other representational acts.

It is precisely this sense of the utopian text as engaging in a particular kind of praxis, a specific representational activity, that I mean to emphasize through my use throughout this book of the phrase *narrative utopia*. This too flies in the face of much of the received wisdom about these works. Utopias are too often read as static descriptions of a place, real or ideal, with "description" being implicitly understood to be the "other" to the temporal, or process, orientation of narrative. However, I argue that in forms like the narrative utopia, description itself serves as what in other contexts we think of as action or plot, so that social and cultural space and communal identity slowly emerge before our eyes by way of a process Roland Barthes calls "semiosis." With this term, Barthes means to distinguish a whole class of texts—providing what might seem at first glance an improbable link between the writings of the Marquis de Sade, Charles Fourier, and Ignatius Loyola—that, unlike the mimetic imperative driving literature and theory, dislocate the problem of reference. Far more significant for these kinds of texts is what

Barthes describes as the "performance of discourse," the very activity of making the world through language.[7] Thus, the classical Enlightenment figure of the map, with its presupposition of a singular "God's-eye view" upon a fixed and stable space, is an inappropriate one for the narrative utopia. Narrative utopias are more akin to traveler's itineraries, or an architectural sketch, tracing an exploratory trajectory, a narrative line that, as it unfolds, quite literally engenders something new in the world.[8]

This implies a dramatic temporal reorientation as well; for if both literary and theoretical representations approach the narrative present in terms of the past, attempting to grasp it as some form of a completed whole, semiotic itineraries or performances like those of the narrative utopia conceive of the present in terms of the future, as something that is incomplete and continuously coming into being. That is, the present, its concerns, desires, and contradictions, rather than being the end of the representational practices of the narrative utopia (as in those of literature or theory), serves as the very raw material from which the narrative performance will generate something original. These productive performances are what made these works so electrifying for their contemporary audiences, confronting them with all the shock of the new. In this book, I want to recapture some of this energy and excitement and thereby help us, too, to begin again to think of the possibilities of the new.

Both this "in-betweenness" and the orientation toward the future account for the cultural pedagogical force of utopian texts. The particular narrative utopias I discuss at length in this book—most centrally, More's *Utopia,* Edward Bellamy's *Looking Backward,* Alexander Bogdanov's *Red Star,* Jack London's *The Iron Heel,* Yevgeny Zamyatin's *We,* Ursula K. Le Guin's *The Dispossessed,* and George Orwell's *Nineteen Eighty-Four*—were, along with numerous other representatives of the genre that I touch on more briefly (including, among others, Francis Bacon's *New Atlantis,* William Morris's *News From Nowhere,* Arthur Dudley Vinton's *Looking Further Backward,* Ignatius Donnelly's *Caesar's Column,* Charlotte Perkins Gilman's *Herland,* H. G. Wells's *A Modern Utopia,* and Aldous Huxley's *Brave New World*), deeply influential in their particular times and places, contributing to, and often directly shaping debates over a wide range of social and cultural concerns. Indeed, one of the most exciting aspects of studying these works in their contexts is witnessing the passionate and engaged public discussions they often provoked. However, in addition to these immediate effects, many of which I elaborate in the coming chapters, the very narrative practices made available by utopian texts helped transform how their readers understood and acted in the world in far more profound ways as well. By inserting something heretofore unknown in the world —an original conception, figure, or what one of More's contemporaries called a "speaking picture"—the narrative utopia generates the cognitive space around which new kinds of lived experiences and theoretical perceptions form. Thus, understanding the past work of narrative utopias has real consequences for how we live and perceive modernity in the new millennium.

Each of the chapters of this book is organized in such a way as to form a kind of "in-between" representation as well, being at once theoretical—mobilizing and exploring the points of contact between a wide range of different discourses—and historical, focusing on how various narrative utopias engage with the concerns of their time and place while participating in the ongoing, long revolution of modernity. Thus, this study in its very form calls into question some of the conventions of current intellectual work, and attempts to clear a space for a new kind of relational-spatial study of cultural texts. I explicitly address these issues in Chapter 1, where I begin by reconsidering what is still too often perceived as the discredited work of genre criticism. I argue first that problems arise when we assume that genre study involves only the creation of textual taxonomies. In order to circumvent these problems, I elaborate an alternative approach to genre that reads it as a fundamental aspect of the self-interpreting "being-in-the-world," or Heideggerean *Dasein,* of any text. Such a self-reflexive awareness becomes evident both in the ways each text in the genre engages with its predecessors and in its particular remaking of the generic institution in response to its particular historical context. Thus, in a manner reminiscent of Heidegger's phenomenological analysis, my approach to genre sets aside the impossible goal of describing definitively the set of necessary and sufficient conditions for membership in the genre—which would be nothing less than a quest after ontological *essences*—and instead explores how such a critical self-awareness defines the genre's *existence.* Like all such institutional beings, genres exist in time, and thus genre provides a means of reviving a kind of historical thinking, stressing the relationship between cultural texts located in different times and places, unavailable in many contemporary critical reading strategies, including those of the New Historicism and a good deal of cultural studies. Through this discussion, I hope to contribute to the project of constructing a richer, multidimensional approach to any cultural text.

The next section of Chapter 1 examines in more detail the particular nature of the representational practices of the narrative utopia. Central to my discussion at this point is the work of the French social philosopher and theorist of space, Henri Lefebvre. Only recently becoming more widely known to an English-reading audience, Lefebvre's innovative studies of the spatiality of contemporary life have been central to many of the most influential recent discussions of modernity and postmodernism. I show how Lefebvre's crowning achievement, *The Production of Space,* and the dialectical tripartite model of space that it develops provide a powerful tool for rethinking the practices of the narrative utopia. However, as I emphasize throughout this book, the spatial mapping of modernity takes place alongside an equally important critical assault on already existing practices and spaces. I thus conclude this chapter by examining some of the theoretical work—including that of the most significant twentieth-century student of utopia, Ernst Bloch—that highlights this dimension of the form. What emerges is a dialectical understanding of the relationship between the temporal and spatial dimensions of the narrative utopia, a dialectic that, I maintain, is at the heart of the experience of modernity as well.[9]

Having established some of the theoretical stakes involved in this project, I begin Chapter 2 with an exploration of the "origins" of this generic institution. Although its roots extend much further back into older traditions of "utopian" thought and representation, the modern narrative utopia has a distinct moment of birth in the 1516 work by the English Christian humanist Thomas More, which at once introduces a new word, literary institution, and conceptual problematic into the European cultural imagination.[10] However, I show that it is not More's original act, but rather a process of "re-authorings" of his narrative undertaken by its subsequent readers—readers among whom I number More himself—that set into place the institutional being-in-the-world of this genre. What these various readers recognized in More's performance was a new tool that enabled them at once to bring into view and participate in the making of a nascent modernity.

One of the most effective theoretical descriptions we have of this particular representational activity is to be found in Louis Marin's important work, *Utopiques: Jeux d'espace.* I also focus in this chapter on Marin's elaboration of the operation he calls "utopian figuration," a way of mapping, through the narrative elaboration of the "speaking picture" of the utopian text, some of the most significant dimensions of an emerging modernity. However, for all the suggestiveness of Marin's analysis, the conception of modernity deployed in his text is marked by a crucial blind spot; thus the latter part of this chapter explores another possible way of reading the project of *Utopia*. Marin implicitly accepts the assumption that the history of modernity is one with a telos, gradually moving toward the realization of a single, universal, sociocultural space and subjectivity, wherein all forms of contradiction and conflict have been abolished. Such a vision is shared by theorists of the modern on both the political left and right, from the most enthusiastic socialist visionaries to the most despairing theorists of iron-cage disciplinarity (and continues today, for example, in many invocations of the implicitly teleological concept of "globalization"). In contrast to this view, I argue that modernity is in fact constituted by a fundamental contradiction between universalism and particularism, between the production of homogenous empty space—capital, the money form, labor, and the juridico-political subject—and the formation of new kinds of local identities and spaces distinguished by what Slavoj Žižek calls "organizations of enjoyment," the "real, non-discursive kernel" materialized through a particular set of social and cultural practices and understood as under constant menace by the Other.[11] The brilliance of More's originary text lies in its mapping of the relationship between these twin dimensions of an emergent modernity, of the constant movement between universalization and particularization, or the de- and re-territorializations of social desire. Thus, in addition to the abstracting and universalizing tendencies so effectively articulated by Marin, we see suddenly exploding forth in More's work a radically new and deeply spatialized kind of political, social, and cultural formation: that of the modern nation-state.

The success of More's work in founding this new genre also helped to establish the nation-state as the increasingly naturalized expression of both the space and the subjectivity of modern history. In Chapter 3, I begin to explore the fortunes of this representational practice during the course of the last century. By the latter part of the nineteenth century, the link between the imaginary community of the utopia and the imagined community of the nation-state had become so firmly established that later expressions of the form now also serve to recontain the anxiety-producing clash of publics that occurs within the spatial and cultural boundaries of the national community. This is exactly what unfolds in Bellamy's phenomenally successful *Looking Backward* (1888). Writing in a moment when the earlier definition of the United States "Republic" was being challenged by the new class, racial, and ethnic "publics" that were then coming to inhabit it, and attempting to walk a line between conservative desires for a retreat to the past and radical calls for the violent overthrow of the present, Bellamy uses the institution of the narrative utopia as a way of imagining a new kind of American national community. While presenting an important early figuration of the contours of emerging practices and institutions, such as those of middle-class consumerism and professionalism, Bellamy also develops a profound reflection on the relationship between collective identity, national space, and *memory*. His text presents a program for overcoming the fractured and conflicting "organizations of enjoyment" of the late-nineteenth-century United States by way of a willed forgetting of those memories and histories that bind individuals and communities to what he views as the dead weight of the past.

While Bellamy's text offers us one last look backward at the older project of the narrative utopia, the two texts that I investigate in Chapter 4, Bogdanov's *Red Star* and London's *The Iron Heel* (both 1908), present a fundamental and far-reaching reconsideration of the practices of this generic institution. Both texts were written as deeply political interventions, and I argue that they succeed precisely to the degree that they also challenge the established practices of the genre. Indeed, I maintain that all of the great twentieth-century works that participate in the generic institution of the narrative utopia are involved in the project of remaking the form so that it will be adequate to a changing experience of modernity. Responding to the political crisis initiated by the defeat of the 1905 Russian Revolution, and negotiating the concerns of their particular social and cultural situations (for London, especially the growing fissure in the American labor movement between the IWW and AFL), Bogdanov's and London's works also mark a growing awareness of the ways that the processes of modernity have effectively sutured global space into a single totality. And yet, neither text can offer an adequate representation, or cognitive mapping, of the kind of collective subjectivity, a universalized organization of enjoyment, that might coincide with such a space. Thus, both works refocus the project of the narrative utopia on the figuration of the kinds of collective subjects that will mediate the passage between these two spatial orders of modern history. In effect, these two works sever the old link between the imaginary community of the narrative utopia and the imagined community of the nation-state. In Bogdanov's text, what takes the place of the nation as the subject of modern history is the idealization of the Proletariat that he elaborates in a monumental philosophical system, the "Tectology," while in London's work, there occurs a much more concrete figuration of the mobile, imagined collective subjects found in places as diverse as the bureaucracies of the corporations and the "state capitalist" socialist parties.

This points as well toward another concern that I explore in this chapter: the role of the intellectual within these imaginary and imagined communities. While I suggest that the narrative utopia has been centrally concerned with the place of intellectual labor from More's founding text onwards, this issue takes on an even greater urgency as the form itself undergoes the dramatic reconstructions we witness in the twentieth century. In an important way, these two utopias illustrate the central tension in the vision of the role of the intellectual that will be much fought over in the coming decades: a withdrawal from action that arises from the determinist idealism hinted at in Bogdanov's work and the determining vanguardism of an intellectual bureaucratic elite promoted in London's text.

The reevaluation of the older project of the narrative utopia continues with Zamyatin's *We* (1920). If the older expressions of the genre present a singular narrative of the spatial history of modernity, one bounded within the confines of the nation-state, Zamyatin's text offers a vision of multiple competing "possible worlds" or historical trajectories for modernity. Equally significant, as a consequence of the events in Zamyatin's own time and place in the years following the Soviet revolution, he comes to regard the nation-state as not only an insufficient space for the potentialities of modernity, but as an actual detriment to its realization: in *We,* the borders of the nation-state now mark a possible horizon of modern history itself. As a way of navigating around this blockage, Zamyatin develops a brilliantly original, permutational schema of possible expressions of the narrative utopia form and, indeed, marks the place of two of the most influential expressions of the genre that appear in the years following the Second World War: the "anti-utopia," and the "open-ended" utopia that proliferates in the early 1970s. A powerful example of the latter is to be seen in Le Guin's *The Dispossessed* (1974), and in the second part of Chapter 5, I explore the significant and little remarked upon convergences between her influential work and Zamyatin's earlier text. I do not want to underestimate the significance of Zamyatin's and later Le Guin's rigorous maintenance of this "horizon" of possibility, especially in light of the perceived political closures of each of their historical situations. Indeed, I show that something quite similar is accomplished on the philosophical front in the contemporary work of Bloch. However, the failure of these texts to offer any concrete figuration of a new spatiality is not without its own cost, something similarly stressed by Antonio Gramsci, whose insights I invoke in the closing pages of this chapter.

Exactly the nature of this price is evident by the time we arrive at one of the single most influential narratives, utopian or otherwise, of the twentieth century: Orwell's *Nineteen Eighty-Four* (1949). This narrative marks another crucial turning point in the history of this generic institution, negating the modernist play of "possible worlds" we see in Zamyatin's and later Le Guin's texts and offering in its place what I call, drawing upon the work of Karl Mannheim, a new form of the "conservative utopia." Orwell's celebrated text, like another key work of this moment, Theodor Adorno and Max Horkheimer's *Dialectic of Enlightenment,* perceives the mass media and industrial forms of global cultural production as a threat to the various autonomous organizations of enjoyment—rational, aesthetic, subjective, domestic, and *national*—that had been so central to the histories of modernity. Their destruction, Orwell concludes, will bring the project of modernity to a close. Moreover, in Orwell's view, it is the rise of what Walter Ong later describes as "secondary orality"—in the form of the new global informational technologies—that now undermines the more than four-century-long hegemony of print literacy, as well as the forms of the imagined community that arose alongside and, indeed, through it.[12] Thus, diverging from the institutional tradition of the narrative utopia, Orwell's work imagines a short-circuiting of the forward momentum of modernity. *Nineteen Eighty-Four* attempts to delink the values of modernity from the very ongoing process of modernization which gave rise to these values in the first place, and promotes instead a nostalgic return both to the older form of the imagined community found in the English nation and the kind of "literate" intellectual critique formed within it. Thus, while providing a double assault on the new mass-media culture and the kinds of "engaged" intellectuals we see, for example, in London's work—a double critique that will play a crucial role in the political intellectual struggles of the Cold War world—his text offers a figurative glimpse of what will become one of the dominant forces of our post–Cold War present: the explosive emergence of nostalgic and antimodern nationalisms. And in mapping the antinomies of a homogenous global mass-media and commodity culture and the violent particularisms of the new nationalisms, Orwell's text effectively blocks out the horizon of our own present experience of modernity.

As I hope will become evident, I conceive of my book itself as another kind of experiment in utopian figuration, or of cognitive mapping: an attempt to create at once a historical and theoretical overview of the work of past narrative utopias, and to produce my own "speaking picture" of a history still in formation, and hence "not yet" available for a final summation. And as with the various narrative utopias I discuss throughout this book, I imagine this project as an invitation to see the histories of modernity in a new way, so that we might also begin to imagine anew the space of our present and future. As this book will show, such imaginings are indeed real, and they will shape, as much as the imaginary communities of the past, the paths we embark upon in our attempts to make our futures.

CHAPTER ONE

Genre and the Spatial Histories of Modernity

Terry Eagleton asks, "What traumatic upheaval of perception is involved in thinking of the political no longer as a question of local sovereignty, of something interwoven with the labor and kinship relations of a specific place, but as an abstract *national* formation?"[1] The debate onto which Eagleton's question opens up—over the origins of the nation-state as both a uniquely modern conceptualization and practice of cultural and social space—has taken on a special urgency in our present, as concerns grow that the nation-state, at once beset by the forces of globalization and of ethnic fragmentation, may already be in the midst of its death throes. In this book, I enter into this important discussion and explore both the origins and the subsequent fate of the nation-state, by way of a reading of the vitally significant and also specifically modern literary genre of the narrative utopia. The story I tell here thus ultimately touches on one of the central concerns of all modern cultures: that of the identity and boundaries of any community. For if it is true that the cultures of modernity are marked by universalist aspirations—the abstract formalisms of liberal democracy, of the marketplace, of the family of man, of human rights—it is equally true that they have given rise to all kinds of particularisms, both original and those older forms newly reborn: those of nationalism, Eurocentrism, racism, and so forth.[2] This contradiction is embedded in the very hyphen that forms the specifically modern and, as we shall see, the deeply spatial concept of the "nation-state": at once a cultural form, that of an "imagined" particular and bounded collectivity, a *nation,* and an abstracting social mechanism, the *state,* regulative and relatively autonomous, as Nicos Poulantzas suggests, with regard to particular class and group economic interests.[3] Moreover, this deep contradiction between universalism and particularism is not the consequence of a conflict between the values of the past and those of the modern; rather, it is, as Slavoj Žižek persuasively argues, "constitutive" of modernity itself.[4] Thus, its legacy will continue to shape whatever kinds of communal formations we participate in making in the future.

I show in the following pages how the narrative utopias of the past negotiate modernity's double demand and thereby engage in an absolutely vital work of what Antonio Gramsci describes as cultural pedagogy: in the narrative utopia, the presentation of an "ideal world" operates as a kind of lure, a play on deep desires, both immediately historical and otherwise, to draw its readers in and thereby enable the form's educational machinery to go to work—a machinery that enables its readers to perceive the world they occupy in a new way, providing them with some of the skills and dispositions necessary to inhabit an emerging social, political, and cultural environment.[5] Thus, rather than focusing on the often-trumpeted failures of the utopian form (its failure, for example, to provide a "realistic," or realizable, program for a radically other form of social existence), I want to look at ways the form not only succeeds, but plays a definitive role in the histories of Western modernity.

Such a pedagogical function also points toward the status of these works as public acts—interventions that address and subsequently help shape the more immediate social and cultural concerns that were central to the moment in which they appeared. From this perspective, Edward Bellamy's *Looking Backward* (1888), a text I examine in more detail in Chapter 3, is comparable in its significance for the nineteenth-century United States only to a work like Harriet Beecher Stowe's *Uncle Tom's Cabin* (these two also sharing the distinction of being the first American fictions with sales surpassing the one million mark); and, as I show, *Looking Backward,* like Stowe's now more widely celebrated narrative, not only presented a powerful crystallization of the upheavals then plaguing American society, it helped mediate the passage between changing definitions of collective national identity. To offer a second example, one perhaps more readily acknowledged by readers today, George Orwell's *Nineteen Eighty-Four* (1949)—a work whose status in the tradition of the narrative utopia is examined in Chapter 6—is one of the few literary texts that could stand as a popular version of what Michel Foucault calls a "founder of discursivity," a work that helps establish the "primary coordinates," or cognitive paradigm, from within which emerge the figures and concepts—notions of the state, the collective, media, politics, power, and finally of utopia itself—that organize the understanding of, and even aspects of the experience of, contemporary social life, a paradigm that in many ways still holds today.[6]

Precisely because they are influential public interventions in their own moment, narrative utopias make particular demands on their later readers. Gary Saul Morson suggests that the narrative utopia requires from these readers an "extraliterary" knowledge, "a measure of familiarity with the social and political issues they traditionally address," in addition to "an understanding of the special semiotic nature of literature, fiction, or particular genres."[7] While Morson notes that such a knowledge is in fact obligated by every literary genre—especially on the part of those subsequent readers interested in reconstructing the past meaning-making capacities of these institutional forms—the narrative utopia distinctively foregrounds such a requirement, thereby, in its very form, disrupting the reification of the category of "autonomous" literature and forcing us to forge links between disparate knowledges.

Moreover, the very generic tradition of the narrative utopia provides us with the opportunity to think about the historicity of the borders defining such distinctions between "fields" of knowledge. For Thomas More, whose work *Utopia* (1516) founds the modern genre, "teaching" and "delighting"—political engagement and linguistic play, social analysis and literary creativity—were all part of the domain of activity of that ideal Renaissance figure, the Christian humanist intellectual, although even in More's case such a unity is realized only in a brief moment in his own life, a window of opportunity during which *Utopia* is composed.[8] However, for the authors of the narrative utopias of the nineteenth and twentieth centuries, the fashioning of the kinds of public interventions represented by the utopia required complex mediations between what were often seen as conflicting political, artistic, and commercial concerns. The utopian space itself thus often serves as the locus where the clashes are staged between the now distinctive roles of the intellectual-writer. Jack London's *The Iron Heel* (1908), as we shall see in Chapter 4, is exemplary in this regard: into his future world, London projects his own sense of conflict between his disparate vocations as intellectual, socialist activist, artist, and successful commercial writer. Thus, narrative utopias not only contributed to the reeducation of their audiences in the ways they imagined the places they inhabited, they helped their authors define, in a new and continuously evolving way, the vocation of the modern intellectual, a project also already begun in More's founding text. In the following pages, I bring into focus these multiple and interwoven stories—about the nation, modernity, knowledge, and intellectuals—stories central to the formation of the world we inhabit today.

THE INSTITUTIONAL BEING OF GENRE

In order to retell these various stories, I also offer another narrative, one focusing on the relationship between the various works that make up the *genre* of the utopia. At the outset, however, I want to stress that I will *not* be engaging in the taxonomic operation—collecting field samples in order to abstract a table of shared characteristics—that is too often associated with genre studies. The rigid taxonomies that result from such operations are open to the same criticism V. N. Volosinov levels against the Saussurean model of *langue:* the system, whether it be the inner structure of language or the formal rules of generic behavior, is "merely an abstraction," one that ignores the place of the specific performance, the speech act or the individual text, in a number of different overlapping and interwoven contexts.[9] However, to call something an abstraction is not to say it does not exist; and Volosinov also warns that to move too far in the opposite direction is to fall into the traps of either "academic positivism," proclaiming "'fact' as the ultimate basis and criterion for any kind of knowledge," or "individual subjectivism," taking the isolated "monologic utterance as the ultimate reality."[10] A far more satisfactory approach, Volosinov maintains, lies not in some fantastic "golden mean" between these two poles, but rather in their dialectical synthesis, "a negation of both thesis and antithesis alike."[11]

The dialectical model I propose here views genre as akin to other collective institutions—languages, cultures, nations, classes, bureaucracies, corporations, and so forth—in that it too possesses what Martin Heidegger names *Dasein,* or "being-in-the-world." As with the particular embodiments of these other institutional forms, the works composing any genre make palpable, in the course of their narrative realization, a self-interpreting "awareness" of what it means to be part of this institution and its history.[12] Such a self-interpretation becomes evident both in the ways each participant in the generic institution engages with the possibilities and potentialities of its predecessors—the existence or being-in-the-world of the individual text placed in a background of shared social practices that are sometimes referred to by the abstraction "generic conventions"—and also in its particular remaking of the institution in response to the desires and interests of its unique historical context.[13]

Thus, in a manner reminiscent of Heidegger's phenomenological analysis, this approach to genre means that we set aside the impossible goal of describing definitively the set of necessary and sufficient conditions for membership in the genre—which would be nothing less than a quest after ontological *essences*—and instead explore how such a critical "self-awareness" itself defines the genre's *existence*. And this in turn will enable us to bring into focus the ways the various works making up the generic institution of the narrative utopia engage simultaneously in a number of what Mikhail Bakhtin describes as *dialogic* relationships: with the traditions of utopian writing that both precede and follow them; with the broader literary and intellectual presents they inhabit; with their variously situated readers; and, finally, with the concerns of the larger cultural and social realities in which they first appear.[14]

If such an understanding of genre provides an indispensable focusing mechanism in my study, it also hints at a more contentious dimension of this project, a challenge to some of the impasses in which literary and cultural studies currently find themselves. These dilemmas are effectively embodied in the influential institutional genre—with a *Dasein* or self-interpreting existence as concrete as that of any other genre—called the New Historicism. Commentaries in the last decade on the New Historicism abound, and I need not rehearse them all again here.[15] However, even a cursory glance at some of the practices and protocols of this exemplary critical genre make more evident the potentialities of the kind of genre study I propose. In its most brilliant manifestations, work in the New Historicism helped dissolve the formalist and idealist border separating the literary text from its context—a divide made most evident in the United States in the various New Critical fallacies and heresies—and in turn exposed some of the reifications involved in the very notion of "literature" itself. Moreover, as Fredric Jameson argues, the new historical practice of constructing homologies—of yoking together disparate and what at first may appear unrelated texts and materials in such as way as to bring to light their common cultural logics—generates an original "aesthetic" of criticism:

> Elegance here consists in constructing bridge passages between the various concrete analyses, transitions or modulations inventive enough to preclude the posing of theoretical or interpretive questions. Immanence, the suppression of distance, must be maintained during these crucial transitional moments in such a way as to keep the mind involved in detail and immediacy.[16]

Jameson's description of the aesthetic of New Historicism, with its emphasis on the importance of the "link" between different sites, also points toward some heretofore unexplored resonances between this literary critical practice and computer hypertext writing, so much so that one might be inclined to see New Historicism as modeling, *avant la lettre* and within the linear two-dimensional plane of print textuality, the modes of representation that only emerge full-blown in the electronic realm.

The accomplishments of the New Historicism, as even this briefest of invocations suggests, have been profound, and in what follows I deploy many of its lessons and innovations. However, what Jameson describes as the New Historicist "valorization of immanence and nominalism that can either look like a return to the 'thing itself' or a 'resistance to theory'" also points toward the kinds of conceptual closures generated by or imported into this critical practice.[17] As is well known, the founding work in the New Historicism was profoundly influenced by the poststructuralist cultural anthropology of Clifford Geertz and others.[18] I would suggest that the "valorization of immanence and nominalism" in the New Historicism, as well as in other related contemporary practices of cultural studies analysis, betrays a double closure not unlike that plaguing classical anthropological and indeed literary notions of a "culture."[19] In other words, the New Historicism develops a practice of reading a culture that has implicit or explicit borders defined in time and space. In its institution of these kinds of temporal closures, the New Historicism also reveals its intellectual kinship with Claude Lévi-Strauss's structuralism, where a representational strategy of homology was earlier practiced: like classical structuralism, and anthropological criticism in general, the New Historicism is deeply synchronic in focus, plotting a relational nexus between texts and materials in a discrete and closed historical locus. Indeed, this is borne out by Stephen Greenblatt and

Catherine Gallagher in their superb discussion of the contours of New Historicist practice in general, and its parallels in particular with the thought of Johann Gottfried von Herder, the German thinker often pointed to as one of the founders of the modern idea of culture:

> This approach accords well not only with our anthropological and cultural interests, but also with our rather conservative interest in periodization (for each of us had been trained to be a specialist in a given area and to take its geographical and temporal boundaries seriously). More important still, Herder's brilliant vision of the mutual embeddedness of art and history underlies our fascination with the possibility of treating all of the written and visual traces of a particular culture as a mutually intelligible network of signs.[20]

Richard Halpern points out that one of the consequences of this, in the particular case of Renaissance New Historicism, is a tendency to abjure entirely questions of the "epochal transitions": "'Modernity' is simply assumed as the ever-receding and unexamined horizon of analysis."[21]

New Historicist practice also tends to import a spatial concept of culture whose borders implicitly coincide with those of the modern nation-state. David E. Johnson has shown that at the heart of the New Historicism stands a conceptualization of the state uncannily like that of Hegel, and much of the work in this critical genre centers on the relationship between "the state (its institutions and discourses) and the individual."[22] Indeed, the privileged cultural sites of New Historicist scholarship—Johnson too points to the English Renaissance, but I would also add to the list Victorian England and the late-nineteenth-century United States—turn out to be precisely those in which these relationships are in the midst of crucial rearticulations. Thus, whatever the radicality and originality of its aesthetic and critical practice, something again I would not want to underestimate, the New Historicism often ends up once more implicitly sanctioning the most sacrosanct boundaries of the discipline of literary studies; and this in turn helps support a curriculum defined largely in the traditional terms of national literatures, the classical periodizations, and even the established canon itself.

The genre study I pursue in this book transgresses these temporal and spatial boundaries in a number of different ways. First, the institution of a genre is one that circulates both within and across the very different institutional identities of national culture, periodizations, and canons, all of which, I would again stress, are like a genre in that their various concrete practices reveal a self-awareness of their existence in the world

as part of an institution. Crucially, this does not mean that I am posit-
ing anything like a stable and potentially recoverable essence of the
genre that transcends and subsumes each of its specific examples: for the
"essence" of a genre, like that of all beings in the world, is its "existence," each of its concrete and particular material manifestations, manifestations that then in turn reshape the institution itself. Thus, my
analysis of each of these works will remain located within the horizon of
and defined in relationship to other institutions such as language, nation, culture, and period, each of which, in a turning of the critical lens,
then appears less an institution in its own right and more the background of shared relationships, or the context, within which any particular performance or "existence" of the genre occurs.

The force of a genre arises from a combination of enough flexibility
to adapt to these different cultural and historical niches with the rigidity necessary to maintain a shared institutional identity across these various contexts. The successful dissemination and subsequent flourishing
of a genre then results from its inherent "portability," its capacity to be
carried into and redeployed in contexts quite different from those from
within which it first emerges. Crucially, this characteristic of a genre is
also shared by the other modern institution that will be of central focus
in this study: that of the nation-state. Indeed, in his deeply influential
study of the development of this particularly modern form of the "imagined community," Benedict Anderson shows how the "modular" nature of the institution of the nation-state enabled it to spread across
radically different contexts, first by forms of "pirating" and later by self-
conscious adoption, ultimately to become, in an increasingly unified
modern world system, "virtually inseparable from political consciousness."[23] The genre of the narrative utopia both resembles the nation-
state in its capacity for dissemination and, as I will demonstrate shortly,
serves as a vehicle by which such transmissions and circulations occur
in the first place.

Thus, what I earlier described as the dialogic nature of any genre enables my approach to produce a different kind of narrative than that
found in the New Historicism and other kinds of analysis founded on
an anthropological or culturalist basis: for in addition to the *historicist*
mapping of a particular cultural site, a discussion of the dialogue between differently located members of the generic institution provides us
with a way of bringing into focus a narrative of *historical* change as well.
Jameson suggests that the force of the study of a genre "clearly lies in the
mediatory function of the notion of a genre, which allows the coordina-

tion of immanent formal analysis of the individual text, with the twin diachronic perspective of the history of forms and the evolution of social life."[24] I would only add to this formulation an additional level of immanence, that of the particular cultural background within which each expression of the genre appears, in order to emphasize the dual perspective—formal and historicist, evolutionary and historical—opened up by an investigation of genre.

Moreover, this points toward one further way that the historical nature of the genre study brings into focus material unavailable to the "immanent and nominalist" perspective of a historicist approach. For it is precisely the operation of dialectical "coordination," of producing relational webs, that illuminates the ways that any particular text is at once located in a range of what Neil Smith calls "scaled spaces."[25] Smith eloquently argues for the necessity, when reading any particular cultural phenomenon, of taking into account its simultaneous embeddedness in a number of different "nested" spatial contexts: body, home, community, city, region, nation, and globe. Smith concludes, "By setting boundaries, scale can be constructed as a means of constraint and exclusion, a means of imposing identity, but a politics of scale can also become a weapon of expansion and inclusion, a means of enlarging identity."[26]

While I draw upon Smith's important insights more directly in reading the narrative utopia's mapping of the spatial histories of modernity, his notion of scaled spaces also can serve as a basis for a reconsideration of the status of the generic text. For any such being-in-the-world as the generic text finds itself occupying and acting on a number of different scaled levels: from the most local or immanent ones of the formal, the biographical, and the local cultural, up through the "imagined" bonds of the national, and finally into the most abstract and yet still concrete level of the mode of production itself, which, in turn, must be understood, as Raymond Williams suggests, in terms of both its "epochal" and "historical" status, or what Marx describes as the one and the many capitalisms.[27] Crucially, however, I do not mean by this model to reinscribe the kinds of isomorphisms between these different levels that one finds, for example, in the structuralist, or New Historicist, or even the older Lukácsian dialectical practice of homology (all of which ultimately can have the consequence of flattening out the differences between each level).[28] Rather, I want to focus on the ways that each manifestation of the genre responds to the problems and concerns particular to each of these semi-autonomous levels. The aesthetic employed in such a reading then will be centered on tracing out the complex *mediations* between them. The end result of all of this will be a multi-dimensional reading of each narrative, plotted across the complexly overdetermined, three-dimensional field formed by the intersection of these synchronic and diachronic axes.

Such a reading will dispense with the illusion of exhaustively mapping each of these particular texts. However, the very open-endedness of the approach to genre that I have outlined above, one that eschews the implicit historical and spatial closures of the various historicist and culturalist approaches, will make it more amenable to a further form of dialogue: one with its own readers, whose subsequent engagements will provide a means of expanding and ultimately dialectically transforming, rather than simply displacing, any discussion begun here.

SPACE AND MODERNITY

It is no coincidence that the modern genre of the narrative utopia emerges full-blown in the early sixteenth century with the celebrated work by More that simultaneously introduces a new word, genre, and conceptual problematic into European and Western culture. More's late-feudal world is one in transition, in the throes of the earliest moments of the traumatic upheavals and sometimes violent dissolutions of traditional and older organizations of social and cultural life, a process marvelously captured in Marx's much-cited phrase "All that is solid melts into air": the long revolution of creative destruction and recomposition of the social body that we have now come to understand as a central dimension of the experience of modernity.[29] This too suggests something significant about the generic tradition to which More's work gives birth: later efflorescences of the form occur in similar moments of transition—the punctuations of crisis, conflict, change, and open-ended potentiality, Walter Benjamin's famous "messianic" holes in time, that mark the uneven, lurching, and deeply contested movement of modernity.[30] Thus, one way to think about the role of these narrative utopias in the transitional moments in which they appear is as what Jameson calls "vanishing mediators": cultural interventions that in retrospect appear as bridges over the "holes in time" between different organizations of social life, and whose particular effectivity disappears once these transitions have been accomplished (I return to this concept in the next chapter).[31] The history of the genre offers one vital way of narrating the historical changes that occur within this long wave of modernity, and in the following chapters, I investigate some of the most influential examples of the genre, and their intricate relationship with the particular transitional times and places in which they appear.

Moreover, the genre of the narrative utopia presents us with a means of reconceiving such a narrative in terms of what I have already described as its "spatial histories." My exploration of the genre of the narrative utopia is thus also intended as a contribution to the emerging interdisciplinary formation centered on the problematics of "space" or "cultural geography," an interdisciplinary research project that includes some key recent work—whose influence marks all of these pages—by, among others, Henri Lefebvre, Michel Foucault, Michel de Certeau, David Harvey, Meaghan Morris, Edward Soja, Anthony Giddens, Mike Davis, Paul Rabinow, Kristin Ross, Allen Feldman, Rem Koolhaas, Manfredo Tafuri, Bernard Tschumi, Paul Carter, Walter Benjamin, Elisabeth Grosz, Edward Said, Edward S. Casey, Smith, Williams, and Jameson. What links the diverse projects of these various theorists together is a shared challenge to the Enlightenment, Cartesian, and Kantian notions of space as an objective homogeneous extension (*res extensa*), distinct from the subject (*res cogitans*), and as an empty container in which human history unfolds; or as Foucault put it, the treatment of space as "the dead, the fixed, the undialectical, the immobile. Time, on the contrary was richness, fecundity, life, dialectic."[32] Against such presuppositions, all of the thinkers named above show how space itself is both a *production,* shaped through a variety of social processes and human interventions, and a force that, in turn, influences, directs, and delimits possibilities of action. Modernity, as Soja writes, is both a historical and a geographical-spatial project, a continuous dissolution and reorganization of the environments, including our bodies, that we all inhabit.[33] A narrative about modernity that takes into account the dialectical interactions between both these historical and spatial dimensions thus will be a far richer one.

The classical privileging of temporality and history over space has its literary analogue in a critical tradition that valorizes the development of character psychology as the highest expression of narrative art. Characters are fundamentally temporal constructs that unfold in a space, or "setting," which, once established, seems to remain constant. Space is often presented in this critical tradition through the metaphor of the "stage" upon which the drama of character development unfolds, and setting is viewed as distinctly secondary in importance to character. Paul Carter notes a similar process at work in the contemporaneous writing of what he calls "imperial history," a narrative form "which re-

duces space to a stage, that pays attention to events unfolding in time
alone. . . . empirical history of this kind has as its focus facts which, in
a sense, come after the event."[34] Finally, in the increasing interiorization
that occurs in certain strands of modernist fiction—which, in turn, have
a marked influence on how we read earlier works as well—setting or
space seems to all but vanish. This occurs in a moment that, as Soja
points out, not coincidentally also saw the subordination of the spatial
problematic in social theory.[35]

However, such an emphasis on individual character is itself deeply
historical and a relatively recent phenomenon: indeed, Susan Stewart offers the reminder that it is only from the Renaissance onward that "a
tendency to replace collective experience with individual experience had
evolved" in the traditions of literary fiction, a gradual displacement that
ultimately gives rise to the new kind of interiorized and individualized
"psychological" literature found in the modern novel.[36] The narrative
utopia, on the other hand, emerges out of an older tradition, that of the
romance. Thus, it probably comes as no surprise that in one of the key
debates—staged over the course of nearly two decades between Henry
James and H. G. Wells—establishing the dominance of the psychological or character emphasis of the modern novel over the very different
concerns of the romance, it is the author of some of this century's most
important narrative utopias and "scientific romances" who, as convention has it, comes out on the losing end.[37]

Going beyond the circular axiological criterion implicit within such
an evaluation (the novel does what the novel does better than the romance does what the novel does), it becomes evident that in the narrative utopia, as within related expressions of the mode of romance, the
experience of space comes to the center of attention.[38] In a discussion of
the narrative functions of the romance, Jameson, drawing upon the
work of Heidegger, suggests that the "romance is precisely that form in
which the *worldness* of *world* reveals or manifests itself, in which, in
other words, *world* in the technical sense of the transcendental horizon
of our experience becomes visible in an inner-worldly sense."[39] The goal
of the romance as Jameson sees it is to spark in the reader a new awareness of what it means to be-in-the-world by highlighting the specific con-
structedness of the geographies and environments such a reader inhabits. That is, if the novel focuses on "character," making us aware of and
even producing the complexities of a modern, centered subjectivity, the
romance attempts to give expression to the "experience" of settings,
worlds, or spaces.[40]

The novel, as in the earlier invention of painterly perspective, posits a fundamental gap between the interior subjective viewpoint and the space upon which it gazes. However, as Hubert Dreyfus points out, "Painters did not paint the world from a perspectival viewpoint until the fourteenth century. Before then, they painted larger what was more important—what they were involved with."[41] Romance, along with these earlier painterly practices—as well as in later recovery projects such Heidegger's "destructive" hermeneutics—return us to a situation before the historical constitution of the centered subject. Hence, character functions in the romance form in a very different way than in the novel: as a formal "registering apparatus" whose movements during the course of the narrative action produce a traveler's itinerary of both the "local intensities" and "horizons" of the space that the narrative itself calls into being.[42]

The ways the particular generic tradition of the narrative utopia helps map the particular intensities and horizons of the nested "scaled spaces" of modernity can be further elaborated by way of a detour through one of the single most significant texts in the contemporary theorization of the spatial problematic: Henri Lefebvre's *The Production of Space* (1974). In this rich and brilliant work of dialectical thinking, Lefebvre maintains that the emergence and extension of capitalist modernity, as well as that of any other historical social formation, occurs through a particular "(social) production of (social) space"—that is, a space that is fundamentally produced by and through human actions, and which is thus "constituted neither by a collection of things or an aggregate of (sensory) data, nor by a void packed like a parcel with various contents, and . . . it is irreducible to a 'form' imposed upon phenomena, upon things, upon physical materiality."[43] For Lefebvre, such a space is a deeply historical one, its moments of apparent stability short-lived and contingent at best: indeed, Lefebvre suggests that one of the great temptations produced by the Enlightenment conceptualization of space as a static construct is that we think of it as a reified thing rather than as an open-ended, conflicted, and contradictory *process,* a process in which we as political agents continuously intervene.

According to Lefebvre, such a space is itself never constituted as a singularity, as other traditions of spatial thought might suggest, such as those of structuralism and phenomenology, with their respective focus on the subjective and objective dimensions of space. Rather, Lefebvre, following the lead of Marx's "regressive-progressive" analysis of exchange, develops a "concrete abstract" tripartite schematization of spatiality that has a special relevance for our discussion here.[44] Lefebvre argues that any socially produced historical space is constituted by a dialectically interwoven matrix of what he calls "spatial practices," "representations of space," and "spaces of representation," each allied with a specific cognitive mode through which we "re-present" it to ourselves (something captured far more effectively in the German term *Darstellung*): respectively, the domains of the "perceived," the "conceived," and the "lived."[45] The first of his three terms pertains to the most abstract processes of social production, reproduction, cohesion, and structuration, and hence bears a striking resemblance to the concerns of the various structuralisms whose "perceptual" apparatus takes on the abstract conceptual systematicity of a *science* (although in making such a comparison we need to keep in mind Lefebvre's own critique of what he views as the consequences of the structuralist privileging of the static notions of "mode of production" and "coherence" at the expense of the more dialectical concepts, "relations of production" and "contradiction").[46] The third set of terms refers, on the other hand, to the space of the embodied individual's cultural experience and the signs, images, forms, and symbols that constitute it: it is this level of space that has been mapped so thoroughly by phenomenology, whose emphasis on the individual's "lived" existential experience of space resonates with that found in this dimension of Lefebvre's work. The middle terms, those of the representations of space or the realm of the conceived, point toward what we more conventionally think of as "space" proper, mediating between and drawing all three of the levels together into a coherent ensemble. Of the social and cultural practices that constitute this dimension of space, Lefebvre writes, "conceptualized space, the space of scientists, planners, urbanists, technocratic subdividers and social engineers, as of a certain type of artist with a scientific bent—all of whom identify what is lived and what is perceived with what is conceived."[47]

In his own profitable engagement with Lefebvre's work, David Harvey replaces the third of Lefebvre's three levels, that of spaces of representation, or the domain of the lived, with the term "the imagined."[48] What I find most suggestive about Harvey's translation is the way it points toward an unremarked-upon convergence between Lefebvre's tripartite schema and the different one of the Real, the Symbolic, and the Imaginary first articulated by Jacques Lacan, and so central, in the traditions of Marxist thought, for the work of Louis Althusser. In Lefebvre's schema as well as that of Lacan, each of the three levels is understood to be dialectically inseparable from the others, although, again in both cases, we can analytically isolate them by way of a genetic, narrative reconstruction of the moment of their respective origins: beginning, in Lacan's case, with the infant's entrance into the Imaginary during what he calls the "mirror stage" and, for Lefebvre, with the primal emergence of "spatial architectonics"—demarcation and orientation, border (inside/outside) and energy flows or "rhythms"—emanating from the phenomenological body itself.[49] This first level of spatiality again in both cases encompasses the particular "pre-" or "non-verbal" insertion of the individual being in the world (but crucially not yet, or not even necessarily ever, a centered subject), and it is this level to which Althusser's famous formulation of ideology alludes: "the imaginary relationship of individuals to their real conditions of existence."[50] At the other extreme, we find that Lefebvre's level of the practice of space corresponds to the Lacanian Real, which Lacan famously argues "resists symbolization absolutely," and which Jameson has suggested is another term for "simply History itself": this level is that of the spatial social totality, a kind of Kantian noumena or Althusser's "lonely hour of the last instance," whose "perception" must always be mediated through the lived-Imaginary and the conceived-Symbolic.[51]

The analytical force of each of these schematizations lies in the distance that is maintained between each of their three terms and the unwillingness of their respective creators to allow one to be folded into the other two. Indeed, both Lefebvre's and Lacan's work stand as powerful rejoinders to the tangential textualization of the world, or what Lefebvre calls the "generalization of the concept of mental space," at play in certain strands of structuralist, semiotic, and post-structuralist theory.[52] However, once again in both cases it is the level of the conceived, of the Symbolic or representations of space, that provides the mediating link between the spaces of the individual and those of the larger social and historical realities she inhabits. This is also the level on which unfolds what Jameson elsewhere calls "cognitive mapping," where the pedagogical practices take place that enable us to inhabit, make sense of, orient ourselves within, and act through any particular space.[53] This, as Lefebvre maintains, is the domain of architecture, urban planning, nation building, and social engineering—and, I want to argue here, of narrative utopias.[54]

Lefebvre describes the spaces of representation in the following terms: "space as directly *lived* through its associated images and symbols, and hence the space of 'inhabitants' and 'users', but also of some artists and perhaps of those, such as a few writers and philosophers, who *describe* and aspire to do no more than describe."[55] The representational strategy that Lefebvre alludes to here, the passive attempt to mirror a world already constituted, is the one that in the long history of aesthetics has been associated with the concept of *mimesis*. Following the lead of Roland Barthes, I would suggest that the narrative utopia, as well as all similar practices of cognitive mapping, are, on the other hand, examples of *semiosis*: "what [it] 'represents' is constantly being deformed by the meaning, and it is on the level of meaning, not of the referent, that we should read [it]."[56] The unfolding of the narrative utopia is thus to be understood as a performance, a *mapping*, or travel itinerary—in short, Carter's "spatial history," "spatiality as a form of nonlinear writing; as a form of history."[57] These "unfinished maps" and "records of traveling" stand in stark opposition to the static, reified, and totalized (something we must always keep distinct from the performative labor of "totalizing") construct of the map.[58]

Or, as Darko Suvin puts it in summarizing Barthes, the narrative utopia offers "a panoramic *sweep* conducted along the well-known, culturally current socio-political categories (geography, demography, religion, constitution, economics, warfare, etc.)."[59] Each of these social categories—whose specificity and distribution, Suvin suggests, enable us once more to read off the narrative utopia its precise historical and cultural immanence—represents one stop on such an itinerary, a designated site whereupon the particular narrative utopia performs its critical symbolic praxis. This narrative production of world is what Tom Moylan describes as the "iconic register" of the utopian text in particular (and of the romance more generally), and in it "can be found the conflicting dialogue between the world as we know it and the better world that is not yet."[60] Finally, Jameson argues that the "object of representation" in a utopia has never been the "realm of freedom" that would exist in a radically other society, the concrete phenomenological contents or Lefebvre's "lived" space of such an other world; rather, the utopia produces, through its narrative work, what he calls the "machine," concentrating and localizing necessity—those structures that enable a social order to (re)produce itself—so that new forms and spaces of freedom can come into being in the first place.[61] The later displacement of this narrative elaboration of the machine by what Marc Angenot calls the "absent paradigm" then marks the transformation of the narrative utopia into science fiction (Wells's *Time Machine* again being both the transitional point and the exemplary text in this regard).[62]

Barthes goes on to argue that the specificity of *narrative* utopias, as opposed to political *science,* lies in the *"imagination of detail . . .* since detail is fantasmatic and thereby achieves the very pleasure of Desire."[63] This also destabilizes the typical distinction between narrative or merely "literary" utopias and plans or programs for "real" utopian communities (and indeed, for Barthes, Charles Fourier is more of a literary figure than a social engineer)—for both narrative forms can now be understood as ways of educating the desire of their readers, enabling them to inhabit the new kind of space that is then coming and called into being. Finally, all of this points toward the way the narrative utopia presents such an emerging space: not through the systematized conceptual structure of theory or science, but rather through the spatialized re-presentational operation that Louis Marin, as we shall see in more detail in our next chapter, calls *figuration.*[64]

ESTRANGEMENT AND THE TEMPORALITY OF UTOPIA

As significant as such a remapping of space may be, it can only come about after the narrative utopia first successfully performs another pedagogical operation: teaching its audiences how to think of the spaces they already inhabit in a new critical fashion. This dimension has been of central concern for much of the best scholarly work on utopia, looking at it as both a genre and as a particularly modern conceptual problematic. For example, Suvin, in turn drawing upon the cultural criticism of Bertolt Brecht and the Russian Formalists, influentially argues that the power of the form lies in its ability to "estrange" or momentarily distance its audience from the norms and values of their particular social worlds, thereby enabling them to experience that reality in its most fundamental aspects as a contingent, artificial, and most, importantly, a deeply malleable human construct.[65] Paul Ricoeur, in a more wideranging examination of the relationship between ideology and utopia, comes to some similar conclusions. Drawing upon his reading of Karl Mannheim's *Ideology and Utopia,* Ricoeur contends that utopia exists in a dialectical relationship with ideology, the latter producing the place or apparent ontological constancy of any social reality, the former an imaginary discursive site "outside" this reality that enables us to look upon the world with a critical eye. Echoing Suvin's description of the utopia's estranging function, Ricoeur writes, "From this 'no-place' an exterior glance is cast on our reality, which suddenly looks strange, nothing more being taken for granted."[66] The utopia thus serves as a constitutive element in the production of modern social reality, a progressive counterblast to the essential conservatism of ideology: "There is no social integration without social subversion, we may say. The reflexivity of the process of integration occurs by means of the process of subversion."[67] In other words, if ideology creates the synchrony or place of a given social reality, then utopia marks its potential for diachrony or historical becoming.

It is in the work of the most important of this century's theorists of the utopian impulse, Ernst Bloch, that we see this conceptualization of utopia worked out in its most elaborate form.[68] Prefiguring Ricoeur's model of the relationship between ideology and utopia, Bloch maintains that the expression of utopian desire in any cultural production takes the form of a surplus of meaning (*Überschuss*) that literally "overshoots" the ideological context in which it is embedded:

> *Ideological surplus arises according to the utopian function in the formation of ideology and above this ideology.* Thus, great art or great philosophy is not only its time manifested in images and ideas, but it is also *the journey of its time and the concerns of its time if it is anything at all,* manifested in images and ideas. From this vantage point, it is new for its time. From the vantage point of all times, it is that which is not yet fulfilled.[69]

Resembling Jacques Derrida's more well-known concept of the *supplément* and its more recent avatar the "specter," Bloch's utopian surplus passes through and disrupts the closure of any historical present, thereby opening it up to the possibilities of historical becoming.[70] Indeed, Bloch contends that any model of the real that fails to take into account the category of becoming represented by the utopian surplus, and which thereby denies the always already "unfinished" nature of any world, society, or culture, falls prey to the mystifications of an ideology that posits a full self-presence of the present, a dilemma that Bloch suggests haunts even the work of fellow Marxists such as Georg Lukács, and which Derrida in turn finds endemic to post–Cold War announcements of the "end of history."[71] In a stinging condemnation of these false realisms, Bloch writes, "Where the prospective horizon is omitted, reality only appears as become, as dead, and it is the dead, namely the naturalists and empiricists, who are burying their dead here."[72] Thus, a fuller cultural hermeneutic, according to Bloch, takes as its task the unveiling of the signs of "nonsynchronic" layers of the past and the present, as well as emergent and potential futures located in any cultural artifact.[73] Of course, this project too will only ever be partially successful, for the Archimedean point of any such a critical totalization similarly will be located in the always deferred, "not-yet-become" unity of the utopian future. (An analogous conclusion, although to quite different ends, is arrived at, as we shall see in Chapter 4, in London's *The Iron Heel*, where the full truth of the present can only be revealed from the perspective of the necessarily absent presence of the utopian future.)

Bloch's utopian hermeneutics have been criticized both for the implicit idealism of its archetypal structures, and for the universalism of the pattern of desires it unveils: for when everything becomes an expression of utopian desire, to what degree does the category of utopia lose its usefulness? However, Bloch's program must be distinguished from the more conventional archetypalisms since it is always uniquely oriented toward an as yet unrealized future. Jameson observes, "For Bloch, indeed, the doctrine of hope has not one, but two basic philosophical adversaries: nihilism and anamnesis; or . . . anxiety and memory."[74] For an example of this latter position, we need look no further than the work of one of the most influential of archetypal critics, Northrop Frye. Frye maintains that the utopia is the comic inversion of the tragic structure of "contract myth" and hence represents the desire for the *restoration* of that "which existing society has lost, forfeited, rejected, or violated."[75] (A similar notion of utopia as memory is to be found in the work of the other great Marxist theorist of utopia, Herbert Marcuse.[76]) Bloch explicitly rejects such an understanding of utopia as nostalgic because it is predicated on the existence of something like an ahistorical "fixed generic essence" or *truth* of human existence that appears at certain times and places and becomes lost in others. Bloch, on the contrary, holds history to be the process of a continuous transformation of both the definition and lived experience of "human nature," a process given its most concrete formulation by the Marxist dialectic: "For Marxism, the *humanum* has the function of a historical goal, not the function of an a priori principle of deduction; it is the utopia, which is not present but is anticipated—it is not something that ahistorically lies at the basis of things as the arch-certainty of history."[77] Bloch, however, does note that in those strains of Marxism where history is treated schematically "as a series of sequential Fixa or even closed 'totalities,'" there appears another "ossified concept of reality," that of the teleological apprehension of history—again a conclusion that bears a striking resemblance to that arrived at by Derrida.[78]

Every manifestation of the utopian Other, what Bloch calls the *No-*

vum—that which is radically and, more important, *unexpectedly* new —as well as its full expression, the *Ultimum,* the "total leap out of everything that previously existed," will thus always be greeted with nothing less than astonishment.[79] This astonishment in the face of the "uncanny" possibilities of new kinds of spaces, worlds, and ways of being can produce its own kinds of existential anxieties. Edward S. Casey has traced out the role of these anxieties in Heidegger's analysis of space and place in *Being and Time* in a way that suggests both the latter's parallels with and the ultimate philosophical and political divergences from Bloch's work:

> Has [anxiety] perhaps arisen in the innocuous situation of speculating about space as something to be understood on the ground of new possibilities of Being? Has Heidegger glimpsed these possibilities and shrunken back from the anxiety they occasion? Has he fled in the face of the ontologically uncanny— the not-at-home of sheer possibility—into the arms of the actual at-home of the instrumental and theoretical realms? Does not his stress on familiarity, as well as on closeness and involvement, directionality and deseverance, and even on exact observation, bespeak a "turn thither" toward the canny, the known, the palpable, and the predictable? Is this not what is signified by the confinement of place and region to the ready-to-hand and of space to the present-at-hand?[80]

These anxieties play a crucial role in the narrative utopias of Bellamy and Alexander Bogdanov, as we will see in Chapters 3 and 4, and they are similarly obsessively tracked in the utopian science fiction of Arkady and Boris Strugatsky—*Roadside Picnic* and *The Ugly Swans,* among others—as well as in such contemporary cultural documents as the film *Independence Day.*[81]

Narrative utopias then serve as one of those important cultural forms that lay bare this horizon of temporal possibility located in any cultural present. However, Bloch goes even further, and differentiates between what he calls "abstract" and "concrete" utopias. The former operates in any historical conjuncture primarily in a compensatory fashion, projecting a simple fulfillment of those specific needs that are felt to be lacking in the present. Many of the fully elaborated aspects of the "good place" (*eu-topia*) in the narrative utopia fall into this category: the vision offered is less of some radically other place than that of a "repaired" present.[82] Bloch maintains that abstract utopias are more real than many expressions of literary realism, precisely because they mark the place of history and becoming in the present that these realisms deny.

However, abstract utopias are plagued by their own shortcomings. They plunge us back into the immediate and local desires that define any present, and thereby diffuse the hope for some fully other existence, this latter condition being an uncanny one in which our sense of our selves and our world would be so thoroughly and utterly transformed that the very desires to which the abstract utopia responds would themselves have become obsolete. To take an example whose relevance will be evident in my discussions of Bellamy's and London's works, the figures of leisure time, escape from work, or the "right to laziness" are all forms of abstract utopia, attempts to "repair" the deep alienation of labor in our present. In concrete utopia, on the other hand, the category of work itself will be so radically transformed as to make unrecognizable the desires to which these figures respond. By projecting "solutions" in the future to the problems of the present, these abstract utopias risk reducing the dialectical complexity of the historical process—wherein change in any one element will have dramatic and unpredictable consequences for the whole (in this Bloch's work would resemble the modeling found in chaos theory of behavior in complex systems)—to "the single, relatively abstract field of social planning."[83]

Bloch's concrete utopia, on the other hand, represents elements of "anticipatory illumination" (vor-schein), or foreshadowing of emergent aspects of such a radically other future: "Concrete utopia stands on the horizon of every reality; real possibility surrounds the open dialectical tendencies and latencies to the very last."[84] As Ruth Levitas succinctly puts it, "While abstract utopia may express desire, only concrete utopia carries hope."[85] However, by breaking the bonds with the present in this manner, the concrete utopia thereby evades all our efforts to apprehend it directly. Instead, the concrete utopian content of any cultural production is manifest as disruptive traces (Spuren), an ineffable horizon that blocks out the space of what in Derrida's terms would be described as the differentially defined "absent presence," or specter, of such a future.[86] Because we lack those cognitive reference points by which we might make sense of its dramatic otherness, the utopia defined in this more radical sense appears only on the extreme peripheries of our conceptual retina, shadow images of a situation whose truth-content necessarily resides somewhere else.

The trace or horizon of the concrete utopia is present even in the fully realized "speaking pictures" of the narrative utopia, as evident in the following illustration from Bellamy's Looking Backward. During the course of his journeys through the social world of the twentieth century, Bellamy's hero Julian West receives a copy of the future author Berrian's *Penthesilia*, held by many to be the crowning literary achievement of the new world. Upon reading this work, West reflects on what he takes to be the necessary impossibility of producing such "great" literature in utopia: "The story writers of my day would have deemed the making of bricks without straw a light task compared with the construction of a romance from which should be excluded all effects drawn from the contrasts of wealth and poverty, education and ignorance, coarseness and refinement, high and low."[87] In other words, the very conditions that made narrative art possible, at least as West understands them, have faded into history. Nevertheless, this work does exist, and, moreover, it has a profound effect, providing West an access into the world of the twentieth century that up until then had been unavailable. (As we shall see in Chapter 4, more traumatic consequences can arise as well from experiencing the alien other literature of utopia).

And yet, while Berrian's text thus also would seem vital to our own readerly understanding of the utopian place, it is presented to us, as it were, under erasure: the only sign we have of its existence is West's statements about its effects upon him. This is because, as Bloch would have it, such an object is, from the perspective of our own historical present, "impossible": only the manifest presence of the lived social totality of which this work is a concrete expression could enable such a representation. Indeed, we might confirm this observation by looking at the disappointing efforts to write this impossible text, such as C. H. Stone's cloying, sentimental *One of "Berrian's" Novels* (1890). The absent text within Bellamy's text thus becomes the sign of the future itself, a prepresentation of that which is not yet existent in the world.[88] The linguistic trace in the text of this impossible artifact thus serves at once as a figural space holder for, and an allegory of, the radical otherness of the utopian future—an otherness that Bellamy's narrative elsewhere fails to bring to life.

Many students of narrative utopias find scandalous Bloch's emphasis on these representational "failures" of the form. We could read Bloch's concern with such representational dilemmas as a sign of the relationship between his philosophical program and that of modernism more generally; and indeed, we shall see a solution to the problem of "representing" utopia strikingly similar to that advanced by Bloch in the properly modernist narrative utopia of Yevgeny Zamyatin's *We*. However, I would like to suggest another more productive way of using what I find to be Bloch's valuable critical distinction. Taking Bloch's insights even further, Jameson comes to the apparently paradoxical and the seemingly classically post-structuralist conclusion that the utopia is a form of the narration that is "about" the impossibility of its own ostensible task. The "deepest vocation" of the narrative utopia, he maintains, "is to bring home, in local and determinate ways, and with a fullness of concrete detail, our constitutional inability to imagine utopia itself, and this, not owing to any individual failure of imagination but as the result of the systemic, cultural, and ideological closure of which we are all in one way or another prisoners."[89] By narrating the necessary failure of any effort to represent the future, the narrative utopia illuminates the outer horizons of just such a systemic, cultural, and ideological enclosure.

I agree that these "failures" are, in part, what make the narrative utopias of the past such interesting objects for contemporary cultural critics, for it is in the elaboration of the "local and determinate" desires for the future that the individual utopian text can tell us a good deal about its own present. However, if we too quickly and uncritically accept as a conclusion that the narrative utopia, like every other form of cultural representation, fails to break free of the gravitational field of the ideologies, or "beliefs," of its moment, we risk losing sight of the unique critical, pedagogical, and representational work performed by the genre. The present, as Bloch reminds us, is not a homogeneous thing, and any notion of its full self-presence is ideological through and through. Indeed, all the critics I discussed above stress that the function of the narrative utopia is to call into question the ideological stability of its present world by illuminating the horizon of nonidentity located within it; or, as Ricoeur nicely puts it, the utopia transforms the closed circle of ideology or belief into an open spiral.[90]

Thus, it is precisely in its failures to "transcend" its present that the utopian text ultimately succeeds. That is, by not becoming an unknowable trace—much like Berrian's fiction, or, in the Strugatskys' *Roadside Picnic,* the alien artifacts littering the landscape of the "Zone," their original function indecipherable for contemporary humanity—the utopian representation enables its readers to think of their shared present in a new way, teaching them to imagine and conceive of it as in continuous process, in formation, and subject to the disrupting, dissolving energies of modernity. Bloch's concrete utopia, as with Berrian's novel and the Zone's artifacts, are like the Althusserian and Lacanian Real, "simply History itself" or that which "resists symbolization absolutely"; the narrative utopia, on the other hand, provides a concrete symbolization of the historical *process*.

In so doing, the narrative utopia plays a vital role in teaching its readers how to become modern subjects. Anthony Giddens argues that the ability to critically estrange or reflexively engage the contemporary arrangement of the world—which Suvin, Ricoeur, and Bloch all describe as a key operation of the utopia—is one of the features by which we can also distinguish the originality of those modern "modes of social life" that emerge in Europe during the fifteenth and sixteenth centuries. (Or as Lefebvre puts it, "The birth of 'modernity' . . . coincided with the beginnings of doubt and questioning; the world we call modern was born with the shattering of the modern world, carrying within its heart the principle of its destruction and self-destruction."[91]) Giddens goes on to note that "traditional" societies also engage in a form of self-conscious monitoring of social and cultural behavior. Moreover, while he draws upon Max Weber's famous differentiation of traditional and modern societies in terms of their consciousness of time as, respectively, a cyclicality and a linear unfolding, Giddens also reminds us to be wary of thinking of traditional societies as static or even resistant to change in some absolute sense. Every generation, he argues, must necessarily reinvent tradition for itself. The real contrast between traditional and modern societies then lies in the scarcity in the former of those "temporal and spatial markers in terms of which [this] change can have any meaningful form."[92] Thus, while the inhabitants of traditional societies reflect on already established norms with the aim of clarifying their applicability to current problems, thereby emphasizing the essential continuity of present cultural forms with the past, in modernity, social and cultural institutions and practices are continuously reexamined, and then ultimately re-formed, in the light of new incoming information. The consequence of this process is to open up the possibility of imagining a disjuncture between what now have become differentiated temporal locales: the past, the present, and the potentiality of the future.[93] (Similarly, Mannheim maintains that the first of his four "utopian mentalities" to emerge in the Western social imagination, the "orgiastic chiliasm" practiced by the German peasants taking part in the Revolution of 1525, played the epochal, transforming role "of providing us with a qualitative differentiation of time."[94])

The space produced in the narrative utopia offers exactly one of those perspectival "markers" by which such a differentiation can occur. In the earliest expressions of the genre, this distance is presented in specifically spatial terms, the utopia narrated, as it is in More's inaugural work, as being located "somewhere else" on the globe. Indeed, it is only in the latter part of the eighteenth century, with the publication of the text that marks what Suvin calls utopia's "shift to anticipation," Sébastien Mercier's *L'An deux mille quartre cent quarante: Rêve s'il en fut jamais* (1771), that the utopia becomes a "uchronia," an explicit *temporal* transformation of the present.[95] The implications of this lag are profound and extend beyond the literary domain, for it suggests that it is precisely the *spatial practices of modernity*—the shattering of long-established patterns of inhabitation by such processes as enclosure and the dissolution of the feudal estates; the new mobility, voluntary and otherwise, of all kinds of populations; and the voyages of exploration and conquest that bring into contact different cultures and societies— as well as the way these are lived by all kinds of people, that create the conditions of possibility for practicing, conceiving, and living temporality and history in wholly new ways. Lukács too suggests a link between the spatial practices of modernity and the emergence of a modern historical consciousness when he notes that it was, among other factors, the "enormous quantitative expansion of war," with the creation and mobilization in the Napoleonic era of new mass armies, that produced "the concrete possibilities for men to comprehend their own existence as something historically conditioned."[96] Space and history are thus once again understood to be inseparably interwoven dimensions of the experience of modernity.

With this conclusion, we have completed the dialectical loop that unfolds in every narrative utopia: beginning with an initial operation of what Gilles Deleuze and Félix Guattari call "decoding or deterritorializing flows"—dissolving, through the estranging critique, older social formations, bonds, values, beliefs, and practices—these works ultimately engage in "reterritorializations," producing new strictures and bounds, "norms and forms," that are then imposed upon and within the social and cultural environment.[97] Only at this point can we begin to formulate an answer to the dramatic question advanced by Eagleton with which I began this chapter: "What traumatic upheaval of perception is involved in thinking of the political no longer as a question of local sovereignty, of something interwoven with the labor and kinship relations of a specific place, but as an abstract *national* formation?" I would answer that it is precisely through its estranging deterritorialization of late feudal culture that More's *Utopia* first opens up the "traumatic wound" in which emerges the reterritorialization that is only later understood to be the form of the modern nation-state. In so doing, More's work enables its readers to think and to act in new ways in their own spaces as well. The specific nature of More's original pedagogical project is the topic of the next chapter.

CHAPTER TWO

Utopia and the Birth of Nations

RE-AUTHORING, OR THE ORIGINS OF INSTITUTIONS

In this chapter, I will be concerned with the births of a number of institutional beings-in-the-world, each of which is bound inseparably to the others: the birth of the genre of the narrative utopia, the birth of the spatial histories of modernity, and the birth of the "conceived space" that takes the form of the modern nation-state. And yet what do we mean when we say we are going to talk about the "birth" of an institution?

The danger involved when endeavoring to answer such a question has been analyzed quite effectively by Nancy Armstrong and Leonard Tennenhouse: in attempting to construct a narrative of "origins," we run the risk of unconsciously projecting backward our own myths, our own fully-formed and naturalized cognitive categories, into a space where these do not yet exist.[1] In such an instance, the dense web of contingencies and particularities, of contradictory actions and desires, that go into the production of a new institution—put simply, its material history— all but vanishes without a trace. Such a dilemma is evident in many discussions of the generic institution of the narrative utopia that begin either with a terminological and typological differentiation of various kinds of "ideal societies" or with a discussion of the ancient Greek or even prehistoric manifestations of the form. In either case, it seems as if the thing itself had always already existed in some natural, ideal realm, patiently waiting for More to give it its name.[2]

Despite these obstacles, the question of the origin of institutions is a central and serious one for any discussion of a genre like that of the narrative utopia. This is so much the case that what I find to be one of the most satisfactory answers, that offered by the Russian Formalist critic Viktor Shklovsky, may appear at first glance to be exceedingly flip: genres, like all institutions, are born by accident; or, as Shklovsky puts it, "The artistic device, artistic invention, are the final crystallization of a slippage, of a chance mutation."[3] As with Armstrong and Tennenhouse's analysis of the origins of the modern institutions of the author, the family, and the nation, Shklovsky here deftly brackets aside the question of intention, or the unspoken assumption that an author like Thomas More must have envisioned, before the actual act of writing, the lineaments of the new institution to which his work would give rise. For Shklovsky, the originary act lies outside of any conscious decision precisely because the particular narrative performance that ultimately produces a new form is itself bounded by and formed within a background of practices, institutions, and relationships particular to its time and place:

> A work of art is perceived against a background of and by association with other works of art. The form of a work of art is determined by its relationship with other preexisting forms. *The content of a work of art is invariably manipulated, it is isolated, "silenced."* All works of art, and not only parodies, are created either as a parallel or an antithesis to some model. *The new form makes its appearance not in order to express a new content, but rather, to replace an old form that has already outlived its artistic usefulness.*[4]

Fortunately, a great deal of scholarly energy has been devoted to enumerating the specific literary institutions within which More operates and to which he responds in the writing of *Utopia:* among them, the Platonic dialogue, the pastoral romance, the dialogue of counsel, the satire, and the travel narrative.[5] Indeed, it is the text's coordination of this variety of older forms—an operation that Fredric Jameson more generally describes as *generic discontinuities,* "not so much an organic unity as a symbolic act that must reunite or harmonize heterogeneous narrative paradigms"[6]—that becomes one of the characteristic features of the "novelistic discourse" (to use Mikhail Bakhtin's related concept) of the narrative utopia. Kenneth Roemer, for example, finds a similar operation at work in Edward Bellamy's *Looking Backward:* "The styles of the book frequently juxtapose characteristics of the popular sentimental novel . . . philosophical and economic dialogues, and religious preaching."[7]

However, it is the last part of Shklovsky's statement that is of special interest to me here—that new forms arise precisely "to replace an old form that has already outlived its artistic usefulness." There are a number of ways to define such "usefulness." For Shklovsky, the useful is to be understood in strictly formal terms, the specific distribution of literary devices needed to produce certain kinds of effects upon readers. Thus, we see a More who begins by endeavoring through the tried and true institutions to produce certain kinds of effects upon his audience, even if the audience might have included at first only himself, engaging in a bit of linguistic play to while away the hours during an unexpected hiatus in an important diplomatic mission to the Netherlands, and perhaps also the man he called "my derlynge," the great humanist, Erasmus. However, somewhere along the way his particular rhetorical performance entered into new and unanticipated territory, and began to generate the textual space from which a new form could emerge.

Shklovsky's approach remains controversial to many contemporary literary scholars precisely because it demolishes accepted institutions of the author, genius, and artistic invention, and injects a dramatic sense of contingency into the literary historical record. At the same time, however, such an approach is not necessarily at odds with an established tradition of More criticism that has long emphasized the linguistic and rhetorical playfulness of this particular and, in this view, singular textual performance. In this latter reading, Utopia is understood to be a nowhere precisely because More neither imagines nor desires it to be the representation of any kind of space in the world; rather, this content is no more than the "motivation," to use another term of the Russian Formalists, for a stunningly virtuoso rhetorical performance, or literary play, on More's part.

In its very best instances, such an emphasis on the formal rhetorical play of More's text highlights exactly the impossibility, by any amount of textual evidence, of ever definitely answering the question of More's own attitude toward the "speaking picture" produced in this work, an attitude, moreover, that changed as his situation dramatically altered in the years following its original publication. There is indeed at play in the text a fundamental undecidability, the significance of which I shall return to momentarily. Ironically, however, this same reading can just as readily be turned on its head and used as a basis for a most definitive answer *to* the question of More's intentions: Utopia "becomes intelligible and delightful as soon as we take it for what it is—a holiday work, a spontaneous overflow of intellectual high spirits, a revel of debate, paradox, comedy, and (above all) of invention, which starts many hares and kills none."[8] In other words, a "genius" of More's stature could never have been so vulgar as to have "seriously" considered the possibility of the social organization outlined by the work's narrator, Raphael Hythlodaeus, whose Greek surname canonically has been translated as "expert in trifles" or "well-learned in nonsense."[9] At most, such a reading maintains, the work is a cry of outrage at contemporary political and economic conditions; and it has been the fault of subsequent misreaders of the text, "later excited men" as one pair of critics describes them, to have taken More much too seriously.[10] Thus, whatever its corrective benefits, this reading too, as much as the most literal-minded approach to the text, ends up betraying its own ideological or mythological horizons, not the least of which includes what became in the second half of the twentieth century the increasingly naturalized suspicion of and assault upon the utopian imaginary itself.

More immediately, however, such a reading projects an extremely limited notion of "play" onto the very different context of More and his fellow Renaissance Christian humanists. Stephen Greenblatt offers a useful challenge to this anachronistic idea of play in his influential discussion of More's text. According to Greenblatt, *Utopia* is only one example of a wider humanist practice of producing "carefully demarcated playgrounds," places wherein one could experiment with ideas that might otherwise lead to dangerous conclusions. Crucially, "This play is not conceived by humanists as an escape from the serious, but as a mode of civility, an enhancement of specifically human powers."[11] Thus, as Greenblatt sees it, this textual space enables More to accomplish the important work of thinking through his own place and sense of self as he stands on the horizon of a new career of service to Henry VIII, as well as, more generally, the relationship between intellectuals and power in a moment when these were in the midst of a dramatic redefinition.[12]

At the same time, this new emphasis on "human powers" points toward a massive tidal shift, which in More's time is experienced as a form of cultural crisis, then underway in Europe. John M. Perlette shows how the very undecidability of the debate that runs through the first book of *Utopia* marks the seriousness with which More takes the powers of rhetoric: "The very fact that they can both propound thoroughly convincing yet thoroughly irreconcilable arguments validates (paradoxically, ironically, and perhaps unintentionally) the rhetorical point of view."[13] Such a seriousness in turn marks a crucial intellectual change experienced not only by More but by the community of Renaissance Christian humanists as well, a change marked by a growing sense of "the contingent nature of language and 'reality' and the concomitant localization, temporalization, relativization, in short, the devaluation of values."[14] This crisis in values helps us mark the historical specificity of More's situation of production, a particularly unstable moment between two different cultural and social paradigms, that of the "universal" axiological forms of the late feudal world and those more relativistic and cultural ones of a still-nascent modernity. In this sense, *Utopia* becomes "useful" as a literary form precisely to the degree that it enables its audiences to think through these various scales of personal, cultural, and epochal transition.

Thus, if a genre first appears as the consequence of a set of historical accidents and contingencies, it becomes an institution only when it comes to occupy a specific niche in its social and cultural environment, performing certain kinds of work more effectively than similar, already existent institutions. It is this process of "selection" (social and cultural rather than natural, of course) that reintroduces a sense of necessity into the process of institutional formation.[15] Michael McKeon maintains,

> Genres provide a conceptual framework for the mediation (if not the "solution") of intractable problems, a method for rendering such problems intelligible. The ideological status of genre, like that of all conceptual categories, lies in its explanatory and problem-"solving" capacities. And generic form itself, the dense network of conventionality that is both elastic and profoundly regulative, is the prior and most tacitly powerful mechanism of the explanatory method of genre. Genres fill a need for which no adequate alternative method exists. And when they change, it is as part of a change both in the need they exist to fill and in the means that exist for its fulfillment.[16]

McKeon's description of the workings of genre is apt as long as we keep in mind that it is not the original performance that produces the institution, but rather the social and cultural context that selects it out precisely because of its particular success at responding to the needs of that moment. Moreover, it is what Gary Saul Morson calls a "re-authoring" of the original text performed by its subsequent readers that actually does the work of establishing the institutionality, or *Dasein,* of the new genre: "In an important sense, it is really the *second* work of a genre that creates the genre by defining conventions and *topoi* for the class. Read in the context of the second and subsequent works, the style of the first becomes the grammar of the class, and its idiosyncratic themes and rhetorical devices are rediscovered as the motifs and tropes of a tradition."[17] In other words, an act of repetition establishes the "historical necessity" of the founding case; or as Slavoj Žižek more generally argues, "The crucial point here is the changed symbolic status of an event: when it erupts for the first time it is experienced as a contingent trauma, as an intrusion of a certain non-symbolized Real; only through repetition is this event recognized in its symbolic necessity—it finds its place in the symbolic network; it is realized in the symbolic order."[18] Thus, in terms of a narration of the birth of a genre, the original intentions of the author as she sets out to accomplish a specific textual performance become less significant: far more important, from the perspective of the later institutionality of the genre, are what these subsequent readers take it to mean. Moreover, a similar act of re-authoring is performed on any works that only now, in an act of historical revision, are "recognized" as genetic predecessors of the newly established genre, Plato's *Republic* being the classic case of such a re-authoring in the institution of the narrative utopia. Something similar happens in the twentieth century to the narrative utopia itself, as it is now "recognized" as both one of the roots of science fiction, and, as Darko Suvin notes, "retroactively, one of its forms. . . . Utopian fiction is the socio-political subgenre of SF."[19]

Amy Boesky has shown more precisely how subsequent readers, such as the first English translator of *Utopia*, Ralph Robinson (1551), and, even more significant, its major seventeenth-century imitator, Francis Bacon in his extremely influential *The New Atlantis* (1627), helped consolidate such an institutionality.[20] However, such a labor of re-authoring actually may have already begun with More himself. *Utopia,* as is now well known, had a rather unique genesis. More completed the second book, encompassing Hythlodaeus's description of the Commonwealth of Utopia, during his extended stay on the continent. Only later, following his return to England, did he compose the first book containing the crucial prefatory debate between Hythlodaeus and the character "More" concerning both contemporary political and economic conditions in Europe and the value of service as an advisor to a monarch.[21] The later addition of this first book conventionally has been understood to be something of a defense mechanism on More's part, either as a means of distancing himself from responsibility for what could have been taken as the scandalous, if not blasphemous and treasonous, claims advanced in the narration of Book 2, or a way of signaling to his readers his own ironic distance from Hythlodaeus's overly enthusiastic endorsement of Utopian life.[22]

However, I would like to advance another reading, and suggest that the first book represents More's reflections on the potential force or "usefulness" of what he too recognizes as an original literary form.[23] If, as Perlette argues, the conclusion of the debate in the first book comes to no resolution or, more precisely, comes to the resolution that there is nothing but competing rhetorical constructions of the good and the true, then what becomes indispensable in such a condition of skepticism are the rhetorical and narrative machines that will enable one to best (re)construct a world—and this (re)construction is, of course, exactly what the second book of *Utopia* offers.

Every reading of *Utopia* that attempts to determine More's own thoughts about the worth of the place of Utopia must necessarily import some fixed normative criterion, a self-coherent core of values imagined to be possessed by More, against which the work's vision is measured. However, as much of the recent scholarship on More's life has demonstrated, his own "values" go through a series of dramatic shifts as his position changes in relationship to a number of institutional settings and historical events: the monastic community in which he participated as a youth, the circle of Christian humanists, the crown, the challenges of Luther, and ultimately the struggle between secular and Church authority. Thus, it may be precisely this absence of any immutable core of values in his own life, as well as the coherent author-subject imagined to possess them, that has led to the after-the-fact acknowledgment in the first book of the potential power of the rhetorical machine that More himself produced: as a pedagogical tool for teaching his audience (to deploy the tripartite schema of Henri Lefebvre that we outlined in the previous chapter) to *conceive,* and subsequently, to live and to perceive their world in a new way. In other words, More himself may have been the first reader to understand the ways that *Utopia* brings into view both the reality and potentiality of historical change, a potentiality that makes the playful modeling of cultural and social space in Book 2 quite serious work indeed. When More himself later denounces his own work—as in his assertion in *Confutation to Tyndale's Answer* that rather than allow the Latin text of *Utopia* or the works of Erasmus to be translated into English, "I wolde . . . helpe to burne them both wyth myne own hands"—he only reconfirms his own understanding of the form's power to foster change.[24] This power was something the leaders of the 1525 German peasants' rebellion, who reputedly quoted from an early vernacular translation of More's work, must have recognized as well.[25] Only when such "changes" exploded all around him in ways he had not anticipated does More belatedly attempt to retreat from his invention. The very success of More's singular textual performance at achieving these various ends led its subsequent readers and imitators to discover in it the origins of a new and particularly powerful modern institution.

UTOPIQUES AND CONCEPTUALIZED SPACE

The debate in the first book points toward a crucial realization about this new form: its capacity not simply to mirror back mimetically a world and its underlying network of values and beliefs, but to provide its readers with what Lefebvre describes as "conceptions" of space and Jameson calls a "cognitive mapping." As we saw in the last chapter, the operations by which the narrative performs such work are twofold: on the one hand, estranging or "deterritorializing," critically dismantling already existent social and cultural norms and forms; and on the other, representational, illuminating crucial dimensions of transformations already underway, the "horizon" Bloch describes as immanent in any present. Moreover, this textual work always already will be pedagogical, providing its readers with some of the skills and dispositions needed to operate in such an emergent social and cultural reality.

Perhaps the single most effective and sustained attempt to grasp the double nature of More's text and the particular narrative and representational strategies that this involves is to be found in the groundbreaking semiological and structural analysis by Louis Marin, *Utopiques: Jeux d'espace* (1973). Marin's rich text has become something of a touchstone in discussions of *Utopia*, as well as deeply influencing the way we read narrative utopias of all kinds, and in this regard, my analysis is not an exception.[26] If I ultimately depart from some of Marin's conclusions, his work nevertheless provides an indispensable strategy for reading narrative utopias that will be drawn upon in all of my subsequent chapters.

Marin begins by observing a deep relationship between the formal narrative operations of *Utopia* and the historical situation from within which it emerges. *Utopia* appears in a moment of historical liminality, or what Marin describes as "the in-between [*entre-deux*] space at the beginning of the sixteenth century of the historical contradiction of the Old and New Worlds"; that is, spatially, between Europe and the Americas, as Hythlodaeus's description of the voyage to the island commonwealth would suggest (a point we shall return to later), and temporally, between late feudal society and an emerging capitalist modernity.[27] Similarly, More's text is itself "in-between," at once part of what precedes and what follows it, and thus not fully of either place. Marin, following the lead of A. J. Greimas, calls this discursive locus the *neutral*: "Neither yes nor no, true nor false, one nor the other. . . . Rather, this neutral is the span between true and false, opening within discourse a space discourse cannot receive" (*Utopics* 7). From the elaboration of this neutral space, Marin later maintains, springs the narrative utopia's "creative energy, its performative force," its capacity, as we shall see, to map out an emerging social and cultural reality.[28]

Thus, Marin argues that we, as later readers of this text, run into tremendous difficulty when we attempt to locate a singular, fixed place or referent for the utopian space, be it located in the past (as, for example, interpretations of Utopia as a picture of a medieval monastery claim), the present (a reading of Utopia as a representation of the places recently contacted by the European voyages of exploration and conquest), or the future (a vision of Utopia as a projection of communism).[29] Marin goes on to demonstrate how More himself quite carefully cuts off any such mimetic paths leading outside the text: first, in the tracing of an elaborate circular symmetry in Hythlodaeus's journey, so that the island of Utopia only comes into existence through an act of spatial-narrative dislocation opening up outside the mapped world; second, in describing the "act" that founds the place of Utopia, the digging of the great trench by King Utopus, so that the utopian space is written into existence through a separation of the "island" from the "world"; and finally (although this actually occurs in one of the prefatory letters written by More's friend Peter Giles to the two books of *Utopia*—letters, in turn, providing additional re-authorings of More's work that help to establish its generic identity) in claiming that a servant's cough covered Hythlodaeus's description of the location of the island, an event that undermines the mythic plenitude, or referentiality, of the voice, and thereby closes the written text back in on itself.[30] Marin concludes, "Utopia is thus the neutral moment of a difference, the space outside of place; it is a gap impossible either to inscribe on a geographic map or to assign to history. Its reality thus belongs to the order of the text (*Utopics* 57). In other words, *"Utopia is not a topography but a topic,"* an argumentative or rhetorical figure designed to undermine continuously the very place from which it emerges (*Utopics* 115).

Moreover, Marin resists the closed, historicist approaches to the work that have become part of the dominant critical paradigm in the decades following the original publication of his work. Crucially, Marin asserts that "Utopia is not a mirror of social reality, whether anamorphotic or through reverse images" (*Utopics* 159). The utopian figure resists the kinds of one-to-one correspondences these reflective or mimetic relationships entail, presenting us instead with a "dislocated" representation of its historical moment, both as it is and as what it will come to be. Although traces of the material historical context from which it emerges are always present in the utopian text—manifest for example, as Jameson maintains, in the play of topical allusions that run throughout, a subtext reconstituted today by way of the scholarly commentary that often accompanies these texts—these traces serve less as the object of the text's representational strategies than the very raw material upon which the narrative operations go to work.[31] Thus, when we attempt to translate the utopia back into the ideological enclosure of its immediate present, as would historicist or culturalist approaches, we discover blind spots, dislocations, erasures, and aporia marring the picture of the Utopian commonwealth. These absences and slippages are crucial, for they signal the productive, critical neutralizations taking place in the narrative unfolding of the utopian figure.

In the same way that the utopian figure resists these attempts to confine it to a particular historical and geographical space, so too it resists reduction to any singular ideological location. As with Ricoeur, Suvin, and Bloch, whom I discussed in the previous chapter, Marin too draws an important distinction between ideology and utopia:

> Ideological discourse expresses historical reality by deadening it and shaping it into a closed system of ideas aimed at presenting a justifying or legitimizing representation of the world. Utopia as a figure inscribed within a fable-producing discourse *puts into play* ideological discourse and its system of representations in the double sense of an implicit critical questioning of them, and a placing of them at a distance or an internal reflection which reveals presuppositions ideology takes as certain and self-evident. (*Utopiques* 249–50; *Utopics* 195)

Ideological discourse, as Marin sees it, operates in a way analogous to myth, as the latter has been famously described by Claude Lévi-Strauss. The explanatory, or "problem-solving," capacity of myth lies in its projection of an imaginary synthesis or mediation between the fundamental antinomies of a society and culture: nature and culture, the individual and society, life and death, female and male, law and order, and so forth. By reducing these terms to a fictional state of noncontradiction ("an impossible achievement," Lévi-Strauss points out, "if, as it happens, the contradiction is real"), myth, like other forms of ideological representation, fixes the place of and provides legitimation for the contemporary social organization.[32]

The displaced or neutral world of the utopia, on the other hand, functions as a *supplément* to this apparent closure, a place wherein these contradictions do not come to a resolution but instead are allowed to play against one another. By fabricating this kind of fictional point of exteriority, the utopia momentarily defamiliarizes the arrangement of the society of which it is a part: what takes on the appearance of a natural order of things in mythic discourse, the apparently immutable laws of individual and social behavior, is revealed in the utopia to be a product of cultural and historical contingency. Refusing noncontradiction, and hence shattering the hypostatization of the present, the rhetorical machine that is the narrative utopia in effect becomes exemplary of what was then an emerging way of thinking about historical time. The utopia marks the potential immanence of the Other, or historical difference, in its own moment.[33]

The differentiations Marin so carefully establishes—between representation and ideology, on the one hand, and utopia on the other—resonate with the distinctions we discussed in the last chapter that Lefebvre makes between "spaces of representation," or the domain of the lived, and "representations of space," that of the conceived. Moreover, the connections go even deeper, as Marin then distinguishes between the discourse of utopia and that of critical theory, the latter described by Lefebvre as "perceived space." Marin maintains that the deconstruction or deterritorialization in the utopian text of the ideological parameters of one social situation clears the space for the construction of something new, the contours of the latter receiving one of its first elaborations in the neutral space represented by the utopia itself. The narrative utopia thereby maps the place of an imminent and concrete future forming *within* the horizons of its present, this emerging history serving as what Marin calls the "absent referent" of the form (*Utopics* 196).[34] The historical originality of the narrative utopia as a genre thus lies in its capacity to mediate between two different cultural and social realities, between the world that is and that which is coming into being.

This mapping occurs through the process Marin refers to as utopic *figuration,* a schematizing, or "preconceptual," way of thinking, taking the form in the utopian text of the "speaking picture," the narrative elaboration of the utopian society.[35] Marin describes such an operation as preconceptual—but it is better understood as pretheoretical, or in Lefebvre's terms, preperceptual—because while crucial aspects of a newly emergent social reality are present in the utopian figure, the relationship between these elements, dispersed as they are throughout the text, cannot yet be articulated. That is, the utopia presents a narrative *picture* of history-in-formation rather than the theoretical *description* of a fully formed historical situation. Thus, if the utopia fiction has an "anticipatory value," a way of marking the place of a future emerging in the present, it does so, Marin contends, "blindly" (*aveuglée*). This is because

> the present of Raphael and of More, the society which they try out *hic et nunc,* does not really allow the construction of the theoretical categories, or the articulation of its theoretical concepts. That will be the epistemological privilege of a new society, of which sixteenth-century England bears the symptoms of its emergence. We perceive then the function of utopic practice, which becomes visible in the play of "epistemological spaces" of the diverse discourses it brings into use: it is the "introducer" of the possibility of theoretical constructions, presented not in all their *theoretical* power—it is incapable of doing so, and the utopian thinker is not a historical prophet—but under the *poetic figurative* form. In other words, utopic practice, through the play of its discursive topics, does not construct a theoretical concept; rather, it sets the scene, the space of representation, the place of figurability, which is its imaginary schema and the sensuous framework. It would be, to speak the language of Kant, the schematizing activity of the social and political imagination which has not yet found its concept; a blind activity, but one that would trace for knowledge and for action the place, the topic, of its concept. A schema in quest of a concept, a model without structure, the figure produced by utopian practice is a sort of zero degree of the concept. (*Utopiques* 211; *Utopics* 163)

Beginning in the early part of the sixteenth century, utopian discourse represents one way for a modernizing society to represent itself critically to itself, a self-narration that, crucially, appears long before "the constitution of the scientific theory of society," by which Marin means Marx's historical materialism (*Utopics* 200).

The implications are profound of what Marin understands to be the relationship between figuration and theory, and, more generally, between what Lefebvre calls representations of space and spatial practice.[36] As Marin sees it, these operations of figuration always historically *precede* the more coherent and systematic "perceptions" of the world found in theoretical discourses; conversely, these theoretical models are only ever constituted retroactively. This latter work is performed through a critical rereading, reconstruction, or re-authoring of the original figurative presentations. In a later reflection on the critical project undertaken in *Utopiques,* Marin states,

> The theoretical discourse about utopia operates (like in dreams, the screen memory) by filling up the gaps and the blanks of the utopian text, of the

utopian space, by producing the systematic elements which are necessary to
make the text intelligible. This production was possible only *après coup,* in
a site supposed to be the true knowledge of the end of history that is the end
of utopia as well.[37]

The appearances of totalization and scientificity that one finds in these
kinds of theoretical discourses are in fact a product of this retrospective
view. The difference between what we might call the open-ended nature
of the figurations produced in the narrative utopia and the closure of
theoretical discourses—the end of history and the end of figurative or
perceptual practices—is suggested by Marin when he writes, "Utopic
practice introduces into the historical narrative and geographical report
the sudden distance by which the contiguities of space and time are broken and through which is discerned, in a flash of lightning, before it is
immobilized in the utopic figure and fixed in the 'ideal' representation,
the *other,* unlimited contradiction" (*Utopiques* 21; *Utopics* 7). Here the
fixing "ideal representation" may be thought of as the theoretical representation, or *Darstellung,* and the "other" as the open-ended possibilities of meaning, of supplementarity, and of historical difference that
the spatial play of the utopian figure makes available in its own present.[38] The danger arises when the perspective is reversed and the theoretical discourse usurps the place of the figuration, thereby transforming
social and cultural processes, the very life-blood of historical movement,
into dead reified entities. For both Lefebvre and Marin then, as for
Bloch before them, the point of final totalization, of absolute theoretical
knowledge, of science, and of the end of history, must always remain in
front of us.[39]

However, what is true for these different forms of *Darstellung* also
holds in the production of social space itself. In other words, the concrete structuration of social space that Lefebvre refers to as spatial practice, space organized into a system or a thing, only emerges over the
course of time as the end-product of the particular creative processes
taking place on the level of representations of space.[40] Moreover, for
these reasons, as Lefebvre himself continually emphasizes, the apparent
stability of these spatial practices or systems is in fact illusory. In a crucial way, it is in spaces of figuration, of the conception of space, or of
narrative—the spaces of architecture, urban planning, and literary
forms like the narrative utopia—where the possibilities for human
praxis and creativity exist. If the spatial practices within which these latter activities occur finally set concrete limits upon them, we can only

ever recognize these limits after the fact, for it is the very actions that take place on the level of conceived space that ultimately help determine what those limits may be. And it is for this reason that we need to take forms like the narrative utopia so seriously. Much more than the rhetorical play or idle day-dreams for which they are too often dismissed, narrative utopias participate in a significant way in the making of their social and cultural realities (which, of course, is not the same thing as saying these realities are not real; rather, it is to assert that the real is historical and always in process). Marin provides us with a way of genealogically approaching these works, of rewriting the moment of narrative figuration in them in terms of a coherent theoretical narrative, one that helps us better understand the place of these texts in the historical production of our own present. While such a rewriting is important precisely because it aids us in choosing our future actions, it should never be taken as a substitute for this crucial work of creating new "conceptions of space," or new utopias: for it is precisely a society without utopias, as Marin suggests, that has reached the "end of history."[41]

CRIME AND HISTORY

Up to this point, I have focused largely upon the broad contours and implications of Marin's methodology. However, the real power and suggestiveness of his genealogical reading lies in the doing, in the particular theoretical "rewritings" of More's work he offers us. Thus, in order to give a sense of the kinds of interpretive energies Marin himself marshals in his readings, I want to trace one thread in the rich interpretive tapestry he weaves from More's work. The example that I look at occurs not in Marin's discussion of the mapping of the island of Utopia that takes place in the second book, but in one of the brief preparatory sketches found in Book 1: the description of "The Commonwealth of the Polylerites in Persia" (More 75).[42] I have chosen this example precisely because it shows how rapidly the institutional being of the genre had become established. Written after the completion of Book 2, these sketches in Book 1 are part of More's own re-authorings of the earlier text, brief experiments, as it were, in what was now already the institutional *genre* of the narrative utopia.

Raphael Hythlodaeus introduces this utopian sketch as part of his rebuttal to the argument that capital punishment represents the most effective deterrent to the crime of theft. After observing that capital punishment runs contrary to the laws of God as well as proving an inducement to murder (for if murder and theft are punished in the same way, why should the thief not feel less compunction about killing his victim, thereby possibly escaping detection?), Hythlodaeus presents the Polylerites as an example of a society that has developed a superior method for dealing with these criminals:

> Now, in their land, persons who are convicted of theft repay to the owner what they have taken from him, not, as is usual elsewhere, to the prince, who, they consider, has as little right to the thing stolen as the thief himself. But if the object is lost, the value is made up out of the thieves' goods, and the balance is then paid intact to their wives and children. They themselves are condemned to hard labor. Unless the theft is outrageous, they neither are confined to prison nor wear shackles about their feet but, without any bonds or restraints, are set to public works. Convicts who refuse to labor or are slack are not put in chains but urged on by the lash. If they do a good day's work, they need fear no insult or injury. The only check is that every night, after their names are called over, they are locked in their sleeping quarters. (More 77)

The question of what might constitute a proper and effective impediment to property crime was an abiding concern in More's England. This is because incidents of theft had risen meteorically, hand-in-hand with a dramatic increase in the numbers of unemployed and potentially unemployable people inhabiting the island. More's great critical insight was to draw a linkage between this development and the processes of modernization already underway in his society. Hythlodaeus notes that the great mass of the unemployed is composed of retainers from the dissolving feudal estates, mercenary soldiers once engaged by the lords, and agricultural laborers who had been displaced from the common lands as these were enclosed for the grazing of large flocks of sheep. This latter development formed the backbone of England's burgeoning wool-exporting industry, and hence served as the motor for what Marx refers to as the "so-called primitive accumulation" of capital in fifteenth- and sixteenth-century England.[43] (Not coincidentally, negotiations over the English wool trade in the Netherlands had required More's real-world journey to the European continent, thereby providing the opportunity for his "introduction" to the fictional explorer Hythlodaeus.)[44] Moreover, as Richard Halpern shows, these displacements—in this case, literal "deterritorializations"—made these subjects available for a new kind of social coding or reterritorialization.[45]

However, before such work can take place, More finds it necessary to engage in another bit of ideological decoding—a decoding of what Northrop Frye calls the tragic inversion of the utopian comedy, the "contract myth" that would find the origins of crimes like theft in nature itself.[46] At this juncture in the debate, Hythlodaeus argues that these various groups had turned to crime not because of inherent character flaws, as his interlocutor maintains, but because their very survival depended on it. Capital punishment thus fails as a deterrent to theft because, as Hythlodaeus earlier remarks, "no penalty that can be devised is sufficient to restrain from acts of robbery those who have no other means of getting a livelihood" (More 61).

Hythlodaeus's "theoretical" discourse works toward demonstrating first that theft is a consequence of unemployment, and second that unemployment can be shown to be a product of a combination of social mismanagement and greed—the greed of those who monopolize public lands for wool-bearing sheep and the greed of those who maintain large armies to fulfill vain dreams of territorial expansion. Hythlodaeus follows this trenchant critique by proposing the following remedy to the current crisis:

> Make laws that the destroyers of farmsteads and country villages should either restore them or hand them over to people who will restore them and who are ready to build. . . . Let farming be resumed and let cloth-working be restored once more that there may be honest jobs to employ usefully that idle throng, whether those whom hitherto pauperism has made thieves or those who, now being vagrants or lazy servants, in either case are likely to turn out thieves. (More 69–71)

Marin points out that Hythlodaeus's plan to reduce crime in England resembles real-world policies advanced by both Henry VII and Henry VIII. And like those first proposed by England's monarchs, Hythlodaeus's reformist solutions are unworkable, for they attempt to fuse incompatible elements of two different social arrangements, "the precapitalist forms of a free market with a feudal structure of socially connected relations of production" (*Utopics* 151). That is, Hythlodaeus argues for both the restoration of feudal agrarianism *and* the expansion of the nascent cloth-producing industry in order to profitably employ all the retainers and soldiers displaced from the feudal estate. However, the estates that had originally engaged the retainers and soldiers formed a key part of the structural basis of feudal society; restoring feudal forms of agrarian production thus would necessitate recreating the estates, which in turn would reinstitute the very positions that the retainers and mercenaries had lost. On the other hand, only the increasingly rapid dissolution of these estates, and hence the social forms to which they gave rise, enabled the emergence of the protocapitalist industries. To create a situation where elements of both the old and the new, the archaic and the modern, exist together, as Hythlodaeus has suggested, proves to be impossible. His reformist solution collapses under the weight of its own internal contradictions, falling into the gap opened up between two different social formations.

Its failure then clears the ground for the appearance of the quite different kind of "solution" exemplified by the Polylerite society. Marin points out a contradiction between More's analysis of the causes of criminality in historical England and his deployment of the example of the Polylerites as a model of an ethically superior way for dealing with theft. For if the causal link that Hythlodaeus traces between theft and contemporary social conditions turns out to be true, then in the land of Polylerites—where scarcity, poverty, and, most importantly, greed are unknown—theft should not exist. A crucial slippage has thus occurred in the process of narration whereby the figure of the thief in historical England loses its signifier in the u-topos of Polylerite society. At the same time, Marin observes, the utopic figure of Persia, which, we are informed, encompasses the Polylerite society in a legal protectorate relationship, likewise has no direct referent in the contemporary conditions of historical England. Thus, we see a dislocation between two different social models: the critical one of historical England, with its tripartite division of the unemployed (thieves), workers, and society (the robbed); and the no-place of the Polylerite land, with its slaves, free citizens, and the encompassing protectorate of Persia guaranteeing the reproduction of the social relations between these two groups. But it is this very dislocation that enables the operations of utopian figuration, or the elaboration of a schema of what would have been in More's day a newly emerging system of social relationships. Indeed, according to Marin, the Polylerite society serves as "the paradigm, not of the ideal system for controlling crime in a real historical situation, but rather of a possible social system, simultaneously real and to come" (*Utopics* 157). In other words, the Polylerite society models before the fact what will turn out to be the real historical "solution" to England's contemporary social and economic crisis.

The key to the nature of the emerging social system figured in More's text is to be found in the description of the life of Polylerite slaves:

> Except for the constant toil, their life has no hardship. For example, as serviceable to the common weal, they are fed well at the public's expense, the

mode varying from place to place. In some parts, what is spent on them is raised by almsgiving. Though this method is precarious, the Polylerite people are so kindhearted that no other is found to supply the need more plentifully. In other parts, fixed public revenues are set aside to defray the cost. Elsewhere, all pay a specified personal tax for these purposes. Yes, and in some localities the convicts do no work for the community, but, whenever a private person needs a hired laborer, he secures in the market place a convict's service for that day at a fixed wage, a bit lower than what he would have paid for free labor. Moreover, the employer is permitted to chastise with stripes a hired man if he be lazy. The result is that they are never out of work and that each one, besides earning his own living, brings in something every day to the public treasury. (More 77)

While there may be no corresponding place for the English unemployed-criminal nexus in the Polylerite utopia, there is, as this passage makes exceedingly plain, a figure for the English worker: that of the slave. Thus, through this figure More at once effectively neutralizes the contemporary crisis of unemployment and creates a figure of the relationship between workers and capital in later historical England. Marin's own rewriting of this figure completes the loop begun in More's text: moving from critical theory (Hythlodaeus's analysis of the historical origins of crime) through utopian figuration (the commonwealth of Polylerites) and back into critical theory, a movement, to use Lefebvre's terms, from perception to conception and back into perception. Crucially, however, the passage through this middle term disrupts any simple identity between the first and the third. This is because in the intermediary term a powerful dislocation has occurred, transforming the very spatial practices that the first theoretical model had been marshaled to describe. It is thus in the utopian figure where the presence of history manifests itself, providing us with a snapshot of its process in motion. Marin illustrates the interweaving of these three moments of *Darstellung,* or what he calls "epistemological spaces," with the diagram shown in figure 1.

As this diagram makes evident, all the elements of a nascent capitalist social order are already at play in the figure of the Polylerite society. Work is represented as a commodity—the only commodity left to the slave—and, more important, as productive of surplus value: "The result is that they are never out of work and that each one, besides earning his own living, brings in something every day to the public treasury." Such a system of unequal exchange is guaranteed by what turns out to be the necessary presence of state power, here represented in the figure of the Persian protectorate. An apparent secondary echo of this new structure of relations can then be read in Book 2's description of Utopia proper:

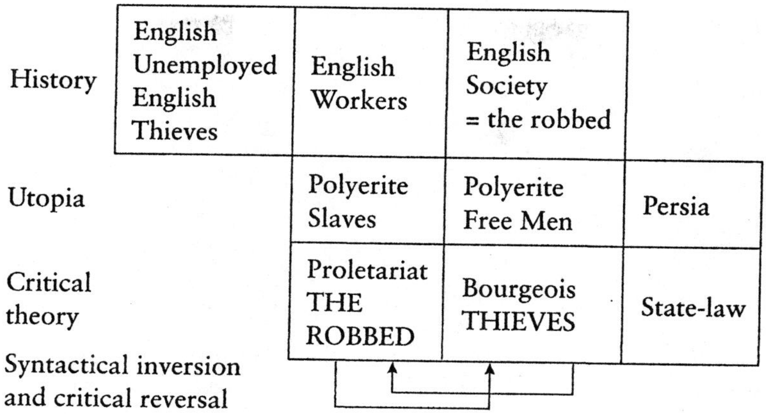

History	English Unemployed English Thieves	English Workers	English Society = the robbed	
Utopia		Polyerite Slaves	Polyerite Free Men	Persia
Critical theory		Proletariat THE ROBBED	Bourgeois THIEVES	State-law

Syntactical inversion
and critical reversal

Figure 1.   Model for the articulation of history, utopia, and critical theory. From Louis Marin, *Utopiques: Jeux d'espaces* (Paris: Les Éditions de Minuit, 1973), 209. Reproduced with permission.

"There is yet another class of slaves, for sometimes a hard-working and poverty-stricken drudge of another country voluntarily chooses slavery in Utopia. These individuals are well treated and, except that they have a little more work assigned to them as being used to it, are dealt with almost as leniently as citizens" (More 185). Here too we see the appearance of a third level of spatiality, that of spaces of representation—the Imaginary, the Ideological, the Mythological, or the way these relationships will be "lived." The ethical "naturalization" of this new set of relationships, implicit in the suggestion that any other situation would be even more undesirable for the worker, the "voluntary" slave, has the effect of dissimulating the fundamental structural inequality between "citizens" and "workers." Again, however, the critical demystification of such a mythology only comes later. Utopic practice is "the schematizing activity of the social and political imagination which has not yet found its concept"; only after the elaboration of a critical theory, or a new perception of space, Marin maintains, does the "concept or structure" of these relationships become intelligible (*Utopiques* 211; *Utopics* 163).

UTOPIA AND THE NATION-THING

Marin's analysis of More's text provides an important entry point for any discussion of later manifestations of the generic institution. However, in the end, Marin himself precludes any continuation of the critical project he has initiated, by questioning the validity of the utopian form once the "political and social imagination" has found its theoretical "voice." In the opening pages of *Utopiques,* Marin states that the methodological focus of his project is at once structural and historical. By historical, Marin means to indicate both the specific placement of More's *Utopia* in the transitional space between late feudal and early modern organizations of European social life, *and* what he takes to be the life span of the generic institution itself. His conclusions concerning the latter are already implicit in his description of utopia as a discursive mode that "designates the as-of-yet empty place of the scientific theory of society" (*Utopiques* 253; *Utopics* 198). On this basis, Marin determines, "Utopic discourse has a sort of critical validity within the ideology of which it is a part: it possesses this validity *historically,* between the moment of the appearance of these material possibilities and the moment the theory is elaborated, which would be, schematically, between the end of the fifteenth century and the first half of the nineteenth" (*Utopiques* 255; *Utopics* 199). According to Marin (and here he appears to be adopting Engels's argument from "Socialism: Utopian and Scientific"), Marx's elaboration in the middle of the nineteenth century of a scientific theory of capitalist society renders obsolete the figurative capacity of the narrative utopia. Although the form continues on in a kind of generic twilight existence, it no longer possesses the same "anticipatory critical value," the power to map figuratively emergent aspects of modern social life (*Utopiques* 256; *Utopics* 200).

I have already pointed out the dangers implicit in this kind of absolute privileging of the scientific, theoretical, or perceptual over the figurative or conceptual: the former, emerging from the place of retrospection, denies the processes of historical becoming at work in any present—a fact, moreover, of which Marin himself seems later to have become aware. However, Marin's original statements also illustrate a number of problems that have vexed Marxist cultural criticism more generally. First, Marin's project exemplifies what Raymond Williams astutely describes as the tendency in some forms of Marxist criticism toward an "epochal" focus: "It is usually very much better at distinguishing the large features of different epochs of society, as commonly between feudal and bourgeois, than at distinguishing between different phases of bourgeois society, and different moments within these phases."[47]

The epochal scale of Marin's analysis of *Utopia*'s mediatory and pretheoretical mappings is perhaps most tellingly evident in a remark following his delimitation of the active life history of the form. Here, Marin speculates, "There exist, no doubt, analogues to utopic discourse, in the discursive formations corresponding to the passage of one epoch to another in the economic formation of society, and in particular in the transition to and shifts from the Asiatic, classical, and feudal modes of production" (*Utopiques* 255–56; *Utopics* 199). Precisely what such analogous discourses might look like Marin does not say, except to note that, whatever their form, they will not be able to manifest, even figuratively, the "topic schema of a scientific theory of society." The assumptions underlying this proposition are then clear enough: utopia functions as a mediatory discourse for Marin only at those historical moments that he imagines on the geological scale of the transition between modes of production. In the subsequent chapters of this book, I focus, on the other hand, more on what Williams calls the "historical questions": both the local cultural and larger structural transformations that occur *within* the "long revolution" of Western capitalist modernity. Thus, by recalibrating what I still find to be the exceedingly powerful hermeneutic machinery Marin makes available to us, I read out of a variety of later utopian texts the genealogical traces of a number of more concrete and local histories.

There is another blind spot in Marin's analysis, one that equally vexes a good deal of traditional Marxist cultural and social analysis. Marin tends throughout *Utopiques* to focus on what have been among the privileged concerns for Marxist criticism: the economic formations of class, the commodity form, and money. And while his reading also illuminates the emergence of such non-economic institutions as centralized state power, these too appear largely subordinate to more properly economic concerns. In short, Marin's analysis is built upon a classical model of base-superstructure causality that then obscures the much more complex, overdetermined relationships between what are in fact various semi-autonomous dimensions of any social formation.

Marin's privileging of the economic basis does enable him to bring into brilliant clarity the ways that More's text offers a narrative figuration of the universalizing and abstracting processes of capitalist modernity—its end being what Georg Lukács calls "reification" and Theodor Adorno, the "identical"—which can then be read, for example, in the homology of commodity logic and liberal democratic citizenship.[48] Such processes evacuate the content from previously existing cultural heterogeneities, deterritorializing older particular hierarchies, roles, and systems of values in order to re-present every element within the new structure as exchangeable with any other: as commodity, as exchange value, as the money form, as juridico-political subject, and so forth. In More's text this emergent tendency is perhaps nowhere more effectively figured than in the image of the quite different forms of dress practiced in historical late-feudal England and protomodern Utopia. On the one hand, Hythlodaeus points toward the legally regulated, sumptuary excesses of the aristocratic classes in Europe, a form of conspicuous consumption meant to reinforce hierarchies of social distinction; on the other, we see in Utopia a form of dress that deploys "one and the same pattern throughout the island and down the centuries, though there is a distinction between the sexes and between the single and married" (More 127). The same process of abstraction also occurs on the level of space itself, as Hythlodaeus describes the cities of Utopia as "all spacious and magnificent, identical in language, traditions, customs, and laws. They are similar also in layout and everywhere, as far as the nature of the ground permits, similar even in appearance" (More 113). More here offers a figuration of the abstraction and homogenization of space—or what Lefebvre calls the production of "abstract space"—that is such a central dimension of modernity.[49]

However, as Žižek points out, this description of modernity and the processes of modernization—one shared by many classical Marxist and liberal democratic theorists alike—represents only one half of a more complex dialectic: "The universal function is founded upon an exception: the ideal leveling of all social differences, the production of the citizen, the subject of democracy [and, of course, the economic subject], is only possible through an allegiance to some particular."[50] Elsewhere, Žižek offers one example of this contradiction that resonates with Marin's reading of the Polylerite section of More's text:

> Freedom, for example: a universal notion comprising a number of species (freedom of speech and press, freedom of consciousness, freedom of commerce, political freedom, and so on) but also, by means of a structural necessity, a specific freedom (that of the worker to sell freely his own labor on the market) which subverts this universal notion. That is to say, this freedom is the very opposite of effective freedom: by selling his labor "freely," the worker *loses* his freedom—the real content of this free act of sale is the worker's enslavement to capital.[51]

Thus, these universalizing processes are, Žižek maintains, inherently unstable. Simply put, there is no steady state for modernity—"The only way for capitalism to survive is to expand."[52] Moreover, as Etienne Balibar notes, these universalizing tendencies themselves produce antagonisms, between various classes for example, that threaten to tear the social structure to pieces.[53] Hence, the need arises for some form of counterbalance to these unstable and antagonistic relationships, an imagined set of particular allegiances and common grounds, or what Žižek describes as a concrete and discrete "organization of enjoyment" that links the members of the social body together into a common identity. And, as both Žižek and Balibar maintain, the explicitly modern form taken by such an imaginary unity, or "reterritorialization," is that of the nation-state.[54]

If Žižek and Balibar present us with powerful theoretical descriptions of the double nature, or "constitutive contradiction," of modernity, More's *Utopia* offers one of its first and most effective narrative figurations. That is, I want to argue that the brilliance of More's text lies in its mapping of the relationship between these twin dimensions of an emergent modernity, of the reflux movement between universalization and particularization, of the de- and re-territorializations of social desires. Thus, in addition to the abstracting and universalizing tendencies so effectively articulated by Marin, what we see suddenly exploding forth in More's work is a radically new and deeply spatialized kind of political, social, and cultural formation—that of the modern nation-state.

The text's figuration of the spatial form of the nation-state occurs during Hythlodaeus's narration of the "birth" of Utopia:

> As the report goes and as the appearance of the ground shows, the island once was not surrounded by sea. But Utopus, who as conqueror gave the island its name (up to then it had been called Abraxa) and who brought the rude and rustic people to such a perfection of culture and humanity as makes them now superior to almost all other mortals, gained a victory at his very first landing. He then ordered the excavation of fifteen miles on the side where the land was connected with the continent and caused the sea to flow around the land. (More 113)

Marin reads this passage as a creation myth about the founding of the social order itself, a narrative depiction of what Freud later will describe more explicitly in works like *Totem and Taboo:* here, More unveils the repressed act of violence against "nature"—the "rude and rustic people" and the physical space of the peninsula itself—that lies at the moment of formation of "culture"—the Utopian citizenry and the island (*Utopics* 105–10). Read in this way, there is no sense in trying to find the place of such an event in the historical record; and yet, as with all mythic events, it is one that, as Žižek points out, "must none the less be presupposed if we want to account for the present state of things."[55]

However, decoding this passage in terms of a universal and ahistorical myth misses what is in fact so particularly modern about the "representation of space" produced by King Utopus. By digging the trench that creates the insular space (*Utopia Insula* in More's Latin original), Utopus marks a *border* where there had previously existed only an indistinct *frontier* between "neighboring peoples," a disjunctive act of territorial inclusion as well as exclusion that Anthony Giddens defines as a crucial dimension of the subsequent spatial practices of the modern nation-state.[56]

The creation of this new kind of spatiality likewise entails the production of a new form of cultural identity, a process similarly narrated in the pages of More's text. Later, during an extended reflection on religious practice in Utopian society, Hythlodaeus presents his audience with this second narrative of origins:

> Utopus had heard that before his arrival the inhabitants had been continually quarreling among themselves. He had made the observation that the universal dissensions between the individual sects who were fighting for their country had given him the opportunity of overcoming them all. From the very beginning, therefore, after he had gained the victory, he especially ordained that it should be lawful for every man to follow the religion of his choice, that each might strive to bring others over to his own, provided that he quietly and modestly supported his own by reasons nor bitterly demolished all others if his persuasions were not successful nor used any violence and refrained from abuse. If a person contends too vehemently in expressing his views, he is punished with exile or enslavement. (More 219–21)

This scene is one of the most celebrated in the entire book, representing for many later readers a call for religious tolerance that had been unknown in Europe, a tolerance that More's own later role as "defender of the faith" would make it impossible for him to put into practice.

This does not mean an embracing of a full-blown secularism, for almost immediately Hythlodaeus informs his listeners that Utopus also "conscientiously and strictly gave injunction that no one should fall so far below the dignity of human nature as to believe that souls likewise perish with the body or that the world is the mere sport of chance and not governed by any divine providence" (More 221). Nevertheless, this passage does effect a crucial decentering of the importance of religion in the construction and maintenance of communal cohesion, a decentering that is then "later" echoed in Book 1 in the suspension of the theological voice in the debate between Hythlodaeus and his interlocutors, a suspension marked in the text by the silence of Cardinal Morton during the entire exchange.[57]

Religious practice on the island does not possess the same unifying force that it had previously in historical Europe precisely because it has given way to a new form of communal identity, one defined first and foremost by spatiality, or the shared sense that one inhabited a single, extended, and bounded place. It is through the common habitation of the island territory and not by their religious allegiances that even Utopians who had never met one another could "imagine" they were one people.[58] Thus, while the spatial and cultural homogeneity of the Utopian cities figures them as part of an abstract universal space, this same feature signals their unity, or shared *national* identity: for their very sameness marks their particularity, their fundamental cultural *difference* from any other such spaces found outside the bounded nation.

The historical originality of such a representation of space is further indicated in the double meaning at play in Hythlodaeus's famous concluding statement, "Now I have described to you, as exactly as I could, the structure of that commonwealth (*Reipublicae*) which I judge not merely the best but the only one which can rightly claim the name of a commonwealth" (More 237). Utopia is not only the one place that could lay the claim to being ordered in the interest of the "public good"—the older definition of the Latin term *respublica* or its subsequent English translation "a common weale"—but is also the single place that was already a "commonwealth" as the term would subsequently be defined, as a synonym for the nation-state.[59]

Although he does produce the representation of space that gives rise to a new kind of spatial practice, there seems to be no place in this geographical and social entity for Utopus himself. Marin carefully shows how the location of the prince "disappears" when we translate Hythlodaeus's description of Utopia into a map: in both the geographical and political layout of the island—a federation of fifty-four cities—and in the capital city of Amaurotum—divided into four equal rectangular districts—there is literally no "site" for the centralized authority of the monarch.[60] Even the name of the capital, Amaurotum or "Shadowy City," suggests the immaterial status of such centers in the space of Utopia.

Marin further shows that money (gold) cannot be found anywhere in Utopia because it is already dispersed throughout the land: Utopians use gold, which is plentiful on the island, for making chamber pots, everyday utensils, the chains of slaves, and stigma for marking criminals (*Utopics* 138; More, 153). Halpern points out that this practice of ritually debasing something that is commonplace in the community suggests a desire that must be suppressed, and which therefore has the contradictory consequence of "transforming social value (gold as the congealed product of social labor: exploration, mining, refining) into a quality of the thing itself."[61] Something similar, I would suggest, takes place with the figure of the king: the sovereign has no place in Utopia precisely because she, he, or it, in the form of national *sovereignty,* is to be found everywhere and in everyone. And instead of this sovereignty being viewed as the product of the unique, spatio-social and political arrangements of the island, it appears as if it too were a fetishized thing itself— a form of what Žižek, drawing upon Lacan, calls the "Nation-Thing."[62]

A similar severing of the link between the spatialized identity and authority of the nation-state and its embodiment in the monarch—a linkage that had been codified during the Tudor reign under the myth of the "king's two bodies"—would play a crucial role in the deposing of Charles Stuart one hundred and twenty-five years after the writing of *Utopia.* Giddens notes,

> It can justifiably be claimed, I think, that neither the fact of a non-monarchical regime, nor the various theories of republicanism and libertarianism associated with the English Revolution could have come about without the prior establishing of a "discourse of sovereignty." As connected to political theory of the time, the concept of absolutism was open to elaboration because it juxtaposed the assertion of the supreme authority of an individual to a more generalized interpretation of state power, in which there was in fact no necessary role for kings or monarchs at all. Once the idea of sovereignty had effectively been turned into a principle of government, the way was open for it to become connected to that of "citizenship"—no longer applied within the confined reach of the urban commune but having as its reference the political "community" of the state as a whole.[63]

Charles I, astute literary critic that he was, recognized the vital role the narrative utopia played in the instantiation of this new kind of spatialized communal organization, declaring in 1642 his fear of "that new Utopia of Religion and Government into which they endeavor to transform this Kingdom"—one, of course, in which he would have no place.[64] King Utopus thus already figurally marks the place of the absolutist monarch in the real history of the formation of the modern nation-state: the monarch serves the role of a "vanishing mediator," dissolving older forms of social and cultural power, that of the feudal estates and the Roman Catholic Church, thereby clearing the space for the emergence of a new kind of centralized social, political, and cultural authority. At the same time, the monarch embodies the "organization of enjoyment" that later becomes articulated in the form of national culture, the latter evident in the nearly cultic worship in the late sixteenth century of the figure of Queen Elizabeth (or even today, in England's persistent fondness for the present "Queen Mum"). The monarch's own place, and the potential "third way" that it represented between late feudal and modern social formations, literally disappears once this extended transitional moment has come to an end.[65]

Reading *Utopia* as offering this kind of figuration of the modern nation-state also enables us to account for another of the major formal characteristics of this particularly modern generic institution. Halpern shows how More's narrative, through its critical neutralization of the "irrational" economy of expenditure and excess that More views as such a destructive aspect of late feudal aristocracy, ends up generating a figuration of the rationalized, zero-degree political economy of the nascent European bourgeois: "The myth of the neutral body or healthy subject, containing its own self-limiting needs, is the dialectical counter-image of the use value, an ideological construct needed to effect the tautological calibration of needs and goods under capitalism."[66] It is this representation of space that then accounts for the sense of Utopia as being outside of history, a social body at an absolute steady state.

While I find Halpern's insight here a persuasive account of one dimension of the figuration of modernity present in More's text, there is a way in which excess, the unassimilable remainder that at once grounds such a steady state and precludes its absolute closure, reemerges on the level of the narrative form itself. This occurs in that dimension of the genre that at once distinguishes it from earlier discussions of an ideal society and makes the reading so tedious for a later public of what were in fact electrifying narratives for their contemporary audiences: the careful and detailed elaboration of various aspects of the practices, behaviors, idiosyncrasies, and values, in short, the culture, of this world—what Suvin calls the "culturally current socio-political categories," Barthes, the "details" of desire, and Jameson, the elaboration of the "machinery," the condensation of necessity, that enables new kinds of freedoms to proliferate around it.[67]

Similarly, in the latter pages of *Utopia*, More establishes another pattern that will be replicated in subsequent manifestations of the genre: rather than coming to any kind of closure, Hythlodaeus's description breaks off, to which "More" can only respond, "I first said, nevertheless, that there would be another chance to think about these matters more deeply and to talk them over with him more fully. If only this were some day possible!" (More, 245). "More deeply" and "more fully" precisely because the depths and fullness of such a discourse, its closure, is finally impossible. That the narrative work of the utopia is a potentially infinite, open-ended one is then suggested in a number of ways in subsequent manifestations of the form: for example, in the "incomplete" texts of Bacon or Jack London, the latter literally breaking off in mid-sentence; in the tendency of narrative utopias to give birth to sequels, such as Bellamy's *Equality*, the rambling second volume of *Looking Backward*; and in the sheer dizzying extent of the utopian writings of Charles Fourier.

It is in this formal practice that More offers us an early figuration of one of the central narrative mechanisms by which the bond that produces the imaginary community is articulated. Žižek points out that such a bond can never be grasped directly, and when asked to describe it, we retreat to strategies that bear an uncanny resemblance to those formally codified in More's text: "All we can do is enumerate disconnected fragments of the way our community organizes its feasts, its rituals of mating, its initiation ceremonies, in short, all the details by which is made visible the unique way a community *organizes its enjoyment.*"[68] Crucially, Žižek maintains that the Nation-Thing can never be reduced to these features, but rather appears as an ineffable excess expressed through them. It is this form of particularization, this excess, that then "categorically resists," as Žižek puts it, the universalizing tendencies of modernization, the production, which we also see at work in More's text, of abstract economic and political-juridical disciplinary subjects.[69]

That More's *Utopia* presents a picture of an England transformed—and not, as first Hythlodaeus and then some later critics maintain, a skewed re-presentation of the communities recently discovered in the New World—was understood by many of the work's first readers. Even the details in the description of the island work to strengthen this connection: the fifty-four cities in Utopia refer to the fifty-three counties and the city of London in historical England; the strange ebb and flow of Utopia's Anydrus River is the same as that of the Thames; and the description of the river's bridge makes it almost identical to London Bridge.[70] However, More's text works to establish an even more fundamental link between these two spatial forms. Jeffrey Knapp argues, "What Utopia and England share is precisely the negativity constituted *in toto* by Utopian insularity . . . 'aparted' England has not only found its negative image in Utopia, but refound through Utopia its own negativity as both an island and an old Nowhere itself."[71] To be a Nowhere is not, however, to be without place. Rather, it is to be a whole unto oneself, an *insula,* a world apart, an enclosed and bordered social, political, and cultural totality; indeed, as Marin emphatically states, "In fact, Utopia never admits anything exterior to itself; it is for itself its own original reality" (*Utopiques* 137; *Utopics* 102). This "otherworldliness" then forms the basis of both a Utopian *and* an emerging English social and cultural identity. In other words, in both Utopia and the "not yet" existent English nation-state that it models, to be in the world is to be represented—at once on the levels of the perceived, the conceived, and the lived—in concretely spatial terms. The history of modernity, as More's work already shows, will be a history that takes place both through and in terms of this spatiality.

The modern genre of the narrative utopia emerges in England at the very beginnings of the transformations that will make the real-world island into the first of the modern nation-states. Indeed, England represents the place where the possibility of "nationness" itself first takes root; as Liah Greenfeld puts it, "The birth of the English nation was not the birth of a nation; it was the birth of the nations, the birth of nationalism."[72] At this crucial historical juncture then, the interchange between the imaginary community of Utopia and the "imagined community" of the nation-state works to instantiate the latter spatial practice in its distinctly modern form. Indeed, in More's text, the nation itself is a product of the operations of utopian figuration: a representation of space that helps shape both the practice and lived experience of space. Because Utopia is Nowhere, *not* a place in the world—or equally importantly, not the identity of any actually existing community—it offers the possibility of redefining what "place" and collective identity might themselves mean. To put it another way, More's *Utopia* helps usher in the conceptual framework or representation of space of "nationness" within which the particularity of each individual nation can then be represented.

The question of what would have enabled such a conception of space suddenly to develop in More's historical moment is a rich and complex one. The elaboration of all the spatial practices, as well as their complex interrelationships, that serve as the preconditions for such a monumental development would comprise another book in itself. However, there is one aspect of contemporary spatial practices that stands out as particularly worthy of emphasis. This is the spatial practice that, in fact, enables Hythlodaeus's own "discovery" of Utopia: "He left his patrimony at home—he is a Portuguese—to his brothers, and, being eager to see the world, joined Amerigo Vespucci and was his constant companion in the last three of those four voyages which are now universally read of" (More, 51).

Again, I do not mean to suggest here that the conception of space found in More's text is one imported from the places contacted through these voyages. Nor do I want to argue that it is imperialism itself that enabled the new spatial *Darstellung* found in More's narrative—although the text itself does famously offer an early figuration of the mythology that would later be used to justify imperial expansion:

> The inhabitants who refuse to live according to their laws, they drive from the territory which they carve out for themselves. If they resist, they wage war against them. They consider it a most just cause for war when a people which does not use its soil but keeps it idle and waste nevertheless forbids the use and possession of it to others who by the rule of nature ought to be maintained by it. (More, 137)

However, as Knapp points out, for more than a century the English lagged behind the Spanish and their other European competitors in the establishment of settler colonies in the Americas, and this led to a "turn inward" in Renaissance English letters, where that which could not yet be accomplished in the world was then achieved in the realm of imagination. Moreover, this "turn inward" was not only imaginary, and already in the sixteenth century (and indeed earlier) the violences rationalized away by More's statements were being turned against those neighboring peoples—the Welsh, the Scots, and the Irish—who would be "forged" together in the formation of the spatial enclosure and organization of enjoyment found in the *British* nation-state (indeed, it is worth keeping in mind that the "plantation system" articulated in More's narrative and later put into such effective practice in the New World was already in place in Ireland by the later sixteenth century).[73]

More significant than either knowledge of the cultures of the Americas or the subsequent colonialism and imperialism practiced there, the fact of *contact* itself provides one of the significant spatial preconditions for the figuration of the nation-state. The self, as Nietzsche points out, is always first defined in relationship to the Other, for it is only by occupying the imagined perspective of the Other that we begin to compile those characteristics, those organizations of enjoyment, by which we define ourselves. The trauma of contact with new worlds only a quarter century before the publication of *Utopia* meant that the figure of this Other began to loom even more significantly than it had before in the European imagination. Contact with the cultures of the Americas suggested, on the one hand, something of the contingency and relativity of European customs, a contingency that in turn is set into play in the rhetorical machinery of More's text and other humanist texts like it. On the other hand, this event also engendered a new need to *define* those things that made the cultures of Europe different from those of the new world and, ultimately, once the bond of the *consensus fidelium,* the foundational European-wide community of believers, had been shattered, different from each other as well. While this new spatial practice did not cause the conception of space figured in More's work, it did play a vital role in opening up the space wherein such a production could occur: Utopia is thus to be located, as Hythlodaeus suggests and Marin bears out, in the space *between* Europe and the Americas, the old world and the new. And much the same thing can be said of the representation of space we now refer to as the nation-state. Crucially, all of this highlights the illusory nature of the nation-state's imagined historical closure: the nation-state is always already part of a *world system,* its particular spatial bounding and collective subjectivity formed in relationship to the other "elements" composing such a system.[74]

More himself would remain profoundly ambivalent about the new conception of space figured in his text. For More at least, the imagined community of the nation had no more worldly substantiality than the imaginary community of Utopia. This is perhaps nowhere more readily apparent than on the level of the narrative's language. The Utopian tongue, no less than that of the English people (the common vernacular speech being, as Benedict Anderson has shown us, of central importance in the formation of a national community) remain largely absent presences in More's text, the latter still written in the "eternal" script-language of Latin, the "tongue" of the European Roman Catholic educated elite. (Although, interestingly, in Giles's prefatory letter we do get the *written* Utopian alphabet, thus, coincidentally, bearing out another of Anderson's central points: that the standardization of the *written* vernacular, by way of the new printing technologies, actually precedes that of the *spoken* national language.[75]) Thus, when England did truly become a "world apart," breaking free of the authority of Rome and consequently shattering once and for all the unity of the *consensus fidelium*—a possibility that Marin sees already inscribed in the later pages of *Utopia* (*Utopics* 183–184)—More would disavow his own earlier narrative vision.

More's resistance to the emerging reality of the sovereign nation-state ultimately cost him his life. Greenfeld reads More's trial following his refusal to acknowledge the king as the supreme head of the *national* church as an expression of the conflict between two incommensurable conceptions of social and cultural space:

> More than four hundred years later, [More's] trial appears profoundly symbolic. Here were the two fundamental worldviews, the pre-nationalist and the nationalist, pitted against each other. And since these worldviews defined men's very identities, no intermediate position was possible between them; there was a cognitive abyss, a clear break in continuity. The unified world Sir Thomas More saw through his inner vision was a vanishing world, and he was a lonely figure among the growing numbers of neophytes of the new, national, faith.[76]

While Greenfeld rightly highlights the conflicting attitudes illuminated by this world historical event, the "break in continuity" between More's own worldview and that which would follow is perhaps not as absolute as she claims: for More's own specific ideological position, at the time of the writing of *Utopia* at least, his "Christian Humanism," represents another kind of "vanishing mediator" bridging the gap between these two different and incommensurable socio-spatial realities.

As Marin and others point out, the solution that More and his fellow Christian humanists imagined to the present social crisis entailed fusing together the religious and secular powers that had been balanced against one another in feudal Europe, with the humanists themselves forming a kind of intellectual leadership caste.[77] It is the mediatory nature of this "solution" that accounts for one of the peculiar qualities of Utopian cultural life. A number of critics have pointed out that Utopian society in many of its aspects resembles a medieval monastery, an institution that More himself had nearly entered in his youth, and which maintained a certain appeal for him throughout his life. As in the monastery, nearly every aspect of Utopian social life is subject to a minute disciplinary regulation and continuous observation. Greenblatt, for example, shows how Hythlodaeus's accounts of both work and travel in Utopia "begin with almost unlimited license and end with almost total restriction."[78]

However, rather than signaling a retreat to the ideals of medieval Catholicism, More's use of the monastery as a model for his fictional social organization produces something completely new; for, as Colin Starnes observes, "this monastic way of life among the Utopians, if this is what it is to be called, was in no way separated from a secular society operating independently and alongside it as in the Middle Ages."[79] Instead, More transforms the *whole* of Utopian society into a monastery, thereby advancing a representation of space that bears an uncanny resemblance to that of another of his contemporaries—ironically, the very man who would become for More, in his role as a defender of the faith, a most hated foe:

> Luther . . . removed the brackets from medieval religious thought. . . . It is because Luther represents a conscious and indeed agonized renewal of the habituated religious thinking of the Middle Ages that he strikes down the artificial isolation of monastic life. His aim is thus a regeneration of religious value or end-orientation; but in so doing, without realizing it, he liberates the nascent rationalism of the monasteries, which are now able to spread to all domains of life.[80]

The famous "medieval communism" in More's utopian fiction functions in much the same way: in Utopian society, More imagines the leveling of the lineaments of the old order, its distinctions of class and caste, its confusing specificities of local "language, traditions, customs and laws," and thereby clears the space for the emergence of a new totalizing organization of social practice that will take place within, and by means of the subject-object of modern history, the nation-state. And like Luther's vision of a truly religious Europe, the other more radical possibilities also figured in *Utopia* vanish as the new social forms take root.

UTOPIA AND THE WORK OF NATIONS

More imagines Utopia as a "world apart" and, in so doing, contributes to the development of a new way of imagining place in *this* world. This way of first conceiving, and later living and perceiving, space will become increasingly dominant over the subsequent course of modern history. If in *Utopia* the imaginary community of the nation-state was itself still a product of utopian figuration, an emerging historical reality blocked out by the narrative operations of the text, by the time of the explosive proliferation of the *English* utopias of the next century—to name only a few of the more well-known examples today, Bacon's *The New Atlantis,* Gabriel Platt's *A Description of the Famous Kingdom of Macaria* (1641), Gerrard Winstanley's *The Law of Freedom in a Platform* (1651), James Harrington's *Oceana* (1656), and Margaret Cavendish's *The description of a new world, call'd The Blazing-world* (1666) (Bacon, Platt, and Harrington's works all directly acknowledging their reliance on More's *Utopia* for their model)—both the institutionality of the genre and that of the nation-state have become firmly established.[81] The subsequent tradition of the utopian narrative takes the nation-state as the object of its estranging critique, while continuing to bolster the sense of the national community as a subject in its own right, as an autonomous agent that performs a vital role in shaping the unfolding narrative of modernity. Thus, even in a work like Bacon's *New Atlantis,* the problem of defining the national community is still at center stage. While it appears that the concerns with society as a whole that were so central to More (and which would once again come to the fore in Winstanley's and Harrington's utopias) have apparently given way to a more particular interest in promoting the institution of the new "natural philosophy," or empirical science, it was precisely through the emerging institutions and ideologies of science that the "modernity," and hence the historical uniqueness, of the society as a whole, the English nation, proclaims itself in the first half of the seventeenth century.[82]

Equally important, it is by way of this relationship between the discursive topos of the utopia and that of the nation that another level of the "situatedness" of the institutional form of the narrative utopia reveals itself: for the very idea of a sovereign national community served as a vital weapon in the ideological arsenal of the emerging European bourgeoisie—precisely the "class," as Marin's work suggests, that composes the citizenry of Utopia. The narrative utopia thus provides this rising class with a mechanism by which to assault the bulwarks of its opponents—first, the ruling alliance of the feudal estates and the Catholic Church, and then later the absolutist monarch and the landed aristocracy—and, in turn, formulate its own, original, historical "place."[83] An awareness of the role of the narrative utopia in helping to instantiate the spatial practices, representations of space, and spaces of representation most amenable to this rising middle class is evident later, for example, in Jonathan Swift's great satiric work *Gulliver's Travels* (1726), for an attack on the generic form of the narrative utopia itself is an important dimension of his conservative assault on the cultural values and practices of this ascending public.[84] The spatialized national subject formulated in the utopian narrative thus serves as one of the original forms of the collective subject of *class*—for it is by way of national identity that the bourgeoisie comes to "identify" itself. In this respect, the narrative utopia appears to play an important role in the formation of the preconditions for the rise of the greatest literary invention of this class, the English novel, whose own subject, as Armstrong and Tennenhouse point out, is nothing less than a transportable version of the interiorized national space.[85]

However, there are in fact two groups of "noncitizens" who appear in Utopia. Thus, if the ambassadors from the distant country of Anemolian represent the older aristocracy of historical Europe (in their attempt to "dazzle" the citizenry of Utopia through "the grandeur of their apparel," they instead become the object of ridicule for even the children of the island [More 155]), then the slaves, as we saw earlier, are the figure for the subsequent Other to the bourgeoisie, the working class. In this respect, More also offers a figuration of another shift that will occur in the project of the narrative utopia. Once the bourgeoisie has become the hegemonic class, and the nation the naturalized form of the social totality, the operations of neutralization that take place in the narrative utopia will be redirected against those groups that threaten the stability of this social and spatial arrangement.[86] The critical deterritorializing energies of the form also come to serve as a dedifferentiating cultural logic, a way of suppressing ethnic, class, and other forms of group heterogeneity in favor of a shared identity determined by the inhabitation of an extended, but bounded, space. At this point, the classical narrative utopia serves as a way to recontain the anxiety-producing clash of publics that occurs *within* the boundaries of the national community.

It is exactly this kind recontainment operation that takes place in Bellamy's *Looking Backward,* the great narrative utopia published more than three and a half centuries after More's work first gave rise to this quintessential modern institution. *Looking Backward* imagines a negation of the conflicting ethnic, racial, and class publics that inhabit the social and cultural landscape of the late-nineteenth-century United States and, in so doing, figuratively blocks out the space from within which will emerge a new kind of national identity—an operation that turns on the simple act of "forgetting."

CHAPTER THREE

Writing the New American (Re)Public

Remembering and Forgetting
in Looking Backward

It is this forgetting—a minus in the origin—that constitutes
the *beginning* of the nation's narrative.
                    Homi K. Bhabha, "DissemiNation"

REMEMBERING

This chapter focuses on the indispensable role that, as Homi K. Bhabha
suggests, "forgetting" plays in the construction of national subjectivity:
"Being obliged to forget becomes the basis for remembering the nation,
peopling it anew, imagining the possibility of other contending and lib-
erating forms of cultural identification."[1] Most of the classical ideo-
logues of nationalism assert that the nation is a form of collective identity grounded in a shared sense of the past. Ernest Renan, for example,
maintains in his influential 1882 lecture, "*Qu'est-ce qu'une nation?*"
(the subject of Bhabha's comments as well), that two things constitute
the "soul or spirit" of the nation, one oriented toward the past and the
other to the present: "One is the possession in common of a rich legacy
of memories; the other is present-day consent, the desire to live together,
the will to perpetuate the value of the heritage that one has received in
an undivided form. Man, Gentlemen, does not improvise. The nation,
like the individual, is the culmination of a long past of endeavours,
sacrifice, and devotion."[2]

Yet, Renan's contemporary, Edward Bellamy, the author of
Looking Backward, 2000–1887 (1888), the single most influential narrative utopia of the nineteenth century, comes to a very different conclusion. While he too holds on to the importance, stressed by Renan, of
devotion and will, the "wish" to perform "great deeds together," as cen-

tral aspects of the unified national self, Bellamy suggests in his narrative utopia that the *divisions* produced by multiple "legacies of memories" have made the realization of any American nation heretofore impossible. For Bellamy, the modern American nation-state can be formed only through a collective act of forgetting, a breaking of the bonds of the past, and a reorientation toward a single future. This shift in focus is stressed in the fictitious Preface to *Looking Backward,* dated December 26, 2000. Here, an unnamed historian from Shawmut College, Boston, writes, "The almost universal theme of the writers and orators who have celebrated this bimillennial epoch has been the future rather than the past, not the advance that has been made, but the progress that shall be made, ever onward and upward, till the race shall achieve its ineffable destiny."[3] The narrative utopia that unfolds after this declaration works to give a form to a nascent "destiny," a new American national subjectivity, that in Bellamy's day still largely remains "ineffable."

As we too celebrate the "bimillennial epoch," it seems appropriate to look backward to the more than a century that has passed since the first publication of Bellamy's narrative utopia, and in so doing, to note a particular act of forgetting that has occurred in the formation of the U.S. literary canon in relation to Bellamy's once-celebrated work. Few books in the history of American literature can rival the contemporary success of *Looking Backward.* Along with Harriet Beecher Stowe's *Uncle Tom's Cabin* and Lew Wallace's *Ben-Hur,* Bellamy's work stands as one of the most widely read and discussed American books of the nineteenth century. In the United States alone, the book sold more than 200,000 copies within two years of publication, 400,000 by the appearance of its sequel, *Equality* (1897), and eventually became the second American work of fiction with sales to surpass the one million mark. It was also widely circulated in Great Britain, and translations were quickly executed in German, French, Norwegian, Russian, and Italian.[4] The book's literary influence was equally tremendous: it spawned a host of imitators, "sequels," and responses, ranging from Ludwig Geissler's simplistic defense of Bellamy's ideas, *Looking Beyond* (1891), to Arthur Dudley Vinton's nasty critique, *Looking Further Backward* (1890). *Looking Backward* is so central to the explosive growth of the literary industry of utopia that Kenneth M. Roemer dates his important survey of American utopian fiction from its publication.[5]

Moreover, the work had a direct impact on the political discourse of its day. *Looking Backward* is one of only a handful of narrative utopias that actually produced a specific political movement, in this case, the one

Bellamy himself christened Nationalism. Although short-lived, the Nationalist Movement influenced both the emerging platform of the larger Populist Party and progressive calls for, among other reforms, the nationalization of public utilities.[6] All of this led the philosopher John Dewey, the historian Charles Beard, and the publisher Edwin Weeks in 1935 to judge Bellamy's narrative of all the works published in the preceding half century second in importance only to Marx's *Capital*.[7]

However, not long after this observation Bellamy's narrative appears to have all but vanished from the American cultural imagination. In an essay first published in the early 1960s concerning the great European "dystopias" of Zamyatin, Huxley, and Orwell, Irving Howe concludes that the very notion of utopia is antithetical to the essential pragmatism of the American character: "Few of us ever having cultivated the taste for utopia, fewer still have suffered the bitter aftertaste of antiutopia."[8] Howe's statement betrays both the "conservative liberalism" of fifties-style American consensus history—a certain Cold War amnesia that enabled many intellectuals to forget the more "radical" (a code word encompassing everything from religious progressives and agrarian populists to anarchists and Marxist-Leninists) cultural producers of the American past—and a high cultural bias that blinds him to the efflorescence of popular anti-utopian and dystopian science fiction literature of his day.[9]

Nevertheless, his observation does usefully remind us of the deep historicity of the utopian literary tradition of which Bellamy's text is a major part. That is, Bellamy's vision of a society restructured in its basic and fundamental form is itself a product of a moment when American society was in the midst of a deep and thoroughgoing reorganization, the consequences of which would shape the ideologies of national identity and the distribution of cultural power well into the next century. One of the great attractions of *Looking Backward* for a late-nineteenth-century audience lay in its comforting portrayal of a new and much-improved social order rising out of the upheavals experienced in the present (although Roemer elsewhere usefully cautions us against us too quickly taking such a "turbulent-times theory," or any other single factor for that matter, as *the* explanation for the book's tremendous popularity and influence, an insight I will develop in other ways as well).[10] By the time of Howe's own quite different cultural present—and perhaps in our own as well—nothing seems more alien than a generic tradition that takes the fundamental malleability of the social order as its starting point.

In the following pages, I want to hold on to this sense of the alienness of Bellamy's narrative utopia, in order to look backward on the unique historical situation from which it emerged. *Looking Backward* was shaped by, and in turn shaped, the cultural, social, and political debates of its day—a moment when the very definition of the American republic was being rapidly transformed by the "new" publics that were coming to inhabit it. If, as Jay Martin claims, the utopia was "the true national novel" in the late-nineteenth-century United States, it was so precisely because the generic institution of the narrative utopia had long served as a privileged vehicle for imagining the modern nation-state.[11] In *Looking Backward,* Bellamy offers a vision of just what a new American nation would look like, a nation that would require, not unlike the amnesia evidenced in Howe's 1950s essay, a fundamental restructuring of the memories, and hence the very identities of the subjects composing it.

THE CONTEMPORARY CUL-DE-SAC

Before developing his "speaking picture" of social life at the dawn of the twenty-first century, Bellamy first provides his readers with his take on the present, capturing in the opening pages of the narrative the sense many Americans had of the precarious nature of their current situation. Employing one of the most famous of the text's many parables, Bellamy's protagonist Julian West—a young, upper-middle-class Bostonian who, after spending more than a century in a hypnotic slumber, magically awakens to the transfigured world of the year 2000—compares 1880s society to "a prodigious coach which the masses of humanity were harnessed to and dragged toilsomely along a very hilly and sandy road" (*LB*, 27).[12] Many of those yoked to this coach fall under the ceaseless prodding of the driver, Hunger, and are brutally crushed under the wheels of the lumbering vehicle.[13] Although the seats at the summit of the coach are "breezy and comfortable," they are equally "insecure"—for, "at every sudden jolt of the coach persons were slipping out of them and falling to the ground, where they were instantly compelled to take hold of the rope and help to drag the coach on which they had before ridden so pleasantly" (*LB*, 27).

This parable, with its deep moral indignation at the terrible spectacle of contemporary capitalist society, also gives voice to other, less immediately evident fears of Bellamy and his Gilded Age audience. The explosive acceleration of industrialization following the Civil War had produced a scale of labor exploitation that seemed to rival that of the now defunct institution of slavery. At the same time, the process of industrial modernization dissolved the underpinnings of an older social order, so that even those whose positions had long been secure now risked being swept up in a maelstrom of riot and poverty. This latter group was composed of the American genteel class of merchants, intellectuals, small-scale manufacturers, clergymen, and gentleman farmers, with roots often extending back to the Jeffersonian republic: a group composed of figures like West, whose income we are told consisted solely of the interest collected on investments made by his great-grandfather; and, in a different fashion, by Bellamy himself, who hailed from a long line of New England ministers (his great-grandfather was a friend and disciple of Jonathan Edwards).[14] From their point of view, the gross social inequities marked out in Bellamy's parable of the coach represented only one aspect of the larger nightmare of industrializing America, that of *disorder*. The current crisis was then as much a product of the laboring class as that of the capitalists, for social disorder also manifested itself in the strikes, work stoppages, and layoffs, which, as West declares, "had been nearly incessant ever since the great business crisis of 1873" (*LB,* 30). (His observation is accurate: the last quarter of the nineteenth century witnessed, in addition to the more spectacular conflagrations like the Great Upheaval and the Haymarket riot, more than thirty-seven thousand strikes involving nearly seven million workers.[15]) Caught in a vise between the ferocious power of the new industrial oligarchy and the increasing militancy of the labor movement, the members of West's and Bellamy's genteel America could only look on as the struggles of the present threatened to give birth to an even greater disorder—that of a new revolution, "a general overturn" of the coach "in which all would lose their seats" (*LB,* 28).

Worst of all, this disorder seemed to be prevalent nearly everywhere on the globe. Mrs. Bartlett, the mother of West's nineteenth-century fiancée, observes that especially in Europe—with the memory of the 1871 Paris Commune still fresh in mind—"it is far worse even than here." She then offers this revealing anecdote: "I asked Mr. Bartlett the other day where we should emigrate to if all the terrible things took place which those socialists threaten. He said he did not know any place now where society could be called stable except Greenland, Patagonia, and the Chinese Empire" (*LB,* 33). The chaos had transformed the present world into a nightmare where the possessing classes suffered from anxiety about the future, and the dispossessed experienced even more material hardships. The two groups were alike, however, in that they were both slaves to a viciously competitive social order. And no resolution to this predicament seemed forthcoming. The promise of social progress which had long served as the rationalization of rapid industrial development had apparently proved empty: as West later reflects, a good number of nineteenth-century observers "believed that the evolution of humanity had resulted in leading it into a *cul-de-sac,* and that there was no way of getting forward" (LB, 188).

The abstract menace of this present situation took concrete form in the figure of the advocate of violent and revolutionary social change. Early in the narrative, West observes,

> The nervous tension of the public mind could not have been more strikingly illustrated than it was by the alarm resulting from the talk of a small band of men who called themselves anarchists, and proposed to terrify the American people into adopting their ideas by threats of violence, as if a mighty nation which had but just put down a rebellion of half of its own numbers, in order to maintain its political system, were likely to adopt a new social system out of fear. (LB, 32)

This linkage between class conflict, violence, and anarchism had been seared into the American national consciousness only two years before the publication of Bellamy's novel with the Mayday events at Chicago's Haymarket Square. During a rally organized by local anarchists to protest police brutality in breaking up a strike at the McCormick Harvester Company, a figure (whose identity and motivations were never ascertained) tossed a bomb from the crowd. A number of police officers were fatally wounded; the survivors charged into the assembled workers, thereby instigating a full-scale riot. The event became a *cause célèbre* in the national press, proof to many of the insidious designs of the growing workers' movement, and served as the excuse for stepping up crackdowns on the organized left, strikers, and other labor agitators.[16]

As Bellamy's West saw it, little good could come from these violent activities. Still speaking from the perspective of the nineteenth century, he opines, "the workingmen's aspirations were impossible of fulfillment for natural reasons, but there were grounds to fear that they would not discover this fact until they had made a sad mess of society" (LB, 31). However, from the viewpoint of utopia achieved, these activities appear in an even more dubious light. Later in the text, West asks Dr. Leete, his host and indefatigable guide to life in the twenty-first century, "What part did the followers of the red flag take in the establishment of the new order of things?" He responds,

They had nothing to do with it except hinder it, of course. . . . They did that very effectually while they lasted, for their talk so disgusted people as to deprive the best-considered projects for social reform of a hearing. The subsidizing of those fellows was one of the shrewdest moves of the opponents of reform. . . . No historical authority nowadays doubts that they were paid by the great monopolies to wave the red flag and talk about burning, sacking, and blowing people up, in order, by alarming the timid, to head off any real reforms. What astonishes me most is that you should have fallen into the trap so unsuspectingly. (LB, 170)

Although a subsequent footnote in the text states that Leete's theory about capitalist sponsorship of anarchism is "wholly erroneous," its voicing illuminates crucial aspects of Bellamy's own assessment of the present situation. By hinting that the supporters of a sometimes violent political praxis might be no more than the paid agents of the opponents of reform, Bellamy points toward a more universally damning supposition: that self-interest rather than the collective good will always turn out to be the prime motivation behind the actions of these political agents—and in this, they become no different than the powers they challenge. Drawing upon the unquestionable force of future retrospection, Bellamy can thus deny any potential efficacy to the political strategies of both the anarchists and the socialists, two movements that were inseparably (and also erroneously) bound in the popular imagination of Bellamy's genteel America. Collective struggle, rather than being a means to social change, proves to be one more of the forces which has led society into its present "cul-de-sac."

Shattering this historical stasis and moving from the world represented in the parable of the coach to the possible world of Dr. Leete's twenty-first century would thus involve the negation in historical America of all such forces, a negation that Bellamy figuratively achieves by refusing these movements any place in the historical narrative. As we shall see shortly, this is but one of the significant lacunae located in *Looking Backward*—absences that will ultimately define the specific class dimensions of Bellamy's project of national reconstruction.

FRAGMENTATION

Bellamy differed little from most late-nineteenth-century, middle-class, progressive thinkers in his fear of the consequences of direct action on the part of the workers.[17] However, the specter of violence was not the only reason for Bellamy's reservations concerning radical politics. A short time after the publication of *Looking Backward*, Bellamy wrote to his patron William Dean Howells, explaining why he chose the name "nationalism" for his nascent political party:

> Every sensible man will admit there is a big deal in a name especially in making first impressions. In the radicalness of the opinions I have expressed I may seem to out-socialize the socialists, yet the word socialist is one I never could well stomach. In the first place it is a foreign word in itself and equally foreign in all its suggestions. It smells to the average American of petroleum, suggests the red flag, with all manner of sexual novelties, and an abusive tone about God and religion, which in this country we at least treat with decent respect. . . . Whatever German and French reformers may choose to call themselves, socialist is not a good name for a party to succeed with in America.[18]

Nor was Bellamy alone in viewing these radical movements as somehow "foreign" to the sensibilities of the "average American." William James, in a letter concerning the Haymarket incident sent to his brother Henry (whose own exploration of the world of the anarchists, *The Princess Casamassima*, was published the same year), writes, "Don't be alarmed by the labor troubles here. I am quite sure they are a most healthy phase of evolution, a little costly, but normal, and sure to do lots of good to all hands in the end. I don't speak of the senseless 'anarchist' riot in Chicago, which has nothing to do with the 'Knights of Labor,' but is the work of a lot of pathological Germans and Poles."[19]

James, like Dr. Leete, errs in his evaluation of the American labor scene. By the mid-1880s the Knights of Labor, with their doctrines of nonconfrontation, voluntary union, and natural cooperation, were fast being supplanted by more aggressive workers' organizations. However, his statement is interesting for another reason: within it, James uncritically accepts the late-nineteenth-century nativist assumption that the radical figure of the anarchist and newly arrived German and Polish immigrants were for all intents and purposes one and the same.[20] For James, Bellamy, and many others as well, the anarchists, socialists, and other new left organizations were dangerous not only because they were violent, but also, and perhaps more importantly, because they were "foreign" to the American way of life.

The same discursive logic is at work in an editorial cartoon first published during the Great Upheaval, the period of extreme labor agitation surrounding the brutal 1877 railroad strikes. The cartoon, with the caption "Waiting for the Reduction of the Army," refers to a growing de-

bate over whether the regular army should be expanded and deployed
as an "internal peacekeeping force" in the urban and business centers.
(Supporters of this proposition included, among others, the president of
the Pennsylvania Railroad, Thomas A. Scott, Congressman James A.
Garfield, and the Reverend Henry Ward Beecher.[21]) The cartoon depicts
a soldier marching on bulwarks, vigilantly standing guard over a pastoral Jeffersonian landscape. In the drawing's foreground, hidden in the
shadows behind a cracked wall, lurk four menacing figures: a knife-
wielding Indian; a labor activist with flaming torch held aloft; a gro-
tesquely caricatured Irish immigrant grasping a stiletto; and finally a
tramp armed with a rifle. Each of the figures in the illustration represents
one of the new and dangerous social groups that had emerged as a result of the dynamic forces then transforming the nation: westward expansion, industrialization, immigration, and unregulated cycles of economic boom and bust.

This cartoon employs a double tropological structure to reveal the
threat inherent in these forces if they remain uncontrolled, a structure
that the popular media would draw upon again and again in the
coming decades. That the Indian should appear to lead the group will
come as no surprise to the reader of Richard Slotkin's study of the
changing uses of "myth of the frontier" during the course of the nineteenth century. Slotkin reveals the process of substitution by which
the racist ideology of the "savage," developed during the Indian Wars
of 1873–76, is transferred to the striking railway workers and the
other members of the "dangerous classes" that inhabited the metro-
politan areas of the United States.[22] At the same time, the metonymic
chain linking the immigrant and the anarchist, already at work in the
James statement we looked at above, now extends even further. All
four figures in this illustration are situated, for the moment, "outside"
the archetypal landscape symbolic of an older America. It is left to the
viewer to surmise that unless the agents of disorder represented by the
Indian, the industrial laborer, the immigrant, and the tramp are recontained, they will soon overrun and destroy the civilized nation. A similar sentiment is evident in *Looking Backward,* specifically in terms of
the last figure in this grouping: "A great number of these seekers after
employment were constantly traversing the country, becoming in time
professional vagabonds, then criminals. . . . [T]his army swelled to a
host so vast and desperate as to threaten the stability of the government"
(*LB,* 163).

Thus, for Bellamy too, the dangerous presence of these cultural,

THE DAILY GRAPHIC

AN ILLUSTRATED EVENING NEWSPAPER

39 & 41 PARK PLACE

VOL. XVI.   All the News, Four Editions Daily.   NEW YORK, FRIDAY, JUNE 14, 1878. $12 Per Year in Advance, Single Copies, Five Cents.   NO. 1633.

WAITING FOR THE REDUCTION OF THE ARMY.

Figure 2.   "Waiting for the Reduction of the Army." *Daily Graphic,* New York, June 14, 1878.

political, and economic Others on the horizon of the American landscape threatened to shatter the tenuous national unity that had been so
recently forged with the conclusion of the Civil War. The divisions of
American society are even manifest in the spatial arrangements of West's
nineteenth-century Boston: "Each class or nation lived by itself, in quar-
ters of its own. A rich man living among the poor, an educated man
among the uneducated, was like one living in isolation among a jealous
and alien race" (LB, 29). Bellamy's choice of phrase here reveals a great
deal: more than the "two nations" of the rich and the poor in Benjamin
Disraeli's Great Britain, the United States had become a cacophony of
competing nations, "jealous and alien races," dissonant publics, and
individual voices. Thus, the great dilemma of the nineteenth-century
United States, as Dr. Leete later informs West, did not lie in the "extraordinary industrial system" of capitalism, but in an epidemic of "excessive individualism" that was by its nature "inconsistent with much
public spirit" (LB, 45).

Although such a "public spirit" had been achieved by the twenty-first
century, Bellamy assures his readers that this did not imply any suspicious internationalism. When West asks Dr. Leete whether European
countries have been similarly transformed, the doctor replies,

> Yes . . . the great nations of Europe as well as Australia, Mexico, and parts of
> South America, are now organized industrially like the United States, which
> was the pioneer of the evolution. The peaceful relations of these nations are
> assured by a loose form of federal union of worldwide extent. An interna-
> tional council regulates the mutual intercourse and commerce of the mem-
> bers of the union and their joint policy toward the more backward races,
> which are gradually being educated up to civilized institutions. Complete au-
> tonomy within its own limits is enjoyed by every nation. (LB, 103)

While Dr. Leete does later state that they "all look forward to an eventual unification of the world as one nation," he quickly adds, "however,
the present system works so nearly perfectly that we are quite content to
leave to posterity the completion of the scheme. There are, indeed, some
who hold that it never will be completed, on the ground that the federal
plan is not merely a provisional solution of the problem of human society, but the best ultimate solution" (LB, 105).

Bellamy himself later reiterates, in the conclusion to his 1890 essay
"Why I Wrote Looking Backward," some of Dr. Leete's sentiments: "It
would be preposterous to assume parity of progress between America
and Turkey. The more advanced nations, ours surely first of all, will

reach the summit earliest and, reaching strong brotherly hands downward, help up the laggards."[23] Today, we can hear in these statements ominous echoes of what would soon become a major ideological justification for U.S. imperialist adventurism in Latin America and Asia, as well as for European policies toward Africa (an apologia for imperialism that finds its roots back in More's *Utopia*). However, the same kind of reasoning was invoked in the late nineteenth century by those who dealt with the dangers of cultural conflict *within* the United States. A typical example of such an approach finds expression in the contemporary federal policy toward American Indians known as the Dawes Severalty Act. Passed only a year before the publication of *Looking Backward,* the Dawes Act required the breakup of designated parts of federal reservations into individual allotments, which were then to be handed over to any Indian who abandoned tribal life to homestead like the white settlers. After a period of working the land in this manner, the Indian automatically would be granted United States citizenship. The supporters of the Act felt that only in this way could Indians be educated into the "habits of civilized life"—an education that, it was hoped, would erase the cultural differences that marked them off from other Americans.[24]

A diverse group of progressive reformers, including Jacob Riis in his influential study of New York City immigrant slums, come to conclusions similar to those of the authors of the Dawes Act: assimilation was the only proper response to the present crisis of diversity besetting the American nation. In *Looking Backward,* Bellamy too attempts to imagine a "dedifferentiation" of the threatening publics that had appeared on the national landscape. By negating these potential sites of conflict, he hoped to produce an achievable figure of a newly unified republic, one that resembled the semi-mythical stable societies found in "Greenland, Patagonia, and the Chinese Empire." This implicit goal of the text is revealed in one of Dr. Leete's many comparisons of nineteenth- and twenty-first-century societies: "The difference between the age of individualism and that of concert was well characterized by the fact that, in the nineteenth century, when it rained, the people of Boston put up three hundred thousand umbrellas over as many heads, and in the twentieth century they put up one umbrella over all the heads" (*LB,* 110–11). In *Looking Backward,* Bellamy shows how these innumerable umbrellas might be sutured into a single harmonious whole. This will entail a special kind of clearing of the national social landscape—an imaginative operation that will erase the threat posed by all these conflicting factions by eliminating the very features that define them as unique.

CONSUMERISM *AND* CLASS

One of the most significant and hotly debated absences at work in Bellamy's narrative is that of labor itself. In order to explain this lacuna, some later readers have suggested that Bellamy's utopia was not oriented toward an imaginary future, but instead literally looked backward to some idealized American past. (Of course, similar assumptions form part of a more general critique of the utopian narrative form, the proponents of which include such noted figures as Northrop Frye and, perhaps more significant here, Leo Marx.[25]) R. Jackson Wilson, for example, maintains that *Looking Backward* "was conceived not in hope or in expectation but in nostalgia."[26] Wilson argues that Bellamy's abstract celebration of technological advancement masks a deeper antimodernism that runs through the narrative, manifest in the text's vivid representations of the lived spaces of the future. The twenty-first-century "world" that West experiences—keeping in mind that in *Looking Backward,* as in all narrative utopias, the experience of place takes on all the force of what in the novel is called event—contrasts dramatically with Dr. Leete's descriptions of it. It is here, Wilson maintains, that we see Bellamy's retreat into a historically regressive vision of *preindustrial* America. (Although this same portrayal of the urban landscape would deeply influence British architect Ebenezer Howard in his designs for the modernist "garden city.")[27] Milton Cantor extends Wilson's line of argument, suggesting that the utopia of *Looking Backward* be read as an idealized recreation of pre-1840 Chicopee Falls, Massachusetts, Bellamy's ancestral home: "Contrasting the old and the emergent, Bellamy continually reaffirmed small-town virtues in an urban society that seemed to threaten values he held dear"—the values of a relatively homogeneous, well-educated, stable, and organic society, with an economic basis of small-scale farmers, merchants, and craftspeople.[28]

For both Wilson and Cantor, the most convincing bit of evidence concerning Bellamy's antimodern longings is the absence in the text of any description of a factory or workplace. Similarly, while West encounters doctors, ministers, educators, administrators, and various service personnel (waiters and the like), he does not come into contact with any member of the laboring ranks of the industrial army—even in the sequel, *Equality,* when he visits one of the great mills of the future.[29] By literally erasing the presence of a heterogeneous, urban, and increasingly immigrant labor force (by the mid-1880s, first-generation immigrants composed more than one-third of all industrial workers), Bellamy could be understood to be recreating the preindustrial world of his youth, a world destroyed by the engines of a modernization he secretly abhorred.

The antimodern reaction was, as T. J. Jackson Lears demonstrates, a significant component of late-nineteenth-century U.S. culture.[30] However, Wilson and Cantor's claim that *Looking Backward* takes part in this movement encounters a number of difficulties, not the least significant of which being its contradiction with the explicit critique of antimodernism leveled *in* the text. In the midst of his description of the changes in the late nineteenth century that would ultimately contribute to the birth of utopia, Dr. Leete emphatically states, "To restore the former order of things, even if possible, would have involved returning to the day of stagecoaches" (*LB*, 53). Moreover, the differences between Bellamy's project and those of more explicitly nostalgic thinkers become even more apparent when we compare *Looking Backward* to the version of utopian pastoralism found in William Morris's *News from Nowhere* (1890). Morris conceived *News from Nowhere* as a direct response to what he famously decried as the "Cockney paradise" of *Looking Backward*. Bellamy's utopia falls short, Morris maintains, because it leaves the fundamental social relations of industrial capitalism untouched; hence, Bellamy reveals himself to be "perfectly satisfied with modern civilization, if only the injustice, misery, and waste of class society could be got rid of" (a critique of the text that later would be reiterated by Ernst Bloch).[31] Morris finds this kind of "half-change" untenable. In his own narrative, he imagines the "warm" utopian conditions under which the very "machinery of life" has been altered so that the exploitation and alienation at the heart of capitalist social relations are eradicated.

However, Morris's delineation of the lived experience of such a society suggests a different source for his vision. In depicting his "epoch of rest," Morris transforms the grim industrial present of England into a fecund pastoral Eden, replete with eternal summer sunshine, a salmon-filled Thames, thatched cottages, and freshly mowed fields. This overt idealization of a redeemed landscape leads Darko Suvin to suggest that *News from Nowhere* represents less an example of the narrative utopia than "the finest specimen of Earthly Paradise story found in modern literature," an heir to the tradition of the medieval dream fable.[32] Suvin's comparison of *News from Nowhere* to a medieval narrative form is in-

structive in that it bears out the fact that Morris's paradise, in its phenomenological or lived form (or in Lefebvre's terms, its spaces of representation), resembles an idealized feudal England *before* the rise of the
modern urban centers and the explosive growth of a complex industrial
society.

Both Bellamy's and Morris's narratives share the vital task of registering the deep historicity, and mutability, of their present situations. Indeed, in this respect, Morris's work is directed less at Bellamy's utopian
vision than at what he took to be the asphyxiating closure of a naturalist empiricism like that of his countryman George Gissing, something
Bellamy reiterates in *Looking Backward* in an allusion to the "profound
pessimism of the literature of the last quarter of the nineteenth century"
(*LB*, 188).[33] However, the two authors diverge dramatically in their
sense of the possibility, or even the desirability, of resuscitating elements
of the *national* cultural past. Morris's historical bifocality, his ability to
look at once forward and backward in the construction of his utopia,
arises from a deep faith in the fundamental continuity of the English
past and present. In another context, Morris suggests that the vision of
his great predecessor Thomas More was so convincing precisely because
More himself was "instinctively sympathetic with the communistic side
of medieval society." Looking backward in this way, More could give
voice to "the longing for a society in which the individual man can
scarcely conceive of his existence apart from the commonwealth of
which he forms a portion."[34] In medieval England, Morris thus finds a
mythic organic unity, the very definition of the healthy nation in the late
nineteenth century, that Bellamy was hard-pressed to find when faced
with his own quite different cultural history.

Indeed, Bellamy explicitly questions whether any such moment of social unity had ever existed in his country. This is nowhere more evident
than in his earlier historical novel, *The Duke of Stockbridge* (1879). In
this work, Bellamy returned to the period immediately after the founding of the republic. Surveying the events surrounding the infamous 1786
rebellion in western Massachusetts of a group of farmers under the leadership of Daniel Shay, Bellamy concludes that the attempt to produce a
national unity in the 1780s was thwarted by social divisions strikingly
similar to those in his own present: the tenuous community established
by the Shayite Captain Perez Hamlin (a figure who stands in for the
older genteel middle class) is undermined by both the landed aristocracy
and the undisciplined, divisive factions of the farmers and laborers.
While clearly intended as a warning against the inevitable failure of any

new revolution, *The Duke of Stockbridge* also demonstrates the undesirability of a return to an earlier moment in American history. The realization of the national community was for Bellamy a project always already located in the future.

Their attitudes toward their respective national pasts were, of course, not the only differences separating Bellamy's and Morris's visions. They also expressed divergent views of the place of work in the radically Other future. Everyone that Morris's dreamer William Guest encounters in this pastoral landscape (with the exception of a crotchety old historian) is happily engaged in explicitly preindustrial forms of labor: the handicraft production of agricultural and artisanal goods for *use* rather than for exchange, with a deep attention paid to the aesthetics of the task. Indeed, many nineteenth-century readers of Morris—especially those in the United States—focused almost exclusively upon this latter aspect of his writing. Ignoring his explicit revolutionary socialism, and uncritically celebrating the "nostalgic aestheticism" found in his work, these readers quickly canonized him as the patron saint of the nascent arts and crafts movement.[35]

These concrete delineations of handicraft and agricultural *production* in Morris's narrative suggest the confusion in Wilson and Cantor's usage of the term "preindustrial society" in describing Bellamy's utopia.[36] Unlike the utopia of *News from Nowhere*—or the no less pastoral vision of Howells's *A Traveler from Altruria* (1892)—the society delineated in *Looking Backward* is *not* preindustrial: for while examples of men and women working may be omnipresent in Morris's ideal state, any representation of the condition of labor is, as both Wilson and Cantor point out, singularly *absent* in Bellamy's narrative, be it that of the industrial present or the preindustrial pasts of Morris's feudal artisans, Howells's yeoman farmers, or the craftsmen of Bellamy's New England youth. Indeed, if we attempt to produce a map of the new world outlined in *Looking Backward,* we quickly realize that we would have great difficulty locating any site of productive labor upon it.

If Bellamy's narrative was simply a glorification of an imaginary preindustrial past, as Wilson and Cantor claim, then this absence would be puzzling. If, on the other hand, we approach the text as a narrative utopia as defined by Louis Marin—as a text engaged in the *figuration* of the as yet untheorized social emergences of the narrative's present— then these empty spaces appear in a quite different light. The conflicts of the late nineteenth century were the result of a particular situation which Bloch generally calls "nonsynchronism"; or, as Herbert Gutman observes, there were co-present in the United States at this time an "older American preindustrial social structure and the modernizing institutions that accompanied the development of industrial capitalism."[37] In *Looking Backward,* Bellamy attempts to mediate a passage between these two different social formations. As with all such mediators, the more radical possibilities hinted at in the narrative, the establishment in the United States of a new postcapitalistic society, vanish once the historical transition has been completed.

The very absence of work in the text signals the nature of the social morass that Bellamy hoped to avoid in his new society: the problem of the modern industrial laborer (the same problem, of course, that led to Morris's antimodern nostalgia). In another context, as is the case for Morris, the effacement of alienated labor, or work as exchange value, might have pointed toward the emergence of a socialist society. However, given Bellamy's own nationalist and nativist anxieties about what he took to be the threatening realities of socialism, as well as the absence of any concrete treatment of how the reorganization of the labor process might be effected, this opportunity vanishes. Instead, the neutralization of the place of work in the text clears a narrative space in which will appear a different, and very modern, social formation: what, for want of a more precise term, has been described as the new "consumerism" associated with an emerging segment of the American middle class.

The contours of this new ethos first emerge in the narrative presentation of the social relations that supplant work in Bellamy's utopia. Interestingly, while *Looking Backward* lacks any description of the processes of production, the narrative pays a good deal of attention to the machinery of circulation. The first time West moves beyond the confines of the Leete home—setting aside, for the moment, his early, delirium-induced *dérive* across the alien spaces of the new city—he accompanies Edith Leete, the doctor's adolescent daughter and West's eventual spouse, on an excursion to one of the numerous shopping centers located "only minutes" from every citizen's abode. West describes in lavish detail this wondrous "distributing establishment":

> It was the first interior of a twentieth-century public building that I had ever beheld, and the spectacle naturally impressed me deeply. I was in a vast hall full of light, received not alone from the windows on all sides, but from the dome, the point of which was a hundred feet above. Beneath it, in the center of the hall, a magnificent fountain played, cooling the atmosphere to a delicious freshness with its spray. The walls and ceiling were frescoed in mellow tints, calculated to soften without absorbing the light which flooded the in-

terior. Around the fountain was a space occupied with chairs and sofas, on which many people were seated conversing. Legends on the walls all about the hall indicated to what classes of commodities the counters below were devoted. Edith directed her steps toward one of these, where samples of muslin of a bewildering variety were displayed, and proceeded to inspect them. (*LB*, 80)

West soon learns that the goods in every such shopping place, regardless of location, are standardized in terms of quality and variety. These items are shipped directly from the producer to a regional warehouse, which West later describes (and in so doing, once more erases the place of productive labor) as "a gigantic mill, into the hopper of which goods are being constantly poured by the trainload and the shipload, to issue at the other end in packages of pounds and ounces, yards and inches, pints and gallons, corresponding to the infinitely complex personal needs of half a million people" (*LB*, 127).

The great spectacle that West here describes resonates with a phenomenon that had in the late 1880s only very recently appeared upon the urban landscape: the giant department store with its unprecedented array of commodities. Although these contemporary "distributing establishments" had only recently come into existence, their impact was immediately felt. In fact, as Alan Trachtenberg notes, the 1880s department store performed a vital pedagogical function: "In department stores, buyers of goods learned new roles for themselves, apprehended themselves as *consumers,* something different from mere users of goods. . . . these places created a unique fusion of economic and cultural values; they were staging grounds for the making and confirming of new relations between goods and people."[38]

These "new relations" form the heart of Bellamy's utopian vision. Immediately following the visit to the store, West discovers the marvels of the musical telephone, which brings into every home an "extraordinary" range of live musical performances. Edith Leete informs West that "the professional music is so much grander and more perfect than any performance of ours, and so easily commanded when we wish to hear it, that we don't think of calling our singing or playing music at all. All the really fine singers and players are in the musical service, and the rest of us hold our peace for the main part" (*LB*, 85). Likewise, when West accompanies the Leetes to the great central dining facility, he learns that the food there is "vastly cheaper as well as better than it would be if prepared at home" (*LB*, 111). (Significantly, the dining facility is not the kind of communal hall we see in More's utopia, but an extension of the privatized bourgeois domestic space: "This is, in fact, a part of our house, slightly detached from the rest. . . . Every family in the ward has a room set apart in this great building for its permanent and exclusive use for a small rental fee" [LB 111].) In both situations, the labor involved in the production of these commodities—the actual performance of music and the preparation of the food—vanishes from the world of the narrative.[39]

Later in the text, Dr. Leete iterates what has become one of the fundamental axioms of twentieth-century society: work is looked upon "as a necessary duty to be discharged before we can fully devote ourselves to the higher exercise of our faculties, the intellectual and spiritual enjoyments and pursuits which alone mean life." However, Dr. Leete goes on to note that "not all, nor the majority, have those scientific, artistic, literary, or scholarly interests which make leisure the one thing valuable to their possessors. Many look upon the last half of life chiefly as a period for enjoyment . . . a time for the leisurely and unperturbed appreciation of the good things of the world" (LB, 136–37). These "good things" are, of course, the vast array of commodities made available by the new system of distribution. The whole of society in Bellamy's utopia thus has been transformed into a giant marketplace, occupied by a population that now functionally defines itself according to the sheer circular formality of the commodity process: the endless consumption of fetishized goods, objects that magically seem to produce themselves, becoming a social end in itself.[40] At the center of such a society stands the cathedral-like department store—an apt symbol for the new "religion of solidarity" that would hold together the utopian social arrangement. Bellamy thus finally negates the crisis of the present by imagining a displacement of the disabled values of the past by social norms that were just beginning to emerge in his day: the utopia of Looking Backward figures a society ordered according to the logic of the commodity, a consumerist paradise wherein the dilemmas of industrialism have been wished away, a world of reified commodities from which every trace of labor has been expunged.

Crucially, however, the lacuna of labor in Bellamy's vision points toward the concrete horizons of this emergent ideology of consumerism. Wilson argues that Bellamy's religion of solidarity "had two direct social consequences, the rejection of industrialism and a tense distaste for workingmen."[41] I would state this another way: Bellamy's utopianism involves an embracing of the fruits of industrial production *and* an erasure of their producers, the industrial worker, as well as their other racial and ethnic avatars. The consumerist world of *Looking Backward* thus prefigures the social circumstances of the new bourgeoisie of an American industrial capitalism, those whom Thorsten Veblen famously labels the "leisure class": the emerging public that alone possessed opportunities for a "lifestyle of consumption" (the ideological foundation of Bellamy's utopian order) that would not be available on a wide scale until much later. I raise this last point as a caveat to those critics who find already in place at the end of the nineteenth century (or even earlier) a full-blown "consumer society." Such a vision of this historical moment is as utopian as the social form elaborated in Bellamy's text. Indeed, as Veblen was among the first to point out, the nascent consumerism of Bellamy's moment is still inextricably linked to expressions of class identity and power. The masses, like the members of the "backwards races," do not appear in the utopia of *Looking Backward* because this form of their education "up to civilized institutions" was, for Bellamy at least, unimaginable.[42] This process of general "reeducation," and with it the actualization of consumer *society*—what has been labeled Fordism—would not occur until nearly a half-century after Bellamy's death.

"THE ASSOCIATIONS OF OUR ACTIVE LIFETIME"

The emergence of this new class order would not be possible without a fundamental restructuring of the mechanisms by which the society is organized. Bellamy's central figure for such a reordering is that of the great "Industrial Army." The principles of modern military organization were, as Krishan Kumar points out, deeply influential for much of the generation of American intellectuals who had lived through the Civil War.[43] (This was especially true in Bellamy's case: enamored with the military life early on, he longed to enter West Point, but was rejected after failing the initial physical examination.) Bellamy saw in the modern military structure exactly the coordination and efficiency that were absent in the disorder of the present; as Arthur Lipow notes, it was the modern military system that provided for Bellamy "the sense of national unity, above and beyond class or party."[44] Dr. Leete states that the society of the nineteenth century is to that of the twenty-first as a "mob, or a horde of barbarians" is to a "disciplined army under one general" (*LB*, 165). Later, during his brief, nightmarish return to the nineteenth century, West announces upon seeing a military regiment pass by, "Here at last were order and reason, an exhibition of what intelligent cooperation can accomplish" (LB, 212).

Society in Bellamy's utopian vision, like this idealized army, is organized into a massive pyramid. The work force is partitioned into ten divisions composed of the numerous agricultural, engineering, and industrial guilds, headed by ten lieutenant generals who alone choose the nation's president. Standing alongside the industrial army are a number of similarly structured allied organizations: that of the "liberal professions"; the autonomous women's guilds (LB, 172–75); and a corps of invalid workers. Only the dissenters and the criminally insane remain outside this all-embracing structure. Although the sick "atavistic" criminal meets with compassionate understanding (and "firm but gentle restraint"), the self-defined outsider is dealt with quite harshly: "A man able to duty, and persistently refusing, is sentenced to solitary imprisonment on bread and water till he consents" (LB, 140 and 95).[45]

The totalizing nature of the social structure imagined by Bellamy has led numerous readers to view his utopia as a precursor to the real-world authoritarian regimes of our century, and a not-so-innocent celebration of the ascendancy of the bureaucratic state. Even a sympathetic reader such as Marie Louise Berneri notes, "we might be tempted to call Edward Bellamy a prophet, rather than an utopian, if he had not been sadly mistaken in thinking that these changes would bring us happiness."[46] However, such a reading runs into problems not unlike those encountered by the view of the utopia as nostalgic for an earlier "simpler" age: rather than rewriting the utopian space in terms of a lost past, this approach inscribes it too rigidly within the confines of subsequent history, reducing Bellamy's utopian figuration, its representation of space, to a kind of futurology. One reading bends the text backward, the other forward, while both ignore its figurative work within its present.

Indeed, Bellamy seems far less concerned with the actual role of the state in the future than he is with the problem of how identity might be produced in a national society unified in some radically new way. Walter Benn Michaels observes that "the industrial army is more committed to producing individuality than to suppressing it. But the individuality it produces is defined by difference rather than independence."[47] In other words, in the utopian order, the self is no longer determined by what Bellamy saw as divisive and finally mutually destructive ethnic, racial, or class categories, but rather by a differentiated

position within a single overarching social taxonomy. Indeed, West realizes, "everybody is part of a system with a distinct place and function," a system from which he alone, for the moment at least, stands
"outside" (LB, 125). These differential identities remain in place even
after the individual has entered retirement: "The associations of our active lifetime," Dr. Leete informs West, "retain a powerful hold on us.
The companionships we formed then remain our companionships till
the end of life. We always continue honorary members of our former
guilds, and retain the keenest and most jealous interest in their welfare
and repute in the hands of the following generation" (LB, 133). Despite
the text's powerful and progressive views of marriage and women's
rights, gender too remains a horizon of preexistent difference beyond
which Bellamy will not pass: Dr. Leete declares, "The lack of some such
recognition of the distinct individuality of the sexes was one of the innumerable defects of your society" (LB, 174). And, as a comparison of
the role of Dr. Leete with those of Edith and the nearly invisible
Mrs. Leete demonstrates, this difference still too readily translates into
hierarchy.[48]

Moreover, once again, Bellamy fails to delineate precisely how this
differential structure operates in the main body of the industrial army.
Instead, he turns most of his energy to mapping the mechanisms by
which distinctions are maintained between these industrial workers and
"the professional classes, the men who serve the nation with brains instead of hands" (LB, 62). During his discourse upon the governing body,
Dr. Leete explains that while members of the "liberal professions"—including educators, artists, and medical practitioners such as himself—
are not eligible for the presidency, "the President has nothing to do with
the faculties of medicine and education, which are controlled by boards
of regents of their own" (LB, 135). Entrance into what amounts to an
autonomous class within this society is strictly controlled: although
higher education is universally available, success in it as well as the subsequent movement into a professional occupation are contingent upon
passing a battery of grueling examinations designed to separate those
who have real aptitudes from those who do not (LB, 63). Later in the
narrative, Dr. Leete describes the effects of these regulatory procedures
upon his own profession:

> Anybody who pleases to get a little smattering of medical terms is not now at
> liberty to practice on the bodies of citizens, as in your day. None but students
> who have passed the severe tests of the schools, and clearly proved their vo-

cation, are permitted to practice. Then, too, you will observe that there is nowadays no attempt of doctors to build up their practice at the expense of other doctors. There would be no motive for that. For the rest, the doctor has to render regular reports of his work to the medical bureau, and if he is not reasonably well employed, work is found for him. (*LB,* 92)

The idea of an expert culture formed by the regulation of practice in medicine, education, law, and similar specialized careers was just beginning to appear in Bellamy's day. Robert H. Wiebe has described the situation of medicine at the middle of the nineteenth century as one in which "almost anyone could, and a great variety did, enter what had once been a profession. Doctors of the people—allopaths, homeopaths, eclectics, and later osteopaths—roamed the land at will. In the seventies, Charles Macune practiced medicine from the same intuition his father had used spreading the Gospel; and a decade later the upright Leonidas Polk set out to make his fortune with a bottled cure for diphtheria."[49] In the early pages of *Looking Backward,* the reader encounters a wonderful example of just such an "irregular" practitioner of the medical arts—Doctor Pillsbury, "Professor of Animal Magnetism," responsible for the hypnotic slumber that will allow West to travel to the year 2000 (*LB,* 35).

However, by the turn of the century, new regulatory procedures, much like those described by Bellamy's Dr. Leete, had begun to take root; backed by increasingly influential professional organizations such as the American Medical Association, these would effectively eradicate the medical species West himself labels "quacks" (*LB,* 35). At the same time, as feminist commentators were quick to note, this regulation of medical practice would effectively undermine the institution of midwifery and other local strongholds of women's medical authority.[50]

The growth of expert culture itself represents only one element of a larger tidal shift that begins in the latter two decades of the nineteenth century and ultimately results in the ascendancy of what Wiebe calls "a new middle class": a large and amorphous group of professionals, educators, administrators, and bureaucrats (and later engineers) that would assume the task of managing the infinitesimal complexities of a specialized technical society. Lipow too notes the dramatic growth of this group in the decades leading up to the publication of *Looking Backward:* "Between 1870 and 1890, the independent professions—medicine, law, dentistry, etc.—more than doubled in size, even though the population as a whole increased by only sixty-two percent."[51] The group of progressive reformers that includes Bellamy himself thus appears, from our position of historical retrospection, to serve as what Raymond Williams elsewhere describes as "one of the advanced formations" of a class, their programs for social reorganization playing the role of an indispensable vanishing mediator between changing definitions of American middle-class identity: those of the genteel Americans I discussed at the beginning of this chapter and the professional-managerial class that emerges full-blown in the twentieth century.[52] *Looking Backward* can then be read as one of the earliest narrative figurations of the emerging "lived" world of this "class" (or, more precisely, class fragment).[53] Mediated through the consciousness of West and the descriptions of Dr. Leete, the world that arises in the text is quite simply the social, cultural, and normative ideologies of this emerging class stratum made concrete.

Needless to say, the conspicuous consumerism we discussed above is also part of the self-identity of this group. These ideologies influence even Bellamy's representation of the material space of the "new" Boston: "At my feet lay a great city. Miles of broad streets, shaded by trees and lined with fine buildings, for the most part not in continuous blocks but set in larger or smaller enclosures, stretched in every direction" (*LB,* 43). Bellamy here offers us a picture of nothing less than the "sub-urban" space, with its parklike setting, large private dwellings, and rigid dichotomy between work and domestic locations, that this new middle class would call home—the prototype of which was just then being set into place on the outskirts of Philadelphia, less than 300 miles from Bellamy's Massachusetts home.[54]

The presence in the narrative of this emergent cultural logic also accounts for the strong assertion in Bellamy's utopia of the dichotomy between the worlds of men and women. Gender difference must be vigilantly reinforced in the twenty-first century precisely because these distinctions, as Dr. Leete himself points out, were increasingly contested in the transitional period of the late nineteenth century. Indeed, even as Bellamy imagines the consumerist world of the Leetes in his utopian romance, the activity of consumption and the tradition of the romance, in the form of the sentimental novel, are increasingly relegated to the domestic sphere of the middle-class woman.[55]

The potential for a "feminization of America" found in *Looking Backward* was not lost on Bellamy's critics. As Arthur Dudley Vinton presents the matter in his unofficial "sequel," *Looking Further Backward,* this feminization expresses itself in a number of ways, including the raising under the Nationalist system of the status of women to "an

equality with man"; the disbanding of the standing army; the closing of
military schools; the abolition of the draft; and even the replacement of
a virile gold standard by mere "symbols of wealth," Bellamy's "credit
cards."[56] However, most dramatically, this emasculation is evident in a
loss of "personal initiative and responsibility": "Born to expect guard-
ianship and support, without either being the result of personal fore-
thought or experience, they could not now, suddenly, appreciate the
need of individual reliance upon themselves" (FB, 52 and 93). These
anxieties are then linked to Vinton's equally disturbing fears of the consequences of racial contamination: early on, his narrator points out that
"owing to the short-sightedness of your remote ancestors you had permitted your country to be over-run with emigrants from the slums of
other nations; they had been given equal rights, socially and politically,
and they had intermarried with your native stock until it became so de-
based that, one hundred years ago, your ancestors were as ready as the
Frenchmen of the eighteenth century to abandon everything for the sake
of an idea" (FB, 31). The disastrous consequences of these developments
become evident when the "yellow hordes" of China (invading, we are
told, in an act of self-defense against the spread of the "pernicious doctrines of Nationalism" [FB, 32]) easily overrun the emasculated nation.
Only West, because of his origins in the heartier world of the nineteenth
century, presents an obstacle to the Chinese armies. However, he too is
ultimately killed in combat, and, in the end, the Chinese forces have
completely encircled the remaining Nationalist territory and are slowly
and methodically tightening the net.

However, the conclusion of this "dystopian" narrative is unusu-
ally upbeat.[57] As in Philip K. Dick's later "alternative history" novel,
The Man in the High Castle, Vinton's view of the consequences of the
successful invasion of the United States by an Asian nation is in fact
deeply ambivalent. The book's narrator, the history professor Won Lung
Li, concludes by summarizing the "benefits" brought by the Chinese
takeover:

> We are no longer a defenseless people, ready to be subjugated by the first
> armed nation that attacks. Our material prosperity was never greater. Our
> soil supports a greater population than it did before. Chinese frugality has re-
> placed the wasteful lavishness that prevailed in private life under the Nation-
> alistic government. Woman no longer competes with man, but has become as
> the Gods intended she should be, the handmaiden of male humanity. What
> was good in Nationalism we have retained. What was bad we have discarded
> and replaced by what is better. Under Nationalism, individualism was re-

duced to a minimum; with us to-day it is honored and given every chance to develop. (*FB*, 187–88)

Even more significantly, we learn that the remaining U.S. territory has reformed, "and the Nationalistic system of government has been changed until to-day it does not so much differ from that which we enjoy" (*FB*, 187). In this conclusion, Vinton's dystopia becomes a version of what Peter Fitting calls a "right-wing utopia," a precursor to later libertarian visions such as Ayn Rand's *Atlas Shrugged* (1957).[58]

However, even setting aside the fact that West's nervous disorder, or neurasthenia, meant that he was already feminized long before he had left the nineteenth-century, thereby making him an unlikely representative of nineteenth-century masculine individualism, the changes he undergoes during the course of the narrative preclude the possibility of his ever taking up Vinton's project of cultural and social restoration. This is because West, unlike his more "backward" contemporaries of the nineteenth century, becomes a full member of the newly forming middle class. This "conversion" literally occurs when Dr. Leete assures West that once his education concerning the institutions of the twenty-first century has been completed, he will enter into a career track designed to exploit his own "expert" knowledge: a special university lectureship on the history of the nineteenth century, the period that the people of the twenty-first century find "one of the most absorbingly interesting" in all of history (*LB*, 126).

West's personal journey thus stands as a powerful allegory of the subsequent historical trajectory of his social public. The older middle class represented by West's genteel Bostonians and Bellamy's New England ancestors would have to be similarly retrained before they could assume a position of cultural authority in the new America. (The same metamorphosis had been chronicled three years earlier, albeit in a different register, in Howells's *The Rise of Silas Lapham*.) However, West's journey from the nineteenth century to the twenty-first would simultaneously entail another kind of change; and it is through the narration of this last process that Bellamy finally accounts for the necessary fate of the other races and classes in the new nation.

FORGETTING

Bellamy joins the social topos of the 1880s with that of the year 2000 by two distinct narrative strands. The first takes the form of a general "history" of the founding of the new social order. When West asks what solution society had come upon for the "Sphinx's riddle" of the labor question, Dr. Leete responds, "It was not necessary for society to solve the riddle at all. It may be said to have solved itself. The solution came as the result of a process of industrial evolution which could not have terminated otherwise. All that society had to do was to recognize and cooperate with that evolution, when its tendency had become unmistakable" (LB, 49). The social event that made such a gigantic leap possible was the emergence, after the Civil War, of the great capitalist trusts. Dr. Leete continues, "The movement toward the conduct of business by larger and larger aggregations of capital, the tendency toward monopolies, which had been so desperately and vainly resisted, was recognized at last, in its true significance, as a process which only needed to complete its logical evolution to open a golden future to humanity" (LB, 53). The process of consolidation subsequently accelerated until, at the beginning of the twentieth century, all corporations merged into a single national entity: "The nation, that is to say, organized as the one great business corporation in which all the other corporations were absorbed; it became the one capitalist in the place of all other capitalists. . . . The epoch of trusts had ended in The Great Trust" (LB, 53–54). Dr. Leete assures West that this transformation involved "absolutely no violence"; the populace even came to admire the very corporations that had caused so much misery, after they "recognized" that these organizations were no more than a necessary step in the upward climb of social progress (LB, 54).

Bellamy here gives a positive liberal spin to a prevailing Spencerian model of social evolution. Spencer himself, unlike some of his more infamous conservative disciples, argued that societies, like organisms, naturally evolved toward larger and larger, more complex entities. This process of social consolidation, if left unhampered, would gradually eliminate all conflict and produce a society of perfect equilibrium and "complete happiness."[59] Spencer's thought thus provides a useful legitimation to Bellamy's own deep distrust of those who sought to transform society through violent actions. However, as we noted earlier, violent conflicts were not the only contemporary block to the necessary process of social evolution: the temperament of "excessive individualism" and the ever more complex differentiation of publics brought about by industrial modernization had led society into its present cul-de-sac. If society were to be changed, then the subjects inhabiting it must be changed as well—a transformation that would involve a much more active process of cultural reeducation than the passive evolutionism that other aspects of the work suggest.

Bellamy would outline such a process of reeducation in the second narrative strand that runs through the text: the story of West's adaptation to twenty-first-century life. The West the reader encounters in the opening pages of *Looking Backward* is an allegorical embodiment of his particular time, place, and social situation. He is concerned with the strife that rends his society, but only because the numerous strikes had prevented the completion of his new dwelling and delayed his marriage to socialite Edith Bartlett. However, these conflicts have had deeper effects on his psyche. We soon learn that he suffers from extreme "nervous excitement or mental preoccupation," which prevents his falling to sleep without the aid of mesmerist Pillsbury (*LB*, 35).[60] Nightly, West descends into a womblike, subterranean concrete vault; shielded from the "never-ceasing nightly noises" of the metropolis, he is hypnotized into slumber, to be awakened the following morning by his servant Sawyer. Then, disaster strikes: the house burns down, and Sawyer is killed the very night Doctor Pillsbury leaves Boston forever. West is lost to human history, until he is discovered by Dr. Leete and, with the doctor acting as the midwife, "born" again into the future world.

After West overcomes his initial incredulity about his current situation, his schooling in the ways of twenty-first-century life commences. While this reeducation spans most of the subsequent narrative, it is punctuated at key junctures by a number of vivid psychic events. The first of these occurs soon after his resuscitation. Although physically fit, West states that his mental balance had been disturbed by his immersion into this radically new society: "The impressions of amazement and curiosity which my new surroundings produced occupied my mind, after the first shock, to the exclusion of all other thoughts. For the time the *memory of my former life was, as it were, in abeyance*" (*LB*, 45; emphasis added).

The stripping away of the old context of the self leads to an even more devastating identity crisis the following morning:

> I think it must have been many seconds that I sat up thus in bed staring about, without being able to regain the clew to my personal identity. I was no more able to distinguish myself from pure being during those moments than we may suppose a soul in the rough to be before it has received the earmarks, the individualizing touches which make it a person. Strange that the sense of this

inability should be such anguish! but so we are constituted. There are no words for the mental torture I endured during this helpless, eyeless groping for myself in a boundless void. . . . I lay there and fought for my sanity. In my mind, all had broken loose, habits of feeling, associations of thought, ideas of persons and things, all had dissolved and lost coherence and were seething together in apparently irretrievable chaos. There were no rallying points, nothing was left stable. There only remained the will, and was any human will strong enough to say to such a weltering sea, "Peace, be still"? (LB, 65–66)

In this remarkable passage, Bellamy evokes the condition of a subject literally pulled from the flow of history. A man without qualities, West dissolves into the primal existential void of "pure being": situated in the gap between past and future presents, West experiences the deterritorialized ungroundedness and loss of selfhood that Gilles Deleuze and Félix Guattari have described as endemic to the "schizophrenic subject."[61]

As this crisis abates, West observes, "The idea that I was two persons, that my identity was double, began to fascinate me with its simple solution of my experience" (LB, 66). A similar doubling occurs at a number of other places in the narrative. During this first identity crisis, West rushes out into the streets of the new metropolis. The few familiar landmarks he comes upon serve only to reinforce the alienness of the city. For West, the past and the future of the place exist simultaneously: "The mental image of the old city was so fresh and strong that it did not yield to the impression of the actual city, but contended with it, so that it was first one and then the other which seemed the more unreal. There was nothing I saw which was not blurred in this way, like the faces of a composite photograph" (LB, 67). Later in the text, West learns that Edith Leete too is a kind of double, the great-granddaughter of his fiancée Edith Bartlett: "My love, whom I had dreamed lost, had been reembodied for my consolation. When at last, in an ecstasy of gratitude and tenderness, I folded the lovely girl in my arms, the two Ediths were blended in my thought, nor have they ever since been clearly distinguished" (LB, 200–201). Each of these doublings then has the effect of "splitting," in Freud's sense, the subject into two distinct entities, its particular nineteenth- and twentieth-century incarnations.[62] Before any new West can be, the older self, like the "original" Boston and Edith, must first perish.

Similar concerns with the double nature of the subject preoccupied Bellamy throughout his early intellectual career. Moreover, in his earlier works, he suggests a deep relationship between a self-interested individualism, like that which had driven late-nineteenth-century society into its present cul-de-sac, and *memory*. In the unpublished essay "The Religion of Solidarity" (1874)—a text, he would later write, that "represents the germ of what has been ever since my philosophy of life"— Bellamy draws upon his religious training to develop a two-tiered Romantic theory of the self, at once individual and disinterested or universal, much in the vein of Shelley or, even more directly, Emerson.[63] And like his great-grandfather's mentor, Jonathan Edwards, Bellamy theorized "that what constituted personal identity is something other than memory: For Edwards, it is nothing less than God; for Bellamy, it is a 'core of being' common to all persons."[64] In his first novel, *Six to One: A Nantucket Idyl* (1878), Bellamy translates this model into the realm of fiction, with a gendering of the universal (feminine) and particular (masculine) aspects of the self that at once recalls and reverses the ethical binary Hegel develops in his reading of *Antigone* and looks forward to such later visions as those found in George Santayana's "Genteel Tradition" or D. H. Lawrence's *Women in Love* and *The Plumed Serpent.*

In both texts too, Bellamy stresses the need for narrowly individual desires to be dissolved into those of a larger collective entity. In "Religion of Solidarity," he writes, "This passion for losing ourselves in others or for absorbing them into ourselves, which rebels against individuality as an impediment, is then the expression of the greatest law of solidarity."[65] And in *Six to One,* protagonist Addie Follet reflects, "She had only, by her lonely life with the sea and her spiritual nature, attained a faculty of sharing to an unusual degree that calming and elevating communion which all the grand forms of nature are ready to pour into any human heart which turns to them in self-forgetfulness for the refreshment that comes from elevation out of the personal sphere."[66]

Bellamy offers a more direct statement of the social value of such a "self-forgetfulness," or memory loss, in his proto–science fiction narratives, *Dr. Heidenhoff's Process* (1878–79) and "The Blindman's World" (1886). *Dr. Heidenhoff's Process* delves into the murky waters surrounding the themes of human suffering, sin, and guilt, a territory most notably mapped in American literature by Nathaniel Hawthorne. (Howells once described Bellamy as "the first writer of romance in our environment worthy to be compared with Hawthorne."[67]) Bellamy develops these themes in *Dr. Heidenhoff's Process* through a pair of parallel narratives. The shorter tale-within-the-tale concerns George Bayley, "a young man of good education, excellent training, and once of great promise," who the previous year "had embezzled a small amount of the funds of a corporation in Newville, of which he was the paymaster, for the purpose of raising money for a pressing emergency."[68] (Interestingly, this embedded narrative appears to have been basis for the short story which would later be adapted into the classic American film about another moment of social and cultural transition, *It's a Wonderful Life*. Even the names of the respective protagonists, except for an inconsequential spelling change, are the same.) Although George Bayley had been fully absolved by both the company and the townsfolk, the "memory" of his disgrace proves more than he can bear. Near the end of a baleful confession before a local religious congregation, Bayley mentions an odd desire:

> The ancients had a beautiful fable about the water of Lethe, in which the soul that was bathed straightway forgot all that was sad and evil in its previous life; the most stained, disgraced, and mournful of souls coming forth fresh, blithe, and bright as a baby's. . . . Just think how blessed a thing for men it would be if such were indeed the case, if their memories could be cleansed and disinfected at the same time their hearts were purified! Then the most disgraced and ashamed might live good and happy lives again. Men would be redeemed from their sins in fact, and not merely in name. (*HP*, 11)

Following on the heels of this reflection, and serving as a kind of counterpoint to it, one of the protagonists of the central narrative, Madeline Brand, confesses to her young suitor Henry Burr, "I wouldn't care to forget anything I've done, not even my faults and follies. I should be afraid if they were taken away that I shouldn't have any character left" (*HP*, 18).

Madeline soon has cause to regret this claim. A big-city soda-jerk named Harrison Cordis arrives on the scene and quickly seduces the naive Madeline. She runs away to Boston, where Henry Burr later discovers her, inconsolate because of the guilt she bears over her "crime." Like George Bayley, Madeline's "heart was pure; it was only her memory that was foul. It was in vain that she swept and washed all within, and was good, when all the while her memory, like a ditch from a distant morass, emptied its vile stream of recollections into her heart, poisoning all the issues of life" (*HP*, 86). Thus, while she agrees to marry Henry, she has become dead to the possibility of true love. This drives him into a fever pitch of anxiety, and, after an especially foreboding interview with the girl, he returns to his dwelling and consumes a powerful sedative.

At this point, the mode of narration shifts dramatically from maudlin sentimentality into speculation. With Henry's return to Madeline the following morning, the reader finds that George Bayley's longed-for Lethe has been become an actuality. Henry reads in a scientific magazine of the wondrous "Extirpation of Thought Processes" recently discovered by Dr. Gustav Heidenhoff: through the application of a galvanic battery to certain sites in the brain, Heidenhoff has found a way to "annihilate" undesirable memories. As Madeline undergoes the process, Dr. Heidenhoff describes to us the astounding benefits of his invention:

> I am fond of speculating what sort of a world, morally speaking, we should have if there were no memory. One thing is clear, we should have no such very wicked people as we have now. There would, of course, be congenitally good and bad dispositions, but a bad disposition would not grow worse and worse as it does now, and without this progressive badness the depths of depravity are never attained. . . . It is memory of our past sins which demoralizes us, by imparting a sense of weakness and causing loss of self-respect. Take the memory away, and a bad act would leave us no worse in character than we were before its commission. (*HP*, 119)

Here, we arrive at the heart of Bellamy's philosophy of memory. The human self, the doctor observes, is an incessantly changing entity, rendering "the difference between the past and present selves of the same individual . . . so great as to make them different persons for all moral purposes" (*HP*, 121). Free the present self from its enthrallment to the past, and you open up an almost infinite possibility of human becoming. Later, in a veritable restatement of Friedrich Nietzsche's vision of the *Übermensch*, Dr. Heidenhoff declares that while his process aids the weak, stronger souls have already achieved this salvation: "They can unloose the iron links and free themselves. Would that more had the needful wisdom and strength thus serenely to put their past behind them, leaving the dead to bury their dead, and go blithely forward, taking each new day as a life by itself, and reckoning themselves daily new-born, even as verily they are!" (*HP*, 125). And indeed, Heidenhoff's observations apparently prove true: when we next see Madeline, she is again "pure" in memory, and joyously looks forward to a future by Henry's side. However, in the tragic closing pages of the narrative, we learn that this redemption is an illusion. Henry, under the influence of the sleeping draught, has dreamt the entire incident. Meanwhile, Madeline, following the example of George Bayley, commits suicide.

In the later short story "The Blindman's World," Bellamy pushes this exploration of the value of memory loss further, now imagining an entire society freed from the burden of the past. An astronomer obsessed

with the red star of Mars is transported from his mortal shell to the
planet's surface. (This journey prefigures the similar voyage of John
Carter in Edgar Rice Burroughs's *A Princess of Mars*.) The beings on the
planet the astronomer encounters are identical with those on Earth,
with one important exception: the denizens of Mars are free of the terrible "disease of memory" and instead possess an amazing "faculty of
foresight." Indeed, Earth appears to be unique in that the mentality of
its residents is oriented toward the past instead of the future; our planet
is thus compassionately referred to throughout the galaxy as the "blindman's world." The difference between the two civilizations is succinctly
summarized for us by a Martian spokesperson:

> All your knowledge, all your affections, all your interests, are rooted in the
> past, and on that account, as life lengthens, it strengthens its hold on you,
> and memory becomes a more precious possession. We, on the contrary, de-
> spise the past, and never dwell upon it. Memory with us, far from being the
> morbid and monstrous growth it is with you, is scarcely more than a rudi-
> mentary faculty. We live wholly in the future and the present.[69]

Thus, recognizing "that the future is as incapable of being changed as
past," the Martians revel in the glory of a being-in-becoming. With all
uncertainty removed from life, the fear of death loses its enervating
sting, while love and friendship are deepened by the anticipation of their
fruits. The experience of this "ideal" culture leaves the visitor with the
cherished fancy that "the people of that happy sphere . . . represent the
ideal and normal type of our race, as perhaps it once was, as perhaps it
may yet be again."[70]

The world that "may yet be again" is, I want to argue, only fully realized in the utopia of *Looking Backward*. Thus, before West can become a full member of such a society, he too must "lose" his older self,
that is, his memory. Late in the narrative, West and Edith Leete have the
following exchange:

> "Ever since that terrible morning when you came to my help, I have tried to
> avoid thinking of my former life. . . . I am for all the world like a man who
> has permitted an injured limb to lie motionless under the impression that it
> is exquisitely sensitive, and on trying to move it finds that it is paralyzed."
>   "Do you mean your memory is gone?"
>   "Not at all. I remember everything connected with my former life, but
> with a total lack of keen sensation. I remember it for clearness as if it had
> been but a day since then, but my feelings about what I remember are as faint
> as if to my consciousness, as well as in fact, a hundred years had inter-
> vened. . . . Can you conceive of such a thing as living a hundred years in four

days? It really seems to me that I have done just that, and that it is this experience which has given so remote and unreal an appearance to my former life." (*LB*, 146–47)

Although West differs from the Madeline Brand of her lover's fantasy in that his conscious memory of past events still exists (a necessity for his future scholarly duties), the two figures are identical in another, more significant regard: in both cases, these memories have lost any *affective* hold, and hence self-activity is no longer shaped by them. West's new self is freed from the gravitational influences of his past, freed, that is, from the bonds of the historical-cultural context from which he emerged. In losing his self in this way, West actually discovers it anew. The people and places of his past are now nothing more to him than "ghosts": later he declares that the "faces and forms that were about me in my former life" had "no longer any life in them" (*LB*, 145 and 196). He is now a tabula rasa, ready to be reinserted into the new social text.

This change is first registered in West's almost magical recovery from his nervous condition. No longer bothered by the incessant "noise" of social conflict and difference in his own time, he sleeps soundly (*LB*, 102). However, the most dramatic evidence of this change is found in the narrative's concluding chapter. West awakens one morning back in the nineteenth century, apparently realizing, like Henry Burr, that his entire vision of utopia was nothing more than a dream. And like Jonathan Swift's Gulliver after his visit to Houyhnhnmland, West soon finds that his experience of utopia has irrevocably changed him: he now finds the disorder, divisiveness and grime of nineteenth-century life to be unbearable. At this point in the narrative then, the places of the two Bostons have been completely reversed—the nineteenth-century landscape has become to the new West as alien, a "foreign city," as the new metropolis was to his former self (*LB*, 211). He desperately flees to the Bartlett home where he attempts to waken them to the nightmare of the present. In this, he fails; rejected by all, including the original Edith, he sinks into despondency. However, *Looking Backward* differs from its predecessor *Dr. Heidenhoff's Process* in that it was intended as a clarion call for future change and not a tragedy, and in the concluding paragraphs of the narrative, West finds himself back in the Leete home. In this case, West's "return" to the past turns out to be the dream.[71] His transfiguration complete, he enters utopia for good.

In these narratives—*Dr. Heidenhoff's Process,* "The Blindman's World," and *Looking Backward*—Bellamy develops a notion of "mem-

ory" that in its major conceptual lineaments recalls what Nietzsche describes as "history" in the second essay in the *Untimely Meditations,*
"On the Uses and Disadvantages of History for Life." Nietzsche writes,
"Man . . . braces himself against the great and ever greater pressure of
what is past: it pushes him down or bends him sideways, it encumbers
his steps as a dark, invisible burden which he would like to disown."
The cure for this ultimately fatal disease, for "a man or a people or a culture," is to struggle to live *unhistorically,* to "sink down on the thresh-
old of a moment and forget all the past. . . . Forgetting is essential to action of any kind."[72] Paul de Man locates in Nietzsche's description of
this latter state nothing less than "the radical impulse that stands behind
all genuine modernity"—a modernity, de Man claims, that, "exists in
the form of a desire to wipe out whatever came earlier, in the hope of
reaching at last a point that could be called a true present, a point of origin that marks a new departure."[73]

For Bellamy the point of the "new departure," and the subsequent
emergence of a truly "United" States, also would be impossible until
the determining dead weight of cultural memory and history, West's
"ghosts" and the "specters" haunting the contemporary national space,
had been conjured away.[74] In the sermon of Mr. Barton, which serves as
one of the crescendos of *Looking Backward,* Bellamy writes, "With a
tear for the dark past, turn we then to the dazzling future, and, veiling
our eyes, press forward. The long and weary winter of the race is ended.
Its summer has begun. Humanity has burst the chrysalis. The heavens
are before it" (*LB,* 194).

In the end, however, Bellamy's radical program for reconstructing the
subjectivity of the Republic falls back within the horizons of the emerging middle-class public that he had elsewhere delineated in his text.
Memory, as Bellamy describes it, is really those "old world" values and
identities—those of the immigrant, the laborer, the Indian, and, indeed,
of preindustrial America—that threatened the national stability he so
desperately desired. Once these constraining, "nonsynchronic" elements
have been eradicated, nothing, Bellamy assures us, could prevent the
emergence of a unified and truly modern society. West then stands as
the prototype of the new national subjectivity, the end-product of the
emerging assimilationist ideology of the "great melting pot"—a caul-
dron in which all memories and all histories are dissolved away.

And yet, what process could induce such a "forgetting" in the great
masses of the population, the members of the Industrial Army whom I
have already suggested remain a marginal presence in the emergent

middle-class vision of the text? In a marvelous recent discussion of Bellamy's text, Jonathan Auerbach provides one answer: "Rather than the industrial army, in fact, schooling serves as the principle from which all else follows."[75] In the opening pages of his narrative, West describes nineteenth-century society as divided into "four classes, or nations . . . of the rich and the poor, the educated and the ignorant" (*LB*, 25). To fill out the *combinatoire* that Bellamy produces here, West is himself, as he notes, a member of the ideal rich and educated nation; the industrial workers and the other new publics inhabiting the American social body are the poor and the ignorant, the "neutral" inversion of this first term; the "robber baron" corporate leaders, rising to power through exploitation of the laboring classes, make up the rich and ignorant; and finally, intellectuals, like Bellamy himself, form the "nation" of the educated and poor—suffering, if not the desperate material poverty of the laboring classes, at least a lack in the social capital possessed by the other group of the middle class.[76] The new educational apparatus thus would play a crucial role in suturing these publics into a unified national body, while at the same time providing a central "opportunity" for intellectuals in the emergent national culture—a role into which West, as a history professor, is then inserted.[77]

However, there is a fundamental difference between the education received by the "professional classes" and that received by members of the Industrial Army. In response to West's complaint that in any situation of universal standardized schooling "a high education must be pretty nearly thrown away on a large element of the population," Dr. Leete asserts, "If indeed, we could not afford to educate everybody, we should choose the coarsest and dullest by nature, rather than the brightest, to receive what education we could give. The *naturally refined* and intellectual can better dispense with *aides to culture* than those less fortunate in natural endowments" (*LB*, 150–51; emphasis added). He goes on to point out that "its universal and equal enjoyment leaves, indeed, the differences between men as to natural endowments as marked as in a state of nature, but the level of the lowest is vastly raised" (*LB*, 151). Here of course Bellamy figures the ideological rationalization on which will be erected a "meritocratic" educational structure, one that enables the maintenance of distinctions between the "professional classes" and the rest of the industrial labor force.

Moreover, as Dr. Leete presents it, this baseline of universal education represents a form of self-defense for those among the "naturally refined": "I know that the poor and ignorant envied the rich and cultured then; but to us the latter, living as they did, surrounded by squalor and brutishness, seem little better off than the former. The cultured man in your age was like one up to his neck in a nauseous bog solacing himself with a smelling bottle" (*LB,* 151). In an act of synesthesia, Bellamy now rewrites the noise, the social cacophony, that had disturbed West's sleep as smells, the "odors" of cultural difference: and as Žižek points out, "what really bothers us about the 'other' is the peculiar way he organizes his enjoyment, precisely the surplus, the 'excess' that pertains to this way: the *smell* of 'their' food, 'their' *noisy* songs and dances, 'their' strange manners, 'their' attitude toward work."[78] If for Bellamy there is no greater hindrance to the formation of this national body than the presence within it of these conflicting noises and smells, then it will be the goal of a universal education to induce a "forgetting" of them. It is this universal education, finally, that turns the perspective of the entire population from their diverse cultural pasts to the unified national future: "There is still another point I should mention in stating the grounds on which nothing less than the universality of education could now be tolerated . . . and that is, the interest of the coming generation in having educated parents" (*LB,* 152). [79]

Ironically, the same institutional educational act of "forgetting" would result in that "coming generation" in the disappearance of Bellamy's own narrative from the cultural memory. Of course, history shows us that the manner in which this process of erasure would proceed was never as "utopian," nor as total, as Bellamy would have liked to believe.[80]

CHAPTER FOUR

The Occluded Future

Red Star *and* The Iron Heel
as "Critical Utopias"

In one of the first significant discussions of the efflorescence of utopian writings in the late 1960s and early 1970s, Tom Moylan coins the term "critical utopia" to describe these new works. Drawing inspiration from the radical political culture and new left movements of the moment, these narrative utopias challenge not only the dominant cultural and social realties from which they emerge, but also the very assumptions and expectations of the generic institution of which they form an integral part:

> A central concern in the critical utopia is the awareness of the limitations of the utopian tradition, so that these texts reject utopia as a blueprint while preserving it as a dream. Furthermore, the novels dwell on the conflict between the originary world and the utopian society opposed to it so that the process of social change is more directly articulated. Finally, the novels focus on the continuing presence of difference and imperfection within utopian society itself and thus render more recognizable and dynamic alternatives.[1]

Moylan's description of the critical utopia resonates with what I noted in my first chapter to be the self-reflexivity that is part of the institutional *Dasein* of any genre. Thus, in this chapter, I would like to build on Moylan's insight, and suggest that elements of the "critical utopia" are in fact already evident in works produced much earlier in the century.

Alexander Bogdanov's *Red Star* and Jack London's *The Iron Heel*, both originally published in 1908, exemplify many of the characteristics of the critical utopia. Like the later texts Moylan examines, these works emerge in response to the major political crisis unleashed by the Russian Revolution of 1905. In both cases, the authors' response to this event would result in a rethinking of the generic institution itself. The events of what Leon Trotsky would later refer to as "a history of fifty days"—the tantalizingly brief moment of the first workers' Soviet and the horrors of the Czarist counteroffensive—coupled, in London's case, with a series of political disappointments that occurred the same year in the United States, demonstrated for each author the untenability of the progressivist faith at the heart of such earlier utopias as *Looking Backward*. As Bogdanov and London now see it, a new utopian order would emerge only from the crucible of revolutionary struggle, and both works issue a call for this kind of radical praxis.

However, the magnitude of the defeat suffered by the insurgency of 1905 would raise another, more disturbing question for these two thinkers: if a great change did seem *immanent* in the conditions of the present, as Bellamy also would have agreed, was it as *imminent* as the author of *Looking Backward* believed? These two later writers' answer to this question is provided in their particular reworking of the genre: both ultimately relegate the narrative elaboration of the utopian space, what Moylan calls the utopian "blueprint," to the margins of the text (this is literally true in *The Iron Heel*). Preserving the utopian space as a "dream" of otherness, the narrative focus of each text is then redirected toward the delineation of the conflicts involved in "the process of social change."

The ultimate "failure" in each work to represent—or in Lefebvre's terms, to conceive—the space of utopia also points toward another fundamental reconsideration underway in the genre. As we will see shortly, both Bogdanov's and London's fictions call into question the fundamental link established in the genre between the imaginary community of the utopia and the "imagined community" of the modern nation-state. As these two authors view the matter, both a new space and a new subject for the continuation of the spatial histories of modernity needs to be called into being. Unable to "conceive" the former, both turn their energies toward giving form to the latter.

Interestingly, Bogdanov's and London's fictions also share a common destiny, in that both were later celebrated and widely circulated in the Soviet Union, especially in the first decade following the 1917 revolution. *Red Star* went through several editions in the years after the revolution, with a press run of 120,000 in 1929, which, Keith Jensen notes, was "a startling figure given the place and the time."[2] London was the most popular American author in the early years of the Soviet Union, and would continue to be so in many of the later socialist states (and elsewhere). Whereas there has never yet been an English-language edition of London's collected work, there were six such editions already published in the Soviet Union between the years 1918 and 1929; and by 1943, there were 567 different editions of his various works, with more than ten million copies sold.[3] Moreover, soon after the revolution a film version of *The Iron Heel* was produced, with a screenplay coauthored by Anatoly Lunacharsky, the first Soviet Commissar for Education and the Arts (alas, no known copy of the film survives).[4] Perhaps most revealing of London's popularity in the early Soviet Union is the well-known story told by Nadezhda Krupskaya of her reading to Lenin, as he lay on his deathbed, London's short story "Love of Life."[5]

The reasons for this success, I will suggest, lie in part in the way each work helps elaborate new "myths" that soon would be dominant not only within the Soviet Union, but in much of the mainstream Communist movement elsewhere as well. In his classic work of ideological semiology, *Mythologies,* Roland Barthes maintains that the fundamental work of "myth" is to naturalize and universalize a certain historical reality, and in so doing mask the political aims involved in any such pedagogical process. Thus, the one kind of language that cannot be mythical is that of revolution: "Revolution is defined as a cathartic act meant to reveal the political load of the world: it *makes* the world; and its language, all of it, is functionally absorbed in this making. . . . Revolution announces itself openly as revolution and thereby abolishes myth."[6] Barthes goes on to argue that to the degree that the "Left is not revolution," that is, in its distance from this active, performative, remaking of the world, it becomes more and more susceptible to the process of mythologization. As a consequence, the Left takes up its own project of preservation, its past achievements becoming images, institutions, and orthodoxies—a depoliticization of its "speech" that "is sooner or later experienced as a process contrary to revolution."[7] Both Bogdanov's and London's narratives would play a crucial role in this process, which Barthes calls "revolutionary ex-nomination." Ironically, in their very efforts to imagine the spaces and organizations of struggle appropriate to the new century, both works would contribute to the ebb of the tide of revolution.

RED STAR AND THE HORIZONS
OF RUSSIAN MODERNITY

Bogdanov's *Red Star (Krasnaya Zvezda)*, although less well-known in the West today, played a central role in the subsequent development of Soviet science fiction and utopian literature. Darko Suvin maintains that *Red Star* "renewed the tradition for left-wing Russian SF, which had been in abeyance since [Nikolai] Chernyshevsky's times"; while Richard Stites notes that Bogdanov's narrative served as a touchstone for the rich outpouring of imaginative literature in the years 1917–29, not the least of which included the celebrated work by Yevgeny Zamyatin, *We (My)*, which I discuss in more detail in the next two chapters.[8] However, Bogdanov had more than simply literary aspirations in mind when writing *Red Star*. This work responds to the various concerns and doubts plaguing socialist intellectuals in the aftermath of the 1905 Revolution. Bogdanov himself was one of the founders of the Bolshevik group of the Russian Social Democratic Workers party. He worked closely with Lenin during 1905, organizing underground activity in their native country. However, the two would diverge in their respective interpretations of the strategic climate following the defeat of the revolutionary insurgency: whereas Lenin supported Bolshevik participation in the newly formed Duma, Bogdanov viewed any such concession as an abandonment of the aspirations of the socialist revolution—the revolution that he was sure would again explode forth sometime in the near future.[9]

An assessment of this contemporary situation is conveyed to the reader through the musings of the protagonist of *Red Star,* the Russian activist Leonid N. After returning from the achieved socialist society of the "Red Star," the planet Mars, Leonid—who, because of his journey, had missed the crushing defeat of the 1905 uprising—reflects,

> We were clearly on our way toward new and decisive battles. The road was so long and so full of twists and turns, however, that many became weary and even began to despair. The so-called radical intelligentsia, whose participation in the struggle had been limited for the most part to demonstrations of sympathy, betrayed the cause almost to a man. There was nothing to regret in that, of course, but despondency and despair had even infiltrated the ranks of my former comrades. That fact alone told me what a trying ordeal revolutionary life must have been at the time.[10]

This real-world malaise provides Bogdanov with the immediate impetus for writing *Red Star*. Bogdanov hoped that his vision of the glories of a realized socialist society might inspire future revolutionary struggle. Indeed, Leonid's Martian host Netti might very well be speaking to the reader of the aims of *Red Star* when she observes that on Earth, "Blood is being shed for the sake of a better future. . . . But in order to wage the struggle one must *know* that future. And it is for the sake of such knowledge that you are here" (*RS*, 47: I, 7).

On a first glance, *Red Star* seems to adhere closely to the form and concerns of the classical narrative utopia. The work opens in the "early days of the great upheaval" of 1905. Leonid, an amateur scientist, literary intellectual, and socialist organizer, encounters a young comrade bearing the strange name of Menni, whom Leonid soon discovers to be a visitor from the planet Mars. When Leonid inquires as to why he in particular has been chosen as Earth's emissary to their world, Menni tells him, "You are to serve as a living link between the human races of Earth and Mars by familiarizing yourself with our way of life and acquainting the Martians with yours" (*RS*, 34: I, 4). Moreover, the reader soon learns that a Russian was chosen for this vital task because of "all the major peoples of the world . . . the pulse of life throbs stronger there, and, more than anywhere else, people are forced to look to the future" (*RS*, 42: I, 7). During the course of the two-and-one-half month-long journey on the etheroneph, the Martian spaceship powered by the radioactive decay of "minus-matter," Leonid's education in the utopian socialism practiced on the red planet commences. Much of the rest of the narrative follows the utopia's familiar pattern, the main body of the text taking the form of a reminiscence written by Leonid wherein his various queries and observations about Martian social life are answered, confirmed, or refuted by a member of the community.

Once on Mars, Leonid encounters a world where the norms of individualism and competitive capitalism have been supplanted by those of collectivism and egalitarian socialism. There are no marks of rank or position among the members of the society. Every individual achievement, whether scientific or artistic, is viewed as the end product of and contribution to the collective's accumulated genius: the only monuments erected in this society mark great historical events and scientific discoveries. Gender inequalities have disappeared, and free love is practiced by all, albeit in a strictly heterosexual fashion (Leonid's unease at his attraction to the Martian medical doctor Netti gives way to exuberant passion only *after* he discovers that Netti is in fact a woman [*RS*, 93: II, 7]). The planet's children are reared together; the life span has been greatly extended and overall physical well-being enhanced through the frequent use of "mutual blood transfusions" (Bogdanov, himself a practicing physician, would die in 1928 while undergoing an experimental self-transfusion with a student suffering from malaria and tuberculosis); and suicide for the old, infirm, and despairing is condoned by society.[11]

Finally, as befits any great utopian vision, money, compulsory work, and artificial limits on personal consumption have been eliminated. Prefiguring the syndicalist PDC of Ursula K. Le Guin's *The Dispossessed,* Bogdanov pictures a centralized Institute of Statistics that maintains planetwide industrial production, guarding against any surplus or shortage of goods by monitoring output and directing the voluntary labor force to the areas where their skills are most urgently needed (*RS*, 65–68: II, 2). Moreover, diverging dramatically from the specialized, professional organization of work envisioned in *Looking Backward,* every worker in the socialist collective of *Red Star* engages in a rich variety of activities during the course of her lifetime, resulting in a broadly skilled, creative, and energetic labor force. The same regard for diversity in every worker's activity later would lead Bogdanov to speak out against attempts to introduce into Soviet factories Taylorist forms of labor organization, reforms that would have the additional consequence of shifting control of the production process from the workers to factory managers.[12]

However, even with these remarkable achievements, Bogdanov's critical utopian vision shows us that the society on Mars remains immersed in the ebb and tide of historical time: for although conflicts between individuals and social classes have passed from the Martian social stage, elements of *negativity,* challenges and barriers that spur human creativity to new invention, remain a dominant presence on the Red Star. This is perhaps nowhere more dramatically evident than in the population's struggles against an unyielding natural environment; as Jensen puts it, humanity's "relationship (struggle) with nature" has become "the basic fact of life and the raison d'etre" of Martian society.[13] The inhabitants of this world are plagued by the problem of scarcity, the dwindling of resources on a planet twice as old as the earth, and the threat of extinction (anxiety over one's individual future having been supplanted in Bogdanov's utopia by a deep and abiding concern with the life of the collective). These various natural challenges provide the impetus for Martian science and technology to advance. Indeed, we soon learn that the struggle with the natural world has played a central, even determining role in Martian history: the very events that begat socialism on Mars— the elimination of private landholding, the collectivization of agricultural production, the eradication of the "pre-modern" peasantry, and, most magnificent of all, the monumental engineering feat involved in the construction of the great canals—were themselves the consequences of a dwindling planetary water supply (*RS*, 54–56: I, 9).[14] (These "historical" themes are developed more fully in Bogdanov's prequel to *Red Star, Engineer Menni* [1913].) Moreover, the rapid depletion of certain vital mineral reserves and a food supply inadequate to the needs of an ever-growing population—artificial regulation of the birth rate or the shortening of the life span are both repugnant to Martians, for they would mean "denying the unlimited growth of life" (*RS*, 79–80: II, 4)—have led the Martians to debate the possibility of undertaking a massive colonization of either the primitive planet Venus or Leonid's own Earth.

The red planet's preeminence in scientific and technological matters is rivaled only by its achievements in philosophy. Indeed, the narrative assures us that every advance in the former realm could not but positively affect the latter. In comparing the dominant modes of thought on the two worlds, the Martian medical doctor Netti notes that while the rich variety of Earth's philosophical systems display a subtlety and complexity absent during the similar stage of Martian development, these systems nonetheless betray Earth culture's "imperfect and fragmented cognition and reflect a deficient level of scientific development. They represent attempts to provide a uniform description of Being by filling in the gaps in scientific experience with speculations." However, she concludes that inevitably "philosophy will be eliminated on Earth as it has been eliminated among us by the monism of science" (*RS*, 118–19: III, 8).

The intellectual roots of this assault on metaphysics—similar to that found in the first chapter of *The Iron Heel*—can be traced to Bogdanov's own fascination with the work of the then widely influential German scientist-philosopher Ernst Mach. Mach believed that he had definitively closed the debate between materialism and idealism by discovering the elements, or "sensations," that constitute the neutral, a priori basis of both matter and mind. (Bogdanov's adoption of Machism would lead to a further erosion of his relationship with Lenin, culminating in a thoroughgoing critique of Bogdanov's thought in Lenin's *Materialism and Empirio-Criticism,* published less than a year after *Red Star.*)[15] When Bogdanov combined Mach's empirio-criticism with a Darwinist evolutionism derived from the work of Mach's countryman Ernst Haeckel (who, as we shall see shortly, also had a considerable influence on the work of London), the result would be the grand, all-encompassing, theoretical "monism"—a kind of philosophical unified field theory, a number of which were popular around the turn of the century—that Bogdanov would call, in a later work of the same title, the Tectology.[16] In his explication of this theory, Bogdanov argues that human society has been directed, from the moment of its inception, by a "hitherto unnoticed principle" of integration, or "Organization."[17] Thus, according to Bogdanov, the realization of total Organization is the universal destiny of all life.

This inexorable evolutionary movement toward Organization also provides the common teleological thread that joins together the distinct human worlds of Earth and Mars. Martian social life differs from that on Earth only in that it has already achieved a more advanced level of overarching, systemic unity. Early in the narrative, Netti informs Leonid that "the common cause of mankind is not yet really a common cause among you. It has become so splintered in the illusions generated by the struggle among men that it seems to belong to individual persons rather than to mankind as a whole" (RS, 44: I, 7). Nevertheless, she assures him that the two humanities are "brothers," for Martian science had "discovered" what Bogdanov believed to be self-evident: the more highly advanced the social type, the more strictly delimited its possible forms of expression (RS, 55: I, 9). Thus, when Earth overcomes its internal divisions, replacing the relative anarchy produced by capitalism with the Organization that is socialism, it will pass from its "adolescence" and enter into a "mature" existence, which, in its major lineaments, would be nearly identical to that of its elder. With the assertion of the homology between the two societies, the narrative's spatial journey folds over into a temporal one, the movement between the two planets paralleling the passage on Earth from the present to a more highly evolved future.[18] Serving as the link between these distinct topoi is the figure of Leonid. Leonid observes that in his role as a socialist activist, he "stood on the border" between the two worlds, "like a split second of the present between the past and the future" (RS, 86: II, 6).

However, the central question that Netti passes over in silence concerns how the Earth will overcome these inherent divisions. And, by the conclusion of the narrative, it still remains unclear how the unification of the two spaces might be accomplished. This dilemma is further borne out by Leonid's individual failure, unlike his predecessor Julian West, to navigate the difficult personal passage into the other world. Indeed, in the final sentences of his manuscript, he observes, "The new life is inaccessible to me, while I do not want the old one, to which I no longer belong either intellectually and emotionally" (RS, 135–36: IV, 5). Leonid remains, for the moment at least, trapped in a zone of dead time, neither of "Earth" nor "Mars," neither a denizen of the present nor of the future. Bogdanov here gives expression to the sentiments of many in the Russian socialist movement in the aftermath of the failed revolution: the restoration of the Czarist regime seemed to signal the derailing of the very engine of history. One of the central questions that Bogdanov attempts to address in *Red Star* concerns how it might once again be put back on track.

Leonid's conclusion that a place in Martian society is unavailable to him is precipitated by two distinct crises. The first, Leonid's "sympathetic" crisis, occurs almost immediately after he acknowledges his position on the "border" between the two worlds. While attempting to gain some understanding of the contours of Martian society through an intense examination of its scientific and artistic texts, Leonid becomes overwhelmed by the utter strangeness of life on the red planet. The principles of Martian scientific reasoning completely evade him, and even "pure fiction" offers no reprieve from a dizzying sense of Otherness: "Its images seemed simple and clear, yet somehow they remained alien to me. I wanted to penetrate them more deeply and understand them more intimately, but the result of my efforts was wholly unexpected; instead of opening themselves to me the images faded into fog-shrouded shadows" (*RS,* 87: II, 6; compare this with West's quite different experience of the literature of utopia.)[19] Lacking the reference points by which he might mentally negotiate this new world, Leonid succumbs to a kind of cognitive-deprivation-induced delirium, hallucinating figures and scenes from his life on Earth. Fittingly, Leonid expresses his desire for Mars in the language of sexual conquest ("to penetrate," "intimately," "opening themselves up to me"), for it will be in a more local sexual adventure that he finds a moment's peace. Plagued by his inability to "know" Mars, Leonid averts a complete descent into madness only by launching into a love affair with Netti.

However, his second crisis proves far less easily resolved. While investigating Netti's abrupt decision to accompany an expedition to Venus, Leonid stumbles upon transcripts of a debate concerning the possible colonization of Earth. He learns to his horror that any such project would entail the annihilation of the indigenous human species. In order to do so, the Martians would deploy the lethal energy produced by the disintegration of minus-matter in the etheroneph engines—a reference perhaps to the "Heat-Rays" of the Martian invaders in H. G. Wells's *The War of the Worlds.* Driven mad by the unbearable knowledge of the

potential extermination of his people, Leonid seeks out and murders the
mathematician Sterni, the leading spokesperson for this colonization
plan. This act concludes his days on Mars. When he next returns to his
senses, he finds himself back on Earth, an inhabitant of a sanitarium in
the northern Russian provinces operated by his friend and revolutionary
comrade, Dr. Werner (whom Jensen suggests is an avatar of Bogdanov
himself).[20]

Leonid's failure to suture the gap separating the temporal "place" of
Earth and that of Mars represents far more than a case of personal in-
adequacy. Indeed, through the depiction of these events, Bogdanov's
text begins to call into question the whole narrative teleo-logic that un-
dergirds utopian discourse as it had hitherto developed in the modern
period: for without a successful mediatory figure, the apparently seamless temporal totality constituted by the places of Earth and Mars begins
to unravel. Mars comes to look less like a figure for Earth's future and
more like the truly Other place, a realm finally inaccessible to Bogdanov's present.

The central causes of this representational crisis come to the surface
in the scene that many readers of *Red Star* have acknowledged to be
the work's high point: the monumental debate on the possible colonization of Earth. The chillingly analytical Sterni begins the discussion
by describing the inhospitable conditions on Venus that preclude any
attempt at a wide-scale resettlement of that planet. On Earth, on the
other hand, no "natural obstacles" exist that might hinder colonization, while the environmental riches of the planet will assure that Martian life flourishes on both worlds. Sterni then carefully details those
features of the native human civilization that make cohabitation between the two worlds impossible. The worst of these traits, or "psychological peculiarities," and the one that most readily distinguishes
Earth from Martian social life, is the form of group self-identification
known as "patriotism":

> This indefinite but strong and deep-seated emotion includes a spiteful dis-
> trust of all other peoples and races, a visceral attachment to a particular way
> of life—especially to the territory with which each people has fused, like a
> turtle with its shell—a certain collective self-conceit and often, evidently, a
> simple thirst for destruction, violence, and plunder. Patriotic fervor in-
> tensifies and becomes extremely acute after military defeats, especially when
> the victors seize a part of the losers' territory. The patriotism of the van-
> quished then takes the form of an intense and prolonged hatred of the vic-
> tors, and revenge becomes the ideal of not just the worst groups—the upper

or ruling classes—but of the entire people, including the best elements among the toiling masses. (RS, 111: III, 7)

Ironically, Sterni maintains, the inhabitants of the Earth might overcome these divisions only in the face of a Martian invasion; then "the entire population of the planet would doubtless find itself united by a common patriotism and merciless racist hatred and resentment toward our colonists" (RS, 111: III, 7).[21]

Patriotism as Sterni here defines it is the pathology endemic to the modern nation-state, and a "common patriotism and merciless racist hatred and resentment" toward the Martians represents the projection of this pathology to a global level. Slavoj Žižek points out that "the element which holds together a given community cannot be reduced to the point of symbolic identification: the bond linking together its members always implies a shared relationship toward a Thing, toward Enjoyment incarnated. This relationship toward the Thing, structured by means of fantasies, is what is at stake when we speak of the menace to our 'way of life' presented by the Other."[22] The Martian menace, as Bogdanov formulates it here, thus represents one form of this Other big enough to suture all of the earth's people into a single national subject, one nation whose "organization of enjoyment" would be that of a common humanity.

A similar process is evident in the writings of Wells, one of the new century's most influential authors of utopian fiction. In the opening pages of his most fully elaborated utopian vision, *A Modern Utopia* (1905), Wells explains why it is necessary now to imagine a utopian space that extends beyond the borders of the insular nation-state:

> No less than a planet will serve the purpose of a modern Utopia. Time was when a mountain valley or an island seemed to promise sufficient isolation for a polity to maintain itself intact from outward force. . . . But the whole trend of modern thought is against the permanence of any such enclosures. We are acutely aware nowadays that, however subtly contrived a State may be, outside your boundary lines the epidemic, the breeding barbarian or the economic power, will gather its strength to overcome you. . . . A state powerful enough to keep isolated under modern conditions would be powerful enough to rule the world, would be, indeed, if not actively ruling, yet passively acquiescent in all other human organisations, and so responsible for them altogether. World-state, therefore, it must be.[23]

Wells then proceeds to delineate a global utopia that represents a triumph of rational organization and centralized planning: a socialist collectivity that gives full reign to the eccentricities of the individual human character, the happiness of the whole secured by a voluntary scientific and bureaucratic elite, the order of the Samurai.[24]

However, Wells never explains how such a global unification first came about. An answer, I believe, is to be found elsewhere in his writings, in his earlier, self-described "fantasias of possibility" and "scientific romances," works that would also contribute to the rise of the new generic institution, science fiction, that will shortly subsume the narrative utopia.[25] In his 1899 short story "The Star," Wells narrates a series of catastrophic events that occur when a rogue planetary body passes near the Earth. In the story's penultimate paragraph, Wells briefly alludes to the consequences of this singular event: "But of the new brotherhood that grew presently among men . . . this story does not tell."[26] Similarly, in *The War of the Worlds* (1899), the narrator states, "It may be that in the larger design of the universe this invasion from Mars is not without its ultimate benefit for men; . . . it has done much to promote the conception of the commonweal of mankind."[27] In both cases, this later "story" is, in effect, the one told in *A Modern Utopia*. The catastrophes imagined in these earlier works thus serve as double "vanishing mediators," enabling the literal production of a global nation-state, "the commonweal of mankind," and freeing up Wells's literary imagination to map it.[28] Wells's influence on the development of later science fiction can be felt up to the present day; and the device of the external mediator as a mechanism for suturing the global totality is still evident in such diverse contemporary works as the science fiction films *2010* (1984) and *Independence Day* (1996), and Alan Moore and Dave Gibbon's graphic novel, *The Watchmen*.[29]

Bogdanov, on the other hand, presents a very different narrative of origins for the Martian global community. Early in his education, Leonid learns,

> At one time . . . peoples from different countries on Mars could not understand each other either. Long ago, however, several centuries before the socialist revolution, all the various dialects drew closer to one another and merged in a single common language. This occurred freely and spontaneously. No one tried to bring it about or even gave it much thought. Certain local peculiarities survived for quite some time, so there existed something akin to individual dialects, but these were fairly comprehensible to everyone. The development of literature finally eliminated them as well. (*RS*, 54: I, 9)

The emergence of a dominant vernacular language, and its subsequent stabilization through print technologies, played, as Benedict Anderson demonstrates, an indispensable role in the development of the modern nation-state.[30] A similar process occurs on Mars, with a crucial difference: the transformation happens all at once and on a planetwide level. Bogdanov's Martians thus become one people, a bounded and autonomous nation, *before* they become citizens of utopia. The difficulties of unifying the new global society into a single collective whole, one of the fundamental goals of the contemporary socialist movement, disappear in the narrative, as this unification emerges as a primal cause that itself is without cause, "No one tried to bring it about or even gave it much thought." Moreover, the natural conditions on the planet, menacing, as I noted earlier, the very survival of the humanoid species, serve as the expression of the Other that sustains this particular unification. (Again, this is similar to what Le Guin will later imagine in her anarchist utopia set on the inhospitable moon-world of Anarres).

It is precisely the absence of this primal global unity that marks the incommensurable gap between the histories of Mars and Earth. There emerges in *Red Star,* as much as in the passage from *A Modern Utopia* quoted above, a recognition of the deep imbrication of the "destiny" or the history of the individual nation-state in a global system of interlocking social entities. The narrative thus suggests that a total change of affairs, the realization of socialist Organization, can come about only through the reordering of this global totality—a process, however, rendered unimaginable as a consequence of the fragmentary "unevenness" of Earth's own social development. Indeed, Sterni observes that on Earth

> the struggle for socialism is split into a variety of unique and autonomous processes in individual societies with distinct political systems, languages, and sometimes even races. . . . Due to all these factors, the question of social revolution becomes a very uncertain one. We must expect not one, but a multitude of revolutions taking place in different countries at different times. In many respects they will probably not even have the same basic character, but the main point is that their outcome is unpredictable and unstable. (*RS,* 113: III, 7)

The narrative's failure to map the spatial contours of the future, quite literally "unpredictable" as the text maintains, is thus directly related to the difficulties of grasping this expanded sense of present history: for in order to describe the totality of the present, all of these societies, "political systems, languages, and sometimes even races," as well as the relationships between them, need to be brought into focus simultaneously.

Ignoring his own note of caution, Sterni does allow himself one speculative turn. What, he wonders, would be the consequence of socialism

coming into existence in only a handful of isolated countries? His answer pinpoints this narrative's critical engagement with the generic institutional tradition that precedes it:

> If this happens, the individual advanced countries in which socialism tri-
> umphs will be like islands in a hostile capitalist and even to some extent pre-
> capitalist sea. Anxious about their own power, the upper classes of the non-
> socialist countries will continue to concentrate all their efforts on destroying
> these islands. They will constantly be organizing military expeditions against
> them, and from among the ranks of the former large and small property-
> holders in the socialist nations themselves they will be able to find plenty of
> allies willing to commit treason. It is difficult to foresee the outcome of these
> conflicts, but even in those instances where socialism prevails and triumphs,
> its character will be perverted deeply and for a long time to come by years of
> encirclement, unavoidable terror and militarism, and the barbarian patriot-
> ism that is their inevitable consequence. This socialism will be a far cry from
> our own. (*RS*, 113–14: III, 7)

The scientist Sterni's cool observation redoubles as tragic prophecy
when we reflect upon the later fate of the soon-to-be inaugurated Soviet
revolutionary experiment—an island in a hostile sea, it too slips into a
"socialism" a far cry from its founding ideals.

Bogdanov's unwillingness to accept a model of a social totality (and
history) confined by the borders of the nation-state is in part a product
of his socialist political agenda. Indeed, the implicit threat represented
by nationalism for any kind of international socialist movement would
become a sad actuality less than a decade after *Red Star* was published,
when the "unity and reality of the Second International" was abruptly
shattered by the divisive nationalist fervor of the First World War.[31]
Equally significant, Bogdanov's own national situation positioned him
within a global system of European nation-states in such a way that the
fictionality of national autonomy would have been apparent. In the eyes
of an advocate of radical change like Bogdanov, with Russia located on
the margins of a European community from which it drew the intellectual energies for its own fitful and uneven project of social modernization, future history appears always already structurally incomplete
when confined within the insular horizons of the nation. The dualisms
that up until then had marked modern Russian history—between East
and West, between the traditions of the cultural past and the uneasy
promise of the future (a dualism that Marshall Berman reads as sym-
bolically manifest in the opposition of Moscow and St. Petersburg)—
thus has been translated in Bogdanov's text into an opposition be-

tween two distinct historical and spatial registers, the national and the global.[32]

Staged within this paradigm of choices, Leonid's failure to bridge the gulf between the two "worlds" appears in a new light. Leonid must not only cross from the present into the future, but also between two completely different orders of historical development, the national and the global. As a descendant of the Russian national bourgeois, Leonid remains too much a product of the former order of history to negotiate the passage into the latter (something similar occurs in *Red Star's* prequel with the figure of the Martian bourgeois engineer Menni). If the narrative utopia first emerges as a way to think, to cognitively map, or to produce a "representation of space" of the autonomous nation-state—and thereby simultaneously to teach its readers to think of themselves as new kinds of subjects—then with the "disappearance" of that autonomy (which again, if always already "imaginary," is nevertheless "real"), there emerges a representational crisis within the genre. Leonid's "failure" thus initiates in *Red Star* a very different project of utopian figuration, one that will be pursued all the more vigorously in *The Iron Heel*. Both texts launch the search for a new "*subject* of history," a collective agency or a particular communal "organization of enjoyment," that could replace the national community, and serve as the mediator in the difficult passage between the fragmentary present and the unity of a global future.

In the "Summing Up" chapter of his manuscript, Leonid recalls an early discussion with Menni, the leader of the Martian expedition to Earth. Leonid questions Menni as to why he alone was chosen as representative of humanity, especially given that he is not even the best example of Russian socialism. Bogdanov uses Menni's analysis of the shortcomings of the other socialist leaders as an opportunity to take a swipe at Lenin, referred to in the text as the "Old Man of the Mountain." The Old Man, Menni informs Leonid, "is exclusively a man of struggle and revolution. Our order would not suit him at all. He is a man of iron, and men of iron are not flexible. They also have a strong measure of inborn conservatism" (*RS*, 134: IV, 5). Even more significant is Leonid's next question: Why did the Martians not select as the Earth's emissary a member of the proletariat, one of those "who constitute the base and main strength" of the revolutionary movement? Menni responds that the workers lack the prerequisite "broad, well-rounded education" that the ideal candidate must possess (*RS*, 134: IV, 5).

Later, back on Earth, Leonid realizes the flaw in Menni's reasoning. His subsequent breakdown, he now theorizes, was rooted in an innate inability to overcome the contradiction between his inner and outer worlds: his experience of insular consciousness and the shared social collectivity he inhabits on Mars. In other words, Leonid reduplicates on the individual psychic level the division between the two spatial registers of history that I discussed above. The isolated bourgeois subject inhabits, and indeed reflects in its very form, the insular realm of national history; while a utopian subjectivity would exist on a wholly different plane altogether. Leonid thus concludes that in his role as a revolutionary intellectual, one who worked primarily "alone or in a one-sided, unequal relationship to his comrades," he had been isolated (again in a way quite similar to his Martian "predecessor," the engineer Menni) from the crucial *experience* of the collective, the very experience that forms the core of the "primitive and uncultivated" life of the industrial worker (*RS*, 135: IV, 5). Any worker would have better adapted to life on Mars because the worker's current existence more closely prefigures that on the Red Star. And what is such an experience but what Žižek describes as the shared relationship toward a Thing, a particular set of "enjoyments incarnated"?

With this conclusion, we witness the first figuration of what would later serve as the linchpin of Bogdanov's universal theory of Tectology: the belief that the proletariat, far more significant than its "merely" epiphenomenal structural position in a capitalist mode of production, had been destined, from the very beginning of human society, to serve as the agent by which the final form of Organization, or social collectivism, would be realized. Here we also see one of the earliest expressions of what would later become Bogdanov's most lasting, and most notorious, contribution to an emerging Soviet Party mythology: the idealization of the worker known as "Proletcult."[33] Thus, in an unexpected way, Bogdanov's vision becomes even further removed from that of "Old Man" Lenin, "exclusively a man of struggle and revolution": for the very text through which Bogdanov attempts to spark a new phase of revolutionary struggle in Russia also generates one of the central figures that will later be used in constructing the orthodox myth of the Soviet Union as the final form of the revolution "achieved."

In the end, however, Leonid's acknowledgment of the irrevocable loss of the "new life" does not lead him to despair. Instead, he launches into renewed action, for he now realizes that only revolutionary struggle can shatter the stasis of the present and create the conditions where the "hated boundary between the past and the future," the two orders of history, finally will be erased. With the cry "Long live the new, the better life!" Leonid brings his manuscript to a close (*RS*, 136: IV, 5).

But rather than providing a satisfactory resolution to the narrative, this conclusion opens a new set of problems. Leonid's endorsement of an individual political voluntarism does not square with the macrological evolutionary determinism of the Tectology: for if a new structure of social Organization, to be implemented by the collective agency of the proletariat, will inevitably arise from the conditions of the present as a matter of historical necessity, what need is there for Leonid's political activities? Indeed, while his actions may shorten the time that it takes for such a utopian situation to appear, there is always the danger that his interventions, unaccounted for in the systemic modeling of the Tectology, might inadvertently *delay* their realization. This oscillation between the two extreme poles of voluntarism and determinism, of subjective and objective determinations of individual action, actually extends back through the whole narrative of *Red Star*. Thus, for example, although Netti can confidently talk of the objective *inevitability* of the maturation of the earth's inhabitants, she can finally prevent their eradication at the hands of her own people only through the subjective ethical assertion that the *potential* for, and not the necessity of, improvement in any species makes it worthy of life. (Of course, why couldn't the same argument for potentiality then be extended to the dinosaurs and other primitive Venusian life forms that invariably will be destroyed during the colonization effort?) While Bogdanov is neither the first nor the last thinker to run up against the philosophical and political dilemmas raised by the contradiction between determinism and voluntarism, they create special problems in *Red Star,* short-circuiting the narrative's stated program of showing our collective future, and throwing the question of revolutionary action back into the realm of individual election.[34]

Indeed, this latter position comes to the fore in the closing pages of Bogdanov's narrative. In an epilogue "written" by Dr. Werner at some indeterminate point after the events narrated by Leonid, we learn that our protagonist does in fact achieve a kind of personal salvation. Wounded during an attack on the enemy forces, Leonid is taken to a field hospital, where Dr. Werner diagnoses his condition as critical. Suddenly, Netti reappears, promising Leonid that his wounds will heal and together they shall return to Mars. While at the hospital, Netti refers to Leonid only by the Martian form of his name, "Lenni"—a sign that Leonid, after successfully passing through the baptism of the revolution, has been rechristened as a full member of the utopian society (*RS*, 139–40; "Epilogue"). When Dr. Werner comes to check in on Leonid the next day, he discovers that both he and Netti have vanished. With these final, almost mystical, notes, *Red Star* comes near to passing from the generic realm of the utopia altogether, and into that of fantasy—for at this point, Mars no longer seems to represent a potential topos of future history, but instead has become the otherworldly place of the religious paradise, a world Leonid can enter only at the moment of his death.

THE LONG REVOLUTION OF *THE IRON HEEL*

In his analysis of conditions on Earth that make global socialism such a difficult project, Sterni notes that a violent counteroffensive would follow on the heels of any revolutionary action: "The ruling classes will rely on the army and sophisticated military technology, and in certain cases they may deal the rebelling proletariat such a stunning blow that the cause of socialism will be frustrated for decades in a number of important states. Such examples have already been recorded in the chronicles of Earth" (*RS*, 113: III, 7). While the specific "example" he has in mind here is again that of real world Russia of 1905, Sterni's observation also reads like a plot summary of London's *The Iron Heel*. However, if *Red Star* displays a shaken confidence in the near imminence of a transformed human future—the "delay" still imagined to be only "decades" long—*The Iron Heel* offers little hope that such a dramatic change of affairs will occur any time soon. Indeed, London's narrative opens up a yawning fissure between the temporal locus of his present and that of the radically other future: the reader learns in the narrative's foreword, written more than four hundred years after the founding of the global socialist Brotherhood of Man, that the utopian society does not appear until after three *centuries* of tyrannical rule by the most repressive regime in all of human history, the capitalist Oligarchy popularly referred to as the Iron Heel.[35] In this, London seems to replicate Marx's shift from the confidence in the imminence of revolution found in *The Communist Manifesto*—a text, I will suggest momentarily, upon which London models his own narrative—to the much longer-range temporal perspectives of the *Grundrisse*.

London's pessimism regarding the possibilities of the near future had its roots in two very different events in the year 1905 that became indelibly linked in his imagination: the defeat of the Russian Revolution, and the outrageous treatment he received at the hands of the U.S. press because of his recent divorce and his espousal of revolutionary socialism during a national lecture tour.[36] The coincidence of these historical and personal setbacks seemed to convince London that capitalist hegemony would continue far into the future. This grim outlook would, in turn, lead to the rebuking of the book by reformist factions within the American socialist intelligentsia (although others, including Eugene Debs and Bill Haywood, still found it quite powerful).[37] Still later, these same thematic elements would be celebrated by readers such as Anatole France and Trotsky, the former seeing in London's narrative a foreshadowing of the setbacks experienced by Western European socialism in the early 1920s, and the latter finding it prescient of the rise of the fascism that inevitably followed upon "the defeat of the proletarian revolution."[38]

London himself would later claim that he never intended for *The Iron Heel* to be taken as a bleak prophecy. Rather, he meant to serve warning of what might occur if socialism failed to achieve a modicum of success in the coming national elections.[39] And indeed, there are points within the narrative that would seem to cut against the grain of the argument that London viewed the Iron Heel's tyranny as an inevitable consequence of the present state of affairs. In this text, London again employs one of his favorite literary devices, the frame-story.[40] The main body of the narrative takes the form of an incomplete memoir written in 1932 by Avis, the wife of the revolutionary leader Ernest Everhard. Her enframed manuscript in turn looks backward to the events in the years 1912–17, the period during which the Iron Heel effected its sweeping reorganization of the social order. Framing her narrative, in turn, is a commentary composed seven hundred years hence by the utopian historian Anthony Meredith. Through the use of this double frame, London's fiction at once accommodates three different perspectives: Everhard's, in the years of the Iron Heel's ascendancy; Avis's, from her retrospective position after his death; and Meredith's, located long after the establishment of a utopian society.

In his foreword to the "Everhard Manuscript," Meredith notes the weird place of the Iron Heel in the process of social evolution:

> The rise of the Oligarchy will always remain a cause of secret wonder to the historian and the philosopher. Other great historical events have their place in social evolution. They were inevitable. Their coming could have been predicted with the same certitude that astronomers to-day predict the outcome of the movements of stars. Without these other great historical events, social

evolution could not have proceeded. Primitive communism, chattel slavery, serf slavery, and wage slavery were necessary stepping-stones in the evolution of society. But it were ridiculous to assert that the Iron Heel was a necessary stepping-stone. Rather, to-day, is it adjudged a step aside, or a step backward, to the social tyrannies that made the early world a hell, but that were as necessary as the Iron Heel was unnecessary. . . . In the orderly procedure of social evolution there was no place for it. It was not necessary and it was not inevitable. It must always remain the great curiosity of history—a whim, a fantasy, an apparition, a thing unexpected and undreamed; and it should serve as a warning to those rash political theorists to-day who speak with certitude of social processes. (*IH*, 320–21)

The phrases used here to describe the Iron Heel—"a step aside, or a step backward," "not necessary," "not inevitable," "unexpected and undreamed"—serve to distance London's vision from the comfortable progressivist teleology found in the tradition of utopian literature represented in the American context by *Looking Backward,* a work London had in mind when working on *The Iron Heel.*[41] Moreover, Meredith's advice to his twenty-seventh-century readers, that a study of the rise of the Iron Heel will dispel any lingering illusion of "certitude" in the evolutionary unfolding of history, is clearly intended for London's readers as well.

But while the Iron Heel regime may not have been a "necessary" stage in social evolution, it plays an indispensable role in the context of London's own narrative of future history. Early in the manuscript, Avis tells us that her reminiscences are being recorded on the eve of the revolution that she believes will finally overthrow the Iron Heel. That is, for her, the temporal horizon is still that of Sterni's decades. However, in his commentary, Meredith informs us otherwise:

The Second Revolt was truly international. It was a colossal plan—too colossal to be wrought by the genius of one man alone. Labor, in all the oligarchies of the world, was prepared to rise at the signal. Germany, Italy, France, and all Australasia were labor countries—socialist states. They were ready to lend aid to the revolution. Gallantly they did; and it was for this reason, when the Second Revolt was crushed, that they, too, were crushed by the united oligarchies of the world, their socialist governments being replaced by oligarchical governments. (*IH*, 324)

The assumptions at work here appear strikingly similar to those of *Red Star.* As in *Red Star,* history is presented as a global rather than an insular national phenomenon, the destiny of each individual nation-state set within a larger, more complex whole. Moreover, Sterni's warning about the fragility of a nation-state-bound socialism, "islands in a hostile capitalist and even to some extent precapitalist sea," becomes, in London's work, an actuality.

Because the flowering of the utopian future, and with it the realization of the next stage of modernity, is understood by these narratives to be a global phenomenon, both focus on the question of how we might move from the present situation of unevenness and fragmentation to a condition of global unity. The description offered by Meredith of the fate of the socialist states provides an important clue to London's imaginary solution to this historical dilemma. With every victory by the Iron Heel —and every victory belongs to it, with only the momentary set-back of the general strike described in chapter 13 —the desired integration of the social body has been extended further, until, with the conquest of the autonomous "de-linked" socialist states, the capitalist Oligarchy dominates the global totality. Thus, despite Meredith's statements to the contrary, the very movement of London's narrative posits the Iron Heel as the *necessary* precondition for the utopian Brotherhood of Man. Meredith later observes that his people "tread the roads and dwell in the cities that the oligarchs built" (*IH*, 469). In the same way, the utopian future will come to inhabit a social whole forged only through the vanishing mediator of three hundred years of Oligarchical rule.

"NAMELESS, FORMLESS THINGS"

However, again as in *Red Star,* the representation of the space of this expanded social totality, either in its Oligarchic or utopian form, proves to be far less readily achieved. Indeed, conspicuous by their absence in *The Iron Heel* are any descriptions, beyond the passing glances offered in Meredith's notes, of either society. While London thus foregoes the spatial-representational project of the classical narrative utopia, he does still draw upon the form's estranging powers. In the very first paragraph of the text, Meredith judges the Everhard Manuscript to be marred by numerous errors, "not errors of fact, but errors of interpretation." The explanation for such flaws lies in Avis's limited subjective and historical position: "She lacked perspective. She was too close to the events she writes about. Nay, she was merged in the events she has described" (*IH*, 319). Meredith, on the other hand, located as he is in utopia achieved, occupies the Archimedean point outside Avis's present. He can thus correct her interpretive errors—shifting misplaced emphasis on certain events and individuals elsewhere, and providing the unifying links between what seem unrelated phenomena—precisely because he can see

the past as a whole in a way that she cannot. For London then, in order
to imagine the future, we must first correctly imagine the present, and
this requires the production of a perspectival point from which the
"detotalized totality" that currently exists might be successfully cognitively mapped.[42]

The desire to discover such a totalizing perspective similarly appears
as a theme within the narrative proper. In the very first chapter of Avis's
manuscript, Everhard delivers an attack on idealist metaphysics that is
reminiscent of the critique of Earthly philosophy presented in *Red Star*.
Everhard is one in a long line of working-class "natural aristocrats,"
Nietzschean "blonde beasts," and evolutionary "supermen" that, in
part, serve as the mouthpiece for London's own beliefs (his speech before the capitalist Philomath Club in chapter 5 reproduces London's lecture "Revolution").[43] As his daughter Joan London notes, in a statement
whose deeper significance will become evident below, "Ernest Everhard
was the revolutionist Jack would have liked to be if he had not, unfor-
tunately, also desired to be several other kinds of men."[44] In this opening debate, Everhard declares metaphysics to be an attempt to explain
"consciousness by consciousness," and in so doing, it remains forever
locked within the solipsistic universe of the individual mind, with "no
place in the real world except in so far as it is phenomena of mental
aberration" (*IH*, 326–28). "Idealistic monists"—from Bishop George
Berkeley in the eighteenth century to Everhard's interlocutors, the the-
ologians Doctor Hammerfield and Doctor Ballingford—are "as remote
from the intellectual life of the twentieth century as an Indian medicine-
man making incantation in the primeval forest ten thousand years ago"
(*IH*, 328). Everhard, on the other hand, claims to practice a materialism
in line with modern science, moving inductively from the "facts of experience" to theory, and from these theories to an overarching systematic philosophy, which Everhard calls "the widest science of all" (*IH*,
329).[45] Everhard's "facts" thus fall on the privileged side of a series of
dualisms that run through the narrative: materialism versus idealism,
health versus sickness, the whole versus the particular, unity versus fragmentation, the modern versus the primitive, science versus philosophy,
socialism versus capitalism, and so forth. Everhard's statements have led
a number of critics to read the first part of *The Iron Heel* as an espousal
of London's idiosyncratic version of historical materialism.[46] However,
although there is a certain resemblance to the critique of idealism found
in Lenin's *Materialism and Empirio-Criticism*, the absence of any kind
of dialectical sensibility in London's thought often results in what Ales-

sandro Portelli more precisely describes as a reduction of Marxism to "a variant of positivism."[47]

The best test in Everhard's philosophical system is a simple pragmatic one: "Will it work?" (*IH*, 333). A provisional answer to the obvious question—to what ends does such a system work?—emerges during the course of the debate with the two metaphysicians. Facts for Everhard are weapons to be launched against his opponents: "He tripped them up with facts, ambuscaded them with facts, bombarded them with broadsides of facts" (*IH*, 332). This "smashing, sledge-hammer manner of attack" then creates conditions in which Everhard's opponents "forget themselves" (*IH*, 328). To "forget" oneself here is to allow the veils of social convention to fall away, and thereby *expose* the "realities" they mask. For example, Everhard shows that, for all its high-minded humanism, the idealist philosophy of Ballingford and Hammerfield is nothing more than an ideological mystification of the injustices of contemporary society. Everhard thus appears to achieve powers of critical perception rivaled only by those of Meredith. Indeed, his uncanny ability to "see" into the real nature of things, and thereby map the path of future history, leads Meredith to marvel that "Everhard's social foresight was remarkable" (*IH*, 468).

The dialectic of exposure and revelation by which Everhard unveils the inner realities of the present is similarly at work in one of the narrative's most memorable scenes, Everhard's passionate exchange with the Philomath Club. The chapter in which this takes place opens with Avis reflecting on Everhard's interpretive gifts: "He became my oracle. For me he tore the sham from the face of society and gave me glimpses of reality that were as unpleasant as they were undeniably true" (*IH*, 368). An "exposure" in this manner of the Philomath Club would stand as Everhard's, and by extension London's, greatest critical achievement. The men of the Philomath Club are, after all, the "lords of society," and thus apparently represent its central and determining power: to see them in their true form would be to grasp the deepest and most "undeniable" truth of the capitalist world order.

Everhard's diatribe against their "mismanagement" of society, combined with his threats of imminent working-class revolt, does produce a kind of revelation, tearing away the "sham" of sociability masking the true nature of the refined capitalist master: "A low, throaty rumble arose, lingered on the air a moment, and ceased. It was the forerunner of the snarl . . . the token of the brute in man, the earnest of his primitive passions. . . . It was the growl of the pack, mouthed by the pack, and mouthed in all unconsciousness" (*IH*, 376). Avis's subsequent conclusion—"I realized that not easily would they let their lordship of the world be wrested from them" (*IH*, 376)—is then reconfirmed in the rejoinder to Everhard offered by Mr. Wickson, one of the leaders of the club: "We are in power. Nobody will deny it. By virtue of that power we shall remain in power." Wickson soon adds, "There is the word. It is the king of words—Power. Not God, not Mammon, but Power" (*IH*, 384).

The desire to reveal to the public the agency controlling capitalist society—or, to use the language of London's contemporary Frank Norris, the capitalist "Force" [48]—is not original to London's utopian fiction. Indeed, a similar dynamic can be found in another work that inspired *The Iron Heel: Caesar's Column* (1890), an apocalyptic future fantasy and utopia written by Ignatius Donnelly, the Minnesota senator and author of the preamble to the Populist Party Platform. [49] Donnelly's work similarly portrays the ominous consequences of the exacerbation of the current social crisis: the collapse of democratic institutions, the establishment of military authoritarianism, and the slide of the great masses of the populace into bestial servitude. And, also like London, Donnelly must struggle to embody for his readers the powers that determine the shape of contemporary society. Thus, the protagonist Gabriel Weltstein describes the cabal of capitalists upon which he eavesdrops as

> the real center of government of the American continent; all the rest is sham and form. The men who meet here determine the condition of all the hundreds of millions who dwell on the great land revealed to the world by Columbus. Here political parties, courts, juries, governors, legislatures, congresses, presidents are made and unmade; and from this spot they are controlled and directed in the discharge of their multiform functions. The decrees formulated here are echoed by a hundred thousand newspapers, and many thousands of orators; and they are enforced by an uncountable army of soldiers, servants, tools, spies, and even assassins. He who stands in the way of the men assembled here perishes. He who would oppose them takes his life in his hands. You are, young man, as if I had led you to the center of the earth, and I had placed your hand upon the very pivot, the well-oiled axle, upon which, noiselessly, the whole great globe revolves, and from which the awful forces extend which hold it all together. [50]

For Donnelly, writing in the early 1890s, it is still possible to believe that an attack on these men would shake the fundamental structure of capitalist society. The information Gabriel Weltstein gathers during his spying mission initiates a chain of events that ultimately leads to the collapse of their rule. However, for a Populist like Donnelly, raised on the traditions of democratic Republicanism and fearing the consequences of direct action on the part of the American workers, such a revolution must be shown to lead not to utopia but to anarchy. Moreover, the ethnic identities of the leaders of the revolutionary "Brotherhood of Destruction"—the Italian Cæsar Lomellini and the "nameless Russian Jew"—signal Donnelly's anxieties, not unlike those of Bellamy, concerning the immigrant-worker-anarchist-socialist complex.[51] In the end, Donnelly locates his utopia elsewhere, in the Oz-like, isolated, agrarian nation-state of Gabriel Weltstein's Ugandan valley.[52] Reversing traditional polarities in this fashion, so that North America becomes the "dark continent" and Africa the locus of future promise, Donnelly's narrative also looks directly back to one of its most important predecessors in the realm of American political fiction: Harriet Beecher Stowe's *Uncle Tom's Cabin,* where the freed slave George Harris effects, albeit to quite different ends, a similar transvaluation of the America-Africa polarity.[53]

However, while the similarities between Donnelly's and London's narratives are striking, their differences are even more significant, precisely because the latter provide important clues as to the fundamental changes that have occurred in the brief historical span separating the two works. In his rejoinder to Everhard's declaration of the imminence of socialist revolution, the Philomath leader Wickson says, "A change, a great change, is coming in society; but haply, it may not be the change the bear [Everhard] anticipates" (*IH,* 383). It is these "great changes" which ultimately undermine in London's work any confidence in the representability of the determining "forces" of modern society. The assertion by Wickson I quoted above—"Not God, not Mammon, but Power"—hints at the nature of the social transformation figuratively mapped in London's text: an abstract "Power" has displaced Donnelly's human agency at the "center" of the modern social structure. Wickson thus summarizes the historical trajectory implicitly driving the narrative of *The Iron Heel:* a trajectory that traces the migration of social hegemony from the traditional authority of the churches (God) through a classical national-market capitalism (Mammon)—still the world of Donnelly's narrative—into some new, as yet untheorized stage (Power).

After his fraught meeting with the Philomath Club, Everhard arrives at a conclusion strikingly similar to that of Wickson:

An unseen and fearful revolution is taking place in the fibre and structure of society. One can only dimly feel these things. But they are in the air, now, to-

day. One can feel the loom of them—things vast, vague, and terrible. My
mind recoils from contemplation of what they may crystallize into. You heard
Wickson talk the other night. Behind what he said were the same nameless,
formless things that I feel. (*IH*, 388–89)

Everhard here suggests that the men of the Philomath Club, unlike the
cabal in *Caesar's Column*, are *not* "the real center" of capitalist society.
"Behind" them lurk other forces, "nameless, formless things," that even
Everhard with his awe-inspiring interpretive talents finds himself unable
to apprehend. Power in London's narrative has become anonymous: to
attack the members of the Philomath Club would do little to challenge
the fundamental structure of society, precisely because these men represent only the manifest presence, the expendable representatives, of a
much larger and invisible force. Indeed, by describing the new social
hegemony with the abstraction "Power," London dislocates it from its
older imagined structural, social, and, for political action, challengeable
locus.[54] Later, when the Iron Heel attempts to gain his allegiance by offering him an appointment to the post of United States Commissioner of
Labor, Everhard again remarks, "Behind it is the fine hand of Wickson,
and behind him the hands of greater men than he" (*IH*, 391). And behind them? Everhard sets into motion a chain of deferrals with no apparent end. As a consequence, any successful representation of the determining forces, or Donnelly's "real center" of the social order, as with
the mappings of the realized futures of the Iron Heel and the Brotherhood of Man, vanishes from the narrative tableau.

A similar logic of deferral also ultimately undermines the totalizing
epistemological project represented by Everhard's materialist philosophy; for the very "facts" that serve as both the motor of Everhard's critical program and the linchpin of his totalizing system likewise remain
absent presences in the narrative. That is, London shows in great detail
what these facts can do, how they allow Everhard to unmask his opponents and intuitively grasp the tremendous changes in the social organization then underway, without ever presenting the facts themselves.
Everhard's philosophical whole, like the social reality he attempts to describe, is thus marred from the outset by a crucial absence at its center—
a kind of gravitational black hole into which the totalizing critical gaze
of this narrative utopia invariably collapses.

Other readers have noted the structural deferrals, gaps, and absences
that mark London's narrative. Portelli, in one of the more careful readings of *The Iron Heel*, adds to the list of absences I have already dis-

cussed—the twin topoi of the future, the totality of the present, and an epistemology that might apprehend either of them—representations of the eventual fate of the protagonists Everhard and Avis, the moment of the victorious revolution, and, most important of all, the role of the working class in all of this. According to Portelli, London employs a narrative strategy whereby "he indicates—by *not* describing them—the essential objects" of his political vision.[55] However, in doing so, London fails in his efforts to situate Everhard at the mediatory point between the present and the utopian future. Consequently, Portelli concludes, *The Iron Heel* represents the inverse of what Louis Marin calls utopian discourse: "Rather than imagining something which political theory cannot yet visualize, [*The Iron Heel*] divulgates a fully developed theory but cannot countenance its consequences."[56] This "consequence" is the proletarian revolution itself—the deeply desired, yet terrifying, reemergence of the repressed elements of the social totality.

There is much that is persuasive in Portelli's discussion of London's work. He provides a suggestive catalogue of the contradictory desires at play in the text, contradictions which ultimately thwart London's efforts to represent a general overturning of the capitalist world order. This said, however, I would like to advance an alternative reading of the play of absences in London's narrative. In the second chapter of this book, I addressed what I find to be the limits of Marin's description of Marx's "fully developed theory" of capitalist society: Marin's "epochal" focus elides the more specific "historical" developments that occur within Western modernity. Similarly, rather than viewing *The Iron Heel* as a work that "cannot countenance the consequences" of the social theory it employs (exactly what that social theory might be and its relationship to Marxism, orthodox or otherwise, is an extremely complex problematic in its own right), I want to argue that the representational absences are themselves part of the narrative's implicit acknowledgment of the insufficiency of the theoretical language then available to describe the social developments inscribed in the text. Much as in its contemporary, *Red Star*, these social developments are connected to the growing recognition that the social totality, its horizons now extending far beyond the borders of the individual nation-state, has emerged in an original and, for the individual at least, cognitively ungraspable new form. The presence in the text of this unrepresentable social object likewise renders obsolete older languages of historical agency—forcing London, again like Bogdanov, to attempt to "reinvent" the subject of history.

"GASEOUS VERTEBRATE"

The most prominent candidate we find in the text for this role of historical agent is the Iron Heel itself. As I suggested above, the absent presence of the Iron Heel escapes, at once on the epistemological, analytical,
and political levels, every effort to "confront" it directly. Thus, whatever
clues the text provides to the nature of this new social subject are to be
located in the allusive figures which stand in the place of the missing
theoretical or, in Everhard's own terms, "scientific" description of it.

One of the most interesting of these figures emerges quite unexpectedly during Avis's account of the eventual fate of many of the work's
characters. Of Everhard's philosophical opponents, Hammerfield and
Ballingford, Avis notes,

> They have been faithful to their salt, and they have been correspondingly
> rewarded with ecclesiastical palaces wherein they dwell at peace with the
> world. Both are apologists for the Oligarchy. Both have grown very fat.
> "Dr. Hammerfield," as Ernest once said, "has succeeded in modifying his
> metaphysics so as to give God's sanction to the Iron Heel, and also to include
> much worship of beauty and to reduce to an invisible wraith the gaseous ver-
> tebrate described by Haeckel—the difference between Dr. Hammerfield and
> Dr. Ballingford being that the latter has made the God of the oligarchs a little
> more gaseous and a little less vertebrate." (IH, 505)

This image of God as a "gaseous vertebrate" comes from the international best-seller *The Riddle of the Universe at the Close of the Nineteenth Century* (1900), written by the German scientist and naturalist
philosopher Ernst Heinrich Haeckel. Though largely forgotten today,
Haeckel's work had a wide-ranging impact on the social thought of the
latter part of the nineteenth and early twentieth centuries. No less a figure than Charles Darwin described him as the single most influential advocate of evolutionary theory working in Germany (it was Haeckel who
in his *General Morphology* [1866] formulated the Biogenetic Law "On-
togenesis is a brief and rapid recapitulation of phylogenesis"); while a
more recent critic contends that Haeckel's theories of racial development served as one of the ideological cornerstones of German fascism.[57]
Although this is the first direct allusion to the work of the German
thinker found in *The Iron Heel,* its influence pervades the whole narrative, playing a role similar to that of Machism in Bogdanov's *Red Star.*
Indeed, Everhard's argument against Ballingford and Hammerfield,
"Philosophy is the science of science, the master science, if you please"

(*IH,* 329) echoes Haeckel's assertion that philosophy was the "queen of the sciences."[58]

Haeckel's work is often lumped together with the "materialist monisms" of his contemporaries Ludwig Büchner, Jacob Moleschott, and Karl Vogt, the three thinkers whom Engels famously described as exemplars of "the shallow and vulgarised form" of materialist thought.[59] However, Haeckel himself took great pains to distance his philosophical project from the "pure" materialism of these philosophers. Early in *The Riddle of the Universe,* Haeckel outlines his basic axioms:

> I. Pure monism is identical neither with the theoretical materialism that denies the existence of spirit, and dissolves the world into a heap of dead atoms, nor with the theoretical spiritualism . . . which rejects the notion of matter, and considers the world to be a specially arranged group of "energies" or immaterial natural forces.
>
> II. On the contrary, we hold, with Goethe, that "matter cannot exist and be operative without spirit, nor spirit without matter."[60]

According to Haeckel, classical materialism remains within a dualistic cosmological paradigm, reasserting the primacy of the material over the ideal, but never questioning the fallacious opposition of these two concepts. His monism, on the other hand, postulates a singular "substance" that is at once both "body and spirit," "matter and energy," "God and nature" (*RU,* 20). (In the world of *The Iron Heel,* this theorem has been given scientific legitimation by none other than Avis's father, a physicist at the State University at Berkeley, California: "his monumental work . . . established, beyond cavil and for all time, that the ultimate unit of matter and the ultimate unit of force were identical" [*IH,* 325]). All the elements of this monistic universe, organic and inorganic, likewise continuously develop according to a rigid deterministic pattern. Evolution—"the inevitable result of selection, and not the outcome of a preconceived design"—should thus be understood as a process, similar to Organization in Bogdanov's Tectology, of "progressive improvement, an historical advance from the simple to the complex, the lower to the higher, the imperfect to the perfect" (*RU,* 266).

On this theoretical basis, Haeckel outlines the various evolutionary modifications undergone by the "God-idea" during the course of human civilization. Haeckel contends that all the known concepts of God can be divided into two categories: the dualist-mystic or theistic group, and the rational-monist or pantheistic group. The dominant theistic religions "represent God to be an extramundane or a supernatural being.

He is always opposed to the world, or nature, as an independent being; generally as its creator, sustainer, and ruler" (*RU*, 287). In the more primitive versions of theism, the gods, and then later the monotheistic God, are believed to think and act like men, only in a more highly developed form; God is thus conceptually transformed into a "vertebrate." The more advanced and abstract theisms do away with the embodied God, and instead worship "pure spirit." "Nevertheless," Haeckel maintains, "the psychic activity of this 'pure spirit' remains just the same as that of the anthropomorphic God. In reality, even this immaterial spirit is not conceived to be incorporeal, but merely invisible, gaseous. We thus arrive at the paradoxical conception of God as a *gaseous vertebrate*" (*RU*, 288).

In the pantheistic tradition, on the other hand, the separation of God and the world no longer holds: "in Pantheism God, as an *intramundane* being, is everywhere identical with nature itself, and is operative *within* the world as 'force' or energy'" (*RU*, 288). As might be expected, Haeckel proposes that only this latter tradition is consistent with scientific monism and the modern "discovery" of the iron-clad laws of substance and evolutionary determinism. Here however, we come up against the fundamental conceptual problem of Haeckel's monism, a dilemma plaguing many philosophical attempts to develop a third synthetic position beyond the opposition of materialism and idealism: how does one *re-present* this a priori being without falling back upon the "imperfect metaphors" drawn from each of the two sides of the initial opposition, especially if, as Lenin argues in *Materialism and Empirio-Criticism*, that the history of philosophy is nothing more than the struggle between these two opposed tendencies?[61] When Haeckel describes "substance" as an evolving combination of "body and spirit," he thus falls into the same patterns as the deistic religions he decries: his substance too resolves itself into a kind of "gaseous vertebrate," a paradox whose dreamed-of resolution might be indicated, but which nevertheless defies description.

Many of the concepts at work in Haeckel's monistic philosophy—the ideas of evolutionary determinism, the languages of force and energy, and so forth—have likewise been shown to be central to the tradition of literary naturalism of which London's work forms a noted part.[62] At the same time, however, and as I pointed out earlier, the Iron Heel Oligarchy shatters the determinism that is also at the heart of Haeckel's philosophy. Again, as Meredith informs the reader in his foreword to the manuscript, the appearance of the Iron Heel short-circuits "the orderly procedure of social evolution," a process of development that London was not alone in believing to be the movement from capitalism to socialism (*IH*, 321).[63] The "unexpected and undreamed" of Iron Heel then emerges as a new kind of *determining* social agency, one that transcends the individuals (like Wickson) composing it, and one that possesses the power to shape "natural" laws instead of being passively shaped by them.

Indeed, the Iron Heel's mastery over the forces of the natural world serves as a recurring motif throughout Avis's manuscript. When the "nascent Oligarchy" instigates a monetary crisis, Avis observes, "They sowed wind, and wind, and ever more wind; for they alone knew how to reap the whirlwind and make a profit out of it. . . . Strong enough themselves to weather the storm that was largely their own brewing, they turned loose and plundered the wrecks that floated about them" (*IH*, 435). Moreover, during her description of the abortive revolution in Chicago which serves as kind of climax to the narrative, Avis suggests the Iron Heel even possesses the power to blur the boundary between the natural and the artificial. The uprising of the masses thus takes on the appearance of a kind of Frankenstein monster, appearing to be a spontaneous "natural" phenomenon, while in actuality being a construct of the Oligarchy: "We of the Revolution . . . thought it was a spontaneous spirit of revolt that would require careful curbing on our part, and never dreamed that it was deliberately manufactured" (*IH*, 525).[64]

Breaking with Haeckel's evolutionary determinism in this manner, London returns to the thought of the German philosopher in an interesting new way, for the Iron Heel as a subject of history occupies the same paradoxical conceptual position as the "gaseous vertebrate" deity in Haeckel's philosophy. That is, the Oligarchy appears as at once irreducibly and contradictorily corporeal and immaterial, as body and spirit. "Nameless and formless," it still has the ability to cast "a shadow of something colossal and menacing" (*IH*, 389). As with Haeckel's "pure spirit," the Iron Heel does not possess a "bodily appearance" and consequently cannot be described or located by individuals such as Everhard (or indeed, London himself). At the same time, however, the "bodily" presence of the Iron Heel is indicated by its actions and voracious *desires:* "The Oligarchy wanted the war with Germany," and "The Oligarchy wanted violence" (*IH*, 458 and 479). Finally, like any other subject, the Iron Heel develops a sense of self-worth: Avis maintains that more than its material achievements—"Prisons, banishment and degradation, honors and palaces and wonder-cities, are all incidental"—"the strength of the Oligarchy today lies in its satisfied conception of its own righteousness" (*IH,* 519).

The mystery of the historical identity of this new, "unnatural," trans-individual agency has been explored by Walter Benn Michaels in his influential study of American literary naturalism. In his reading of Norris's *The Octopus,* Michaels shows that the new entity which for the early twentieth century unveils "the monstrosity of personhood, the impossible and irreducible combination of body and soul" is nothing less than Norris's Octopus, the capitalist corporation.[65] (This too suggests a deeper connection between London and Norris: Norris's intellectual journey from a fascination with the nature-culture opposition in *Vandover and the Brute* and *McTeague* to his subsumption of this opposition in the "corporate fiction" of *The Octopus* is paralleled by London's own movement from the concerns of *The Call of the Wild* and *White Fang* to those of *The Iron Heel.*) Meredith makes explicit the identity of the Oligarchy as a corporate subject. When Everhard declares, "What its nature may be I refuse to imagine," the utopian historian Meredith observes that even though they too were unable to understand its nature, "There were men, even before his time, who caught glimpses of the shadow." Meredith quotes no less a source than Abraham Lincoln, who prophesies, "I see in the near future a crisis approaching that unnerves me and causes me to tremble for the safety of my country. . . . Corporations have been enthroned" (*IH,* 389).

Thus, between the vision of capitalist power in Donnelly's *Caesar's Column* and that in *The Iron Heel* lies the "unexpected" realization of what Bellamy had "dreamed"—the formation, beginning in earnest in the United States in the 1890s, of the first truly transnational, monopolistic trusts: "The biggest new combination, U.S. Steel, formed in 1901 from 150 smaller corporations, was capitalized at over $1 billion. U.S. Steel was so large, it could dictate prices; competition in the steel industry virtually disappeared."[66] Completely abolishing any illusion of the "natural" world of the free market, the rise of the corporation heralded dramatic changes in the contemporary organization of social life. However, unlike Bellamy, who thought the unfettering of the corporate order would presage the emergence of the utopian future, London views this "mutation" in the logic of capitalism as pushing any such future even further away. While the rise of the corporation did make possible the unified global society, or the "world market" (*IH,* 473) that London took to be the precondition for a utopian society, this development also relegated (both literally and figuratively) The Brotherhood of Man to the margins of the text, the light of the transformed future occluded by the massive and immovable absent presence of the Iron Heel: "'What's the matter with America?'—were the messages sent to us by our successful comrades in other lands. But we could not keep up. The Oligarchy stood in the way. Its bulk, like that of some huge monster, blocked our path" (*IH,* 463).

If the rise of the corporation made it increasingly difficult for London to imagine a restructuring of the social whole, this historical "event" nevertheless provided him with the opportunity to speculate on the nature of some of the inevitable changes in social relationships. One of the more significant of these changes would concern the situation of writers and other artists, all of whom had become servants under free-market capitalism to the volatile and unpredictable tastes of middle-class consumers. Everhard informs Avis that the tremendous surplus profits garnered by the Iron Heel will be reinvested in public works and the arts: "When the oligarchs have completely mastered the people, they will have time to spare for other things. They will become worshipers of beauty. They will become art-lovers. And under their direction, and generously rewarded, will toil the artists. The result will be great art; for no longer, as up to yesterday, will the artists pander to the bourgeois taste of the middle class" (*IH,* 469). (Compare this to the free-market vision of the arts we find in *Looking Backward,* where every artist "must pay for the privilege of the public ear, and if he has any message worth hearing, we consider that he will be glad to do it.")[67] For a literary producer like London himself, who had come to feel his own work to be constrained by the vagaries of the literary marketplace—a central theme in his next novel, the semi-autobiographical *Künstlerroman, Martin Eden* —there would be a great deal that was attractive in such guarantees of patronage.

Even more curiously, London imagines that this new situation might also provide a resolution to the troubling contradiction between his literary and *political* vocations, a dilemma made manifest in his refusal to accept a desired assignment to write an exposé on mill conditions in the southern United States because he was afraid of the consequences for future book sales. For in the world of the Iron Heel, it is possible to be both a successful artist *and* a political activist. Meredith notes, "The flower of the artistic and intellectual world were revolutionists. With the exception of a few of the musicians and singers, and of a few of the oligarchs, all the great creators of the period whose names have come down to us, were revolutionists" (*IH,* 513).

While such an envisioned situation might indeed resolve some of London's own dilemmas, it opens up a far-reaching ambiguity concerning the nature of the revolutionary organization that London imagined might challenge the authority of the Oligarchy. Although Everhard, much like Bogdanov's Leonid, will claim that his revolutionary movement finds its "roots and strength" in the working class, the passage quoted above suggests that the blossoms put out by this strange plant will in fact be free of those roots. Indeed, in the figuration of the revolutionary bloc, London will imagine a situation in which the complexities of class and social positionality at work in his own present have disappeared; and, in so doing, he clears the ideological space for the emergence of another new kind of social agency, one that rivals in significance, but is also deeply interwoven with, the capitalist corporation.

SIMPLIFICATION AND THE NEW SUBJECT OF HISTORY

In *The Communist Manifesto*, Marx describes the nineteenth-century "epoch of the bourgeoisie" as unique in world history because it "has simplified the class antagonisms: Society as a whole is more and more splitting up into two great hostile camps, into two great classes directly facing each other: Bourgeoisie and Proletariat."[68] It is this process of "simplification" that serves as a necessary precondition for world revolution, and Marx carefully narrates precisely how such a situation is coming about. However, what is for Marx a development imminent in the present has become for London a deferred future destiny. In order to show how we *might* arrive at such a desired situation, the narrative of *The Iron Heel* repeats the historical trajectory traced in *The Communist Manifesto*, adopting it to the particular conditions of the early-twentieth-century United States.[69]

I have already suggested the central structural role the Oligarchy plays in the development of future history: by drawing together into a unified whole the fractured and unevenly developed global totality, the Iron Heel serves as a mediating link between London's own present and the unrepresentable utopian Brotherhood of Man. At same time, however, the narrative also focuses on the process of simplification that occurs within the United States. When Everhard exclaims, "Confusion thrice confounded! . . . How can we hope for solidarity with all these cross purposes and conflicts?" (*IH*, 474), he describes what had become a central dilemma for American leftist politics in the early part of this century (as well as in other times and places): how to build a unified,

anticapitalist, revolutionary bloc out of myriad competing and conflicting social groups. In the narrative laboratory of *The Iron Heel*, London formulates a tentative resolution to this crisis. Through a carefully staged sequence of shorter narratives embedded in the overarching
whole, London imagines the negation of each of the specialized and
conflicting publics occupying the social stage of the first decade of the
twentieth century until, finally, all that remains is a generalized binary
opposition of forces—London's own version of Marx's "two great hostile camps."

Approaching the narrative in this manner casts new light on the
opening confrontation between Everhard and the clergymen, Hammerfield and Ballingford. By "demonstrating" that the doctrines of organized religion are no more than ideological "buttresses of the established order," London strips any autonomy from the traditional
authority of the churches. Indeed, when Everhard tells Hammerfield,
"go ahead and preach and earn your pay" (*IH,* 335), the narrative has
already begun to prepare the reader for the central thematic statement
later uttered by the oligarch Wickson, "Not God, not Mammon, but
Power": for Everhard's observations show that the historical residuals of
a once socially determinate religious authority are now beholden to the
more powerful interests of capitalism—a truth further reinforced by
Avis's later description of the position of the two men after the establishment of the Iron Heel.

Religious authority does make a subsequent appearance in the narrative, in the quite different guise of Christian "charity," or philan-
thropy. Everhard's devastating assault on the religious idealism of Hammerfield and Ballingford has a dramatic impact on the lives of both of
the witnesses to it, Avis and the Catholic Bishop Morehouse. When
these two accuse Everhard of exaggerating for effect the injustices of the
present social order, he "challenges" them to investigate first-hand the
nightmarish realities created by industrial capitalism (*IH,* 337–47).
Avis's discoveries launch her career as a revolutionary and also lead to
her eventual marriage to Everhard. The Bishop's "journey through
hell," on the other hand, has a quite different outcome: recognizing for
the first time the great disparity between the preachings of the Christian
church and its social practices, he attempts to suture this gap through a
program of individual charity.

Religious practice in this latter manifestation thus serves as one of
the first targets in London's programmatic assault on what he took to be
the inefficacy of partial, or "reactionary socialist," political strategies.

If the more conventional naturalist novel struggled to recontain the desires for social change implicitly imbedded in the philanthropic project by folding it back within the confines of human nature or individual psychology, London, whose expressed goal in *The Iron Heel* is to legitimate revolutionary struggle, shows how these kinds of ethical gestures, when cast onto the larger social stage, invariably mutate into political ones.[70] Before an assembly convened to discuss the question of "public immorality," the Bishop issues a plea for an institutional reform of the church, which would include, among its other goals, the conversion of "the palaces of the Church" into "hospitals and nurseries for those who have fallen by the wayside and are perishing" (*IH*, 394). From London's "revolutionary" perspective, the Bishop's program is at best reformist in design, misguidedly aiming at the symptoms of social illness rather than its deep structural causes; or as Everhard later more colorfully puts it, "charity" is "a poulticing of an ulcer. Remove the ulcer was [Everhard's] remedy" (*IH*, 447). The Bishop's project—London's version of what Marx calls "clerical socialism"—is thus doomed from the outset.[71] As Everhard predicts, the Bishop's well-heeled audience responds to his call for Christian charity by ordering him locked in a sanitarium. Later, when the protagonists again encounter the Bishop, he still pursues what Everhard and Avis now both judge to be a naively ineffective, if nonetheless heroic, charitable agenda, administering to the needs of those inhabiting "the monstrous depths of the tenements" (*IH*, 450).

The next set of embedded narratives, or ideologemes, deals with those social groups—small-business owners, manufacturers, and merchants; farmers; and democratic politicians—whom London associates with the more recent past hegemony of bourgeois capitalism: in Wickson's triad, these interests are assembled under the aegis of "Mammon." All of these already had been relegated by London to the dustbin of history in an earlier tribute to Rudyard Kipling, one of the authors who had a deep influence on the stylistic development of the young London.[72] In his essay, London writes,

> The nineteenth century, so far as the Anglo-Saxon is concerned, was remarkable for two great developments: the mastery of matter and the expansion of the race. Three great forces operated in it: nationalism, commercialism, and democracy—the marshalling of the races, the merciless, remorseless *laissez faire* of the dominant bourgeoisie, and the practical, actual working government of men within a very limited equality.[73]

Kipling was the great artist of this historical milieu. However, the past is the operative tense here, for London had opened his essay with the

declaration that Kipling "is dead, dead, and buried."[74] While London
meant with this statement to mark the chronological passage of one century into another, he also already points toward the larger sociological
shift that will become the subject matter of *The Iron Heel*. Kipling is
"dead" precisely because the social realities of which he writes—nationalism, *laissez-faire* commercialism, and democracy—no longer play
leading roles in the drama of world history. The new world would need
new poets, a position for which London argued himself to be ideally
suited.

The depiction in *The Iron Heel* of the "passing" of the epoch of the
bourgeoisie, or, in the U.S. context, the older, middle-class strata whom
we have already encountered in our discussion of *Looking Backward*,
begins in the chapter entitled "The Machine Breakers." Everhard meets
the "owners or part-owners in small factories, small businesses, and
small industries—small capitalists, in short" whose "unanimous complaint was against the corporations and trusts" (*IH*, 399). Their political solutions to this challenge—government ownership of the rail-
roads, telegraphs, and public utilities, graduated income taxes, and free
markets (the real-world solutions of the Progressives and Populists)—
made these groups for London the early-twentieth-century equivalent
of what Marx called "Petty-Bourgeois Socialists."[75] And London, again
following what he took to be Marx's lead, presents them as a historically reactionary force.[76] Everhard compares them to eighteenth-
century English Luddites when one of their members, the appropriately
named Mr. Calvin—a dairyman and, significantly, a representative of
the Grange Party (Donnelly's Populists)—queries, "Why can we not return to the ways of our fathers when this republic was founded?" (*IH*,
406). Later, Mr. Calvin too will make explicit the class identity of this
group: "It is a case of life and death for us of the middle class" (*IH*, 419).

Interestingly enough, Everhard's response to Calvin's question differs
little from that which would have been given by Bellamy's Dr. Leete.
Everhard declares that the inexorable process of social evolution has
rendered such a retreat impossible: "The sun of the small capitalists is
setting. It will never rise again. Nor is it in your power even to make it
stand still. You are perishing, and you are doomed to perish utterly from
the face of society. This is the fiat of evolution. It is the word of God.
Combination is stronger than competition" (*IH*, 406–7). The middle
class, he notes, is being ground out of existence between the "two great
forces" of the capitalist corporation and labor (*IH*, 419). With the subsequent ascendancy of the Iron Heel, his adumbrations prove to be cor-

rect, as those representatives of the middle class the reader has encountered are shown to be driven down into the swelling ranks of the oppressed mass.[77]

As the economic power base of the older middle class collapses, so do those political institutions that were the products of its rule. Donnelly had concluded *Caesar's Column* by arguing that only a reform-minded political party, put into power through the electoral process, might properly confront the social ills of the industrial order. The second half of his narrative had already "proven" that any attempt at direct action on the part of the masses would lead only to anarchy. In *The Iron Heel*, on the other hand, London seeks to demonstrate the insufficiency of Donnelly's variety of reformism. Later in the narrative, we learn that following the collapse of William Randolph Hearst's Democratic Party— its platform, Meredith informs us, an impossible oil and water mixture of "an emasculated socialism combined with a nondescript sort of petty bourgeois capitalism" (*IH,* 454)—the only thing that prevents the Socialists from taking control of the government is "the brief and futile rise of the Grange Party" (*IH,* 455). Like its real-world counterpart—the agrarian People's Party, or Populism, whose meteoric rise abruptly halted with the disastrous elections of 1896—this political force flares up in the midst of the rocky transition between two orders of capitalist society.[78] Moreover, while the fictional Grangers do capture a dozen state governments and a large number of congressional seats in the 1912 election, their ascension to national prominence also comes to an abrupt end: "The incumbents refused to get out. It was very simple. They merely charged illegality in the elections and wrapped up the whole situation in the interminable red tape of the law. The Grangers were powerless. The courts were the last recourse, and the courts were in the hands of their enemies" (*IH,* 479). Ironically, the very movement in which Donnelly had placed so much hope for the aversion of violence becomes in London's narrative the spark that ignites a nightmarish inferno of destruction. In a scene that prefigures the climactic slaughter of the Chicago Commune, the expropriated American farmers are tricked into open revolt by agents of the Oligarchy, until, Avis writes, "Every Granger state was ravaged with violence and washed in blood" (*IH,* 480). In the larger narrative schema of *The Iron Heel,* this development does double work: for conflicts between agrarian and urban interests are similarly resolved with the conquest of the countryside by the forces of the Iron Heel.

Of course, the duly elected Socialists fare no better than their Populist counterparts. In a scene that recalls the 1886 events in Chicago's Haymarket Square (Meredith makes this connection explicit), Everhard and his fellow Socialist congressmen are arrested after a bomb tossed by another agent of the Oligarchy explodes in the House of Representatives (*IH,* 486–93). Although Everhard and his revolutionary comrades do later escape, this scene completes London's fantasized "final consummation" of the old order (*IH,* 478).

At this point, London appears to have fully unencumbered the social stage for the pure "ideal type" of struggle between the two great collective forces of the capitalist corporation and the working class. And yet, London now curiously goes to great efforts to divorce his imaginary revolutionary group from the class in whose interests it purportedly acts. London quite carefully shows that the members of this organization come from a number of different social strata. While Everhard himself may claim his origins in the working class, Avis—whose transformation into an agent of the revolutionary vanguard comprises a significant portion of the plot of *The Iron Heel*—is the daughter of a middle-class physics professor.[79] And later, the reader learns that one of the most important converts to the "Cause" is Philip Wickson—son of the leader of the Philomath Club! Indeed, Meredith informs us that "Many young men of the Oligarchy, impelled by sense of right conduct, or their imaginations captured by the glory of the Revolution, ethically or romantically devoted their lives to it" (*IH,* 516). Crucially then, Everhard becomes a leader of the revolution *not* because of his working-class origins, but precisely to the degree that he can "transcend" them; or, as Portelli puts it, "even though Ernest speaks *for* the working class, he does not speak *from* it. He 'represents' it much as the Party 'represents' the masses."[80]

The "representation" of the working class—by Everhard's party *in* the text and by London *through* the text—is indeed one of the narrative's more vexing issues. In order to bring into focus the multiple facets of this dilemma, we need first to set into place the *third* event of 1905, along with the failed Russian Revolution and the response to London's lecture tour, that fundamentally shaped the thematic structure of *The Iron Heel:* the opening of an insurmountable fissure in the summer of that year between the radical and reformist elements of the American labor movement. On the one side of the gulf stood the militant Industrial Workers of the World (the IWW, or Wobblies) with their DeLeonite industrial unionism, confrontational tactics, and inclusive championing of the rights of all workers, skilled and unskilled, regardless of race or gender; on the other, Samuel Gompers's American Federation of Labor (AFL), advocating political moderation and an exclusionary craft and trade unionism, while seeking a middle ground between the demands of labor and capital. Both the "left" and the "right" labor fronts were powerful presences in London's contemporary California. While some of the IWW's most celebrated successes were in the western United States, the AFL, through its avatar of Patrick Henry McCarthy's Building Trades Council, represented a massive political and social force in the San Francisco Bay area.[81]

The narrative's vision of the working class organizes itself around the two extremes represented by the IWW and the AFL. With its explicit advocacy of radical revolutionary socialism, the narrative appears to adopt the stance of the IWW.[82] And indeed, in one of the work's more prescient moments, London offers a trenchant critique of what he viewed to be the consequence of the concessionary politics of the group of workers that Daniel DeLeon had famously called the "labor aristocracy." In an earlier short story, "The Dream of Debs," London had shown how a nationwide general strike, carefully orchestrated on the part of organized labor, could lead to full-scale social collapse and, eventually, the founding of a new order. (London here was probably embellishing upon the mass walkouts of 1901—San Francisco would not experience a real general strike until 1934, eighteen years after his death.[83]) Similarly, the general strike which takes place in *The Iron Heel* represents the only successful challenge to the Oligarchy we witness. When the United States announces war with Germany, the socialists, fusing all aspects of the labor force into a single oppositional force, paralyze the nation for one week: "The pulse of the land had ceased to beat. Of a truth the nation had died. There were no wagons rumbling on the streets, no factory whistles, no hum of electricity in the air, no passing of street cars, no cries of news-boys—nothing but persons who at rare intervals went by like furtive ghosts, themselves oppressed and made unreal by the silence" (*IH*, 461).

While the strike succeeds in averting the war and even leads to the overthrow of the German Emperor, it has quite different consequences in the United States. The Iron Heel ensures that such a coalition can never be formed again by "subsidizing" the key skilled unions, railroad and foundry workers, engineers, and machinists: "The members of the favored unions became the aristocracy of labor. They were set apart from the rest of labor. They were better housed, better clothed, better fed, better treated," even to the extent of being moved from the now threatening urban centers to new peripheral communities that resemble the working-class suburbs that flourish after the Second World War (*IH*, 473). London bitterly blamed the "betrayal" of the socialist movement by organized labor—whom Everhard ruefully describes as "the flower of the American workingmen" (*IH*, 467)—for indefinitely extending the struggle against capitalism.[84] Indeed, upon learning of the intentions of the great unions, Everhard proceeds to offer his own despairing prediction of the centuries-long rule of the Iron Heel (*IH*, 467–70).

However, while decrying the political strategies adopted by big labor, London actually appears much closer to them than the more radical IWW in his views of the masses of the unskilled urban proletariat. This is perhaps most dramatically evident in the wildly apocalyptical, climactic chapters entitled "The Roaring Abysmal Beast," "The Chicago Commune," "The People of the Abyss," and "Nightmare."[85] Goaded into action by false information issued by the Iron Heel's agents-provocateurs, the people of Chicago launch a premature rebellion, only to be brutally slaughtered by the Oligarchy's military forces. Avis, who has been sent to the city to investigate the rumors of the Iron Heel's activities, unexpectedly finds herself in the middle of the rioting mass, of which she offers this startling description:

> It surged past my vision in concrete waves of wrath, snarling and growling, carnivorous, drunk with whisky from pillaged warehouses, drunk with hatred, drunk with lust for blood—men, women, and children, in rags and tatters, dim ferocious intelligences with all the godlike blotted from their features and all the fiendlike stamped in, apes and tigers, anæmic consumptives and great hairy beasts of burden, wan faces from which vampire society had sucked the juice of life, bloated forms swollen with physical grossness and corruption, withered hags and death's-heads bearded like patriarchs, festering youth and festering age, faces of fiends, crooked, twisted, misshapen monsters blasted with the ravages of disease and all the horrors of chronic innutrition—the refuse and the scum of life, a raging, screaming, screeching, demoniacal horde. (*IH*, 535)

Avis then proceeds to mark the boundaries separating the revolutionists from the members of this bestial mass. When she meets one of the members of the latter group, she observes, "in his face was all the dumb pathos of the wounded and hunted animal. He saw me, but there was no kinship between us" (*IH*, 546). And earlier, Avis had suggested that these masses represented as great a threat to the revolution as the Iron Heel itself.[86] In order to justify the revolution's decision to "sacrifice" the people of Chicago—the Oligarchy simply beat them to the punch in this—Avis summarily states, "The abysmal brute would roar anyway,

and the police and Mercenaries would slay anyway. It would merely
mean that various dangers to us were harmlessly destroying one another" (*IH*, 524).[87] (A similar un-Debsian identification between the dis-
organized proletariat masses and the capitalist overlords interestingly
occurs in "The Dream of Debs": both groups are shown to be equally ill
equipped to deal with the events of the general strike, each ultimately de-
scending to the level of animals.)

The most immediate source for this portrait of the unskilled urban
working class as the bestial Other is London's own notorious nativist
and racist sentiments. Joan London recounts that when challenged by
the members of the Oakland socialist club over his attitudes toward the
Japanese (see especially the ugly 1904 essay "The Yellow Peril"), her father exclaimed, "I am first of all a white man and only then a Socialist!"[88] London's belief in the essential superiority of the "Nordic peoples" would distinguish them in his mind even from other European
immigrant groups, a fact his later fiction sadly bears out. Like Jacob Riis
and Upton Sinclair, London equates the brutalized bestial elements of
the working class with the recently arrived Southern and Eastern European immigrants—a group from whom London is quite careful to distinguish the "proletariat" Everhard: "He had been born in the working
class, though he was a descendant of the old line of Everhards that for
over two hundred years had lived in America" (*IH*, 338). London here
thus turns from the inclusive class politics of the more radical elements
of the American labor and socialist movements and embraces the nativist prejudices then popular with large sections of the national public.[89] (Similarly, the large numbers of recently arrived Italian immigrants
were also largely excluded from the powerful organized labor groups in
San Francisco.)[90]

Given what he took to be the unattractiveness of both the left and
right versions of working-class politics, London, in the creation of his
fiction of the revolutionary vanguard, altogether jettisons the Marxist emphasis on the centrality of the working class. In so doing, *The
Iron Heel* seems to differ little from other texts in the wider generic tradition of literary naturalism; a tradition whose organizational framework, as Fredric Jameson notes in his discussion of George Gissing's
The Nether World, "is not that of social class but rather that very different nineteenth-century ideological concept which is the notion of 'the
people,' as a kind of general grouping of the poor and 'underprivileged'
of all kinds, from which one can recoil in revulsion, but to which one
can also, as in some political populisms, nostalgically 'return' as to some

telluric source of strength."[91] (The persistence of this double image of the "people," reconfigured for the different situation of a "postindustrial" or "service" economy, is evident in such contemporary "naturalist" works as the popular film, *Fight Club* [1999].)

Both aspects of this double vision of the "people" do emerge during the course of the events narrated in *The Iron Heel*.[92] In his speech before the Philomaths, Everhard presents the people as a vital engine of social change:

> "Such an army of revolution," he said, "twenty-five millions strong, is a thing to make rulers and ruling classes pause and consider. The cry of this army is: "No quarter! We want all that you possess. We will be content with nothing less than all that you possess. We want in our hands the reins of power and the destiny of mankind. Here are our hands. They are strong hands. We are going to take your governments, your palaces, and all your purpled ease away from you, and in that day you shall work for your bread even as the peasant in the field or the starved and runty clerk in your metropolises. Here are our hands. They are strong hands!" (*IH*, 376)

The great irony here is that the only hands we see are those of the revolutionary vanguardist Everhard: "And as he spoke he extended from his splendid shoulders his two great arms, and the horseshoer's hands were clutching the air like eagle's talons" (*IH*, 376). Indeed, the only other member of the "working class" the reader has encountered thus far, the *former* mill worker Jackson, is distinguished precisely by his missing left arm (*IH*, 348–51). Thus, lacking the virtuous strength so hyperbolically manifest in Everhard, these other elements of the working class are rendered by London in the pathos-filled terms of Charles Dickens, Riis, or his own earlier documentary study of London's East End, *The People of the Abyss* (1903): "One thing was plain, Jackson's situation was wretched. His wife was in ill health, and he was unable to earn, by his rattan-work and peddling, sufficient food for the family. He was back in his rent, and the oldest boy, a lad of eleven, had started to work in the mills" (*IH*, 351). Even more ironically, London seems here to have forgotten the insights of *The Communist Manifesto* that had played such a key role elsewhere in his text, for the narrative's vision at this point coincides with that of the utopian socialists of the first half of the nineteenth century, of whom Marx observed, "In the formation of their plans they are conscious of caring chiefly for the interests of the working class, as being the most suffering class. Only from the point of view of being the most suffering class does the proletariat exist for them."[93]

However, the double negation of the place of the working class in the text also testifies to more personal anxieties on the part of London him-self. London's knowledge of what it meant to be part of the "most suf-fering class" was direct: that is, London did not have to imaginatively "identify" with the condition of the unskilled laborer because he had ex-perienced it first-hand in his own youth. An important clue to what he understood this condition to be can be found in Avis's horrific descrip-tion of the people of the abyss: "dim ferocious intelligences with all the godlike blotted from their features" (*IH,* 535). As we have already seen, to be "godlike" is, in a way, to be like the capitalist corporation, a self that is at once irreducibly both body and spirit. It is exactly this kind of corporate self into which London as the writer and intellectual-worker has made himself; as Jonathan Auerbach puts it, "If corporations were beginning to assume the attributes of persons (thanks to court rulings on trusts during the 1880s), then perhaps authors, by way of a magical naming, could be made to resemble corporations."[94] The unskilled in-dustrial laborer, on the other hand, is not a person: for that individual lacks the spiritual-intellectual aspects of identity, and has been reduced to the sheer brute materiality of the *working* body.

The threat of being transformed into a mindless body recurs as a theme throughout London's work. In the early short story "The Law of Life," it appears in its most frightening form, as an inexorable ontolog-ical destiny—to become like the corporation then would also mean one could ward off death. However, London's later description of his semi-autobiographical hero Martin Eden's labor in a steam laundry shows how this reduction can also be *social* in nature, a part of the nascent pro-cess of capitalist workplace reorganization that would soon be described as Taylorism:[95]

> All Martin's consciousness was concentrated in the work. Ceaselessly active, head and hand, an intelligent machine, all that constituted him a man was devoted to furnishing that intelligence. There was no room in his brain for the universe and its mighty problems. All the broad and spacious corridors of his mind were closed and hermetically sealed. . . . He had no thoughts save for the nerve-racking, body-destroying toil.[96]

The negation of the place of the working class thus also expresses Lon-don's deep desire to guarantee his own position and, consequently, his personhood: for by erasing the working class from the narrative world, London can assure that he could never fall back into this condition. (The "fear of falling" looms as prevalent theme in works as diverse as "Love of Life," "The Red One," and *The People of the Abyss.*[97]) This may also account for why London has Avis and not Everhard witness the destruction of the Chicago Commune. For if Everhard is in part a heroic projection of London himself, then placing him in the city would bring the threat of the voracious abyss too near for comfort. However, given that two of the possible paths by which such a process of negation might occur—the figuration of the socialist utopian future in *The Iron Heel* and romantic individualism in *Martin Eden*—prove to be failures (for Martin too ends up a soulless body[98]), the question arises, where will such an "escape" lead?

The contours of an answer had already been sketched in London's 1903 autobiographical essay, "How I Became a Socialist." Here, London recounts how the adventures of his youth had "effectively hammered out" of him a "rampant individualism" and replaced it by a kind of organic "unscientific" socialism.[99] Crucial to this transformation was the young London's realization that the seemingly inexhaustible strength of his body would one day fail him. He tells us that at that moment he "swore a great oath":

> All my days I have worked hard with my body, and according to the number of days I have worked, by just that much I am nearer the bottom of the Pit. I shall climb out of the Pit, but not by the muscles of my body shall I climb out. I shall do no more hard work, and may God strike me dead if I do another day's hard work with my body more than I absolutely have to do. And I have been busy ever since running away from hard work.[100]

A similar victory is achieved in London's short story "The Apostate." In this story, London again looks at how industrial labor transforms the person, this time a young boy working in a jute mill, into a mindless body. Like London himself, the boy escapes, becoming an "apostate" to the religion of a nascent Taylorist industrial organization. Moreover, the boy's rebellion is taken to its logical extreme, becoming a rejection not only of work, but of movement itself: "What makes me tired? Moves. I've ben movin' ever since I was born. I'm tired of movin', an' I ain't goin' to move any more."[101]

In his discussion of this story, Mark Seltzer argues that "London's apostate is one case study in the neurasthenic inversion of the work ethic."[102] I agree with Seltzer's observation, and think the same could be said of the conclusion reached in the essay "How I Became a Socialist." However, there is a crucial fact about the late-nineteenth-century "epidemic of nervousness" that Seltzer does not point out: the specific *class* dimensions of the illness. As T. J. Jackson Lears shows, the neurasthenic experience of the distancing of one's own body was explicitly coded in the late nineteenth and early twentieth centuries as the "disease of choice" of the new urban middle class.[103] Thus, the decision on the part of both the fictional boy and the real-world London to become neurasthenics should be understood as nothing less than an expression of the desire to ascend into this nascent middle class. In short, London transfers the energies of one kind of movement, that of the working body, into another, social mobility.

Here then we arrive at the "solution" to the problem of class in *The Iron Heel*: for by negating the place of the working class in the narrative, London creates a "revolutionary" bloc that, in all its major lineaments, emerges as another figure for the new, urban, middle-class strata. Everhard's absorption into this group signals London's own desire to break absolutely with his past. However, the precise class space that London's "revolutionary" vanguard occupies is quite distinct from that of the merchants, small-scale businessmen, farmers, and intellectuals of the older American middle class (the place of this nineteenth-century bourgeoisie already having been neutralized in the text); nor is London's figure precisely the same as the professional-managerial bloc that emerges in Bellamy's *Looking Backward*. Peter Dobkin Hall points out that "had the channelling of occupations in the late nineteenth century been a simple matter of professional specialization, the overall social impact would have been fragmentation rather than integration." Instead, the consolidation of the new national corporate capitalist structure

> depended in the final analysis on the existence of administrative cadres capable of confronting immense organizational tasks, on sources of information from which intelligent practical decisions could be made, and on the development of ongoing efforts to improve the art of administration, to gather and digest economic and social information, and to comprehend and deal with the consequences of new economic, social, and political realities.[104]

In other words, the appearance of the transnational corporate entity was not possible without the simultaneous development of an administrative, informational, and regulative *bureaucracy* to operate in and through it, a group that London figuratively delineates in the form of the revolution's vanguard collective.[105]

Indeed, all the features that London attributes to his revolutionary bloc likewise describe the new bureaucratic social group. Its members are drawn from across older social class boundaries (a fact, Hall shows us, that would be accomplished through a rapid restructuring of the American university system).[106] Activity in the revolutionary vanguard, as in the modern bureaucracy, is organized according to specialized occupations, while both employ a complex surveillance technology and a massive information-gathering network. Avis informs the reader, "It was necessary for us to keep an eye on friend as well as foe, and this group of madmen was not too unimportant to escape our surveillance" (*IH*, 507). Perhaps most important, the goals of the bureaucratized "revolutionary" bloc appear less the unimaginable transformation of society than the institution of a new rationalized social order. Here then the aims of the Iron Heel and the revolutionists converge. The Iron Heel, Avis informs us, "mastered the surging millions, out of confusion brought order, out of the very chaos wrought its own foundation and structure" (*IH*, 475). The revolutionists too are "struggling to overthrow the irrational society of the present and out of the material to build the rational society of the future" (*IH*, 372). Both can achieve this end only through the control and manipulation of the great social mass. Again Avis writes of the actions of these organizations, "All was unseen, much was unguessed; the blind fought the blind; and yet through it all was order, purpose, control" (*IH*, 484). Anonymity and the desire for order and control: both the revolutionary group and the Iron Heel share these fundamental aspects of the modern bureaucracy.

Reading London's figure of the revolutionary vanguard in this way clears up one of the more puzzling features of the narrative: its portrayal of the ostensibly distinct organizations of the Iron Heel and the revolutionists as being so deeply interwoven. After the old order has collapsed, Avis tells us, "There was no trust, no confidence anywhere. The man who plotted beside us, for all we knew, might be an agent of the Iron Heel. We mined the organization of the Iron Heel with our secret agents, and the Iron Heel countermined with its secret agents inside its own organization. And it was the same with our organization" (*IH*, 484–85). They are linked in this way precisely because the two groups form part of a single figure that stands in for the newly emerging social realities of the twentieth century.

Equally significant, the appearance of this figure in the narrative allows us finally to understand why the occasion of the successful revolution must remain absent in the text. Max Weber, in his ground-breaking studies of the rise of bureaucratic power, held that this new social "machine makes 'revolution,' in the sense of the forceful creation of entirely new formations of authority, technically more and more impossible."[107] For the same reasons, "revolution" becomes an impossible project for the text. The only revolution that could appear would be, as Weber goes on to argue for bureaucratic societies in general, a *coup d'etat:* a redistribution of state social power rather than a more radical change of form. Thus, like Bogdanov's text, London's work offers a devastating figuration of exactly those forces that make the longed-for revolution an increasingly receding horizon.

However, a fleeting recognition of the closure of this horizon of possibility seems to emerge late in the text. In the work's final chapter, Avis writes, "And hand in hand with this, Everhard and the other leaders were hard at work reorganizing the forces of the Revolution. The magnitude of the task may be understood when it is taken into"; to which Meredith appends the following note, "This is the end of the Everhard Manuscript. It breaks off abruptly in the middle of a sentence" (*IH*, 553). Refusing narrative closure in this fashion, London manages to hold open at least the possibility of the "task" that the very logic of his narrative made it impossible for him to represent. In this too, London points forward to the emergence of another more properly modernist solution to the problem of utopia's representation. This solution achieves its most full-blown expression, a little more than a decade after the publication of *Red Star* and *The Iron Heel,* in Zamyatin's *We*—the text that is the focus of my next chapter.

CHAPTER FIVE

A Map of Utopia's "Possible Worlds"

Zamyatin's We *and*
Le Guin's The Dispossessed

> To understand the past we cannot see it exclusively in terms
> of the past, we must also see it in terms of the future. Marx
> demonstrated this, as did others. But if what is possible is
> not certain, if there are several possibilities, how are we to
> consider the present? With a certain irony.
>
> *Henri Lefebvre,* Introduction to Modernity

RECLAIMING *WE* FOR UTOPIA

One of the most significant lessons of the literary criticism of the last few decades has been that the currently accepted meaning of any text is a product of the interpretive institutions and communities acting upon it. Fredric Jameson suggests that we never really encounter textual meaning "as a thing-in-itself. Rather, texts come before us as the always-already-read; we apprehend them through sedimented layers of previous interpretations, or—if the text is brand-new—through the sedimented reading habits and categories developed by those inherited interpretive traditions."[1] Stanley Fish further observes that some interpretations, for a variety of reasons, succeed so well that we no longer view them as arguments about the meaning of a work, but instead take them as "simple assertion(s) about the world" itself.[2]

Such sedimented reading habits have long shaped the way readers approach Yevgeny Zamyatin's *We (My)* (1920). It has become something of a critical commonplace, for example, to regard *We* as one of the first and most successful of the twentieth century's *anti-utopias:* the subgenre of the narrative utopia that takes as the target of its critical estrangements not the histories of its present, but the desires and programs of the very generic institution from which it emerges. Indeed, in Western Europe and the United States—where it was first published, in translation, in 1924—*We* for a long time was known primarily as the model for the masterpiece of the anti-utopia, George Orwell's *Nineteen Eighty-Four*.[3] (Of course, the critical rewriting of *We* followed a quite different trajectory in the former Soviet Union, where the text was not officially published until 1988 and had previously circulated only in manuscript and, later, in the clandestine *samizdat* press.) The Anglo-American treatment of *We* as the prototype of the anti-utopia most likely arose from a number of sources: it might well have begun with Orwell's own discussion of the text and, later, would have been bolstered by efforts to recover literary precursors to Cold War attitudes toward the Soviet Union in particular and socialism in general. Indeed, Richard Stites observes, "When Zamyatin's book was revived and reissued in the early 1950s in the West—coinciding with late Stalinism, the publication of Orwell's *1984* . . . and the emergence of the theory of totalitarianism—many took Zamyatin's nightmare to be simply an accurate rendition of Soviet reality from the very beginning."[4]

Even in our own post–Cold War universe, where these older political struggles no longer have the same urgency, reading *We* as an exemplary anti-utopia still has its attractions. Such an interpretation "re-authors" a version of the text consonant with contemporary *fin-de-siècle* attitudes toward the various utopian projects of the earlier part of this century. Indeed, the anti-utopian narrative form seems especially attractive to a historical moment in which we have become deeply suspicious of even the hope of radical social change—there being very little that is "new," for example, in the now already shopworn New World Order. While the narrative utopia gives voice to the desire for an overarching transformation of contemporary society, its anti-utopian inverse attempts to short-circuit this same desire by presenting the "inevitable" consequence of any attempt to realize large changes in the world. Or, as Irving Howe succinctly puts it, "Not progress denied but progress realized, is the nightmare haunting the anti-utopian novel."[5] Thus, even many of the recent interpretations of *We* that seek to find a glimmer of hope in the text accept the critical assumption that Zamyatin's work casts a cold eye on efforts to imagine a radically other tomorrow; as a result, they locate the narrative's vision of redemption not in a transformed future, but in some mythical idealized or archetypal past.

One of the unfortunate consequences of the interpretation of *We* as an anti-utopian narrative is that it sets the work at odds with what we know of its author's own life-long utopian desires. As Darko Suvin points out, "Zamyatin thought of himself as a utopian, paradoxically more revolutionary than the latter-day Bolsheviks."[6] Thus, while Zamyatin would express it in different ways at different times, he appears to have consistently held a very modernist faith in the need for a total transformation of both society and the subjects that inhabit it. Early in his life, Zamyatin's desire for a radical change of affairs led to his participation in the 1905 revolution and his subsequent arrest for political activities. Later, his utopian hopes would be sublimated into literary forums, finding expression in such essays as "Tomorrow," and the celebrated "On Literature, Revolution, Entropy, and Other Matters." Moreover, despite his well-documented persecution at the hands of an increasingly inflexible intellectual establishment, Zamyatin remained until the end of his life committed to the utopian ideals he regarded to be embodied in the Bolshevik revolution. Zamyatin's biographer Alex Shane notes,

> The heretic Zamjatin's objections to the Bolshevik dictatorship and to the dogmatic glorification and canonization of October did not represent a disillusionment with the Revolution; they were rather the logical consequence of his conception of heresy and his belief in never-ending revolution. For him the October Revolution always remained a positive, elemental force that did not need the protective armor of dogma and deification.[7]

Shane's insights are confirmed by a glance at Zamyatin's celebrated 1931 letter to Stalin requesting permission to leave the Soviet Union, to begin what would be a painful exile in Paris. In the letter, Zamyatin writes that while he is now resigned to await the day when "it becomes possible in our country to serve great ideas in literature without cringing before little men," he remains confident that such a "time is near, for the creation of the material base will inevitably be followed by the need to build the superstructure—an art and a literature truly worthy of the revolution."[8]

Such biographical evidence by itself should never be taken as proof of any interpretation of such a complex text as We. Formalist criticisms, of both the Russian and American varieties, long have cautioned against confusing an author's beliefs with the thematic vision of her text. Moreover, we run an additional risk, one that is especially pressing in the case of We, of reducing the complex heterogeneity of the narrative into a univocal, positive or negative, representation. Mikhail Bakhtin sees a related dilemma plaguing the criticism of the earlier Russian writer, Fyodor Dostoevsky. Bakhtin argues that "everyone interprets in his own way Dostoevsky's ultimate word, but all equally interpret it as a *single word*, a *single* voice, a *single* accent," thereby creating a unified monological voice in Dostoevsky's texts that purportedly reflects the author's consciousness.[9]

Bakhtin's observations about Dostoevsky's work have a special relevance for a discussion of Zamyatin's *We*, because a long and interesting critical literature has mapped Zamyatin's thematic and philosophical reliance upon Dostoevsky's oeuvre, especially *Notes from Underground* and *The Brothers Karamazov*.[10] Bakhtin's criticism similarly provides us with the tools to uncover more formal similarities between the works of each author. In his study of Dostoevsky's "poetics"—an inquiry begun about the same time that Zamyatin was writing *We*—Bakhtin contends that Dostoevsky breaks with the tradition of European realism and generates a wholly new narrative practice that Bakhtin calls the "polyphonic novel." What Bakhtin argues of Dostoevsky's work—and especially to the degree that Bakhtin is in fact developing a theory of the modernist narrative proper—also holds for Zamyatin's *We*: unlike the realist narrative, *We* does not present "a multitude of characters and fates in a single objective world, illuminated by a single authorial consciousness; rather a *plurality of consciousnesses, with equal rights and each with its own world,* combine but are not merged in the unity of the event."[11] Moreover, in both writers, realist concerns with time are displaced by an emphasis on a narrative space in which several fictional worlds simultaneously coexist and interact.[12] In fact, Zamyatin's narrative may be distinguished from utopian/anti-utopian texts like Edward Bellamy's *Looking Backward* or Orwell's *Nineteen Eighty-Four* in that it does not configure within its narrative confines a singular monolithic utopian locus, be it ideal or nightmare. Instead, *We* generates a plurality of what Suvin elsewhere describes as the *"Possible Worlds* of utopian fiction." These worlds are variously arrayed narrative topoi emerging from all kinds of utopian texts: fictional universes that are dramatically distinct from, yet still inextricably bound to, the empirical and ideological realities of the text's readers.[13] In mapping the relationship between "Possible Worlds," ranging from the fluid utopian "horizon" to the absolute closure of the true anti-utopia, *We* also dramatically revises the generic institution of the narrative utopia—a reworking operation that, at the same time, has interesting things to tell us about the historical context in which Zamyatin himself operates. *We* thus comes to occupy a crucial junctural point not only in the tradition of Russian utopian and science fiction literature, but in the global generic institution of the narrative utopia as well.[14]

THE CITY AND THE COUNTRY

The events of *We* are set during the thirtieth century—although the literary critical term "setting" is not quite accurate here, because as I suggested in the first chapter, *We,* like all narrative utopias, is in fact really *about* what is conventionally called setting. Early on, the reader learns that the planet's population has been reduced by 80 percent and the rural environs returned to their primitive state as a consequence of a destructive, two-hundred-year-long war waged "between the city and the village."[15] Later the war is described as the conquest of the country by the city: "And almost from the very sky, down to the ground—black, heavy, swaying curtains: slow columns of smoke, over woods, over villages. Stifled howling—black endless lines driven to the city—to be saved by force, to be taught happiness" (*We,* 164; 28). Most immediately, Zamyatin here refers to struggles of the recent civil war in the Soviet Union, the peasant insurgency movements of 1920–21, and the increasing ideological inflexibility concerning the national peasantry developing among some party intellectuals, the disastrous consequences of which would become evident soon enough.[16]

At the same time, however, the opposition between the city and the village serves a broader duty in the narrative. Raymond Williams has shown us, albeit in the different context of England and Great Britain, the central figural role the opposition between the "city and the country" plays in the consciousness of a society in the midst of the liquidating upheavals of social modernization: the densely built environment of the urban industrial center serves as the material emblem of the dramatic transformations wrought by the historical forces of modernization (of which the Soviet revolution is one expression), while the city's "Other," the rural countryside, comes to stand for the already-existing, traditional, agrarian, and, in the case of Zamyatin's Russia, feudal social organization against which these energies are directed.[17] Moreover, T. R. N. Edwards reminds us that the city-country antithesis would have implied for readers in Zamyatin's time "the historical Russian dilemma of choice between West and East," the dilemma also at work, as we saw in the last chapter, in Alexander Bogdanov's *Red Star.*[18]

The conflict between these two forces was exacerbated during the foreshortened process of modernization unfolding in the immediate postrevolutionary Soviet Union. Throughout his work, Zamyatin evidenced little nostalgia for a traditional rural existence—nor does *We* revive the simplistic attack on industrialism and celebration of the peasant life found in L. B. Afanasev's earlier *Journey to Mars* (1901) or the contemporary peasant utopias of Apollon Karelin, Alexander Chayanov, and Peter Krasnov.[19] During a youthful exile from St. Petersburg, the city that Marshall Berman calls "the clearest expression" found on Russian soil of the fraught national experience of modernity, Zamyatin gained a first-hand experience of the "idiocy of rural life," an experience that he would put to use in his ruthlessly satirical work, *A Provincial Tale* (1913).[20]

In *We,* however, Zamyatin first turns his critical gaze onto the other element of this dialectic—the social spaces of the modern city. The city that the reader finds in *We* is unlike any yet built: Zamyatin's "One State" (*Yedinoe Gosudarstvo*)—an array of perfect geometric forms constructed, like the massive "Green Wall" which separates the city from the outside world, of "impregnable, eternal glass"—is the realization of the modernist dream of the new super-rational "machine for living." This design at once recalls Nikolai Chernyshevsky's vision of the crystal palace and prefigures real-world, glass-box urban architectures such as those of Mies Van der Rohe and the CIAM group.[21]

The equation of the contemporary metropolis with the "ideal place" has a long and honored intellectual pedigree, extending back at least to Plato's *Republic*.[22] And yet, as the very name of the "utopia" in *We,* the One State, already suggests, Zamyatin marks a second, more significant, level of reference at work in the modern institution of the narrative utopia: beginning with the founding text of the modern genre, Thomas More's *Utopia,* the imaginary "no-place" both occupies and helps define the same locus contained by the imagined horizons of the central political, economic, and cultural vehicle of social modernization, the nation-state. Thus, while Zamyatin's critical attention is largely occupied by the contemporary consequences of the bounding of history within these borders, he never turns it against the broader critical estranging and constructive possibilities of the utopian imaginary itself. Or, to put this another way, Zamyatin's vision of the One State—and, as we shall see shortly, of the world of the Mephi as well—takes the form of the *dystopia,* the "bad place," and not a more generalized *anti-utopia:* the former presents a critique of the limitations of a specific form of imagining place, the latter a rejection of this cognitive act altogether.[23] (As we shall see in the next chapter, Orwell employs this latter strategy to powerful effects.) Taking as one of its most important tasks the unveiling of the limitations of the older generic logic that binds the utopia to what is now understood to be a constricting and false social totality, Zamyatin's *We* turns the reflexive gaze of the utopian form back in on itself and, in so doing, transforms the representational "failures" of Bogdanov's *Red Star* and Jack London's *The Iron Heel*—their inability to represent a space that would stand as the utopian other of the present global social totality—into an aesthetic and even a kind of political victory.

Social life in the One State, as in the physical spaces of its urban environment, has been rationally organized in every one of its dimensions. The ideological underpinnings of this "perfect" social structure has been derived in a large part from the ideas of Frederick Winslow Taylor, the American modernist superhero (or villain), whose time-motion studies of workplace efficiency and "principles of scientific management" had already by the 1920s begun to profoundly transform social and cultural life around the globe.[24] In the world of the One State, Taylor's scientific principles serve as the basis for the "Table of Hours," a precise, detailed schedule of the movements of each of the city's "numbers," its ten million inhabitants. In the opening pages of *We*, one of these numbers, the protagonist, D-503, describes the daily routine in his "ideal" world:

> Every morning, with six-wheeled precision, at the same hour and the same moment, we—millions of us—get up as one. At the same hour, in million-headed unison, we start work; and in million-headed unison we end it. And, fused into a single million-handed body, at the same second, designated by the Table, we lift our spoons to our mouths. At the same second, we come out for our walk, go to the auditorium, go to the hall for Taylor exercises, fall asleep. . . . (*We*, 12; 3)

Working toward a common goal are all the institutions and practices of the One State—the collectivization of both manual and intellectual labor; the strict regulation of free time (with the significant exceptions of daily Personal Hours and sexual intercourse, which D-503 admits to be a flaw in the social equation); the standardized dress of the gray-blue "unifs"; and the ritual celebration of the fusion of the individual into the group. Each of these practices aims, first, to assure the satisfaction of the society's material wants (unlike Orwell's Oceania, deprivation is unknown in the One State); and second, to secure the stable functioning and smooth reproduction of the current order of things by generating a mechanical unanimity among the needs and desires of the State's inhabitants.

The potential consequences of the industrial modernization process now known as "Taylorization"—human activity reduced to the repetitious monotony of the machine—served as a popular contemporary theme, at the heart, as we saw in the last chapter, of London's fiction and also of later works such as Karel Čapek's science fiction drama *R. U. R.* (1920) and Fritz Lang's expressionist film classic, *Metropolis* (1926).[25] (Indeed, the passage quoted above could serve as a summary of the famous opening sequence of Lang's film.) However, in *We*, as in these related visions, the modern world produced by these processes is not simply dismissed out of hand. In fact, early in the narrative, the mathematician and engineer D-503 paints a stirring portrait of the socio-spatial environments of his ideal modernist city. The whole narrative comes to the reader through D-503's diary notes, and any reflection offered on the social order is always already mediated through his consciousness. He intends his diary to serve as a paean to the "mathematically perfect life of the One State," which will then be placed aboard the spaceship *Integral* as it embarks on its imperial mission of spreading perfection throughout the solar system (*We*, 2; 1). D-503's deepest libidinal responses to his social environment are thus to be found in his descriptions of the spaces of the One State:

> In the morning I was at the dock where the *Integral* is being built, and suddenly I *saw*: the lathes; the regulator spheres rotating with closed eyes, utterly oblivious of all; the cranks flashing, swinging left and right; the balance beam proudly swaying its shoulders; the bit of the slotting machine dancing up and down in time to unheard music. Suddenly I saw the whole beauty of this grandiose mechanical ballet, flooded with pale blue sunlight. (*We*, 3–4; 2)

This aestheticization of modern technology indicates a relationship on the part of D-503 to the world of the city-state that belies what little we know of his personal history. D-503 speaks in this evocation less like a lifelong resident of the One State than someone only recently thrust into this estranging environment, seemingly still awestruck by the utter originality of this social space. Thus, while this passage may do duty, as has been suggested, in Zamyatin's critique of the Proletarian Poets, mocking their use of what rapidly would become a conventionalized imagery of the industrial order, its very presence in the text, as in the otherwise conventional work of the Proletarian Poets, cannot help but remind the contemporary reader of the utter estranging newness in Zamyatin's time of the spatial forms unleashed in the modern city and the experience of being enframed within them.[26] Indeed, I would suggest that D-503 at this moment could also be taken as a stand-in for the engineer and artist Zamyatin himself, whose own libidinal investments in his modernizing world are expressed in the very narrative form of We. Zamyatin's use of an elliptical, stream-of-consciousness narrative voice and symbolist and expressionist imagery signal both his rejection of the "closed" canon of the literary past and his affirmative commitment to the potential of the modernist new.[27]

However, Zamyatin's self-conscious, modernist technique points at the same time toward a deeper ambivalence running through the narrative. The very uniqueness of the form of We, those signatory elements of style that mark its special identity as a narrative object, can also be understood as a gesture of defiance directed at the standardization of contemporary life—be it that of the emergent state bureaucracy of the postrevolutionary Soviet Union or the entrenched bourgeois capitalism that Zamyatin came to loathe during his earlier years in Great Britain.[28] Moreover, this same dynamic is replicated in the narrative in another crucial way: D-503 emerges as another kind of modernist monument, a unique identity that comes to stand out from the homogenized mass. Soon after encountering the mysterious female number I-330—the embodiment in the text of the principles of both individual and social revolution—D-503 begins to deviate from the daily routine laid out by the Table of Hours. Further unprecedented events rapidly follow. D-503 has his first "dream," and is soon diagnosed as having contracted the dreaded "soul-disease." As D-503 describes it in his own richly suggestive language, such a condition marks the development of an interior self, an individual identity now distinct from the social aggregate: "The plane has acquired volume, it has become a body, a world, and everything is now inside the mirror—inside you" (We, 89; 16).

The emergence of this new interiority is extremely upsetting for D-503. He is wracked by anxieties as he comes for the first time to doubt the perfection of his world. His psychic trauma is further exacerbated by I-330, as she challenges his fragile new identity by guiding him through a series of increasingly transgressive adventures. At a climactic moment in the narrative, I-330 leads D-503 outside the walls of the One State and introduces him to the garden world of the Mephi people. This "world" appears to be the antithesis of D-503's modernist city: while in the State D-503 notes only the "gray-blue unifs" of the numbers, here he discovers "black, red, golden, bay, roan, and white people"; while inside

the Green Wall he sees a rationally ordered artificial space, here he encounters the chaos of the natural environment; while in his society
mathematical rationality rules, here prerational desires are given full
play; and, finally, whereas in the State he is part of an integrated collective whole, here the full realization of his new-found individuality comes
dramatically home: "I was I, a separate entity, a world. I had ceased to
be a component, as I had been, and become a unit" (We, 156–57; 27).
The pastoral primitive "world" of the Mephi thus represents a quite different figuration of the premodern "countryside" than that earlier invoked by D-503. At this point, the valences between the terms of the
modern city and premodern countryside have been reversed: the latter is
now the positive pole, as the world of the Mephi seems to promise the
possibility of individual self-realization unavailable within the (en)clo-
sure of the One State.

During the visit to the Mephi, I-330 first reveals her own plans. She
will foment a revolution, which D-503 will aid by giving her control of
the *Integral*. In the end, however, the menace to his old world proves to
be more than D-503 can bear. He rejects her revolutionary challenge to
the One State and, in a fit of anxiety, submits himself to the Office of the
Guardians, the State security force. There he undergoes a fantasectomy,
a medical procedure that excises the physical centers of the imagination
within the brain, the imagination serving in the text as another figural
locus of the autonomous self. This operation cures D-503 of his "madness," and he subsequently betrays the revolution. The narrative ends
with a now fully reintegrated D-503 observing the execution of I-330
and offering his chilling reflections on the "inevitable" victory of a now
absolute State.

Crucially, the subject position occupied by D-503 at the narrative's
conclusion is quite different from the one he inhabits in its opening
pages. In the beginning, D-503 is a textbook example of the subject produced by what Louis Althusser describes as ideological interpellation:
D-503 is "hailed" by the One State, and believes he freely "consents" to
sacrifice his individuality to the greater good of the social collective.[29] If
the society of the State seems absolutely static at this point, it is only so
in appearance. In fact, as the narrative quickly demonstrates, the State
is haunted by the possibility of oppositional activity, for it is in the very
nature of the ideological "choice" given to D-503 to leave open other
potentially transgressive options. Or, to use another language, Zamyatin shows in *We* that there can be no such thing as a "fully sutured," or
absolutely closed, ideological totality.[30] Indeed, it is D-503's decision to

follow an alternative and ultimately oppositional path that serves as the motor driving the narrative action.

This dynamic is symbolized in the narrative by the figure of the imaginary or complex number, the square root of negative one, $\sqrt{-1}$ (*We*, 39–40; 8). D-503, who erroneously refers to this as the "irrational number" and "irrational root" (*irrationsional' nyy koren'*), finds the concept so exasperating precisely because it is a "challenge" to his mathematical understanding of the world that arises from within the very logic of that understanding itself. Moreover, his confusion of the imaginary number with the very different irrational one—a mistake of which the engineer Zamyatin must have been aware—suggests both D-503's and the One State's identification of the imagination with irrationality: for both represent a way of looking at the world other than the officially sanctioned one. (I return to the issue of "irrationality" in the next chapter.) However, in mathematics as in society, as D-503 only too painfully comes to realize, both the imaginary and the real, the rational and the irrational, the simple and the complex are equally important dimensions of reality. During the course of the narrative, D-503 discovers that he too has become a complex and "irrational" number: an alien subjectivity, endowed with that dreaded thing imagination, that ironically emerges from the very State ideologies intended to render such a development impossible.[31]

This structurally produced potential for opposition necessitates that the invisible leaders of the State deploy surveillance technologies (the glass walls, the recording membranes in the streets) and disciplinary apparatuses (the State security forces and the torture bell) to assure the continued acquiescence of all members of the social body. And yet, despite these precautions, rebels such as I-330 activate the latent potential embedded in D-503 and other members of the society. Only with the conclusion of the narrative is the fragility of ideological and repressive control no longer a concern, as the excision of D-503's imagination likewise removes any possibility for opposition.

These fundamental changes experienced by the "character" of D-503 during the course of the narrative serve as important clues to the play of "Possible Worlds" in *We*. Each of the three conditions that we have thus far examined—D-503 as a happy functioning member of the State, D-503 as the conflict-ridden individual, and D-503 as the "nonself"—articulates a different utopian Possible World. Indeed, in *We*, the individual D-503 serves as a synecdoche for the social whole, a figure for the various potential social bodies of which he is always already a part.

Zamyatin thereby emphasizes the fact that the "worlds" of his text—
and, in fact, of all utopian texts—are never just inert containers that individuals passively inhabit, but complex, continuously evolving spatial
constructs that emerge at the intersection of the subject's point of view
and the observed social object—that is, as another form of Henri Lefebvre's "conceived" space. These worlds and their spaces change as the
individuals that interact within and through them change; and, as we
will see made evident in *We,* every present world is surrounded by a
range of residual and emergent alternatives.

HAPPINESS AND FREEDOM

Before we can look at the specific spatio-ideological configurations of
each of these utopian worlds, I need first to lay into place the other crucial figural opposition that is at work in *We:* the opposition between
freedom and *happiness.* In a key passage, with roots in the "Grand
Inquisitor" section of Dostoevsky's *The Brothers Karamazov,* the poet
R-13 observes that the tension between these antinomies lies at the very
foundation of human civilization:

> That ancient legend about paradise . . . Why, it's about us, about today. Yes!
> Just think. Those two, in paradise, were given a choice: happiness without
> freedom, or freedom without happiness. *There was no third alternative.*
> Those idiots chose freedom, and what came of it? Of course, for ages after-
> ward they longed for the chains. The chains—you understand? That's what
> world sorrow was about. For ages! And only we have found the way of
> restoring happiness. (*We,* 61; 11; emphasis added)

This antinomy, as it emerges in Zamyatin's narrative, bears an uncanny
resemblance to that which Ernst Bloch later maps in *Natural Law and
Human Dignity.* Through a detailed examination of key texts in the
history of Western ethical thought, Bloch shows that two separate and
complementary fields of "utopian" ethical thinking have emerged:
those, respectively, of social utopia and natural law (*Naturrecht*). While
both aim at producing a more humane society, they diverge in their primary emphasis. Bloch summarizes their differences as follows:

> Social utopias are primarily directed toward *happiness,* at least toward the
> abolition of misery and the conditions that preserve or produce such misery.
> Natural law theories, as is so readily apparent, are primarily directed toward
> *dignity,* toward human rights, toward juridical guarantees of human security
> or freedom as categories of human pride. Accordingly, social utopias are ori-
> ented above all toward the abolition of human *suffering;* natural law is ori-

ented above all toward the abolition of human *degradation*. Social utopias want to clear away all that stands in the way of the *eudaemonia of everyone;* natural law wants to do away with all that stands in the way of *autonomy* and its *eunomia*.[32]

This opposition between the needs of the society and the desires of the individual can be rewritten in terms of the even more fundamental antinomy of subject (individual) and object (society). In many classical ethical discussions, one pole—more often than not the latter—is privileged over the other, a decision with real political and social consequences. However, this division of ethical thought and the apparent oppositions that it produces is, according to Bloch, fundamentally illusory, for the simple reason that "there can be no human dignity without the end of misery and need, but also no human happiness without the end of old and new forms of servitude." Bloch then locates the dialectical resolution of what he now rewrites as a *contradiction* in the transformed and expanded utopian thinking in Marxism and socialism, "insofar as it simultaneously seeks to come to grips with the person and the collective, and to the extent that—far from the normalized masses of men, near to unalienated solidarity—it seeks to contain the one within the other."[33]

We similarly attempts to map the problems that arise when one of these goals, namely, that of "happiness," becomes so prominent in the minds of social planners that it all but eradicates any consideration of "freedom" or "dignity." D-503 comes to realize that a self-stabilizing social body, where the problems of collective need have been resolved—as in the case of the One State—comes into being only by way of a negation or repression of the individual's desire. To put it another way, the space of the State appears only on the condition that its subjects accept what D-503 calls an "ideal unfreedom" (*We*, 4; 2). Later in the text, I-330 ironically asserts, "And happiness . . . Well, after all, desires torment us, don't they? And, clearly, happiness is when there are no more desires, not one . . . What a mistake, what ridiculous prejudice it's been to have marked happiness always with a plus sign. Absolute happiness should, of course, carry a minus sign—the divine minus" (*We*, 184; 31).

Here, drawing upon nineteenth-century thermodynamics theory, especially that found in the work of German physicist Julius Robert von Mayer, Zamyatin expands the freedom-happiness antinomy into a cosmology.[34] Energy, the dynamic force of creation and destruction, desire and movement, is equated with freedom, while entropy, stasis and the cessation of desire, is inscribed under the sign of happiness. The "divine minus," negative 273 degrees, is the point, according to the second law of thermodynamics, of final entropy, the "heat death" of the universe—an image that also resonates with the haunting final pages of H. G. Wells's *The Time Machine*.[35] (There is also a similar image to be found at the conclusion of Bogdanov's "prequel" to *Red Star, Engineer Menni,* although the differences between Wells's and Bogdanov's responses to this inevitability are instructive indeed.)[36] I-330 implies that a fully achieved happiness is possible only in the absolutely static, posthistorical social order—Claude Lévi-Strauss's "cold" society located at the end, rather than the dawn, of the modern world—a world Zamyatin portrays for us *only* in the final pages of the text.

D-503 himself earlier prefigures I-330's conclusion: "The ideal (clearly) is the condition where nothing *happens* any more" (*We,* 24; 6). However, as Zamyatin so skillfully demonstrates, such a "victory" is a pyrrhic one, for the realization of the absolute happiness represented by the "divine minus" will, for all intents and purposes, render the very notion of happiness obsolete. In such a condition, the State's *raison d'être* disappears. Ironically then, as the rational State moves increasingly near its ideal, it simultaneously slips back into the condition represented for it by the other "divine minus" of the text—the "irrationality" or, more precisely, the "complexity" of the square root of negative one. The destructive arc of modern rational society back into the nonrational, here so effectively mapped in *We,* will be later more extensively elaborated in the form of the "dialectic of Enlightenment" described by Theodor Adorno and Max Horkheimer.[37]

Of course, the converse of this happiness-unfreedom couple is also true: as D-503 increasingly becomes an autonomous subject, he loses his earlier happiness. In the narrative, as the energy-entropy passage makes clear, identity and desire are inextricably woven together. Indeed, D-503's expressions of selfhood are precipitated by his sexual desire for I-330, a motif that will play out in a quite different fashion in *Nineteen Eighty-Four.* As D-503 discovers his "self," his interests increasingly come into conflict with those of the State. More significant, he experiences a growing sense of isolation from the collective whole. At the once-joyous celebration of group fusion, D-503 now can only observe, "I had no place here—I, the criminal, the poisoned one. Never again would I merge into the regular, precise, mechanical rhythm, never again float on the mirrorlike untroubled sea" (*We,* 83; 15). Alienation, anomie, and angst: D-503 exhibits all the unhappy symptoms of a very modern existential crisis.

Moreover, this cycle repeats itself in other characters, and throughout the One State as a whole. For example, O-90, D-503's former "approved" sexual liaison, becomes jealous of his involvement with I-330. Finally, in a desperate attempt to regain "control" of D-503, she commits the antisocial act of an unapproved pregnancy. Later, as the epidemic of individuality spreads throughout the State, open anarchy bursts forth. Ironically, this occurs during the celebration of the Day of Unanimity, the ritualistic reaffirmation of social unity. Again, only with the absolute negation of the self and its desires, occurring at the conclusion of the narrative, is a semblance of order restored.

THE PLAY OF POSSIBLE WORLDS

The two major conceptual antinomies that we have examined thus far—those of "city and the country" and "happiness and freedom"—are similarly interwoven within the deep narrative structure of We. As Williams points outs, spatial figures such as the "city" and the "country" are themselves always already ethico-political ones. In this regard, We is no exception. On the one hand, Zamyatin's narrative suggests that the very physical locus of the idealized modern city—a strictly regulated, super-rationalized organization of human space—works to create a condition of unfreedom. Michel de Certeau similarly maintains that the modernist discourse of the metropolis, which operates in a way intimately linked to the generic utopian discourse of the nation-state, aims at "the creation of a *universal* and anonymous *subject* which is the city itself: it gradually becomes possible to attribute to it, as to its political model, Hobbes's State, all the functions and predicates that were previously scattered and assigned to many different real subjects—groups, associations, or individuals."[38] When the city and state achieve this kind of closed, absolute, anonymous subjectivity, the multiple, conflicting, and deeply human subjective desires by which Zamyatin defines freedom disappear. And, of course, this is exactly what occurs in the "ideally unfree," machinelike spaces of the One State.[39] De Certeau further argues that the *espace propre* of the city attempts to "repress all the physical, mental and political pollutions that would compromise it"—the very kinds of "pollutions" that the State finds in the irrational number, D-503's emergent subjectivity, and the burgeoning revolt of the numbers.[40]

On the other hand, We also shows that the world of the Mephi represents *only* the negation, or antithesis, of the "happiness" found in the One State. A number of readers have attempted to locate a "true" utopian ideal for the text in the garden world of the Mephi. Alexandra Aldridge, for example, contends that *We* expresses a deeply nostalgic and antimodern longing for the restoration of a lost connection between humanity and the natural world. She further argues that Zamyatin draws upon a mytho-poetic polarity between City and Garden, the urban and the Arcadian utopia. The narrative demonstrates the disastrous consequences inherent in the former of these two possibilities and finds salvation in the latter—here expressed in the figure of the Mephi people. Aldridge writes, "In the drift toward 'entropy' the forces of 'energy' have been overwhelmed. . . . Therefore, the only option left is to reverse the entropic process, to regenerate humanity by starting over in a state of benign anarchy, in the unfettered greenery of the Garden."[41] In a similar vein, Gorman Beauchamp argues that the text's political philosophy is closest to a Bakuninesque destructive anarchism: anti-bureaucratic, anti-statist, anti-Marxist, and implicitly anti-collective, Zamyatin locates his utopia in a radical individualism personified by the Mephi. Beauchamp notes, "As with the 'proles' in *1984,* whatever hope the novel holds lies with the primitives, with the savages beyond the Wall who have escaped the yoke of Reason."[42]

This generation of the world of the Mephi as the dialectical negation of the "utopia" of the One State recapitulates a process that in fact occurs throughout the institutional history of the genre. Lyman Tower Sargent points out two different strands of imagining the ideal world that predate Thomas More's founding work in the genre: he calls these "utopias of sensual gratification or body utopias," the older of the two practices, and "the utopia of human contrivance or the city utopia." The former is exemplified in the folk fables of the Land of Cockaigne and the latter by Plato's *Laws.*[43] However, with More's founding of the modern genre of the narrative utopia, these two poles come into dialectical coordination, the former quickly being repositioned as the negation of the latter. Thus, in response to More's "utopia of human contrivance," François Rabelais offers in *Gargantua* the sensual, bodily world of the Abbey of Thélème (or, as Richard Helgerson provocatively points out, even more dramatically in the unrestrained freedom evident throughout the earlier *Pantagruel,* a text in which More's Utopians also make a direct appearance).[44] Similarly, as we saw in Chapter 3, William Morris's equally sensual and pastoral vision of an "epoch of rest" arose as a direct "reply" to Bellamy's *Looking Backward;* and, finally, a similar dialectical couple is formed between Ursula K. Le Guin's *The Dispossessed* and Samuel Delany's *Triton.* The brilliance of Zamyatin's work, then, lies in its incorporation of both thesis and antithesis within itself. By so doing, Zamyatin is able to point toward the limits, the *dystopian* propensity, when either possibility is taken as an end in itself.

The false promise of the romantic primitivist utopia also has been suggested by Williams in his outstanding short study of Orwell's *Nineteen Eighty-Four*: "This stale revolutionary romanticism is as insulting as the original observation. It is the rising of the animals, as in the fable. . . . Orwell created the conditions for defeat and despair."[45] Interestingly enough, the other most famous "anti-utopia" of the twentieth century, Aldous Huxley's *Brave New World*, employs a similar opposition, this time presented as that between an urban, authoritarian, consumer society and the primitive world of the Savage's reservation. Of course, for the often bitterly cynical Huxley, neither appears that attractive.[46] In the narrative of *We*, Zamyatin offers his own critique of the limitations of this form of modernist primitivism and the Romantic notion of the individual that accompanies it. One of the prominent physical features that distinguishes the Mephi from the numbers of the State is their coat of "short, glossy fur" (*We*, 156; 27). When we turn back to the earliest pages of the narrative, we discover that I-330 is first drawn to D-503 because she recognizes in him a potential Mephi, externally manifest in what D-503 calls the "stupid atavism" of his "hairy, shaggy . . . ape's hands" (*We*, 7; 2). Later, as D-503's existential crisis grows, he feels himself dividing into two individuals: "The former one, D-503, number D-503, and the other . . . Before, he had just barely shown his hairy paws from within the shell; now all of him broke out, the shell cracked" (*We*, 56; 10). The physical identification of the torment-ridden D-503 with the Mephi then reveals the existential price of a return to the lost anarchic, premodern world: the sacrifice of the kinds of security and collective identity that the emergence of the State made possible. Indeed, the Mephi represent the very negation of the concept of "society" itself, a Rousseauistic retreat to a fictional, isolated, monadic existence. Thus, *both* the realm of freedom and happiness, the modern city and the premodern countryside, appear, within the structural context of the narrative, as fundamentally limited ethico-political constructs, each lacking the positive elements found in the other.

These four interwoven figures—the modern city and *premodern* countryside, freedom and happiness—together map the thematic coordinates within which the narrative of *We* unfolds. In order to visualize more concretely the relational lines of force running through the narrative—relations of contradiction (happiness-freedom; city-countryside)

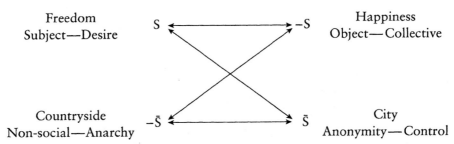

Figure 3.   Greimasian diagram of the four major thematic coordinates of
Zamyatin's *We.*

and of negation (freedom-city; happiness-countryside)—I want to draw
upon the analytical resources of the "semiotic rectangle," first developed
by the French semiotician A. J. Greimas.[47] A Greimasian diagram of the
relationship between these four coordinates would appear as shown in
figure 3.

This diagram of the narrative's major thematic coordinates suggests
that no one of these simpler figures alone composes any of the text's utopian "Possible Worlds." Rather, each World emerges as a more complex
synthesis of the two terms composing each side of the rectangle. The res-
olutions produced on the left and right sides of the rectangle represent
the two Possible Worlds I have detailed thus far. On the right side appears the "utopian" World of the One State, especially as D-503 delineates it in the narrative's opening pages. As I noted above, the D-503 of
this first World accepts and even celebrates the negation of individuality, the anonymity and control, that makes possible the security and
ideal unfreedom of the State. (As a point of comparison, remember that
D-503, unlike Orwell's later Winston Smith, at first sees no conflict between the observations expressed in his journal and the values of the
State.) On the left-hand side, we have the Worlds D-503 discovers only
after his encounters with I-330: the World of the Mephi and that of his
own existential crisis. While in such a situation, D-503 is largely autonomous of the strictures of the social collective, his "free" choices
shaped by newly emergent desires, he is also wracked by the internal
pangs of selfhood as he begins to move along a path that he recognizes
will place him in opposition to the State and his society. With just these
two Worlds in place, we might summarize the argument of Zamyatin's
narrative as follows: a rational (national) social order is predicated on
the violent repression of the self and its desires; conversely, the expres-

sion of these individual desires means the loss of the feelings of security produced by the sense of integration in a stable, unified society. (In many ways, the same contradiction is in play in *Looking Backward*.)

The same opposition of Possible Worlds may then be plotted along the historical trajectory that gave rise to the One State—a "contract myth" for the utopian society.[48] As the poet R-13 informs D-503, it was the experience of an unbearable freedom, coupled with the traumatic absence of security and social stability, that led to the "original" revolutionary founding of the State. Thus, in D-503's existential crisis, as well as in the broader anarchy emerging in the city after the destruction of the Green Wall (*We*, 217–21; 37; I exclude the revolutionary movement of I-330 for reasons that will become clear shortly), we witness nothing less than the *reemergence* of the historical condition preceding the existence of the One State—an unsettled and open-ended condition that bears a striking resemblance to that of Zamyatin's own historical present. The cancellation of this unhappy situation calls the "ambiguous utopia" of the One State into being. The "utopia-of-the-nation-state" envisioned in *We* is thus the inverted or, to use Louis Marin's term, the "neutral" image of the crisis-ridden present in which Zamyatin produces *We*. In the One State, the exhilarating and equally terrifying sense of freedom experienced in the immediate postrevolutionary moment has been recontained, only to result in a situation where there is no fear precisely because there is no longer any possibility for fundamentally remaking society.

If we restrict our attention exclusively to the conflict unfolding in the narrative between these two Possible Worlds, we end up with a version of Zamyatin's text that resonates with the mythic contract narrative that places the repression of instinct at the founding of society, a myth more famously elaborated a decade later by Sigmund Freud. (Not surprisingly, *We* readily lends itself to Freudian critical approaches, wherein the struggles of D-503 and I-330 are rewritten as the internal conflict between an overly vigilant, rational superego and unbounded instinctual desire.)[49] Moreover, with this version of *We* in hand, we must ultimately come to grips with the conclusion, advanced, for example, by Istvan Csicsery-Ronay Jr., that the world of happiness-city and that of freedom-countryside are "formally equal," and that the narrative thus provides us with no "ethical or axiological basis" for preferring one over the other. As a consequence, Csicsery-Ronay goes on to argue, the narrative of *We* can be read as a version of a myth about the opposed ontological constants structuring human existence.[50]

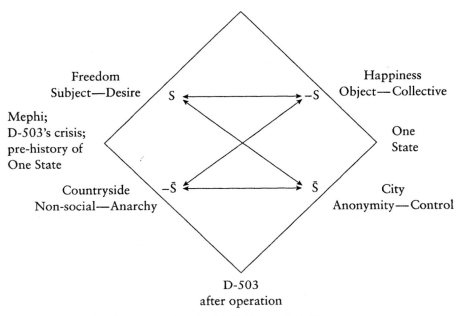

Figure 4. The play of Possible Worlds in Zamyatin's *We*.

Given only these two Possible Worlds to work with, I find Csicsery-Ronay's conclusions persuasive; indeed, as I have already argued, *We* balances the shortcomings inherent in each of these two worlds against those found in the other. However, here is where the application of Greimas's analytical machinery to Zamyatin's narrative becomes so invaluable, precisely because it requires us to acknowledge the potential existence of *two other* Possible Worlds in the text. Before going any further then, I must elaborate the fully realized complex of terms at work in the narrative (figure 4), leaving for the moment blank the "complex" resolution to the problem posed by the text.

  We have already touched on the Possible World that fills what Greimas calls the "neutral" position, the resolution of the "negative" opposition of the countryside and the city, or unhappiness and unfreedom —the world that emerges only in the narrative's concluding pages. As Antonio Gramsci reminds us, whenever a state's hegemony is challenged, it often responds by bringing the full weight of its repressive machinery to bear. In this regard too, the One State proves to be no exception. With the threat of I-330's rebellion growing, the State demands that all of its citizens undergo the fantasectomy procedure or face execution in the glass bell. Consequently, D-503's new subjectivity, with all its pain and potentiality, is brutally torn away. This change is reflected in the very tone of the final chapter, where D-503's once vibrant, expressive language flattens into a dull recitation of "nothing but facts" (We, 231; 40). He now occupies a fixed position within an absolute grid of State power. D-503 thus suffers a death of the self equivalent to the literal execution of I-330. And, with this double murder, the window of revolutionary opportunity, and the promise of a liberatory transformation of the social order, appears to have been violently slammed shut. Such a situation would be, according to Bloch, the moment for final despair—or, as Jameson notes in his discussion of Bloch's work, "from a temporal point of view, what characterizes death is precisely its structure as that instant in which no future (and no hope) is any longer possible."[51] The closure of both subjective and objective historical possibilities—and hence the simultaneous neutralization of the categories of happiness and freedom, of the potential of either collectivity or individuality—produces total stasis, absolute entropy.

By emphasizing this position, we could see in Zamyatin's narrative a bleak pessimism rivaling that of its great successor *Nineteen Eighty-Four*. However, one position in our map of *We*'s Possible Worlds remains unfilled: that of the complex resolution, the negation of the negation, or the "impossible" synthesis of the positive opposition of happiness and freedom. The placeholder for such a potential utopian world is to be found in the narrative's figure of the *"infinite revolution."* This central figure is first invoked during the exchange between D-503 and I-330 that follows upon the revelation of the plan to seize control of the *Integral*:

I jumped up. "It's unthinkable! Absurd! Don't you realize that what you're planning is revolution?"

"Yes, revolution! Why is this absurd?"

"It is absurd because there can be no revolution. Because our—I am saying this, not you—our revolution was the final one. And there can be no others. Everyone knows this. . . ."

The mocking sharp triangle of eyebrows. "My dear—you are a mathematician. More—you are a philosopher, a mathematical philosopher. Well, then: name me the final number."

"What do you mean? I . . . I don't understand: what final number?"

"Well the final, the ultimate, the largest."

"But that's preposterous! If the number of numbers is infinite, how can there be a final number?"

"Then how can there be a final revolution? There is no final one; revolutions are infinite. The final one is for children: children are frightened by infinity, and it's important that children sleep peacefully at night . . ." (We, 174; 30)

This passage offers one of the fullest visions found in the narrative of the "World" of the infinite revolution. In the very concept itself, Zamyatin combines a call for a definitive and total break with the conditions of the present ("revolution"), and an open-ended extension of such a transformative process into any possible future ("infinite"). This then is counterposed to the State's own understanding of history, here summarized by D-503, as a closed teleological process in which the historical narrative reaches its climax with the realization of the "perfect" structures of the One State and therein comes to a conclusion.

The implied resemblance between the historical vision of the One State and that found in the classical utopian narrative is no accident, for We is as clearly "modernist" in its conceptualization as it is in form. In We, the linear causality of the classical utopia, wherein singular past and future conditions are joined together by a narratable chain of events, has been displaced by the kinds of complex causal models at work in Heisenberg's quantum mechanics. Every present in Zamyatin's narrative opens up onto a number of futures, a range of Possible Worlds—the utopia/dystopia of either the One State or anarchic individualism, the anti-utopia of D-503's fate, and the utopian horizon of the infinite revolution—that are less the products of objective historical laws than the consequence of human agents acting upon and within their environments. What We sacrifices in the progressivist confidence expressed in the classical utopia, it compensates for by holding open a place for the utopian potential of revolutionary human action.

The vehicle for the actualization of this utopian possibility is to be found in the narrative *not* in D-503, but in I-330. Far more than a "device" employed to activate the latent subjectivity stirring within D-503, she serves as the guiding force and major theoretician of the "World" of the infinite revolution. The different positions occupied by these two characters are further borne out by their respective fates. On the one hand, D-503 rejects both the pains of subjectivity and the possibility of transformation: he determines to sacrifice himself to the State in order to "resurrect" the old world of happiness. It is important here to keep in mind the exact unfolding of events in the penultimate chapter. Although in the end D-503 is seized and forced to undergo the operation against his will, he *freely* enters the Office of the Guardians with the expressed goal of confessing his sins. After he fails in this attempt—he realizes that he has told his story to an agent of the revolution—he flees to the underground station, where he is captured (*We*, 225–29; 39). I-330, on the other hand, steadfastly refuses to recant, even under torture. In the end, she remains true to the utopian promise of the revolution.[52]

Similarly, it is through I-330 that Zamyatin reveals the dialectical nature of his concept of infinite revolution. Soon after their return from the Mephi, I-330 refuses D-503's desperate plea that they "go together there, beyond the Wall, to those . . . whoever they are" (*We*, 163; 28). In so doing, she definitively rejects any anti-revolutionary, and ultimately anti-utopian, retreat into an idealized anarchic primitive world. Although momentarily taken aback by her refusal, D-503 soon comes to his most important insight: "Who are they? The half we have lost? H_2 and O? And in order to get H_2O—streams, oceans, waterfalls, waves, storms—the two halves must unite. . . ." (*We*, 163; 28). D-503 here offers a crudely materialist, yet nevertheless narratively crucial, analogy of the dialectical process: two independent entities come together in such a way that each maintains its unique identity while producing a qualitatively Other substance. As the very imagery of this passage suggests, the product of such process will be dynamic, energetic forces: the waves and storms are less ends in themselves than the means of further transformations.[53] The vision of social change offered in the text likewise becomes a deeply dialectical one. The way "beyond" the situation of social closure does not lie in the simple "return" to a state of "freedom" represented by an impossibly idealized primitive garden, but in overcoming those social contradictions—the city and the countryside, freedom and happiness, energy and entropy, imagination and reason, desire and satisfaction, and finally, the individual and society—that prevent the emergence of a wholly and unexpectedly new situation.[54] Real happiness is impossible without freedom; however, the concept of freedom too will remain empty, as much in our own present as in Zamyatin's, without the elimination of those conditions that block the equality, or happiness, of all.

It is never fully explicated in the text of *We* precisely what the "worldness" of this dramatically different human situation might be. Nor could it be. Such a radically Other World, "the total leap out of everything that previously existed," as Bloch elsewhere argues, escapes any attempt to represent it from the perspective of the "present"—both Zamyatin's own historical moment and the "present" of the One State.[55] Lacking the cognitive reference points by which such a situation might be surveyed, the utopographer becomes much like the physicist attempting to represent a four- or five-dimensional object within the confines of three-dimensional space: these objects can be "seen" only in strange geometric models, shadow images—registered, as it were, on the extreme periphery of our conceptual retina—of something whose "truth-content" necessarily resides elsewhere.[56] Zamyatin's "solution" to the real historical contradiction of the individual and the collective is thus purely a *formal* one, the creation of a textual figure for something that by definition can be indicated but not seen. Nevertheless, the absent presence of the figure of the infinite revolution serves a crucial role in the play of Possible Worlds in *We*. Such a figure, what Suvin, echoing Bloch, labels the world of the "utopian horizon," critically illuminates that which is "not yet" available to any of us.

Moreover, the restored presence of this fourth possibility renders the apparently pessimistic, "anti-utopian" conclusion of the narrative far more ambiguous. Let me first quote the final two paragraphs in full:

> This [the execution of the rebels] cannot be postponed, because in the western parts of the city there is still chaos, roaring, corpses, beasts, and —unfortunately—a considerable group of numbers who have betrayed Reason.
>
> However, on the Fortieth cross-town avenue, we have succeeded in erecting a temporary barrier of high-voltage waves. And I hope that we shall conquer. More than that—I am certain we shall conquer. Because Reason must prevail. (*We*, 232; 40)

The first-person point of view employed throughout the text now forces us to call into question the truth-content of this claim. For at this point, D-503's postsubjective perspective is exactly identical with that of the State ("we have succeeded," "we shall conquer"). He is thus unable to imagine any other resolution to the situation. However, from the external, unknowable perspective of the still-struggling "numbers who have betrayed Reason," quite different possibilities arise.

Zamyatin hints in the penultimate chapter that he too recognizes the imaginative bind generated by a closed, self-present totality such as the One State. While in hiding, D-503 encounters a physicist who claims to have calculated the closed spherical dimensions of the universe and thereby proven that infinity does not exist. The physicist then extends these conclusions into the realm of epistemology. He proclaims, "Everything is finite, everything is simple, everything is calculable." To which D-503 simply responds, "Just listen to me! You must—you must give me an answer: out there, where your finite universe ends! What is out there, beyond it?" (*We*, 230; 39). Of course, no answer is forthcoming.[57] Finally, Zamyatin leaves one significant character unaccounted for in the narrative's conclusion: O-90, D-503's former lover, who has gone "outside" the city to bear her child among the Mephi. This figure—at once the *supplément* of the finite ideational world of the One State and the utopian emblem of the continued presence of the worldness of the future—forestalls the grim closure suggested at the narrative's end.

The rich mapping in *We* of these utopian Possible Worlds can also be read as a powerful figure of the complex historical conjuncture out of which the text itself emerges. However, only when all the narrative's multiple spaces are set into place can we begin to grasp the manner in which Zamyatin's text responds to the concrete possibilities illuminated by the then-still-active conflagration of the Soviet revolution. Zamyatin does not judge the revolutionary process to be a failure, nor does he reject the modern world and advocate a retreat to an idealistic anarchic individualism. Rather, the existential crisis of D-503 can be read, in part, as an attempt to come to grips with the historical crisis emerging in the Soviet Union of the 1920s. Leading out from this explosive rupture in the historical continuum, Zamyatin maps two potential roads. Along the first lies the One State, wherein the revolutionary struggle collapses into a process of rationalized modernization undertaken within the confines of a bureaucratic nation-state. (Although Zamyatin, unlike his predecessor Alexander Bogdanov and his successor Le Guin, does not directly acknowledge the ways that the "wall" isolating the state would be as much a product of the Western capitalist nations' policy of encirclement as it was a decision on the part of the leaders of the new society.) The dangers along this first road are also twofold. First, the emphasis on objective social transformations can too easily ignore the complex desires of particular subjects; or, in Bloch's language, in the realization of social utopia, the concerns of natural law and human dignity will be forgotten.[58] Second, the process of change might terminate in an even bleaker "fully other" situation, in which the motor of history has ground to a halt, and the utopian impulse itself has been extinguished. It is this last road, as we shall see in the next chapter, that Orwell maps with greater precision.

However, Zamyatin, while recognizing the real limitations involved in the attempt to bound history within the nation-state, still holds out the possibility of a global change in human affairs. Zamyatin thus uncovers a second way leading out of his present, the road of the "infinite

revolution"—an explosive continuation and dialectical expansion of the
process of social transformation begun in the Soviet Union, a process
that will clear the space for the emergence of an unexpectedly new human situation (and if we accept Beauchamp's claim about the Bakuninesque resonances of the Mephi world, we might also find in Zamyatin's
text an allegory of the reunion of the two factions that divided the First
International). We need only hear in this last formulation the faintest
echoes of the concept of "permanent revolution" advocated by the even
more celebrated Soviet exile, Leon Trotsky, to understand which road
history did not take.[59]

WE'S LEGACY: *THE DISPOSSESSED*
AND THE LIMITS OF THE HORIZON

If Zamyatin's work ultimately fails to achieve this latter political triumph, it does succeed in illuminating vital new possibilities in the
generic institution of which it is a part. I would further argue that Zamyatin's text prefigures the achievements—and, as I will suggest momentarily, also the limitations—of the celebrated "rebirth" of the genre
that occurs in the late 1960s and early 1970s. Some of the first inklings
of this later revival are to be found in works like R. A. Lafferty's *Past
Master* (1968), a text whose critical engagement with the generic traditions of the narrative utopia (its central character being "Thomas
More" himself transported to another world a thousand years after his
death) also deftly invokes the radical political energies and utopian hope
of the late 1960s; and Monique Wittig's *Les Guérillères* (1969), an-
nouncing as it does, the new centrality of issues of gender in the genre.
At its height in the mid-1970s, this flourishing of the genre produced
such works as Mack Reynolds's *Looking Backward, from the Year 2000*
(1973), Joanna Russ's *The Female Man* (1975), Ernest Callenbach's
Ecotopia (1975), Marge Piercy's *Woman on the Edge of Time* (1976),
and Samuel Delany's *Triton* (1976). The outer limits of this period in the
genre's history could be marked by the publications of the founding
works in cyberpunk, most centrally, William Gibson's *Neuromancer*
(1984), and Margaret Atwood's *The Handmaid's Tale* (1985)—the latter
standing in relationship to the seventies flourishing of feminist utopias
as did the work on which it was in part modeled, *Nineteen Eight-Four,*
to the histories of utopian thought and writing in the first part of the
twentieth century.[60]

Situated at the center of this revival, and one of the most influential and debated works of the moment, is Ursula K. Le Guin's *The Dispossessed* (1974). The connections between Zamyatin's and Le Guin's narratives, although rarely noted in discussions of this text, are in fact suggested by Le Guin herself. In an essay first presented in the year before the publication of *The Dispossessed* and concerned with the dangers of "market censorship" in science fiction writing, Le Guin praises Zamyatin's heretical stance, at once "independent, ironic, and critical," and notes that she considers *We* "the best single work of science fiction yet written."[61] Moreover, the description of Zamyatin himself that opens the essay makes him sound as if he were another model (along with physicist and family friend Robert Oppenheimer) for Shevek, the central protagonist of *The Dispossessed*.

Le Guin's figuration of her utopia occurs through a narrative strategy Jameson calls "world-reduction." The anarchist utopia on the planet Anarres comes into being through a process of simplification, a weeding-out of the various forms of natural, social, and cultural clutter that hinder our ability to recognize that which possesses authentic value. Jameson maintains that this formal strategy in turn "becomes transformed into a sociopolitical hypothesis about the inseparability of utopia and scarcity."[62] (It is exactly this equation of utopia and scarcity that Delany challenges in *Triton*, a narrative utopia, or what he calls an "ambiguous heterotopia," written in part as a response to Le Guin's work.[63])

This hypothesis is confirmed when we accompany Shevek back from the moon-world of Anarres to the Earthlike home planet of Urras, from which his ancestors, followers of the anarchist philosopher and activist Odo, had fled more than a century and a half earlier in order to found their new society. At first Shevek is overwhelmed by both the fecundity of natural resources—on his world there are no large animals and only a limited number of plant species—and the wealth of material goods produced by the societies of this world. However, he soon comes to realize the terrible price paid for such an abundance of "possessions:"

> They all looked, to him, anxious. He had often seen that anxiety before in the faces of Urrasti, and wondered about it. Was it because, no matter how much money they had, they always had to worry about making more, lest they die poor? Was it guilt, because no matter how little money they had, there was always somebody who had less? Whatever the cause, it gave all the faces a certain sameness, and he felt very much alone among them.[64]

Shevek discovers that in a society based upon accumulation and exploitation, no one is ever truly free; on Anarres, by contrast, "Our men and women are free—possessing nothing, they are free. And you the possessors are possessed. You are all in jail. Each alone, solitary, with a heap of what he owns. You live in prison, die in prison" (*TD,* 228–29). Le Guin's contrast of the "worlds" of Anarres and Urras then serves as what Suvin describes as a "parable of de-alienation:" "The Dispossessed means thus literally—in its more beautiful, semantically richer, and thus more forceful English—the De-Alienated, those rid of alienation both as physical reification (by things and impersonal apparatuses) and as psychical obsession (by demons and what Marx calls fetishes)."[65]

Le Guin's narrative also exemplifies the process Marin calls utopian neutralization, the figure of Anarres's scarcity emerging as the inverse image of the material abundance of a post–World War II U.S. consumer society—the latter lying suddenly exposed, in the estranging light of the utopian critique, as the very root cause of the condition of "unfreedom," the lives of quiet desperation, experienced by the inhabitants of late-imperial America. Moreover, as in the works by Bogdanov, Wells, and London examined in the last chapter, Le Guin's narrative emphasizes that such a neutralization now must necessarily take place on both a national *and* a global plane. The figure of the planetary utopia of Anarres thus similarly "reduces" the geopolitical complexities of its other, Urras, whose tripartite superpower division is not unlike that of our world in the 1970s. The first "world" Shevek visits, the nation-state A-Io, has a political and economic system closely resembling contemporary U.S. liberal democratic capitalism. However, while this kinship may lead us to conclude that the superpower A-Io is simply a stand-in for the contemporary United States, Le Guin disrupts any such one-to-one allegorical correspondence by showing us the residuum of the aristocratic and absolutist past of the nation, as well as its current world-leadership role in environmental conservation.[66] The second world, the nation-state Thu, is akin to the Soviet Union, practicing as it does authoritarian socialism, which makes it, Shevek is told, "even more centralized than the State of A-Io" (*TD,* 136). Finally, a third world is represented in the text by the nation-state Benebili, "a military dictatorship, run by generals. It was a large country in the western hemisphere, mountains and arid savannahs, underpopulated, poor" (*TD,* 201). During Shevek's visit, a military conflict between A-Io and Thu flares up in Benebili. Shevek's host makes explicit the connection of this event to then-contemporary struggles in Vietnam, Central America, and other "hot spots" in the Cold War world when he asserts, "We've outgrown the kind of barbarism that used to bring war into the heart of the high civilizations! The balance of power is kept by this kind of police action" (*TD*, 275).[67]

While Le Guin thus uses the world of Anarres to develop an effective estranging critique of both contemporary U.S. society and the larger geopolitical order in which it is embedded, the utopia on Anarres is itself, as the book's subtitle stresses, an "ambiguous" one. If the world of Urras is akin to the One State in Zamyatin's text—both being defined by the combination of happiness, or material abundance and security, and unfreedom—then the world of Anarres is closer to that of Zamyatin's Mephi. Indeed, Carl Freedman links the Odonian anarchism practiced on Anarres with the major tenets of Bakunin, and thereby recalls the similar connection Beauchamp offers between these ideas and the world of the Mephi.[68] Even more significant, as with Zamyatin's Mephi world, the society on Anarres does not escape its text's critical, interrogative gaze. *The Dispossessed* unfolds through a double narrative structure, which, by way of alternating chapters, interweaves the story of Shevek's voyage to and experience on Urras with that of the crucial events in his earlier life on Anarres that led to his monumental and controversial decision to visit the *ur*-world. In the course of this latter narrative, the reader learns that problems have arisen in Anarres's anarchist society largely as the result of a strict policy of isolationism adopted more than a century and a half earlier. Although trade does occur between the two worlds, no one from one has ever yet visited the other. Moreover, the people of Anarres choose not only to cut themselves off from Urras, but also from the larger interplanetary federation, the Ekumen, established by the ancient civilization of the interstellar-traveling Hainish—a federation that, we soon discover, also includes our own "real" world, Terra, albeit three hundred years in the future.[69]

Also as in Zamyatin's narrative, images of "walls" appear throughout Le Guin's text, beginning with the opening sentence, "There was a wall" (*TD*, 1). Because of these self-imposed walls, the inhabitants of Anarres lack the kind of critical perspective that contact with other worlds would enable—and here, Le Guin is also making a more general appeal for the importance of utopia and science fiction. Hence, most of its inhabitants are unable to see the bureaucratic and cultural rigidities that have set into their ostensibly open society: "The social conscience completely dominates the individual conscience, instead of striking a balance with it. We don't cooperate—we *obey*. . . . We fear our neighbor's opinion more than we respect our own freedom of choice. . . .

We've made laws, laws of conventional behavior, built walls all around ourselves, and we can't see them because they're part of our thinking" (*TD*, 330–31). Shevek, along with the group of dissidents surrounding him, takes up the task of "unbuilding" these walls, and in so doing, attempts to restore to Anarres the original promise of its revolution.

At the same time, there is another constant threat to the success of this utopian society, one that Shevek and his comrades find less easy to overcome. During the years of Shevek's young adulthood, an extended drought begins, culminating in a global famine and a more general social crisis. During an especially grim moment, Shevek finds himself reflecting on

> the reality of hunger, and about the possible inadequacy of his society to come through a famine without losing the solidarity that was its strength. It was easy enough to share when there was enough, even barely enough, to go round. But when there was not enough? Then force entered in; might making right; power, and its tool, violence, and its most devoted ally, the averted eye. (*TD*, 256)

These periodic exacerbations of the world's condition of scarcity threaten the utopian society on Anarres in other ways too. Shevek later notes that these kinds of crisis situations generate new ossifying structures within his society's central regulative mechanisms: "Every emergency, every labor draft even, tends to leave behind it an increment of bureaucratic machinery within PDC, and a kind of rigidity: this is the way it was done, this is the way it is done, this is the way it *has* to be done" (*TD*, 329).[70]

If Jameson is correct in his claim that there is a constitutive relationship between the condition of scarcity and the utopian place of Anarres, then a disabling performative contradiction appears to emerge in Le Guin's utopian discourse. On the one hand, the very condition of scarcity that enables the utopian world to come into being represents, at the same time, a permanent threat to its continued existence. Conversely, if this threat is eradicated and living conditions on Anarres are made more secure, we can only conclude that this utopian alternative would dissolve away as well, folding Anarres back within the world of Urras, with all the inequalities and unfreedoms that its condition of abundance produces.

However, the figurative work of Le Guin's text does not end here. Again, like Zamyatin's *We*, *The Dispossessed* generates a fourfold *combinatoire* of utopian Possible Worlds. Late in the narrative, the reader learns that it is our world of Terra that actualizes the nightmarish possible future of which Shevek sees dim hints on Anarres. Although on Anarres scarcity is a natural condition, on Terra it has been produced by the actions of humanity, rampant consumption of natural resources, greed, selfishness, and warfare, all but annihilating the planet.[71] Although humanity has survived, it has done so only at a tremendous cost:

> Well, we had saved what could be saved, and made a kind of life in the ruins, on Terra, in the only way it could be done: by total centralization. Total control over the use of every acre of land, every scrap of metal, every ounce of fuel. Total rationing, birth control, euthanasia, universal conscription into the labor force. The absolute regimentation of each life toward the goal of racial survival. (TD, 348)

This condition of radical scarcity combined with total unfreedom produces a cold, static, and apparently absolutely sutured world not unlike that inhabited by D-503 in the concluding pages of We. Shevek tells the ambassador from Terra, after she relates the preceding vision, "You do not believe in change, in chance, in evolution. You would destroy us rather than admit our reality, rather than admit that there is hope!" (TD, 349–50).

The inversion of the world of Terra, its utopian neutralization, is that of the Hainish, tantalizingly illuminated only in the text's closing pages. On board a Hainish ship bound for Anarres, Shevek appreciatively observes the phenomenological richness, or what Lefebvre calls lived space, of the vessel's interiors: "Inside, it was as spacious and solid as a house. The rooms were large and private, the walls wood-paneled or covered with textured weavings, the ceilings high" (TD, 380). For all its apparent similarity to the spaces he has encountered on Urras, Shevek notes a significant difference: "Its style had neither the opulence of Urras nor the austerity of Anarres, but struck a *balance,* with the effortless grace of long practice" (TD, 381; emphasis added). Crucially, the Hainish offer an image of an achieved balance not only of the design practices of these two cultures, but also of what is best in each of their Possible Worlds. Along with the capacity to produce this kind of material elegance, the "long practice" of the Hainish has taught them a great deal about the value of individual freedom, and for this reason too they find Shevek an attractive figure. Shevek's host Ketho informs him that the Hainish "have been civilized for a thousand millennia. We have histories of hundreds of those millennia. We have tried everything. Anarchism, with the rest. But *I* have not tried it. They say there is nothing new under any sun. But if each life is not new, each single life, then why are we born?" (TD, 385). Thus, if the world of Terra is the embodiment

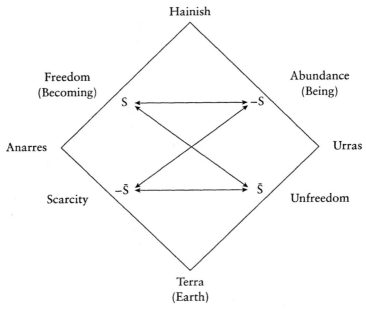

Figure 5.   The play of Possible Worlds in Le Guin's *The Dispossessed.*

of an experience where hope has been completely negated, then that of the Hainish represents its endlessly lived, and relived, possibilities.

With this figure, Le Guin's narrative closes its circle, and Shevek is able to return home anew, confirming his earlier insight, "You *can* go home again . . . so long as you understand that home is a place where you have never been" (*TD,* 55). A Greimasian mapping of the relationships among the text's four worlds, paralleling the similar mapping we generated from Zamyatin's text, would appear as shown in figure 5.

With both the worlds of Anarres and Urras presented as "ambiguous" (respectively, the problematic if constitutive nature of scarcity; and the absence of authentic freedom), the real goal of the narrative now appears to be the production of the space in which might occur the dialectical unification of the two worlds.[72] Early on, Shevek expresses a similar idea: "We ignore you; you ignore us. You are our history. We are perhaps your future. I want to learn, not to ignore. It is the reason I came. We must know each other. We are not primitive men. Our morality is no longer tribal, it cannot be" (*TD,* 75). And later, on finally encountering the full contradictory reality of A-Io, the suffering masked by its material splendor, he realizes, "a thinking man's job was not to deny one reality at the expense of the other, but to include and connect" (*TD*, 284–85). This motif replicates itself elsewhere in the narrative as well, as, for example, in the physicist Shevek's quest to discover a "General Temporal Theory," unifying the theoretical models of Simultaneity and Sequency and thereby overcoming the fundamental antinomy of being and becoming: "Becoming without being is meaningless. Being without becoming is a big bore." (*TD*, 224). The discovery of this General Temporal Theory also would produce another kind of unification, enabling the invention of the ansible, a device through which the far-flung worlds of the Ekumen could communicate instantaneously (*TD*, 276). And, as Robert Philmus points out, the resolution of this temporal opposition is enacted in both the narrative's form, with its converging double strands, and in Shevek's dawning awareness of the paradoxical "possibility that seemingly broken promises can be kept."[73]

By the conclusion of *The Dispossessed*, a joining of the worlds of Anarres and Urras likewise appears to be in the offing. On Anarres, Shevek's allies tell him, "Things are a little . . . broken loose," as people have started to ask questions of their world, and in general have begun once again "to behave like anarchists!" (*TD*, 384). Similarly, Shevek's presence on Urras—as a now-concrete embodiment of the reality of difference for the most direly "dispossessed" of this world—combines with widespread dissatisfaction over labor conditions and indignation over the institution of a war draft, and sparks a new period of revolutionary struggle in A-Io. Although the state's disciplinary apparatuses ruthlessly squelch the uprising—Le Guin's figuration of the worldwide period of state reaction that had set in by the early 1970s—the novel nevertheless leaves us with a powerful image that suggests, as in the last pages of *We*, that a horizon of possibility always remains open:

> When they came, marching in their neat black coats up the steps among dead and dying men and women, they found on the high, grey, polished wall of the great foyer a word written at the height of a man's eyes, in broad smears of blood: DOWN
>
> They shot the dead man who lay nearest the word, and later on when the Directorate was restored to order the word was washed off the wall with water, soap, and rags, but it remained; it had been spoken; it had meaning. (*TD*, 302)

The narrative as a whole then concludes with another appropriate image of hope, Shevek arriving at the launch port on Anarres as a new day dawns (*TD*, 387).

Crucially however, the narrative also breaks off at exactly this point, without showing us what the lived experiences and spaces of these "new days" might look like.[74] With this gesture, then, Le Guin achieves a victory similar to that we have seen in *We*: utopia, as the promise of the radically new, has been dislocated from a locus in the being of either Anarres or Urras, much as in Zamyatin's work it has been moved from the worlds of the Mephi and the One State; and, as Bülent Somay suggests of Le Guin's novel, in both cases, "The movement away from the utopian locus is therefore not towards the familiar but towards a horizon beyond it."[75] In each case, the world of this horizon remains decidedly an absent presence in the text, its realized, concrete form glimpsed perhaps only fleetingly in the figure of the Hainish.[76] Precisely because, as Somay goes on to argue, this horizon is "there and approachable" but "can never be reached," it eludes every effort to represent it concretely.[77]

Zamyatin's and later Le Guin's re-authorings thus both succeed, on the one hand, in radicalizing the genre, eliminating any teleological residuum that would suggest any particular representation of space, especially that of the utopia of the imagined national community, might stand as the ultimate goal of modern history. Moreover, both texts offer a powerful narrative realization of what Bloch calls the "concrete utopia," maintaining a specific horizon (happiness and freedom; freedom and abundance) that enables both a critical perspective on the present and a sense of direction in which to move in the future. This too is what E. P. Thompson, writing in the same moment as Le Guin and about another work in this critical lineage, Morris's *News from Nowhere,* means by his description of utopia as the "education of desire": "This is not the same as 'a moral education' towards a given end: it is, rather, to open a way to aspiration . . . to an uninterrupted interrogation of our values and also to its own self-interrogation."[78]

And yet, in order to achieve these important goals, both narratives must sacrifice a dimension of the double pedagogical agenda that made the generic form such an important vehicle for "thinking" the experience of modernity. In Chapter 1, I pointed out that the classical narrative utopia enables its readers at once to experience their own present as immersed in the liquidating transformations and discontinuities of historical time—a critical, estranging, or deterritorializing energy—*and* to imagine the social and cultural environments they inhabit in concrete and particular new ways—what I have been variously calling the narrative utopia's operations of reterritorialization, figuration, semiosis, cognitive mapping, spatial history, or the elaboration of representations of space. Zamyatin's work, and later utopian fictions like Le Guin's, sunder these two conjoined operations: while maintaining the former, more properly temporal dimension of the form—its capacity to teach us to think the present historically—both works defer the project of developing a particular figuration of a radically new kind of space.

Gilles Deleuze and Félix Guattari further unpack the deeply dialectical relationship between these two poles, in specifically spatial terms, in their conceptual opposition of the "striated"—territorialized, state, sedentary, being, optical space—and the "smooth"—deterritorialized, frontier, nomad, becoming, haptic space. They point out that it is always necessary to "remind ourselves that the two spaces in fact exist only in mixture: smooth space is constantly being translated, transversed into a striated space; striated space is constantly being reversed, returned to a smooth space."[79] Later in this "plateau," they further develop this insight: "Nothing is ever done with: smooth space allows itself to be striated, and striated space reimparts a smooth space, with potentially very different values, scope, and signs. Perhaps we must say that all progress is made by and in striated space, but all becoming occurs in smooth space."[80] Finally, in the concluding pages of this plateau, they offer another reminder, one with great significance for our discussion here: "Of course, smooth spaces are not in themselves liberatory. But the struggle is changed or displaced in them, and life reconstitutes its stakes, confronts new obstacles, invents new paces, switches adversaries. Never believe that a smooth space will suffice to save us."[81] Similarly, Lefebvre, in the same year that Le Guin publishes *The Dispossessed,* acknowledges the importance of diversions (*détournements*), reappropriations or poachings of space; however, he too concludes, "Diversion is in itself merely appropriation, not creation—a reappropriation which can call but a temporary halt to domination."[82]

What vanishes in these two great narrative utopias, then, is a development of both sides of this dialectic. Or, to put this another way, while these utopian texts maintain hope in the "abstract," they refuse to tell us anything concrete about the particular Thing, the alternative experience of space and collectivity, to which we will inevitably give our "allegiance."[83] I suggested earlier a correspondence between Zamyatin's figure of the "infinite revolution" and Trotsky's concept of the "permanent revolution," and thus Gramsci's comments on the latter can help us better grasp the possible limitations of Zamyatin's and Le Guin's still indispensable re-authorings of the genre. Gramsci writes, "The theoretical weaknesses of this modern form of the old mechanism are masked by the general theory of permanent revolution, which is nothing but a generic forecast presented as a dogma, and which demolishes itself by not in fact coming true."[84] Over and against a potential all-or-nothing "generic" proposition, Gramsci calls for a different kind of political pedagogy, a "war of positioning," a careful step-by-step building up of an alternative hegemony. Such an educational project will necessarily involve the kinds of figurative and conceptual operations that have been such an important part of the genre of the narrative utopia.

Although such a project is fraught with risks, if we do not take it up, we may end up in a position akin to that of Franz Kafka's man "before the Law," waiting for an entry that will never come. Zamyatin's dreamed-of day when "it becomes possible in our country to serve great ideas in literature without cringing before little men" never did arrive. In the end, Gramsci suggests, this "modern form of the old mechanicism" may provide an education of a very different sort. Gramsci does acknowledge that in times of political paralysis, when the road forward appears blocked—and in this category, we can surely include Zamyatin's and Le Guin's moments, witnessing as they did the transformation of the Bolshevik revolution into a national-state bureaucratic project of modernization and the defeat of the radical political forces of the 1960s—models of historical thinking that are mechanistic and deterministic, on the one hand, and messianic or abstractly hopeful, on the other, have great value:

> When you don't have the initiative in the struggle and the struggle itself comes eventually to be identified with a series of defeats, mechanical determinism becomes a tremendous force of moral resistance, of cohesion and of patient and obstinate perseverance. "I have been defeated for the moment, but the tide of history is working for me in the long term." Real will takes on the garments of an act of faith in a certain rationality of history and in a primitive and empirical form of impassioned finalism.[85]

However, Gramsci goes on to argue that if such a "naive philosophy of strength" is forced to be sustained for too long, it invariably mutates into "a cause of passivity, of idiotic self-sufficiency. This happens when they don't even expect that the subaltern will become directive and responsible."[86]

The force of Gramsci's conclusion will be evident in the work of the author I examine in the next chapter. While Zamyatin, Le Guin, and those who follow them present one kind of re-authoring of the genre, George Orwell offers another, very different one.

CHAPTER SIX

Modernity, Nostalgia, and the Ends of Nations in Orwell's *Nineteen Eighty-Four*

"It would be nice," he said, "if we could fight the whole battle by writing."

That sounded like a deep heart-felt sigh, like a mild, resigned protest against politics which becomes the second, worse nature of every human being who practises it seriously over a long time.

György Dalos, 1985

The writer is *situated* in his time; every word he utters has reverberations. As does his silence.

Jean-Paul Sartre, "Introducing Les Temps modernes*"*

It has become something of a commonplace to point out that our *fin-de-millennium* culture has given birth to a diversity of narratives of endings: the ending, among other things, of modernity, master narratives, and ideology; of philosophy and critique; of modernism, the avant garde, and the aesthetic; of feminism, gender, and sexuality; of liberalism, humanism, and the bourgeois subject; of industrialism, Fordism, and the welfare state; of Marxism, socialism, and communism; of the Cold War; and even of history itself. As the work of two of the more well-known proponents of this last narrative, Jean Baudrillard and Francis Fukuyama, bears out, it often isn't an easy thing to place the tellers of these apocalyptical tales on traditional political spectrums.[1] A similar blurring of older political positioning occurs in the case of a narrative of ending that similarly has taken on a certain urgency in the last decade, a narrative concerning the exhaustion of what Liah Greenfeld calls "the constitutive element of modernity," the modern nation-state. Concerns over the future fate of the nation-state, understood as beset at once by the homogenizing forces of an incipient globalism and the centrifugal energies of neo-ethnic "tribalisms," often make strange bedfellows of thinkers on the left and the right.[2]

However, as in the case of many of these millenarian fantasies, the contemporary narrative about the end of the nation-state "resonates like an old repetition. . . . The same question had already *sounded*."[3] Also, paradoxically enough, such repeated stories can serve as often as not to strengthen the hold of precisely the thing they claim has come to an end. This is very much the case in George Orwell's *Nineteen Eighty-Four* (1949), the influential, midcentury narrative of the nation's end that I examine in this chapter. Ironically, the significance of Orwell's work has seemed to wane with the conclusion of the Cold War struggles in which it played such a central role, apparently giving credence both to Irving Howe's suggestion that Orwell's "desperate topicality" would mean his work could not "survive [its] time," and Harold Bloom's dismissal of *Nineteen Eighty-Four* as a "literary period piece" whose "defense . . . cannot differ much from a defense of period pieces in clothes, household objects, popular music, movies, and the lower reaches of the visual arts."[4] However, I want to argue that the continued relevance of Orwell's work lies in the early figuration it offers of one of the most central and hotly debated issues of our own present: that concerning the relationship between the processes of *globalization*—especially in the forms of a U.S. corporate, cultural, and consumer hegemony, and new media technologies—and the persistence and even resurgence of nationalist particularisms.[5] Jürgen Habermas notes, "The nation-state, conscious of its historical achievements, stubbornly asserts its identity at the very moment when it is being overwhelmed, and its power eroded, by processes of globalization."[6] While Habermas is speaking of conditions in the last years of the twentieth century, I will show that Orwell's text enacts precisely this dynamic, in the particular case of the English nation, decades earlier.

Moreover, Orwell's work resonates with our present for another reason. His fears concerning the future of the nation-state are situated within a broader set of anxieties about the threat posed to a linked set of autonomies—the subject, the critical intellect, literacy, the private sphere, and the aesthetic—that similarly have been central features of the cultures of modernity. Orwell's imaginary solution to this crisis, a solution that would have very real effects on many lives, involves delinking those things he valued in modernity from the processes of modernization that had given rise to them in the first place. In so doing, Orwell effects a mutation in the institutional being of the narrative utopia, producing what I call, following the lead of Karl Mannheim, the "conservative utopia." Thus, it is precisely *Nineteen Eighty-Four's* "desperate topicality," its insight into the continued spectral existence of the nation-state form, that guarantees the work's significance in our present. If *Nineteen Eighty-Four* is, as Bloom notes, a period piece, it is of a period from whose repetitious history we have yet to awake.

FROM UTOPIAN MODERNISM TO NATURALIST UTOPIA

Nineteen Eighty-Four is best known as a work that heralds another kind of ending as well. For many readers, Orwell's text is the single most persuasive illustration of the closure of the modern "vision of utopia" itself—this "vision" now being understood to encompass both the desire for a radically Other future and the project of producing the cognitive maps by which such a desire might be realized.[7] Even for Orwell himself, an avowed humanitarian socialist until the end of his days, his often-stated aim of clearing the stage for some uniquely *English* socialism—a project that, in turn, has roots in the utopian writings of William Morris—required a full frontal assault on the systemic and systematizing discourse of the utopia.[8]

The project that would be undertaken in *Nineteen Eighty-Four* was already announced by Orwell four years earlier in an essay on what he perceived to be the obsolescence of the work of H. G. Wells, one of the other great English utopian thinkers of the century. Wells, Orwell maintains, understands history as "a series of victories won by the scientific man over the romantic man," those abstracting, universalizing forces associated with modernization—"science, order, progress, internationalism, aeroplanes, steel, concrete, hygiene"—inexorably sweeping away the atavistic remnants, the particular organizations of enjoyment, of all previous modes of social and cultural life.[9] Wells's "singleness of mind" and "one-sided imagination," his unflappable belief in universal rationality and progress, made him one of the most celebrated visionaries of the first decades of the century. However, by the 1940s, the same qualities "that made him seem like an inspired prophet in the Edwardian age, make him a shallow, inadequate thinker now."[10] Wells's equation of science, technological development, and global modernization with

a rational, orderly, and utopian future had been demonstrated false by
the emergence of authoritarian regimes in Germany and the Soviet
Union. Indeed, in Nazi Germany, the greatest intellectual achievements
of the modern world are conjoined with ideas and beliefs "appropriate to the Stone Age." Wells "was, and still is, quite incapable of understanding that nationalism, religious bigotry and feudal loyalty are far
more powerful forces then what he himself would describe as sanity."
Thus, Orwell concludes, "Wells is too sane to understand the modern
world."[11]

This polemical target is made explicit in *Nineteen Eighty-Four*
through the fictional text-in-the-text that provides both the reader and
Orwell's protagonist Winston Smith with a theoretical description, or
what Henri Lefebvre calls a "perception of space," of the social order in
the year 1984: *The Theory and Practice of Oligarchical Collectivism*,
reputed to be authored by the former Ingsoc (English Socialist) Party
leader Emmanuel Goldstein, a figure in part modeled on Leon Trotsky.
From this text, Winston Smith learns,

> In the early twentieth century, the vision of a future society unbelievably rich,
> leisured, orderly and efficient—a glittering antiseptic world of glass and steel
> and snow-white concrete—was part of the consciousness of nearly every lit-
> erate person. Science and technology were developing at a prodigious speed,
> and it seemed natural to assume that they would go on developing.[12]

Of course, the world we have experienced by this point in *Nineteen
Eighty-Four* turns out to be something else altogether: a "bare, hun-
gry, dilapidated place," where terror, physical and emotional deprivation, and hatred suture a nightmarish social order (*NEF*, 155). Later,
Smith's inquisitor, O'Brien, a member of the ruling Inner Party and the
internal disciplinary apparatus, the Thought Police, tells him that this
"new" world stands as "the exact opposite of the stupid hedonistic
Utopias that the old reformers imagined" (*NEF*, 220). Artificial scarcity
and strictly enforced hierarchies produce a utopian "Possible World"
not unlike the version of the One State or the Terra figured, as we saw
in the previous chapter, in the closing pages of Zamyatin's and Le Guin's
texts. We could say then that where these narratives end, Orwell's is just
beginning.

The nature of the relationship between *Nineteen Eighty-Four* and
Zamyatin's earlier work, and especially the degree to which Orwell "borrowed" from *We*, has long been debated.[13] Although Orwell reportedly
did not read *We* until 1945, well after he had begun formulating the idea

for *Nineteen Eighty-Four*, he knew of it as early as 1943, and it is clear that he adopted some elements of the earlier work into the design of *Nineteen Eighty-Four*.[14] Many of these borrowings are evident in the structure and plot of his work. For example, like Zamyatin's D-503, Winston Smith records his thoughts about his present social order in a diary, although, significantly, Orwell dispenses with Zamyatin's first-person point of view. Similarly, the burgeoning oppositional sentiments of the protagonists in both works are fired by illicit sexual affairs, again instigated in both cases by the woman.[15]

These connections between the texts suggest that we might likewise be able to map *Nineteen Eighty-Four* against Zamyatin's schema of utopia's "Possible Worlds." To do so, however, moves us even further from the understanding of *We* as one of the first "anti-utopias" of this century: for rather than simply attacking the historical mission of the classical narrative utopia, Zamyatin's text now appears as a kind of narrative laboratory in which a whole system of expressions of the genre are evaluated, each encompassing unique cognitive possibilities, values, and epistemologies of history, and each marked by a distinctive set of representational limits. Orwell's narrative, on the other hand, occupies only one of these "worlds" mapped in Zamyatin's text, the position that involves a negation of the entire generic institution itself.

In an early diary entry, Winston Smith salutes what he acknowledges to be his unknown, and necessarily unknowable, audience:

> To the future or to the past, to a time when thought is free, when men are different from one another and do not live alone—to a time when truth exists and what is done cannot be undone:
> From the age of uniformity, from the age of solitude, from the age of Big Brother, from the age of double think—greetings! (NEF, 26–27)

The absent world to which Winston Smith directs his attention in this passage, the world "when men are different . . . and do not live alone," could be read as loosely corresponding to the horizon-world of *We*, I-330's "infinite revolution," the "place" of the leap beyond the antinomies of "freedom" and "happiness." (However, Orwell's ambiguity about the temporal locus of this place is crucial, as we shall see shortly). The "known" society of Smith's Oceania, on the other hand, the "age" of uniformity and solitude, wherein both the rich experience of individual identity and the pleasures of collective unity have in effect disappeared, stands in relation to this absent situation as a neutral Other— Orwell's equivalent of Zamyatin's cold society, the gray-on-gray world "outside" of history that D-503 occupies in the concluding pages of the narrative. Thus, both Zamyatin and Orwell share a vision of the truly nightmarish situation as one in which history itself has "ended": the most terrifying feature of Oceanic society lies precisely in the ruling Party's seeming ability to extend its domination infinitely into the future, "to arrest progress and freeze history at a chosen moment" (*NEF*, 167).

However, *Nineteen Eighty-Four* diverges from *We* in that *every* road "forward" in Orwell's text seems to end in this final point of closure. The play of utopian Possible Worlds elaborated in Zamyatin's narrative is reduced in *Nineteen Eighty-Four* to a single, homogeneous, monolithic enclosure, the "World" of Oceania. Oceania represents what L. S. Dembo defines as the "totally undetotalizable totality": "a world, in fact, in which pure form has triumphed and become monstrous, a totality proof against detotalization, a synchrony free of all diachrony . . . a changeless, fixed entity dedicated to the elimination of history."[16] Fittingly, when Winston Smith's long-dreamed-of Golden Country, "the place where there is no darkness . . . the imagined future," is actualized in the narrative, it too is subsumed within the Oceanic nightmare, taking form in the torture chamber in O'Brien's Ministry of Love (*NEF*, 87 and 189). The horizons of historical difference and multiple possibilities that had been integrally located *within* Zamyatin's narrative—in the figures of the Mephi, I-330, the infinite revolution, O-90, and even, at times, D-503 himself—appear in *Nineteen Eighty-Four* as an *exterior* frame to the main body of the text. This exterior "world" is occupied by the unknown and unknowable reader to whom Smith addresses his diary, by the unidentified "author" of the famous Appendix, "The Principles of Newspeak," and even, perhaps, the "historical novel" *Nineteen Eighty-Four*, based, as some readers have suggested, on Winston Smith's diary.[17] Winston's ambivalence in locating the temporal place of his imagined reader (future or past), coupled with what some critics view as the banal "familiarity" of the "voice" of the scholarly Appendix—that is, written in the "future," it nevertheless uses the academic prose style of the past—already suggests that the only place imagined to exist outside the world of Big Brother might be Orwell's own immediate past or, at best, a future that looks very much like it. (I will return again to this crucial point.)

The dissimilarity between the vision of the future history in the two texts likewise manifests itself on the level of narrative form. The self-

consciously modernist, open, or "polyphonic" form of *We* is replaced in
Nineteen Eighty-Four by the often-celebrated "plain speech," naturalist
prose style that Orwell had been gradually perfecting in the sequence of
early novels from *Burmese Days* (1934) to *Coming Up for Air* (1939)
and in his well-known works of reportage. This prose style also points
toward the direct influence on Orwell of an earlier naturalist writer, the
nineteenth-century English novelist George Gissing, then largely unread,
for whom Orwell had on more than one occasion acknowledged a deep
and abiding admiration.[18] There is even evidence that Orwell had Gissing's work in mind when developing his vision of Oceania. In one of his
last essays published before his most famous text, Orwell describes the
Victorian England pictured in Gissing's fiction in terms that bear an uncanny resemblance to the "future" world of *Nineteen Eighty-Four*:

> The grime, the stupidity, the ugliness, the sex-starvation, the furtive debauch-
> ery, the vulgarity, the bad manners, the censoriousness—these things were
> unnecessary, since the puritanism of which they were a relic no longer upheld
> the structure of society. People who might, without becoming less efficient,
> have been reasonably happy chose instead to be miserable, inventing sense-
> less taboos with which to terrify themselves.[19]

The socialist beliefs held by both Gissing and Orwell meant that such a
situation must be presented as the consequence of human "choice," and
hence open to the possibility of change. However, by elaborating their
fictional worlds through the prose style of literary naturalism—an asphyxiating empirical mode of representation that locates each aspect,
each form, and each group in a single, fixed place in the social world,
what Frank Lentricchia describes as "the secretarial imagination"[20]—
both Orwell and his predecessor produce pictures of social reality from
which has been squeezed dry the very lifeblood of historical possibility,
the sense of the mutability of any present that had been a central feature
of the narrative utopia from its beginnings.[21]

This difference between the sense of historical possibility offered in
We and *Nineteen Eighty-Four* is further reinforced by the deployment
in each text of, respectively, a first- and third-person narrative point of
view. In *We,* the adherence to a circumscribed subjective voice, that of
D-503, has, by the conclusion of the narrative, opened up at least the
possibility of perspectives different from the one presented to the reader.
(A similar effect is achieved through the use of a montage structure
in the Hungarian author György Dalos's *1985,* a brilliant "sequel" to
Orwell's narrative that presents a powerful open allegory of the Post-

Stalinist thaw in the Soviet Union as well as subsequent history in the East Bloc as a whole.[22]) Orwell's clinically detached, third-person narrative voice, on the other hand, generates an apparently seamless totalized picture of the World of Oceania, thereby eliminating precisely the horizons of difference that had been so important in Zamyatin's text. In terms of the more local history of English utopian fiction, *Nineteen Eighty-Four* also brings us full circle: for if Morris's "reinvention" in the late nineteenth century of the utopian form comes, in part, as a response to the dead empirical reality projected by the naturalist narratives of a writer like Gissing, then Orwell outflanks Morris by introducing the same sense of narrative closure into the utopian form itself.[23]

The relative degrees of narrative openness and closure we find in *We* and *Nineteen Eighty-Four* also points toward fundamental differences in the political and epistemological aims of these two texts. Orwell's vision of the future, as with that of every other utopian thinker we have examined thus far, was intended first and foremost as a pointed political intervention in the situation of his own present. Although Cold War polemicists might simply assert that *Nineteen Eighty-Four* mirrored life in the Soviet Union (a project Orwell had already accomplished in the quite different form of the dark allegorical tale *Animal Farm* [1945]), more perspicacious readers of the text, including Orwell himself, have tirelessly pointed out that it was not meant as a "prophecy" of what must pass, much less a portrait of a world already existing, but rather as a "warning" of what could be unless certain trends in the present were checked. In this respect, the text becomes akin to its other key predecessor, Jack London's *The Iron Heel*. These trends, in all their social, political, and cultural complexity, could for Orwell be described by a single word: totalitarianism. Thus, in his famous late essay "Why I Write" (1947), Orwell could assert, "Every line of serious work that I have written since 1936 has been written, directly or indirectly, *against* totalitarianism and *for* democratic socialism, as I understand it."[24]

What Orwell "understands" democratic socialism to be is most explicitly elaborated in the second part of *The Road to Wigan Pier* (1937), a work that, along with the pamphlet *The Lion and the Unicorn: Socialism and the English Genius* (1941), contains some of his most thoroughgoing reflections on socialism and on English socialists, always two quite different things in Orwell's mind.[25] In *The Road to Wigan Pier*, Orwell asserts that socialism first and foremost "means justice and common decency." Thus, "Socialism cannot be narrowed down to mere economic justice . . . a reform of that magnitude is bound to work immense changes in our own civilisation and . . . way of life."[26] Earlier in the same book, Orwell complains that "middle-class" socialists—by which he often seems to have meant nearly *every* other socialist in Great Britain—have, with few exceptions, misapprehended the *total* nature of the change in the current state of affairs that the establishment of a true democratic socialism would bring about. If socialism means the end of class society, then, for the middle class, "to abolish class-distinctions means abolishing a part of yourself. . . . What is involved is not merely the amelioration of working-class conditions, nor an avoidance of the more stupid forms of snobbery, but a complete abandonment of the upper-class and middle-class attitude to life."[27]

While the commitment to the negative dimension of the two-part agenda announced in "Why I Write"—the critical assault on all manifestations of totalitarianism—is clearly taken up in *Nineteen Eighty-Four,* this latter, more positive project of "retotalization," of attempting to imagine what a different socialist future might look like, disappears without a trace. Indeed, the very narrative logic of *Nineteen Eighty-Four* works to undermine the possibility of envisioning the historical process through which democratic socialism as Orwell had professed to understand it might come into being. *Nineteen Eighty-Four,* as we shall see momentarily, inexorably drags the reader to the conclusion that every effort to effect a total change of the present, to institute a utopia—be it those advanced along the lines of a progressive, technocratic, liberal reformism like that of Edward Bellamy and Wells, or those that follow a program of revolutionary action—invariably gives rise to total systems of domination, systems wherein, ultimately, even the potential for change might be eliminated. In Orwell's text it is the possibility of this kind of future and not the past or even the present that "lies like a nightmare on the brains of all the living," and it is against its realization that the text directs its critical force.

However, by eliminating every other possible utopian horizon from the presentation of such a future world, *Nineteen Eighty-Four* leads its readers to equate this vision with that of the future as such. Orwell's narrative thus seems to arrest the dialectic of hope and fear that works its way through the fiction of Zamyatin. With the only remainder being a terrible fear, *Nineteen Eighty-Four* appears to have short-circuited the very ideology of historical movement that had heretofore served as the foundation of the narrative utopia form.

ORWELL AND MANNHEIM:
NINETEEN EIGHTY-FOUR AS "CONSERVATIVE UTOPIA"

However, if the narrative topos developed in *Nineteen Eighty-Four* does indeed occupy a place on Zamyatin's generic schema, we can expect Orwell's work similarly to express only one of a number of competing possible ideologies of history. In order to elaborate more precisely how these ideologies of history relate to the generic system that I outlined in the previous chapter, I want to turn momentarily from the texts of Zamyatin and Orwell, and focus instead on Karl Mannheim's corresponding mapping of what he calls the "ideal types" of the utopian mentality.[28] In *Ideology and Utopia,* published later in the same decade as *We,* Mannheim, like Zamyatin, postulates four species of utopian cognition—what he calls Orgiastic-Chiliasm, the Liberal-Humanitarian Idea, the Conservative Idea, and the Socialist-Communist Utopia. He then plots the relationships between each of these forms along two intersecting axes. On the first, or temporal, axis Mannheim shows how each "mentality"—a kind of cognitive framework through which a determinate, ascending social group apprehends its world—emerges in historical succession. This story begins on the very horizon of modernity itself, with the Chiliasm of Thomas Münzer and his followers in the 1525 Peasants' War, and extends up through the development of the Marxist *Wissenschaft* in the latter part of the nineteenth century. According to Mannheim, each subsequent mentality modifies and adapts the conceptual machinations of its predecessors, the entire narrative climaxing with the development of the total system of thought of the Socialist-Communist Utopia.

The fundamental problems that arise in Mannheim's historical narrative have been amply commented upon: his work elides the question of its own "disinterested" place in relationship to these "committed" modes of thought, while, at the same time, it creates its own teleology, whose conclusion, with the final diminishing of the gap of "noncongruence" between utopia and reality, *a priori* precludes the emergence of new kinds of utopian thought (and, by extension, the new kinds of oppositional publics that accompany them).[29] However, Mannheim also projects this schema along a second typological axis. All four mentalities, he argues, exist together in his own present, each also representing a critical "counter-utopia" to its three competitors, as well as being the repository of a distinctive "time-sense," or mode of historical consciousness. Understood in this way, Mannheim's schema of these "ideal types" appears less a mechanism for pigeonholing every individual expression of utopian thought and more what he himself describes as a heuristic "methodological device" for "reconstructing" the outer limits of the "ideal type" of the political imagination of his own day—abstract horizons of possibility that, he writes, "are present in reality although not always obvious," and which would then include his own "disinterested" analysis as well (*IU*, 202 and 210).

The time sense of Mannheim's Orgiastic-Chiliastic, Liberal-Humanitarian, Conservative, and Socialist-Communist mentalities can be summarized, respectively, as the *kairos*, or what, in a different context, Walter Benjamin describes as the *Jetztzeit*, the "now-time"; progress; duration; and structural discontinuity.[30] Thus, while the chiliastic mentality emphasizes the "absolute presentness" of the current moment, always already ripe with the possibility of the explosive emergence of a radically Other human situation, the liberal idea views its present as a discrete point on a gradually unfolding *telos* moving toward the realization of a universal Ideal. History for this latter mentality represents the process of a regular and unbroken diminishing of "the gap between the imperfection of things as they occurred in a state of nature and the dictates of reason by means of the concept of progress" (*IU*, 215 and 222). For the communist-socialist mentality, on the other hand, each present situation is viewed as an expression of a complexly integrated and self-contained structure of economic, social, cultural, and ideological forms and relationships, which in turn are to be distinguished from those forms and relationships that are part of quite different past and future structures. History for this mentality is understood as a "series of strategical points" that mark past and potential future moments of discontinuity between one social mode and another (*IU*, 244).

However, the conservative mentality unfolds in a somewhat different direction. This form of utopian thought differs from all these others in that, as Paul Ricoeur emphasizes, it "discovers its 'idea' after the fact," coming to theoretical self-realization only in the face of transformational agendas of the other mentalities.[31] Thus, Mannheim maintains that the conservative mentality is first and foremost a form of counterutopia, its primary antagonist being "the liberal idea which has been translated into rationalistic terms. Whereas in the latter, the normative, the 'should' is accentuated in experience, in conservatism the emphasis shifts to existing reality, the 'is'" (*IU*, 234–35). More important, Mannheim argues,

The time-sense of this mode of experience and thought is completely opposed to that of liberalism. Whereas for liberalism the future was everything and the past nothing, the conservative mode of experiencing time found the best corroboration of its sense of the determinateness in discovering the significance of the past, in the discovery of time as the creator of value. . . . Consequently not only is attention turned to the past and the attempt made to rescue it from oblivion, but the presentness and immediacy of the whole past becomes an actual experience. (*IU*, 235)

Such an outlook can still be described as "utopian" because, as with the other three mentalities, it too "is incongruous with the state of reality within which it occurs": the conservative mentality maintains this ideal of the full self-presence of the past in the present precisely in a moment when the possibility of such an unbroken continuity begins to disappear—that is, in a moment of dramatic historical upheaval (*IU*, 192).

Mannheim's descriptions of these utopian time-senses have been further expanded upon by Hayden White, who shows how each of these four mentalities also expresses an ideological "conception of the historical process and of historical knowledge" associated with one of the fundamental modes of political thought that dominate the nineteenth and the first half of the twentieth centuries: anarchism, liberalism, conservatism, and radicalism. Crucially, according to White, each of these different political agendas is oriented toward a different temporal topos.

Conservatives are inclined to imagine historical evolution as a progressive elaboration of the institutional structure that *currently* prevails, which structure they regard as a "utopia"—that is, the best form of society that men can "realistically" hope for, or legitimately aspire to, for the time being. By contrast, Liberals imagine a time in the *future* when this structure will have been improved, but they project this utopian condition into the *remote* future, in such a way as to discourage any effort in the present to realize it precipitately, by "radical" means. Radicals, on the other hand, are inclined to view the utopian condition as *imminent*, which inspires their concern with the provision of the revolutionary means to bring this utopia to pass *now*. Finally, Anarchists are inclined to idealize a *remote past* of natural-human innocence from which men have fallen into the corrupt "social" state in which they currently find themselves.[32]

All four of these ideologies of history are similar, according to White, in that they are "cognitively responsible," a term he borrows from Stephen C. Pepper "to distinguish between philosophical systems committed to rational defenses of their world hypotheses and those not so committed."[33] That is, unlike "authoritarian" systems of knowledge whose truth claims rest on the more or less unquestioned authority of some sort of external agency—be it divinity, a charismatic leader, or a certain group or class—each of these political and cognitive positions are, to varying degrees, epistemologically self-reflective, engaging in an ongoing public debate with their opponents, while struggling to produce totalizing explanatory systems that might account for the " 'data' un-covered by investigators of the social process working from alternative points of view."[34] Crucially, White's definition greatly expands the pa-rameters of what is thought of as a "rational" mode of cognition. Thus, for example, while the cognitive position of anarchism finds its roots in older chiliastic beliefs, and shares with Rousseau's romanticism a cele-bration of the autonomy of the individual in her natural state (a cele-bration that, according to White, also feeds into the Fascist idealization of the *volkisch* past), modern political anarchism differs from these re-lated forms of belief in that "it seeks to provide rational justifications for its irrational posture."[35]

Mannheim's typology of the utopian mentalities and their respective time-senses, coupled with White's further elaboration, provide another way to map the similarities and differences in the respective agendas of *We* and *Nineteen Eighty-Four*. Both Orwell and Zamyatin (along with their contemporary, Benjamin) aim the critical energies of their texts against what, in Mannheim's terms, we would call the liberal utopia and its "progressive" time-sense: the utopia for Zamyatin represented by the figure of the One State, and for Orwell by what he understood to be Wells's vision of history. This liberal, progressive view of history is like-wise associated with the set of social processes yoked together under the term *modernization*—the reorganization of older forms of social life that accompany the development of a money economy, industrialism, urbanization, secularization, and all the other forces that give rise to the modern West—for which the nation-state had long served as the primary vehicle. (Interestingly, both Zamyatin and Orwell had earlier written narratives that directly attacked the ills of a modern English urban-industrial society, Zamyatin's *The Islanders* and Orwell's *Keep the Aspidistra Flying* [1936] and *Coming Up for Air*.) Both *We* and *Nine-teen Eighty-Four* (and to this list we can add Aldous Huxley's *Brave New World*) further work to show that the quantitative changes intro-duced as a result of modernization—efficiency, increased productivity, electrification, the shrinking of space as a consequence of new trans-portation technologies—do not necessarily end in a qualitative better-

ing of human existence. Indeed, perhaps even more readily evident for
Orwell than either Zamyatin or Huxley, the processes of social modernization have in fact resulted in a nightmarish deterioration of contemporary social and cultural life.

However, Zamyatin's and Orwell's narratives again diverge dramatically in the consequences each draws from this critique of modernization. In *We,* the critical assault on the "liberal utopia" was undertaken
with the ultimate aim of opening up the possibility of an alternative path
along which a different kind of reorganization of society might be accomplished—the path represented by the textual figure of the "infinite
revolution." In *Nineteen Eighty-Four,* on the other hand, this path disappears, for such a possibility violates what Orwell now holds to be a
nearly ontological "truth" about human society. This truth is related to
Winston Smith through Goldstein's book:

> Throughout recorded time, and probably since the end of the Neolithic Age,
> there have been three kinds of people in the World, the High, the Middle, and
> the Low. They have been subdivided in many ways, they have borne count-
> less different names, and their relative numbers, as well as their attitude to-
> ward one another, have varied from age to age; but the essential structure of
> society has never altered. Even after enormous upheavals and seemingly ir-
> revocable changes, the same pattern has always reasserted itself, just as a gy-
> roscope will always return to equilibrium, however far it is pushed one way
> or the other. (*NEF,* 166)

This passage reiterates the lesson already drawn in Orwell's earlier grim
allegorical fable, *Animal Farm.* Any effort to radically change society
—the "one way or the other" now representing for Orwell the two
faces, fascism and Stalinism, of the same totalitarian coin—does nothing more than create new rulers whose subsequent reign in fact may be
far more horrific than that which they supplant. In the conclusion to the
earlier fable, the "Pigs" have become indistinguishable from the "Men"
that they had replaced.[36] Likewise, in a review of Arthur Koestler's *The
Yogi and the Commissar,* published only months after *Animal Farm,*
Orwell writes, "Throughout history, one revolution after another—
although usually producing a temporary relief, such as a sick man gets
by turning over in bed—has simply led to a change of masters."[37] Thus,
even before the writing of *Nineteen Eighty-Four,* Orwell had become
like those "middle-class" English socialists he had so vehemently de-
nounced in *The Road to Wigan Pier:* making the strictures of class society identical with history itself, he finds himself unable to imagine even
the possibility of another form of human existence.

Indeed, the collapse of the radical alternative offered in Zamyatin's text leaves for Orwell only one other option available. Zamyatin's narrative also presents a third possibility, that of the "anarchist utopia," represented in the text by the world of the Mephi. Such an option does not even appear in Orwell's text, no doubt in part reflecting the commonly held assumption of the middle of the twentieth century that anarchism had all but vanished as a viable political possibility: a "fact" of which Orwell, who had witnessed the brutal suppression of the POUM anarchists during the Spanish Civil War, was well aware.[38] Thus, for Orwell, the "best," or more accurately, the least bad, imaginable arrangement of human affairs can be found only in the *past*. Whereas the normative locus from which Zamyatin and later writers like Le Guin launch the critique of their own presents is finally located in the future— in a "not yet" existing, radically Other human situation—Orwell, for whom such a horizon of possibility no longer exists, reverses direction, looking, as does Winston Smith, "to the past" for the values that ground his critical narrative project (*NEF*, 146). In this way, *Nineteen Eighty-Four* becomes an example of Mannheim's "conservative utopia."[39]

Orwell was not the first to write this kind of utopia. Indeed, in Chapter 3 we saw how Arthur Dudley Vinton's *Looking Further Backward* draws upon the critical force of conservative gender, race, and class norms in order to attack the program for remaking American national identity plotted in Bellamy's *Looking Backward*. However, Orwell's text differs from these earlier conservative utopias in that rather than assaulting a particular political agenda or representation of future history, *Nineteen Eighty-Four* attempts to create a "counter-utopia" to the historical vision of the utopia as such. Paradoxically, Orwell engages in this negation of the "modernity" of the narrative utopia, its incessant marking of the historicity of the present, as part of a desperate gambit to save the project of modernity from itself.

THE CRISIS OF MODERN REASON

We can begin to ascertain what Orwell understood to be the "past" that he undertook to defend in this way, as well as the nature of the developments in his own present against which he was defending it, by way of a final comparison between *We* and *Nineteen Eighty-Four*. In his review of *We*, Orwell points out that the target of Zamyatin's criticism "is not any particular country but the implied aims of industrial civilisation." In this sense, *We* appears similar to *Brave New World*. However,

Orwell finds Zamyatin's book "superior" to Huxley's in that the former demonstrates an "intuitive grasp of the irrational side of totalitarianism—human sacrifice, cruelty as an end in itself, the worship of a Leader who is credited with divine attributes."[40] The same understanding of the deep "irrational" nature of fascism made London's *The Iron Heel* such an effective work for Orwell as well.[41]

Here, too, Orwell significantly misreads the narrative program of *We*, for, as Zamyatin's work makes abundantly clear, "irrationality" is *not* part of the province of the One State, but rather of the Mephi and of D-503 during his crisis of burgeoning individuality. Irrationality, as it is represented in Zamyatin's narrative, denotes less the negation of reason than, as White similarly argues, a unique mode of cognition in its own right. Indeed, each of the utopian Worlds mapped in *We* also embodies a distinctive species of rationality—a specific, "cognitively responsible" way of apprehending, evaluating, redescribing, and hence constructing the world in which one lives.[42] Irrationality, or what Zamyatin refers to as "imagination," is the private term in this schema, a way of thinking deployed by the isolated individual, and, by way of the Mephi, linked to the "world" of an anarchic, Rousseauistic, presocial existence: a kind of Blakean "innocence" counterposed to the "experience" of the One State. In these terms, the character in *Nineteen Eighty-Four* who might be said to occupy the space of the "irrational" is not O'Brien, nor even the absent-present, semidivine "personhood" of Big Brother, but Winston Smith himself. Indeed, as O'Brien informs Winston, "You would not make the act of submission which is the price of sanity. You preferred to be a lunatic, a minority of one" (*NEF*, 205). This latter equation of the "irrational" with sickness and abnormality—D-503's "soul disease" and Winston Smith's lunacy—makes sense only when perceived from within the strictures of a completely different mode of cognition, that which is defined as normal by and for the dominant social order.

Zamyatin's definition of what constitutes the "normal" mode of thought in the One State is similarly linked to his critique of the social logics of modernization. The One State embodies in a pure form the processes Zamyatin already saw at work in his own modernizing present. This form of reason or rationality—mathematics, regularity, order, conformity, routine, stability, and efficiency, all manifest in the "perfect" physical and social environments of the One State—has become a self-present end in its own right, all but eradicating the goal, the "bettering" of human life, toward which it had originally been instituted. Reducing everything and everyone to an equivalency, the rationality of the One State eliminates the kinds of rich diversities of human individuality, or irrationality, that Zamyatin views as being embodied in the figure of the anarchic, presocial world of the Mephi. Zamyatin emblematizes this opposition in the contrast of the standardized, gray-blue "unifs" of the State's Numbers with the multihued coats of the Mephi people.

Zamyatin's representation of the dilemmas of the "rational" mode of cognition, which he suggests are endemic to contemporary society, also resonates with what Max Weber describes as the process of "disenchantment" and "rationalization" of the modern world, or what Max Horkheimer and Theodor Adorno will later call "instrumental reason": the replacement of religious or mythic explanations of the natural world with a science and philosophy aimed at an increasingly precise manipulation and finally domination of that world. But more like Adorno and Horkheimer than Weber, Zamyatin postulates the possibility of another kind of thinking, that associated with the "not yet" existing topos of the "infinite revolution": a mode of apprehension wherein the oppositions marked out in the text—irrationality and instrumental reason, individual and society, subject and object, freedom and happiness—have been reconfigured within an expanded and conceptually flexible "dialectical" reason. "This is the constant dialectical path which in a grandiose parabola sweeps the world into infinity. Yesterday, the thesis; today, the antithesis; and tomorrow, the synthesis."[43] If my diagram of the text's "Possible Worlds" is correct, then the thesis is the "irrationality" of the Mephi; the antithesis, the instrumental reason of the One State; and the synthesis, the dialectical reason associated with the world of the infinite revolution.

The dialectical reason linked to the topos of the infinite revolution is situated as the unrepresentable "complex" point subsuming into itself the contradiction of these other two modes of cognition; while the final place on Zamyatin's schema of utopian Possible Worlds, that of the post-fantasectomy D-503, represents the complete negation of all of these other modes. Indeed, it is only in this final world where the concept of "cognitive responsibility" is rendered meaningless as D-503 quite literally loses his mind and is thus rendered incapable of making any kind of judgment independent of the authority of the One State. This situation, that of what we might call "nonreason," would represent an "impossible" world outside the historical context in which Zamyatin produces We. Moreover, such a world would occupy the "neutral" place in the Greimasian map we elaborated in the previous chapter, the position

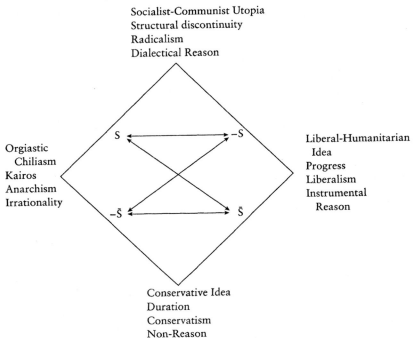

Figure 6.   Correspondences between Mannheim's utopian mentalities and their time-senses, White's map of political ideologies, and four species of rationality, mapped on the Greimasian diagrams from Chapter 5.

that, as Louis Marin usefully reminds us, "creates the paradoxical idea of a part of a whole, but outside of the whole, of a part that would be a supplement to the complementary parts of the totality whose sum exhausts it."[44] Thus, a mapping of the four corresponding, but *not* homologous (i.e. reducible to each other), schemas elaborated in this chapter—Mannheim's utopian mentalities and time-senses, White's political positions, and these four species of rationality—onto the Greimasian representation of the play of Zamyatin's utopian Possible Worlds we elaborated in the previous chapter would take the form shown in figure 6.

The final, purely negative world, like that of the infinite revolution, exists in Zamyatin's text as a formal rather than a concrete spatial possibility, a figural space holder for something else that Zamyatin finds finally unrepresentable. However, for Orwell, positioned on the other side of the great gulf of the Second World War, the utter negation of these various modes of rationality, and thus the negation of modernity itself, has become much more than an imaginative possibility, taking on a concrete expression in real-world totalitarian societies. That Orwell understood totalitarianism to amount to a cancellation of modern rationality is borne out by his incessant equation of German fascism and Stalinist communism with the Roman Catholic Church, the dominant organization of the "premodern" European world. All three, Orwell maintains, require the same blind acquiescence to authority that is fundamentally alien to the pursuit of rational "truths."[45] Goldstein's book further reinforces this identification of Oceania with the Catholic Church, stressing, among other aspects, their similarity in employing "adoptive" rather than "hereditary" hierarchical organizations (NEF, 173). O'Brien too, whose name suggests his descent from Catholic Ireland, appears as the figural embodiment of Orwell's earlier pronouncement: "One of the analogies between Communism and Roman Catholicism is that only the 'educated' are completely orthodox."[46] Nevertheless, the society of Oceania represents an original historical variant on this older organizational structure, the totalitarian social form as Orwell understands it serving as the vehicle for the actualization of a potential condition "beyond" modernity.

One of the more significant recent theorizations of the relationship between Western modernity and a new order of rational cognition can be found in the work of Habermas. Also drawing upon the description of modernity first advanced by Weber, Habermas argues that the secularization of European society was accompanied by the breakdown of the unified Christian worldview and its accompanying traditional (habitual and ritualized) social practices. In the place of the "substantive reason" of this old world, there gradually emerged three distinct and autonomous spheres of rationality. These in turn become increasingly abstracted from the contingencies of everyday life so that each could develop according to its own discrete internal logics. Habermas labels these spheres the cognitive-instrumental, the moral-practical, and the aesthetic-expressive: the domains of science; jurisprudence, ethics, and politics; and art. Each is focused, respectively, on questions of the true, the good, and the beautiful. The "project of modernity," as codified in eighteenth-century Enlightenment philosophy, aims at unlocking the specific potential of each of these spheres in order to "promote not only the control of natural forces but also understanding of the world and of the self, moral progress, the justice of institutions and even the happiness of human beings."[47] This optimistic agenda comes crashing down,

Habermas maintains, only with the cataclysmic events of the first half of the twentieth century.

The broken promise of modernity in the twentieth century also serves as one of the central themes in Orwell's final work. Moreover, with Habermas, Orwell maintains that this catastrophe happens not because of flaws internal to the structures of modern reason; rather, it occurs as a result of the actions of a whole new class of political elites. This thesis is figurally embodied in the narrative unfolding of *Nineteen Eighty-Four*. In his role as the "Last Man in Europe" (the work's original title), Winston Smith becomes the embodiment of Western modernity. His "re-education" into Oceanic society thus progresses by way of a dismantling of each of the spheres of rationality—that of truth, goodness, and beauty—clearing the ground for the new kinds of cognition demanded by totalitarian regimes like that of Oceania.

The domain of the first of these spheres coincides with what Orwell himself refers to as "common sense," and takes a figural form in the mathematical equation "two plus two equals four." The distance between Zamyatin's and Orwell's narratives again can be measured by the quite different symbolic valences each invests in this figure: while in *We,* as in Fyodor Dostoevsky's *Notes from Underground,* this mathematical figure symbolizes the procrustean, de-differentiating force of modern society's instrumental reason, for Orwell, it signifies a bedrock of "self-evident" knowledge upon which all other questions of value and taste ultimately can be grounded.[48] Thus, in one of his earliest diary entries, Winston Smith writes, "Freedom is the freedom to say that two plus two make four. If that is granted, all else follows" (*NEF,* 69).

The guarantee that this mode of rationality continues to operate as a kind of universal foundation lies, according to Habermas, in its position of abstraction "outside" the contingencies of the "lifeworld," or everyday realm of intersubjective social interaction. Thus, in order to demolish the fixity of this fundamental mode of knowledge, the ruling elite of Orwell's Oceania must draw it back into the mundane social-subjective plane. They achieve this end by denying the existence of any external realm of objective rational knowledge. Indeed, "reality," according to the Party, is not something waiting for an intentional human consciousness to apprehend properly, but the very thing produced by that consciousness. O'Brien himself states as much at various points throughout the extended torture-interrogation that occurs in the latter part of the narrative: for example, "Reality exists in the human mind, and nowhere else"; and later, "We control matter because we control the mind. . . . We make the laws of nature" (*NEF*, 205 and 218).

When Winston Smith, acting as a kind of heir to London's Ernest Everhard, points out the idealist fallacy in such a proposition, O'Brien counters with the assertion, "This is not solipsism. Collective solipsism, if you like. But that is a different thing; in fact, the opposite thing" (*NEF*, 219). A theory of individual solipsism presupposes the existence of an autonomous subject, "free" to invent its own divergent realities, the "irrationality" I discussed above. However, it is precisely this kind of free subjectivity that the Party in Oceania works to eradicate. The Party not only makes the laws of the external natural world, it attempts to create "human nature" as well (*NEF*, 222). The extended and meticulously detailed torture of Winston Smith thus represents what Lionel Trilling calls "a hideous parody on psychotherapy," a methodical breaking down of Winston Smith's "deviant," or individual, or irrational, sense of reality so that he may be ultimately resocialized into the contingent reality of this postrational future.[49] "You will be hollow," O'Brien tells Winston. "We shall squeeze you empty, and then we shall fill you with ourselves" (*NEF*, 211). As Richard Rorty astutely puts it, the Party forces Winston to "realize that he is no longer able to use a language or be a self," except for those languages and senses of self authorized by his society.[50] Winston Smith's later acknowledgment that he can in fact "believe" that two plus two may sometimes equal five signals the first step in this process of destroying his autonomous self, a process that culminates in his betrayal of Julia (*NEF*, 213 and 236).

"Common sense" in the world of Oceania is thus shown to be a construct of the dominant social groups. While Orwell himself might accept that common sense in every society is in a large part an expression of the "general direction imposed on social life by the dominant fundamental group,"[51] he views this "new" form of totalitarian hegemony as unique in its absolute nature, its intransigent unwillingness to tolerate even the most infinitesimal degree of deviation from prescribed orthodoxy (at least, significantly, for the members of those groups, the Inner and Outer Parties, from whom this orthodoxy is demanded): "By comparison with that existing today, all the tyrannies of the past were half-hearted and inefficient. The ruling groups were always infected to some extent by liberal ideas, and were content to leave loose ends everywhere, to regard only the overt act, and to be uninterested in what their subjects were thinking" (*NEF*, 169). Without a transcendental standard guaranteeing statements like "two plus two equals four," truth itself becomes infinitely mutable, able to be redefined as the needs of the state change.

Earlier in the narrative, after he has finished reading the first and third chapters of Goldstein's book, Winston Smith ponders the fact that while the information in the book provides him with an understanding of "how" the world of Oceania has come into being, it does not yet allow him to understand "why" (*NEF*, 179). Similarly, through the description of the processes by which "pure reason" and common sense are dismantled in Oceania, the reader learns the "how" of the establishment of a new kind of absolute and total social hegemony; but by themselves these processes do not account for the "why." The answer to this latter question—fittingly provided by O'Brien, who may be the "true" author of Goldstein's book—marks the collapse of the second of the spheres of modern rationality, that of a legal-ethical framework, the transcendental *cogito* of good and evil, by which various kinds of individual behaviors and political systems are evaluated. Winston Smith's explanation of why the Party requires absolute domination still draws on an older modern notion of ethical ends, and in turn echoes those earlier justifications of social control famously elaborated by the very modern figures of Dostoevsky's Grand Inquisitor and Zamyatin's poet R-13:

> He knew in advance what O'Brien would say: that the Party did not seek power for its own ends, but only for the good of the majority. That it sought power because men in the mass were frail, cowardly creatures who could not endure liberty or face the truth, and must be ruled over and systematically deceived by others who were stronger than themselves. That the choice for mankind lay between *freedom and happiness,* and that, for the great bulk of mankind, happiness was better. That the Party was the eternal guardian of the weak, a dedicated sect doing evil that good might come, sacrificing its own happiness to that of others. (*NEF*, 216; emphasis added)

However, O'Brien emphatically rejects any such rationalization of the Party's actions, and in so doing signals its break with this second sphere of rationality: "The Party seeks power entirely for its own sake. We are not interested in the good of others; we are interested solely in power. Not wealth or luxury or long life or happiness; only power, pure power" (*NEF*, 217).

Orwell's Nietzschean-style ontology of power was derived most immediately from the work of the conservative social theorist James Burnham. Burnham had earlier argued that the fundamental goal of the new Machiavellians—a global "managerial elite" composed of those in the bureaucratic, administrative, and organizational strata of the emerging superstates—would be "to maintain its own power and privilege."⁵² As we saw in Chapter 4, a similar concept can be found in London's earlier *The Iron Heel*. For London, too, "power" served as a figure for what he understood to be an emerging "postcapitalistic" social organization, dominated by the "unrepresentable" agency of the new transnational corporations. And yet, because London still struggled to hold open the possibility of imagining a resistance to this expression of pure power, he posited an oppositional force, his revolutionary vanguard, over and against the Iron Heel oligarchy. It is only from our later historical perspective that we see how these dispersed utopian figures actually consolidate in the emerging reality of the corporate-bureaucratic structure. Moreover, London's vision of challenging power through power— Ernest Everhard asserts, "Power will be the arbiter, as it always has been the arbiter"—similarly requires London to suppose that the actions of the Iron Heel, as well as those of the revolutionary vanguard, will be underwritten by a very modern ethics: "They, as a class, believed that they alone maintained civilization. It was their belief that if ever they weakened, the great beast would ingulf them and everything of beauty and wonder and joy and good in its cavernous and slime-dripping maw. . . . I cannot lay too great a stress upon this high ethical righteousness of the whole oligarchical class."⁵³

However, in Orwell's Oceania, as in Burnham's vision of an emerging global managerial order, the totalizing consolidation of the social text already has been accomplished. Thus, O'Brien can dispense with the modern conception of a political ethics based on considerations of what constitutes the "best" organization of human society, and in its place announce a pure instrumentality of power: "Power is not a means; it is an end. One does not establish a dictatorship in order to safeguard a revolution; one makes the revolution in order to establish the dictatorship. The object of persecution is persecution. The object of torture is torture. The object of power is power" (*NEF*, 217). The power to rule for O'Brien—and crucially, Orwell suggests, for any individual or group that attempts a radical reorganization of society—reveals itself to be nothing but a pure will-to-power, an unmediated expression of Nietzschean *ressentiment* and rage directed against everything that remains heterogeneous to the closed reality of Oceania.⁵⁴ O'Brien tells Winston Smith that "The individual only has power in so far as he ceases to be an individual" (*NEF*, 218)—that is, once he or she ceases to be a form of what Adorno calls the "non-identical," the form of difference that defines the term "freedom" for both Orwell and Zamyatin.⁵⁵ The violence wielded by O'Brien thus facilitates the extension of the form of universal identity represented by Oceanic social power. Torture is only the means by which Julia and Winston are forced to "escape from identity," first transformed into sheer undifferentiated objects, "bodies in pain," and then reconstituted as "subjects" whose desires are identical with those of the absolutely sutured hegemonic order (*NEF*, 218).[56]

The "free self" is only one of a group of figures representing this kind of heterogeneity that we find in *Nineteen Eighty-Four*. Indeed, if the final "act" of Orwell's three-part narrative produces a despairing vision of the utter obliteration of all forms of autonomy, then the second act serves as its more "utopian" counterpoint, tracing Winston Smith's movement through a progressive series of encounters with a variety of just such figures of heterogeneity, beginning with the action that establishes his autonomous identity, the writing of the diary. The narrative's figures for this kind of non-identity also include the natural world outside of the city of London; the lost "Golden Country" of Winston Smith's youth and the place to which he and Julia return for their first sexual encounter; Julia's physical sexuality; the glass sphere containing a piece of Indian Ocean coral that Winston discovers in Mr. Charrington's antique shop; and, perhaps most significant of all, the small room above Charrington's shop, a space wherein Julia and Winston momentarily re-create the private domestic interior that had been eliminated by an Oceanic regime of constant surveillance.

What is most striking about these figures is the degree to which they all share attributes of what throughout the long revolution of Western modernity had come to be defined as features of the *aesthetic,* the third of Habermas's spheres of modern rationality. For example, we learn that the "undeclared" purpose of the Party's assault on eroticism "was to remove all pleasure from the sexual act" and replace it with a kind of sublime terror (*NEF*, 57). Winston Smith later rediscovers this kind of pleasure through Julia's sexual body and through the everyday physical comforts of their shared domestic space. Secondly, Winston Smith's description of what makes the glass *objet d'art* a "beautiful thing," a process of aestheticization that erases its more mundane instrumental functions, recalls the Kantian definition of the aesthetic object as that which possesses "purposiveness without purpose": "The thing was doubly attractive because of its apparent uselessness, though he could guess that it must once have been intended as a paperweight" (*NEF*, 81).[57]

Finally, and perhaps most important for Orwell's purposes, these aesthetic objects serve as self-contained, autonomous monads—Winston Smith describes the sphere as "enclosing a tiny world with its atmosphere complete" and later the room "a world, a pocket of the past where extinct animals could walk" (*NEF,* 122 and 124). These self-contained worlds instigate in Winston Smith what Herbert Marcuse would later describe as aesthetic *anamnesis:* "The room had awakened in him a sort of nostalgia, a sort of ancestral memory" (*NEF,* 82). Early in the narrative, Winston Smith reflects, "Always in your stomach and in your skin there was a sort of protest, a feeling that you had been cheated of something you had a right to" (*NEF,* 52). The aesthetic object alone provides the truth-content of these feelings. Offering a means of access to the now-repressed reality of the historical past—"If [the past] survives anywhere," Winston tells Julia, "it's in a few solid objects with no words attached to them, like that lump of glass there" (*NEF,* 128)—the aesthetic object becomes a material embodiment of the *memory of happiness* in a world where such happiness no longer exists.

However, the very objects Orwell chooses to serve as these material embodiments of a vanished happiness suggest that the aesthetic in *Nineteen Eighty-Four* operates more precisely as a form of *nostalgia.* Unlike Marcuse's theory of Platonic *anamnesis,* the recollection of a moment of a "prehistoric happiness" before the establishment of a repressive civilization, Orwell's memory of happiness looks backward to a very specific moment in the *English* national past.[58] These objects become the "Thing" incarnate, a concrete manifestation of the shared "organization of enjoyment" that, as Slavoj Žižek points out, fuses together the imagined community of the nation (and crucially, as he also suggests, is imagined to be under constant "menace" by some Other).[59] Charrington informs Winston that the glass paperweight "wasn't made less than a hundred years ago," and the furnishings of the domestic interior recall the same period (*NEF,* 81). Both are thus also products of the time of Orwell's own childhood. The better world toward which Winston Smith looks back longingly is located in the moment that, not coincidentally, coincides with the high-watermark of Great Britain's power—a moment which by the conclusion of the Second World War seems to have vanished forever. Indeed, in the "postwar" world of *Nineteen Eighty-Four,* the very signifier "England" has been erased, and in its place a name given that indicates its now peripheral function as a military outpost for some larger geopolitical entity: "Even the names of countries, and their shapes on the map, had been different. Airstrip One, for instance, had not been so called in those days: it had been called England or Britain" (*NEF,* 30). Thus, if the autonomous aesthetic object enables the creation of Winston Smith's own "free" subjectivity, it does so only by recalling another kind of autonomy, that of the "English" or (imperial) "British" nation-state, the two, as the previous passage makes evident, always already identical in Orwell's mind.[60] (This is *not*, however, a view shared by all of Orwell's contemporaries; something a reading of fellow socialist Lewis Grassic Gibbon's great trilogy, *A Scots Quair*, to take only one example, readily makes apparent.)

It is this "memory of happiness" that O'Brien and his Thought Police find most intolerable. As Winston Smith points out, as long as such aesthetic or nostalgic objects exist, the Party's domination remains incomplete: "What mattered was that the room over the junk shop should exist. To know that it was there, inviolate, was almost the same as being in it" (*NEF*, 124). These self-contained material embodiments of the past serve as the irrefutable proof of the possibility of another, better, situation, and consequently provide the normative ground from which Winston Smith can critique the horror, deprivation, and poverty of Oceanic life. O'Brien's final victory thus requires the violent negation of these reference points and a corresponding shattering of the apparent autonomy of the aesthetic realm: when the Thought Police invade the sanctity of Winston and Julia's domestic space, they literally smash the glass sphere, prefiguring the way O'Brien later will violate the inviolability of their bodies and minds (*NEF*, 183). Seizing "control of the past" in this way, O'Brien comes to dominate completely the present and seemingly every imaginable future.

MODERNIZATION AGAINST MODERNITY: THE CULTURE INDUSTRY AND "SECONDARY ORALITY"

If the aestheticized object embodies in the text a deeply menaced memory of happiness, its mirror inverse, that which does the menacing, is the "bad" official culture of Oceania. Crucially, it is by way of this face of the Oceanic machinery of domination that Orwell expands his diagnosis of totalitarianism beyond what he took to be the social reality of the more properly authoritarian regimes and into emerging conditions in Britain and beyond. Indeed, the originality of *Nineteen Eighty-Four* lies not simply in its production of a language by which Western Europe and the United States could "conceive," to use Lefebvre's term, existence in one of the already existing authoritarian societies, but also in its figuration of the role of mass culture in the creation of an emerging *global* social formation, one which Orwell's contemporaries in the Frankfurt School describe as the total "administered society."

The theme of an opposition between a corrupt contemporary culture and some more authentic and nostalgically longed-for cultural past had already been treated at various places in Orwell's earlier work. In his prewar novel *Coming Up for Air,* for example—a work that in some important respects serves as a full-costume dress-rehearsal for *Nineteen Eighty-Four* (as did Zamyatin's *The Islanders* for *We*)—protagonist George Bowling yearns, much like Winston Smith, for a past era before the horrors of the present, "the time before the war, before the radio, before aeroplanes, before Hitler."[61] This startling image, juxtaposing a figure of mass culture, the radio, with that of the leader of fascism, also appears in Orwell's celebrated 1940 essay "Inside the Whale": "To say 'I accept' in an age like our own is to say that you accept concentration camps, rubber truncheons, Hitler, Stalin, bombs, aeroplanes, tinned food, machine guns, putsches, purges, slogans, Bedaux belts, gas masks, submarines, spies, provocateurs, press censorship, secret prisons, aspirins, Hollywood films, and political murders."[62] Such lists recur again and again throughout Orwell's writings, reinforcing the identification of authoritarianism (machine guns, putsches, purges, press censorship) with a new mass culture (tinned food, aspirins, Hollywood films), an identification that likewise plays a central role in *Nineteen Eighty-Four.* As for the recurring references to "aeroplanes" as another destructive agent of modernization, they seem to point toward, as with England's rechristening as "Airstrip One," a similar process of abstraction that erases the particular identity of English national culture: to "accept" the airplane means to accept that Great Britain has become an abstract landscape you "fly" over rather than a concrete one within which you become immersed.

The institution in *Nineteen Eighty-Four* responsible for this new form of cultural production is Winston Smith's own place of employment, the Ministry of Truth, "which concerned itself with news, entertainment, education, and the fine arts" (*NEF,* 8). The Ministry of Truth, in conjunction with the Ministries of Love (concerned with law and order, the domain of O'Brien's Thought Police), Peace (warfare), and Plenty (economics), regulate every aspect of Oceanic social life. This initial overview of the Ministry of Truth is soon followed by a far more detailed description of the various operations performed by this massive institution, one of the longest such descriptions offered anywhere in the book. Orwell's portrayal performs an important cognitive mapping operation, placing Winston Smith's specific work, which involves the "rectification" of old newspaper reports so that they concur with current Oceanic state policy, in relation to a sprawling integrated industry whose final "product" is nothing less than the whole of Oceanic culture:

> And this hall, with its fifty workers or thereabouts, was only one sub-section, a single cell, as it were, in the huge complexity of the Records Department. Beyond, above, below, were other swarms of workers engaged in an unimaginable multitude of jobs. There were the huge printing shops with their sub-editors, their typography experts, and their elaborately equipped studios for the faking of photographs. There was the teleprograms section with its engineers, its producers, and its teams of actors specially chosen for their skill in imitating voices. There were the armies of reference clerks whose job was simply to draw up lists of books and periodicals which were due for recall. There were the vast repositories where the corrected documents were stored, and the hidden furnaces where the original copies were destroyed. And somehow or other, quite anonymous, there were directing brains who coordinated the whole effort and laid down the lines of policy. . . . And the Records Department, after all, was itself only a single branch of the Ministry of Truth, whose primary job was not to reconstruct the past but to supply the citizens of Oceania with newspapers, films, textbooks, telescreen programs, plays, novels—with every conceivable kind of information, instruction, or entertainment, from a statue to a slogan, from a lyric poem to a biological treatise, and from a child's spelling book to a Newspeak dictionary. And the Ministry had not only to supply the multifarious needs of the Party, but also to repeat the whole operation at a lower level for the benefit of the proletariat. There was a whole chain of separate departments dealing with proletarian literature, music, drama, and entertainment generally. Here were produced rubbishy newspapers, containing almost nothing except sport, crime, and astrology, sensational five-cent novelettes, films oozing with sex, and sentimental songs which were composed entirely by mechanical means on a special kind of kaleidoscope known as a versificator. There was even a whole subsection—*Pornosec*, it was called in Newspeak—engaged in producing the lowest kind of pornography, which was sent out in sealed packets and which no Party member, other than those who worked on it, was permitted to look at. (*NEF*, 38–39)

The production of culture in Oceania has been totally reorganized along the lines of the corporate-industrial-bureaucratic complex of Burnham's managerial society. And, as in London's earlier vision of the corporation, its controlling centers, its "directing brains," are unimaginable, cognitively unmappable. The extent to which what amounts to a self-propelling "culture industry" has come to dominate every aspect of Oceanic cultural life is represented in the text by the institution's work on language itself, in the creation of the infamous "Newspeak" vocabulary: "The purpose of Newspeak was not only to provide a medium of expression for the world-view and mental habits proper to the devotees of Ingsoc, but to make all other modes of thought impossible" (*NEF*, 246).

Orwell's critical investigations of these new cultural forms differ from those of contemporary critics like T. S. Eliot in that Orwell attempts to draw a distinction between the "popular" culture of the "people" and an industrial "mass" culture, a distinction that would then also influence the early work of Richard Hoggart and Raymond Williams, two of the founders of British cultural studies.[63] An authentic "popular" is celebrated throughout Orwell's *oeuvre*. George Bowling nostalgically reflects on the penny candies and popular novels of his youth; Orwell himself writes appreciatively of the culture of the "common man," of the homes of Northern England miners, boy's weekly magazines, "suet puddings and the red pillar-boxes," the fiction of Charles Dickens, postcard art, and early detective novels; and, even in *Nineteen Eighty-Four,* Winston Smith admires a prole washerwoman's ability to transform the "dreadful rubbish" of a machine-generated tune into "an almost pleasant sound" (*NEF*, 115). Indeed, even the text's objects of nostalgia—the glass paperweight, the room above Charrington's shop, and so forth—are expressions of the "popular" rather than the "high" cultural forms that are more often held to be the repositories of a critical aesthetic truth. The danger then, as Orwell sees it, lies not in the popular itself so much as in the displacement of these older *local* expressions of authentic cultural practice by a new form of global mass culture production, for which the earlier figures "radio," "tinned foods," and "Hollywood films" all serve as synechdoches.[64] That is, as evident in the long passage cited a moment ago, Orwell suggests that the unprecedented centralization of the *means* of producing culture will ultimately eliminate, in its very totalizing structural form, the possibility of any form of local cultural autonomy.

In depicting Oceania's institutionalization of culture in this way, Orwell drew on both contemporary wisdom about the bureaucratization of cultural production in the Soviet Union and Nazi Germany, and his own first-hand experiences of the British Broadcasting Corporation during the Second World War.[65] However, as the parallels between the following passage from Orwell's 1946 essay "The Prevention of Literature" (as well as elements in the long description quoted above), bear out, he also meant to bring to mind the mass culture complex of the

United States, for which the Hollywood studio system had become the privileged referent:

> It would probably not be beyond human ingenuity to write books by machinery. But a sort of mechanising process can already be seen at work in the film and radio, in publicity and propaganda, and in the lower reaches of journalism. The Disney films, for instance, are produced by what is essentially a factory process, the work being done partly mechanically and partly by teams of artists who have to subordinate their individual styles.[66]

The significance of this additional level of reference for the narrative program of *Nineteen Eighty-Four* does not fully emerge until later, in the midst of a brief exchange between Winston Smith and Mr. Charrington. When Winston expresses his interest in purchasing the glass paperweight, Charrington informs him, "Now, if it so happened that you wanted to buy it, that'd cost you four dollars. I can remember when a thing like that would have fetched eight pounds" (*NEF*, 81). This casual substitution of pounds for dollars immediately undermines any notion that Oceania is an extrapolation of a purely "English" authoritarian state. Rather, the Oceanic superstate *is* a figure for the United States, in relation to which England, or "Airstrip One," has been demoted to the status of a minor regional outpost. And indeed, with the then-recent signing of the Bretton-Woods Agreement, U.S. currency had in effect displaced the pound, becoming the official standard for the global, postwar market. We can thus begin to see that for Orwell the aesthetic object is an image of an authentically *English* past, while its negative other, *American* mass culture, represents those contemporary forces that have destroyed this idealized moment of national cultural autonomy: it is specifically by way of its cultural industry that the U.S. has, as Orwell earlier put it, "swallowed" up England.[67]

In *Nineteen Eighty-Four*, Julia informs Winston Smith that in the culture industry of Oceania, "Books were just a commodity that had to be produced, like jam or bootlaces" (*NEF*, 108). However, it is in the "free" commodities of the Oceanic media, most especially through the omnipresent telescreen, that the potential leveling force of mass culture becomes most nightmarishly evident. In Orwell's reading, the global cultural hegemony represented by the U.S. cultural industry became possible only with the development of a whole new set of media technologies. Indeed, for Orwell, the total integration of both social space and the individual psyche occurs by means of these technologies.[68] By effortlessly passing over every older border (as with the related trans-portation technology of the airplane), these new media allow the products of the culture industry to penetrate deeper into all aspects of everyday life and, consequently, to destroy every form of autonomy, be it cultural, political, or individual: "With the development of television, and the technical advance which made it possible to receive and transmit simultaneously on the same instrument, private life came to an end" (*NEF,* 169). This vision of the invasive force of the new mass media culture permeates the whole of *Nineteen Eighty-Four,* so that even the constant monitoring by the telescreen becomes a figure not for an actual regime of surveillance performed by the state, but rather for the kinds of internal self-regulations learned by the media's consumers: think, for example, of Winston and Julia's response to the telescreen in the moments before they are captured.[69] Indeed, the media's power to undermine the older, sacrosanct border between the private and public spheres is made evident only a few pages later, when a picture on the wall of Winston and Julia's domestic sanctuary falls away to reveal the telescreen that now seemingly has always already invaded this space (*NEF,* 182).

What was most disturbing for Orwell about this new form of cultural production was its antipathy to the modes of critical cognition he considered to be among the supreme achievements of European modernity. This kind of degraded culture not only had the cumulative effect of desensitizing the individual until she could no longer distinguish between good and bad (the consumption of mass-produced Victory Gin has rendered Winston Smith unable to taste the complexities of red wine [*NEF,* 141]), it replaced the focused critical cognition provided by the true aesthetic object with an endless stream of distractions. In an earlier essay, Orwell argued that this effect was the real aim of the new forms of mass media:

> In very many English homes the radio is literally never turned off, though it
> is manipulated from time to time so as to make sure that only light music will
> come out of it. . . . This is done with a definite purpose. The music prevents
> the conversation from becoming serious or even coherent, while the chatter
> of voices stops one from listening attentively to the music and thus prevents
> the onset of that dreaded thing, thought.[70]

The radio that is "literally never turned off" reappears in *Nineteen Eighty-Four* as the telescreen, for which "there was no way of shutting it off": providing an inescapable and endless stream of white noise, it too effectively eliminates the "dreaded thing," critical thought (*NEF,* 6).

This constant distraction further assures the continuation of the cur-

rent form of Oceanic society. To be so distracted is to be unable to recognize what has been stolen from your world or to give conscious expression to "the mute protest in your own bones, the instinctive feeling
that the conditions you lived in were intolerable and that at some other
time they must have been different" (NEF, 63). Articulating the inartic-
ulate in this way, Winston Smith goes on to iterate one of the central
themes of Nineteen Eighty-Four: "It struck him that the truly characteristic thing about modern life was not its cruelty and insecurity, but
simply its bareness, its dinginess, its listlessness. Life, if you looked
about you, bore no resemblance not only to the lies that streamed out of
the telescreens, but even to the ideals that the Party was trying to
achieve" (NEF, 63). Many readers of Nineteen Eighty-Four have been
struck by the care with which Orwell develops this theme in his description of the everyday details of Oceanic life. From the "vile wind"
and "swirl of gritty dust" of the narrative's opening lines to the clogged
sinks and broken elevators of Victory Mansions, the "oily-tasting" gin,
and the "spongy pinkish stuff" in the lunch stew, the phenomenological
density, what Howe calls the "hallucinatory immediacy," of Orwell's
narrative conveys the quality of Oceanic life as powerfully as any of the
longer narrative passages.[71]

But these textual details serve as much figurative as realist purposes,
becoming another means by which Orwell can critically comment upon
the nature of contemporary life. That Orwell meant this to be a judgment on the false promise of the whole of an emerging industrial and
mass media culture, and not, as sometimes has been asserted, simply
conditions in wartime and postwar England (let alone those in the Soviet Union, or Great Britain under a postwar labor government), can be
reconfirmed both by our earlier discussion of the parallels between the
fiction of Orwell and Gissing and by another glance back at Coming Up
for Air. Entering a cafe, George Bowling observes, "No real food at all.
Just lists of stuff with American names. . . . A sort of propaganda float-
ing round, mixed up with the noise of the radio, to the effect that food
doesn't matter, comfort doesn't matter, nothing matters except slickness
and shininess and streamlining." Only when he bites into a frankfurter
does George Bowling get beyond this world of "appearances" and into
the "essence" of the thing: "It gave me the feeling that I'd bitten into the
modern world and discovered what it was really made of. . . . Rotten fish
in a rubber skin. Bombs of filth bursting inside your mouth."[72] As I suggested earlier, it is the function of the aestheticized remnants of a quite
different cultural past to verify the "truth-content" of these visceral re-

actions: as concrete emblems of a lost happiness, they provide the normative ground from which this kind of critique of the present can be articulated.

Interestingly, the negative terms in Orwell's formulation of the new mass media culture, especially the way it destroys autonomy and memory, resonate with what Walter J. Ong describes as central aspects of premodern "oral cultures." Indeed, in a statement that sounds as if it were taken directly from the pages of *Nineteen Eighty-Four,* Ong notes that "oral societies live very much in a present which keeps itself in equilibrium or homeostasis by sloughing off memories which no longer have present relevance."[73] Ong's theoretical discourse converges in even more significant ways with Orwell's figurative one in the former's description of the "secondary orality" of the new mass media technologies, primarily radio and television. These, Ong argues, have begun to displace the four-century-long hegemony of print literacy:

> Secondary orality is both remarkably like and remarkably unlike primary orality. Like primary orality, secondary orality has generated a strong group sense, for listening to spoken words forms hearers into a group, a true audience, just as reading written or printed texts turns individuals in on themselves. But secondary orality generates a sense for groups immeasurably larger than those of primary oral culture—McLuhan's "global village." Moreover, before writing, oral folk were group-minded because no feasible alternative had presented itself. In our age of secondary orality, we are group-minded self-consciously and programmatically.[74]

Again, this description sounds very much like the vision in Orwell's text of the social collectivity "serialized," to use Jean-Paul Sartre's term for this process, in front of the telescreen.[75] However, what in Ong's work represents the utopian promise of some new, as yet unimaginable human collective existence, appears in *Nineteen Eighty-Four* as an unmitigated catastrophe. The current double crisis so powerfully narrated in Orwell's work—the crisis of Western modernity and English national cultural autonomy—is presented as the product of a continued process of social and cultural modernization, here embodied in the displacement of print literacy, and the modes of cognition it enabled, by emerging technological media. Crucially, as Benedict Anderson reminds us, these two crises are deeply interwoven, as print literacy at once played a central role in the consolidation of modern rationality, the autonomous subject, and the "imagined community" of the nation-state.[76]

Thus, Orwell, with his nostalgic remembrance of the world made possible by print literacy and national culture, stands as a kind of inverted Ong who, much like Claude Lévi-Strauss in *Tristes Tropiques*, looks back to the experience of collective unity and the unalienated closeness to the "human lifeworld" of oral cultures with something bordering on reverence (a form of life, he argues, that may reappear with secondary orality). However, if the hegemony of print literacy has begun to be displaced in Orwell's present, this does not mean that the "literate" intellectuals must vanish as well. Indeed, as we shall see shortly, *Nineteen Eighty-Four* offers a deeply influential figuration of the role of these intellectuals in the new postnational, postliterate culture they are now forced to inhabit.

"IF THERE WAS HOPE . . .": ORWELL'S INTELLECTUALS

But what of those who have never had this "happiness" to lose in the first place? The Oceanic culture industry that Orwell presents in *Nineteen Eighty-Four* is directed primarily at the members of the Outer Party, the "middle" of the three classes in Oceania, and that fraction of the population responsible for the intellectual labor of this complex bureaucratic society. For the far larger lower class, the "proles"—comprising 85 percent of the superstate's population of three hundred million—the distracting effects of "bad" Oceanic culture are unnecessary: "Heavy physical work, the care of home and children, petty quarrels with neighbors, films, football, beer, and, above all, gambling filled up the horizons of their minds. . . . The great majority of proles did not even have telescreens in their homes" (*NEF*, 61–62).

The differences between these two forms of cultural production, replicated in the division of the Ministry of Truth into two separate units, is perhaps best exemplified by the prole's passion for the lottery: "The Lottery, with its weekly pay-out of enormous prizes, was the one public event to which the proles paid serious attention. It was probable that there were some millions of proles for whom the Lottery was the principal if not the only reason for remaining alive. It was their delight, their folly, their anodyne, their intellectual stimulant" (*NEF*, 73). Cruelly, the Lottery, as with the pornography packaged by the Ministry of Truth, promises a happiness that in fact will never be delivered: "Winston . . . was aware (indeed everyone in the Party was aware) that the prizes were largely imaginary. Only small sums were actually paid out, the winners of the big prizes being nonexistent persons" (*NEF*, 73). However, the proles lack even the "memory" of happiness, for they are the group who, by definition, always already have been the victims of the most suffering: "It is an abiding characteristic of the Low that they are too much crushed by drudgery to be more than intermittently conscious of anything outside their daily lives. . . . From the point of view of the Low, no historic change has ever meant much more than a change in the name of their masters" (*NEF*, 166–67). Thus, when provided with only the most ephemeral image of happiness, the Proles are satisfied; the more complex distractions required of the culture produced for the Outer Party are finally unnecessary.

With this point, we arrive at the important question of the role of the figure of the proles in the narrative schema of *Nineteen Eighty-Four*. Many readers conclude that Winston Smith's famous declaration of faith was one shared by Orwell himself: "But if there was hope, it lay in the proles" (*NEF*, 73). Winston Smith later reconfirms this hope in a crescendo of romantic revelation only moments before his arrest by the Thought Police. Observing a prole woman working "outside" their domestic sanctuary, Winston Smith reflects:

> The woman down there had no mind, she had only strong arms, a warm heart, and a fertile belly. . . . And the people under the sky were also very much the same—everywhere, all over the world, hundreds or thousands of millions of people just like this, people ignorant of one another's existence, held apart by walls of hatred and lies, and yet almost exactly the same— people who had never learned to think but were storing up in their hearts and bellies and muscles the power that would one day overturn the world. If there was hope, it lay in the proles! (*NEF*, 181)

This passage nicely summarizes the kinds of populist sentiment that runs throughout Orwell's political and social writings. The prole woman, and the class for which she is the stand-in, represents the only force that might challenge the rule of O'Brien's Inner Party. More precisely, Orwell suggests throughout the narrative that it is their *bodies* that will constitute a significant point of contestation in the new world system.

Julia's rebellion also occurs on the level of her body, and O'Brien's defeat of her involves remaking her body (indeed, un-sexing it) rather than her mind: "He knew now what had changed in her. . . . It was that her waist had grown thicker and, in a surprising way, had stiffened" (*NEF*, 240). This linkage between Julia and the image of the proles also reveals the fundamental dilemma of Orwell's variety of populism. Both figures are treated as if they were only bodies: Julia is "only a rebel from the waist downwards," the washerwoman has "no mind," and the proles "had never learned to think" (*NEF*, 129 and 181). Indeed, the same could be said of every woman that appears in the text, from the washer-

woman to the prole prostitute, Winston Smith's mother, and his ex-wife:
presented as a union of either the maternal or the sterile and the sexu-
ally promiscuous or the frigid, together they form a veritable *combinatoire* of patriarchal assumptions about women as mindless bodies.[77]

However, without the ability to think, there could be no general, as
opposed to individual, challenge to the conditions of the present, for
critical "thinking," as Orwell saw it, was the necessary precondition of
any form of political action. Thus, Winston Smith comes to the paradoxical conclusion that "until they become conscious [the proles] will
never rebel, and until after they have rebelled they cannot become conscious" (*NEF,* 61). And nothing in *Nineteen Eighty-Four* suggests any
way out of this paradox. All we are left with in the end is what Raymond
Williams calls a "stale revolutionary romanticism," a weak challenge indeed to the far more terrible judgment found in Goldstein's book:
"From the proletarians nothing is to be feared. Left to themselves, they
will continue from generation to generation and from century to century, working, breeding, and dying, not only without any impulse to
rebel, but without the power of grasping that the world could be other
than it is" (*NEF,* 173).[78]

The only person who seems to possess this "power of grasping that
the world could be other than it is" is Winston Smith. (O'Brien can do
this as well; but, as we shall see shortly, his knowledge works to quite
different ends). Indeed, Winston Smith and the proles, the critically
aware individual and the unconscious collective body, emerge as inverted images of one another. This is borne out early in the narrative,
when Winston Smith encounters an old man in the prole quarter, and
engages in his sole conversation with a member of this class (excluding,
of course, his often one-sided discussions with the gender-prole Julia[79]).
Recognizing the old man as one of the few people remaining alive who
might remember what conditions were like before the ascendancy of the
Party, Winston Smith asks him to compare life then to that in the present. When the old man can recite only scattered personal memories and
reflections, Winston despairs, "The old man's memory was nothing but
a rubbish heap of details. One could question him all day without getting any real information" (*NEF,* 78). This leads him to conclude,

> Within twenty years at the most, he reflected, the huge and simple question,
> "Was life better before the Revolution than it is now?" would have ceased
> once and for all to be answerable. But in effect it was unanswerable even
> now, since the few scattered survivors from the ancient world were incapable
> of comparing one age with another. They remembered a million useless

things . . . but all the relevant facts were outside the range of their vision. They were like the ant, which can see small objects but not large ones. And when memory failed and written records were falsified—when that happened, the claim of the Party to have improved the conditions of human life had got to be accepted, because there did not exist, and never again could exist, any standard against which it could be tested. (*NEF,* 79)

To think is thus to be able to totalize, to assemble a dispersed field of observations and facts into a "relevant" whole, in order to make comparative evaluations of the validity of one arrangement of society over and against another. Ironically, this despairing assessment of the prole's incapacity to engage in this kind of critical activity, either on an individual or collective level, comes only moments before Winston Smith discovers the crystal paperweight in Charrington's shop, the very thing whose quite different kind of "uselessness" provides, as we saw earlier, the "standard" by which such a judgment could be made. Critical consciousness, the ability to draw these kinds of evaluations, thus emerges in Orwell's narrative less as the product of one's social position or life experience than as a form of aesthetic cognition. The double-pronged threat of contemporary social reality—that of sanctioned state violence and a global culture industry—is directed not against a critical collective consciousness that seems to have always already vanished from the world, but against those individuals, like Winston Smith, who possess this kind of aesthetic insight. They alone stand as a barrier to the creation of a new absolute hegemony.

This vision of the intimate connection between individual autonomy, aesthetic capacity, and critical consciousness cannot but be at least in part the expression of a certain class position, in this case, that of Orwell himself. The reason for this despairing portrayal of the political potential of a working-class collectivity finds its origins in a number of factors in Orwell's own intellectual biography, most immediately in his growing disillusionment with what he took to be the apathy of the working class after its failure to take what he saw as the ideal opportunity of the early days of the Second World War to create an authentically English socialist movement.[80] Moreover, as Williams and others suggest, Orwell's elimination of the possibility of political action on the part of the proletariat also signals his final failure to get outside the ideological field of the "lower upper-middle class" of which he was a part: the "administrative middle class of imperialist Britain" who, while not part of the ruling elite, nevertheless shared their values and attitudes, and who thus remained uneasy, not unlike the members of the upper-middle-class Bloomsbury group (whom Orwell despised), about the potential threat represented by a politically active working class.[81] The displacement of an active, class-based politics by a passive, individual, aesthetic-critical cognition can also be read as an expression of this same cluster of beliefs and anxieties.

However, Orwell's portrayal of the "disappearance" in England of a working-class consciousness also indicates something of a significant historical development in its own right: the attenuation of older forms of national class struggle, within the first world at least, that came hand-in-hand with the institution of a widespread capital-labor *détente* and the emergence of new extensive forms of consumerism—processes that together form that key aspect of late modernist culture and society that has been described as the regime of high "Fordism."[82] Indeed, as early as *The Lion and the Unicorn,* Orwell had already suggested that the outlook of the "old-style 'proletarian'" was rapidly vanishing as a new system of "indeterminate social class" emerged:

> In Slough, Dagenham, Barnet, Letchworth, Hayes—everywhere, indeed, on the outskirts of great towns—the old pattern is gradually changing into something new. In those vast new wildernesses of glass and brick the sharp distinctions of the older kind of town, with its slums and mansions, or of the country, with its manor-houses and squalid cottages, no longer exist. There are wide gradations of income, but it is the same kind of life that is being lived at different levels, in labour-saving flats or council houses, along the concrete roads and in the naked democracy of the swimming-pools. It is a rather restless, cultureless life, centering round tinned food, *Picture Post,* the radio and the internal combustion engine. It is a civilisation in which children grow up with an intimate knowledge of magnetoes and in complete ignorance of the Bible. To that civilisation belong the people who are most at home in and most definitely *of* the modern world, the technicians and the higher-paid skilled workers, the airmen and their mechanics, the radio experts, film producers, popular journalists and industrial chemists. They are the indeterminate stratum at which the older class distinctions are beginning to break down.[83]

Both in terms of group identity and culture then, "class" in England has apparently given way to a formation of a new, undifferentiated "mass," a vision of the contemporary social world that would become increasingly prevalent in the postwar intellectual scenes of both England and the United States. However, in the more immediate narrative context of *Nineteen Eighty-Four,* the figure of working-class consciousness becomes something like Winston Smith's other aestheticized objects, one of those nostalgically longed-for aspects of a now-vanished cultural past.

By imagining the disappearance of this older kind of collective consciousness, Orwell also was able to dispense with what would have been for him an even more uncomfortable development in the interwar and postwar worlds: the emergence of an organized, indigenous decolonization effort. While Orwell had remained throughout his intellectual career an unabashed critic of the policies of the British empire and a vocal supporter of those who wished to end direct imperial rule, he was also consistently critical of indigenous independence movements, especially the nationalist organizations of Ireland and India.[84] "In the age of the tank and the bombing plane," he had written in the early days of the Second World War, "backward agricultural countries like India and the African colonies can no more be independent than can a cat or a dog." As he sees it, the proper way to end empire would be to replace direct administration with a system of alliances and partnerships, a system ultimately shaped by the dictates and interests of the former imperial core.[85] Those indigenous independence movements that called for the immediate and total withdrawal of Britain from their lands thus challenged any such imagined orderly restructuring of the globe, and consequently threatened England's own cultural identity as well.[86] However, in the world of *Nineteen Eighty-Four* no such movement can exist, for the entire population of the former colonial territories is presented as nothing more than an extension of the unconscious laboring body of the three global powers: "All of the disputed territories . . . contain a bottomless reserve of cheap labor. Whichever power controls equatorial Africa, or the countries of the Middle East, or Southern India, or the Indonesian Archipelago, disposes also of the bodies of scores of hundreds of millions of ill-paid and hard-working coolies" (*NEF*, 154–55). By imagining that the "coolie" peoples were bodies even more passive than the Oceanic proletariat (an image that goes back at least to Joseph Conrad's *Lord Jim*), Orwell could effectively wipe away any threat they might represent—with the unfortunate consequence of perpetrating the older belief that those who had until then ruled the colonial territory were precisely those who could still decide what was best for them.

This double neutralization of the place of the proles, in both their first- and third-world avatars, likewise is registered in the absence in the narrative of any examination of the deep economic structure, or, to use an old Marxist metaphor, the materialist "base" of the new social order.[87] Such an absence is most immediately apparent in the omission of a detailed treatment of the two administrative units, the Ministries of Plenty and Peace, whose respective domains are those of economic production and warfare. Indeed, the only "appearance" of these two institutions occurs in Goldstein's book, where they are shown to be locked into a self-consuming loop: "The primary aim of modern warfare . . . is to use up the products of the machine without raising the general standard of living" (*NEF,* 155). By not further mapping these institutions, Orwell again elides the place of the proles, for they are, after all, both the material producers of this society and the most aggrieved victims of interstate violence. Equally significant, the absence in the narrative of any treatment of production and warfare (or interstate relations) transforms the representation of the world of Oceania into another kind of aestheticized object, a cultural system that has been cut loose from its material moorings.

This "detotalization," the freeing up of the cultural sphere from its material contexts, then enables one final and quite different project of utopian figuration to take place in *Nineteen Eighty-Four.* We have already seen such a project marked out in shorthand form in Orwell's extended description of the interior spaces of the Ministry of Truth: as with the gradually widening narrative perspective that enables us to situate Winston Smith within the massive, complex totality of the Ministry of Truth, so too the narrative action of *Nineteen Eighty-Four* provides Orwell with the means to "think" his own place as an intellectual and as a writer in an emerging global cultural system. By imagining this cultural sphere as one from which have disappeared any vestiges of determining social, economic, or political structures, Orwell eliminates in advance the possibility of something like a cognitive standpoint emerging in relationship to one's always already structurally positioned subjectivity, be it in terms of class, or gender, or the imperial world system. All the intellectuals in *Nineteen Eighty-Four* are in this sense "free-floating," figures for roles one might inhabit as one chooses. The mapping of what Orwell understood these choices to be then becomes one of the most significant and influential of the "utopian" programs of *Nineteen Eighty-Four.*

While this narrative fiction of intellectual choice enabled Orwell to dispense with what had been the nagging problem of the social determinations of his own views, it more significantly provided him with the opportunity to confront and finally exorcise what he saw as two dangerous potential roles for the intellectual, those he labels the extremes of "passivity" and "commitment." Orwell earlier explicated each of these possibilities in his great essay on the intellectual and literary history of the twentieth century, "Inside the Whale." In this essay, Orwell argues

that the contemporary writer-intellectual is caught in an apparently ir-
resolvable bind. On the one hand, he can become "not only individualistic but completely passive," adopting "the viewpoint of a man who believes the world-process to be outside his control and who in any case
hardly wishes to control it." In summarizing the intellectual outlook of
this position, Orwell creates one of the more famous of all the images in
his work: "Seemingly there is nothing left but quietism—robbing reality of its terrors by simply submitting to it. Get inside the whale—or
rather, admit you are inside the whale (for you *are,* of course). Give
yourself over to the world-process, stop fighting against it or pretending
that you control it: simply accept it, endure it, record it."[88]

Over and against this first position—exemplified for Orwell by such
younger writers as Henry Miller—stands the frightening possibility of
political commitment, of deploying one's intellectual talents in the service of one of the larger collective movements whose declared purpose
is the transformation of society. However, according to Orwell, the literary history of the thirties had already shown the disastrous consequences of this latter choice: "For any writer who accepts or partially
accepts the discipline of a political party is sooner or later faced with
the alternative: toe the line, or shut up." In either case, the writer-
intellectual must give up the possibility of producing art, for "Literature
as we know it is an individual thing, demanding mental honesty and a
minimum of censorship." Because literature is by definition "a product
of the free mind, of the autonomous individual," in a political climate
hostile to both freedom and autonomy such an "art" will soon cease to
exist.[89]

The figures of the passive and committed intellectual appear again in
different forms in *Nineteen Eighty-Four.* The former is represented by
what we might call the "normal" intellectual worker in the culture industry of the Ministry of Truth: those who possess the skills to produce
"culture," but who nevertheless willingly embrace the established norms
of Oceanic society.[90] The character who most readily exemplifies this
position is Winston Smith's friend and colleague Syme, one of the authors of the eleventh edition of the Newspeak dictionary. While Syme
can wax eloquent about the complex theoretical principles underlying
the invention of a new language, a language ironically designed to prevent this very kind of eloquence, he nevertheless becomes "venomously
orthodox," and even celebratory, when it comes to describing the horrific realities of Oceanic life: "He would talk with a disagreeable gloat-

ing satisfaction of helicopter raids on enemy villages, the trial and confession of thought-criminals, the executions in the cellars of the Ministry
of Love" (*NEF*, 44).

The opposite extreme, that of the even more dangerous, committed
political intellectual—for even the orthodox Syme, precisely because
"He sees too clearly and speaks too plainly," ends up in the Thought Police's prison (*NEF*, 47)—finds its embodiment, of course, in the figure of
O'Brien. As the perfect authoritarian, he stands as the model of the committed political intellectual produced by this century:

> The heirs of the French, English, and American revolutions had partly be-
> lieved their own phrases about the rights of man, freedom of speech, equal-
> ity before the law, and the like, and had even allowed their conduct to be
> influenced by them to some extent. But by the fourth decade of the twentieth
> century all the main currents of political thought were authoritarian. The
> earthly paradise had been discredited at exactly the moment when it became
> realizable. Every new political theory, by what ever name it called itself, led
> back to hierarchy and regimentation. (*NEF*, 168)

Crucially for Orwell, these committed intellectuals, irrespective of their
political beliefs, make impossible the utopian transformation of the social order. Through a complete transvaluation of older modern values,
"enlightened and progressive" thought has come to mean the toleration
and defense of such practices as "imprisonment without trial, the use of
war prisoners as slaves, public executions, torture to extract confes-
sions, the use of hostages and the deportation of whole populations"
(*NEF*, 169). In the figure of O'Brien, we thus see the final falling away
of any remaining ideological veils that might occlude the "true" purposes of this kind of intellectual. For the political intellectual, all
thought is directed toward a single end: the establishment and maintenance of a seemingly unbreakable domination.

However, with the essay "Why I Write," published a short time before *Nineteen Eighty-Four,* Orwell imagines a third option between
these two extremes: that of the intellectual who can "make political
writing into an art."[91] This synthetic possibility would involve creating
an engaged art, but one generated from a position of political autonomy,
a way of critically analyzing the modern world later summed up by
Trilling in the phrase, "the Politics of Truth."[92] As the very title of Orwell's essay suggests, this position is very much tied up with the technologies of print literacy. Thus, a figure of this intellectual appears in
Nineteen Eighty-Four in the "writer" Winston Smith, author of the diary that is coextensive with portions of the book *Nineteen Eighty-Four.*

(The diary form itself is, we should keep in mind, one of the most significant inventions of print literate cultures, the vehicle for both the development of the modern novel and of the interiorized, autonomous subjectivity so much celebrated in Orwell's text.) The very act of writing itself then comes to stand as a figure of resistance—if finally not opposition—to the new, mass-mediated present.

Orwell shows this figure also to be inescapably part of the massive institutional structure of the Oceanic culture industry. Orwell's description of the totalizing nature of mass media culture eliminates even the possibility of a place outside this system, the kinds of outsides that Zamyatin represents in the Possible Worlds of the Mephi and the infinite revolution, and that Le Guin represents in those of Anarres and the Hainish. Indeed, what seems to have vanished altogether in Orwell's vision is the horizon of radical difference, or historical possibility—the very "location" in modern society that was occupied, as I have argued throughout this book, by expressions of the narrative utopia form. Imagining a utopia is part of the work of the committed intellectual, and in recoiling from such a commitment, Orwell rejects even the effort of envisioning a different kind of future.

Still, it would be incorrect to say that the possibility of difference has disappeared completely from Orwell's text, for it is precisely such an Otherness with which Winston Smith makes contact in his experience of the aestheticized emblems of a lost happiness. His aesthetic sensibility, his writerly activities, and his ability to gain access to the past and thereby generate a stable normative position from which he can critically evaluate the present, make Winston Smith himself a short-lived locus of nonsynchronous heterogeneity within the horizonless world of Oceania: that is, he is an analogon of an authentic modernity in a place where it appears no longer to exist.[93] Orwell's message, then, is that in a world where the strong form of "revolution" has become an option to be avoided at all costs—for it was this desire for radical change that gave rise to the committed political intellectual in the first place—critical "rebellions," what Gianni Vattimo describes as "weak" interventions, are the only form of political action left viable.[94]

If for Winston Smith there is a certain attraction in becoming a passive intellectual—at one point we learn that "Winston's greatest pleasure in life was in his work," because in its difficulties and intricacies he could "lose" his anxiety-ridden "self" (NEF, 39)—it is the position of the committed intellectual that represents for him a far greater and more dangerous temptation. That O'Brien was meant to represent another

potential intellectual avatar of Winston Smith and, by extension, of Orwell himself is borne out in Winston Smith's reflections on the experience of reading Goldstein's book: "In a sense it told him nothing that
was new, but that was part of the attraction. It said what he would have
said, if it had been possible for him to set his scattered thoughts in order. It was the product of a mind similar to his own, but enormously
more powerful, more systematic, less fear-ridden. The best books, he
perceived, are those that tell you what you know already" (*NEF,* 165).
What distinguishes both Winston Smith and O'Brien from cultural
workers such as Syme is their shared capacity for critical thought. However, unlike Winston, O'Brien can possess such a knowledge and at once
utterly sublimate its truth-content to a will-to-power. Paradoxically but
not contradictorily, for O'Brien two plus two can at once equal and not
equal four: "The stars can be near or distant, according as we needed
them. Do you suppose our mathematicians are unequal to that?" (*NEF,*
219). The nightmarish possibility of such a "lunatic dislocation" of the
mind—what Orwell took to be required by the exigencies of contemporary political action—precipitated one of his most infamous and influential coinages: *doublethink,* the ability simultaneously to acknowledge and deny any system of truths (*NEF,* 176–77).

If O'Brien resembles Winston Smith in a shared capacity for critical
reflection, Winston becomes more and more like O'Brien as he appears
to near his goal of actively challenging the Party. Winston's initial contact with O'Brien comes about because of his desire to join the mythical
revolutionary organization, the Brotherhood (a play, perhaps, on London's Brotherhood of Man). When O'Brien informs him that such an organization does exist, Winston declares his willingness to perform any
action they might require of him:

> "You are prepared to cheat, to forge, to blackmail, to corrupt the minds
> of children, to distribute habit-forming drugs, to encourage prostitution, to
> disseminate venereal diseases—to do anything which is likely to cause de-
> moralization and weaken the power of the Party?"
> "Yes."
> "If, for example, it would somehow serve our interests to throw sulphuric
> acid in a child's face—are you prepared to do that?"
> "Yes." (*NEF,* 142)

Later, in the Ministry of Love torture chamber, O'Brien asks Winston if
"you consider yourself morally superior to us, with our lies and our cruelty?" When Winston answers in the affirmative, O'Brien simply plays
back a recording of this earlier exchange (*NEF,* 222–23). The grim les-

son in all of this is clear: the political represents the negation of the ethical conception of good or evil because any form of overt political action
ultimately degenerates into an expression of an instrumental will-to-
power. The only way the intellectual can avoid such a danger is by maintaining his autonomy from any political group formation. Ironically
then, Winston Smith's utter abnegation at O'Brien's hands is also a form
of "salvation": in being rendered completely powerless, Winston Smith
is redeemed once and for all from the temptations of political power.[95]

In the same way, the narration of Winston Smith's thwarted efforts to
overcome the terrible reality of his present—a failure shared, without
exception, by every one of Orwell's fictional protagonists (a fact that
also suggests another link between Gissing's naturalist fictions and Orwell's work)[96]—becomes a kind of victory for Orwell himself. Indeed,
the demonstration of the inevitability of the will-to-power in every political intellectual and the danger of what might occur if these agents are
left unchallenged was to be one of the single most powerful lessons for
many of the early readers of *Nineteen Eighty-Four*. The text was thus a
significant boon to efforts in both Great Britain and the United States to
discredit any form of intellectual political activism and, in fact, to rethink the whole role of the public intellectual.[97] Of course, with the
then-recent and thoroughgoing delegitimation of fascism throughout
the Western world, "political" had become simply a code word for socialism. Thus, ironically, and perhaps contrary to his desires, Orwell the
"socialist" thinker created one of the most powerful tools for the systematic assault on socialism, while the persona of the "good" intellectual that he presents both in *Nineteen Eighty-Four* and in the example
of his own life—the autonomous thinker, the "man who tells the truth,"
celebrated by Trilling—served as a model for what Thomas Hill Schaub
calls the new "conservative liberal" intellectuals who, like Trilling himself, played such an important role in shaping the American intellectual
climate of the postwar moment.[98] Thus, even more ironically, in the
hands of these conservative liberal intellectuals, the anti-Americanism of
Orwell's critique, if not its assault on mass and media cultures, vanishes
as well, as his work becomes a crucial tool in their forging of a conception of an "authentic" American national and intellectual character, one
where, as Orwell had already put it in 1941, "Patriotism and intelligence will . . . come together again."[99]

Such a notion of intellectual autonomy is itself illusory, the effect of
a self-willed negation of the shaping material contexts of any intellectual
position. Indeed, the restoration of these contexts has been an important

part of recent efforts to rethink the postwar intellectual scene.[100] Nevertheless, it was an illusion that was as necessary as that required by the other conservative "utopian" figure that inhabits *Nineteen Eighty-Four*: the aestheticized image of the English nation-state. On the one hand, this utopian image of the English past permitted a retreat from a present in which a variety of forces threatened England's national cultural identity, "the breeding barbarian or the economic power" that Wells had warned of in *A Modern Utopia* more than four decades earlier.[101] On the other hand, however, Orwell could create such an image only by ignoring the material conditions that enabled such a possibility of "happiness": those realities of class and imperial exploitation that Orwell the socialist and critic of empire rightly found unbearable.[102] "England" in the late nineteenth and early twentieth centuries was no longer simply a nation-state among nation-states: it was the hegemonic center of the capitalist world system, what Giovanni Arrighi calls "the third (British) systemic cycle of accumulation." According to Arrighi, this cycle comes to a close in the years of the Second World War, as the United States displaces Great Britain from its hegemonic position, whereupon a fourth systemic cycle begins. Orwell's anxieties about the "end" of English autonomy can also be understood as a response to this larger historical shift.[103]

Disappearing in the present and never having really existed in the past, Orwell's figure of the autonomous nation becomes as "utopian" as the one we first saw in Thomas More's founding work in the genre, a figure whose historical "actuality" exists only inside the text. The real nightmare in *Nineteen Eighty-Four* thus turns out to be nothing less than history itself—the history of the future, to be sure, but also the painful histories of the English past and its place in a new global present. Through *Nineteen Eighty-Four*, Orwell attempted to escape all of these histories; but his very success in doing so ironically assured that he would play a central role in shaping the intellectual history of the coming decades. That is, if Orwell wished to forget history, history finally could not forget him.

Notes

INTRODUCTION

1. Raymond Williams, *The Long Revolution,* rev. ed. (New York: Harper & Row, 1966), ix. Epigraph from page x.

2. See the exhibition catalogues, *Utopie: La quête de la société idéale en Occident,* ed. Lyman Tower Sargent and Roland Schaer (Paris: Bibliothèque nationale de France/Fayard, 2000); and *Utopia: The Search for the Ideal Society in the Western World,* ed. Roland Schaer, Gregory Claeys, and Lyman Tower Sargent (New York: New York Public Library/Oxford University Press, 2000).

3. Etienne Balibar, "The Nation Form: History and Ideology," in Etienne Balibar and Immanuel Wallerstein, *Race, Nation, Class: Ambiguous Identities,* trans. Chris Turner (New York: Verso, 1991), 93.

4. Benedict Anderson, *Imagined Communities: Reflections on the Origin and Spread of Nationalism,* rev. ed. (New York: Verso, 1991). Also see the collection of essays, including a number of responses to Anderson's work, in Gopal Balakrishnan, ed., *Mapping the Nation* (New York: Verso, 1996).

5. Liah Greenfeld, *Nationalism: Five Roads to Modernity* (Cambridge: Harvard University Press, 1992), 18.

6. For example, Krishan Kumar prefaces his study of narrative utopias with the following disclaimer: "On the whole, utopias are not very distinguished for their aesthetic qualities as works of literature. . . . What is interesting about them, and what I have concentrated on, is the nature and quality of their ideas about individuals and societies. It is chiefly as contributions to social thought that I consider them." *Utopia and Anti-Utopia in Modern Times* (Oxford: Basil Blackwell, 1987), ix. Gary Saul Morson also discusses some earlier failures to

take account of the "literary" dimensions of these works in *The Boundaries of Genre: Dostoevsky's Diary of a Writer and the Traditions of Literary Utopia* (Austin: University of Texas Press, 1981), 67–74.

7. Roland Barthes, *Sade, Fourier, Loyola*, trans. Richard Howard (New York: Hill and Wang, 1976), 36.

8. For the distinction between the representational strategies of the map and those of the itinerary, see Michel de Certeau, *The Practice of Everyday Life*, trans. Steven Randall (Berkeley: University of California Press, 1984), 118–22. For a marvelous phenomenological history, showing how traveler's itineraries, among other practices, constitute space, see Paul Carter, *The Road to Botany Bay: An Essay in Spatial History* (London: Faber and Faber, 1987). The notion of "spatial history" developed by Carter is, as I suggest in the next chapter, similar in many ways to the processes at work in forms like the narrative utopia.

9. Beginning from his vital research into the urban, geographical, and spatial dimensions of capitalist modernity, David Harvey has recently come to some similar insights about the dialectical, "spatiotemporal" dimensions of utopias. See *Spaces of Hope* (Berkeley: University of California Press, 2000).

10. For two important discussions of these roots, see Robert C. Elliott, *The Shape of Utopia: Studies in a Literary Genre* (Chicago: University of Chicago Press, 1970); and Lyman Tower Sargent, "The Three Faces of Utopianism Revisited," *Utopian Studies* 5, no. 1 (1994): 1–37.

11. Slavoj Žižek, *Tarrying with the Negative: Kant, Hegel, and the Critique of Ideology* (Durham, NC: Duke University Press, 1993), 201–2.

12. Walter J. Ong, *Orality and Literacy: Technologizing of the Word* (London: Methuen, 1982), 136.

1. GENRE AND THE SPATIAL HISTORIES OF MODERNITY

1. Terry Eagleton, foreword to *The Emergence of Social Space: Rimbaud and the Paris Commune*, by Kristin Ross (Minneapolis: University of Minnesota Press, 1988), xiii.

2. For a discussion of the "modernness" of expressions of racism, see Etienne Balibar, "Is There a Neo-Racism?" as well as the other essays collected in Etienne Balibar and Immanuel Wallerstein, *Race, Nation, Class: Ambiguous Identities*, trans. Chris Turner (New York: Verso, 1992).

3. Nicos Poulantzas, *Political Power and Social Classes*, ed. and trans. Timothy O'Hagan (New York: Verso, 1978), especially 190–94.

4. See Slavoj Žižek, *Looking Awry: An Introduction to Jacques Lacan through Popular Culture* (Cambridge: MIT Press, 1991), 154–69; and his further elaboration on these ideas in *Tarrying with the Negative: Kant, Hegel, and the Critique of Ideology* (Durham, NC: Duke University Press, 1993), especially 200–237.

5. See Antonio Gramsci, *Selections from the Prison Notebooks*, ed. and trans. Quintin Hoare and Geoffrey Nowell Smith (New York: International Publishers, 1971).

6. Michel Foucault, "What Is an Author?" in *The Foucault Reader,* ed. Paul Rabinow (New York: Pantheon Books, 1984), 101–20.

7. Gary Saul Morson, *The Boundaries of Genre: Dostoevsky's* Diary of a Writer *and the Traditions of Literary Utopia* (Austin: University of Texas Press, 1981), 79.

8. Stephen Greenblatt notes, "*Utopia* appears almost timeless, reaching effortlessly back to Plato and forward to our own age, but its existence is nonetheless the result of a daring grasp of a single propitious moment: five years earlier or later More could not have written it." See *Renaissance Self-Fashioning: From More to Shakespeare* (Chicago: University of Chicago Press, 1980), 58.

9. V. N. Volosinov, *Marxism and the Philosophy of Language,* trans. Ladislav Matejka and I. R. Titunik (Cambridge: Harvard University Press, 1986), 67.

10. Ibid., 62 and 84.

11. Ibid., 82.

12. See Hubert Dreyfus, *Being-in-the-World: A Commentary on Heidegger's* Being and Time, *Division I* (Cambridge: MIT Press, 1991), 15.

13. For a persuasive account of the more general ways any "narrative version" is situated in a particular horizon of aims and interests, see Barbara Herrnstein Smith, "Narrative Versions, Narrative Theories," in *On Narrative,* ed. W. J. T. Mitchell (Chicago: University of Chicago Press, 1981), 209–32.

14. Mikhail M. Bakhtin, *The Dialogic Imagination,* trans. Caryl Emerson and Michael Holquist (Austin: University of Texas Press, 1981). Morson too notes the way such works enter into "intra-" and "inter-generic" dialogues; see *Boundaries of Genre,* 79. Peter Ruppert argues for an Iserian reader-response approach to narrative utopias, emphasizing how the open-ended meaning of the narrative utopia emerges through the dialectic between the mutually interdependent reader and text. He maintains that "we discover the essential value of these texts, not in any properties in the texts themselves, but in their startling and provocative effects on readers," and later concludes, "Literary utopias, in other words, are effectively open because they underline the importance of our own performance—our own decision-making role—as readers"; see *Reader in a Strange Land: The Activity of Reading Literary Utopias* (Athens: University of Georgia Press, 1986), 24 and 51. Although Ruppert's readings of individual texts are insightful, his approach runs the risk of transforming both the text and the reader into idealized abstractions.

Darko Suvin, in an important essay on the "pragmatics" of utopian studies, offers a useful emendation to such a model by stressing the concrete sociohistorical situatedness of both sides of this dialectic, before proceeding to outline how "the interaction between the fictional elements presented in a text and the presuppositions of the implied reader induces in the readers" the realization of one specific form of what he describes as utopia's "Possible Worlds"; see "Locus, Horizon, and Orientation: The Concept of Possible Worlds as a Key to Utopian Studies," *Utopian Studies* 1, no. 2 (1990), 78. (Originally published in a modified version in *Utopia e Modernita: Teorie e prassi utopiche nell'eta moderna e postmoderna,* ed. Giuseppa Saccaro Del Buffa and Arthur O. Lewis [Rome: Gangemi editore, 1989], 47–65.) I will draw upon Suvin's insights in this essay again in my discussion of Zamyatin's *We* in Chapter 5. For a more general discussion of the ways in which all cultural artifacts serve as a series of notations enacted by an active reader-consumer, see Raymond Williams's influential, "Base and Superstructure in Marxist Cultural Theory," in *Problems in Materialism and Culture* (New York: Verso, 1980), 31–49, as well as the further expansion of these ideas in *Marxism and Literature* (Oxford: Oxford University Press, 1977).

One of the most interesting and significant ongoing explorations of various, concretely situated readers of utopian fictions is to be found in Kenneth M. Roemer's forthcoming *Utopian Audiences: How Readers Place Nowhere*. For some of Roemer's already published research, focusing in particular on various readers of Bellamy's *Looking Backward* (including the author himself), see his "Perceptual Origins: Preparing American Readers to See Utopian Fiction," in *Utopian Thought in American Literature*, ed. Arno Heller, et al. (Tübingen: Gunter-Narr Verlag, 1988), 7–24; "Getting 'Nowhere' Beyond Stasis: A Critique, a Method, and a Case," in *Looking Backward, 1988–1888: Essays on Edward Bellamy*, ed. Daphne Patai (Amherst: University of Massachusetts Press, 1988), 126–46; "The Literary Domestication of Utopia: There's No *Looking Backward* without Uncle Tom and Uncle True," *American Transcendental Quarterly* n.s., 3, no. 1 (1989): 101–22; and "Utopian Literature, Empowering Students, and Gender Awareness," *Science-Fiction Studies* 23 (1996): 393–405. For related discussions, see Lee Cullen Khanna, "The Text as Tactic: *Looking Backward* and the Power of the Word," in *Looking Backward, 1988–1888*, ed. Patai, 37–50; and Francis Robert Shor, "The Ideological Matrix of Reform in Late-Nineteenth-Century America: Reading Bellamy's *Looking Backward*," in *Utopianism and Radicalism in a Reforming America, 1888–1918* (Westport, CT: Greenwood Press, 1997), 3–25. Finally, Tom Moylan discusses the similar reading protocols of science fiction in *Scraps of the Untainted Sky: Science Fiction, Utopia, Dystopia* (Boulder, CO: Westview Press, 2001).

15. See for example, Brook Thomas, *The New Historicism and Other Old-Fashioned Topics* (Princeton, NJ: Princeton University Press, 1991); the essays collected in *The New Historicism Reader*, ed. H. Aram Veeser (New York: Routledge, 1989); Carolyn Porter, "Are We Being Historical Yet?" *South Atlantic Quarterly* 87, no. 4 (1988): 743–86; Richard Halpern, *The Poetics of Primitive Accumulation: English Renaissance Culture and the Genealogy of Capital* (Ithaca, NY: Cornell University Press, 1991), 1–15; and a number of the interesting commentaries published in issues of *Arizona Quarterly* in the early 1990s.

16. Fredric Jameson, *Postmodernism, or the Cultural Logic of Late Capitalism* (Durham, NC: Duke University Press, 1990), 188.

17. Ibid., 190.

18. Greenblatt discusses the influence of Geertz's *The Interpretation of Cultures* on the development of the New Historicism in Catherine Gallagher and Stephen Greenblatt, *Practicing New Historicism* (Chicago: University of Chicago Press, 2000), 20–30. Also see Greenblatt's founding text in this critical genre, *Renaissance Self-Fashioning*, 3–4.

19. For important readings of the emergence of this spatial concept of cul-

ture in early-nineteenth-century French architectural debates, see Paul Rabinow, *French Modern: Norms and Forms in the Social Environment* (Cambridge: MIT Press, 1989), 53–57; and in the context of the early-twentieth-century U.S., see Susan Hegeman, *Patterns for America: Modernism and the Concept of Culture* (Princeton, NJ: Princeton University Press, 1999). For other recent challenges to the closed anthropological concept of culture, see Arjun Appadurai, *Modernity at Large: Cultural Dimensions of Globalization* (Minneapolis: University of Minnesota Press, 1996); and James Clifford, *Routes: Travel and Translation in the Late Twentieth Century* (Cambridge: Harvard University Press, 1997).

20. Gallagher and Greenblatt, *Practicing New Historicism*, 7. Also see Raymond Williams, "Culture," in *Keywords: A Vocabulary of Culture and Society*, rev. ed. (New York: Oxford University Press, 1985), 87–93.

21. Halpern, *Poetics of Primitive Accumulation*, 12.

22. David E. Johnson, "Voice, the New Historicism, and the Americas," *Arizona Quarterly* 48, no. 2 (1992): 88.

23. Benedict Anderson, *Imagined Communities: Reflections on the Origin and Spread of Nationalism*, rev. ed. (New York: Verso, 1991), 80–81, 135.

24. Fredric Jameson, *The Political Unconscious: Narrative as a Socially Symbolic Act* (Ithaca, NY: Cornell University Press, 1981), 105.

25. Neil Smith, "Homeless/Global: Scaling Places," in *Mapping the Futures: Local Cultures, Global Change*, ed. Jon Bird et al. (New York: Routledge, 1993), 87–119.

26. Ibid., 114.

27. See Williams, "Base and Superstructure in Marxist Cultural Theory," 38. The model of the generic text I am developing here also draws upon the multidimensional Marxist allegorical hermeneutic that Jameson describes in *The Political Unconscious*, chap. 1.

28. Porter describes the New Historical practice as one of "analogy"; see "Are We Being Historical Yet?" 761–62. For a critique of Lukács's practice of homology, see Williams, *Marxism and Literature*, 101–7.

29. The growing literature on the topic of modernity is immense. In addition to those dealt with more extensively in the following pages, a few recent discussions that I found especially useful include Marshall Berman, *All That Is Solid Melts Into Air: The Experience of Modernity* (New York: Penguin Books, 1988); Jürgen Habermas, *The Philosophical Discourse of Modernity: Twelve Lectures*, trans. Frederick Lawrence (Cambridge: MIT Press, 1987); David Harvey, *The Condition of Postmodernity* (Oxford: Basil Blackwell, 1989); Henri Lefebvre, *Introduction to Modernity: Twelve Preludes, September 1959– May 1961*, trans. John Moore (New York: Verso, 1995); Nancy Armstrong and Leonard Tennenhouse, *The Imaginary Puritan: Literature, Intellectual Labor, and the Origins of Personal Life* (Berkeley: University of California Press, 1992); and Giovanni Arrighi, *The Long Twentieth Century: Money, Power, and the Origins of Our Times* (New York: Verso, 1994). Habermas has recently taken up the question of the role of the nation-state in modernity in the essays collected in the section, "Is There a Future for the Nation-State?" in *The Inclusion of the Other: Studies in Political Theory*, ed. Ciaran Cronin and Pablo De Greiff (Cambridge: MIT Press, 1998), 103–53.

30. Walter Benjamin, "Theses on the Philosophy of History," in *Illumina-tions: Essays and Reflections,* trans. Harry Zohn (New York: Schocken Books, 1969), 253–64. Also see Jacques Derrida's recent development of this concept in *Specters of Marx: The State of the Debt, the Work of Mourning, and the New International,* trans. Peggy Kamuf (New York: Routledge, 1994).

31. See Fredric Jameson, "The Vanishing Mediator; or, Max Weber as Storyteller," in *The Ideologies of Theory: Essays, 1971–1986,* vol. 2 (Minneapolis: University of Minnesota Press, 1988), 3–34; as well as the further development of this concept in Žižek, *Tarrying with the Negative,* 226–32.

32. Michel Foucault, *Power/Knowledge: Selected Interviews and Other Writings, 1972–1977* (New York: Pantheon Books, 1980), 70.

33. Edward. W. Soja, *Postmodern Geographies: The Reassertion of Space in Critical Social Theory* (New York: Verso, 1989). This is the first volume of Soja's trilogy, which now also includes *Thirdspace: Journeys to Los Angeles and Other Real-and-Imagined Places* (Oxford: Blackwell, 1996); and *Postmetropolis: Critical Studies of Cities and Regions* (Oxford: Blackwell, 2000).

34. Paul Carter, *The Road to Botany Bay: An Essay in Spatial History* (London: Faber and Faber, 1987), xvi.

35. Soja, *Postmodern Geographies,* 31–35.

36. Susan Stewart, *On Longing: Narratives of the Miniature, the Gigantic, the Souvenir, the Collection* (Durham, NC: Duke University Press, 1993), 4. Similarly, see Erich Auerbach, *Mimesis: The Representation of Reality in Western Literature,* trans. Willard R. Trask (Princeton, NJ: Princeton University Press, 1968).

37. For the texts of this classic debate, see Leon Edel and Gordon N. Ray, ed., *Henry James and H. G. Wells: A Record of Their Friendship, Their Debate on the Art of Fiction, and Their Quarrel* (Urbana: University of Illinois Press, 1958). I discuss the particulars of this debate, as well as another attempt, which will be of special interest to readers of this book, to "prove" definitively the superiority of Jamesian novelistic fiction—David Bleich's *Utopia: The Psychology of a Cultural Fantasy* (Ann Arbor, MI: UMI Research Press, 1984), in my essay, "World, History, and the Romance: Looking Back on the Wells-James Debate" (forthcoming).

One issue I cannot adequately address in this book is the complex relationship between the narrative utopia, the novel, and the later genre of science fiction. As the briefest of a prolegomenon, I would suggest a double horizon for any future investigation. On the one hand, Wells's own name for his founding work in the genre points toward a fundamental continuity between utopia and science fiction, both expressions of the particular narrative dynamics of the prose romance. Thus, Jameson observes that, whereas science fiction eschews the pleasures and demands of canonical forms of literature, those of complex psychological portraits of "realistic" characters and "well-formed plots," within these works "the collective adventure accordingly becomes less that of a character (individual or collective) than that of a planet, a climate, a weather, and a system of landscapes—in short, a map. We thus need to explore the proposition that the distinctiveness of SF as a genre has less to do with time (history, past, future) than with space"; see "Science Fiction as a Spatial Genre: Generic Discontinuities and the Problem of Figuration in Vonda McIntyre's *The Exile Waiting*," *Science Fiction Studies* 14 (1987): 58. Conversely, science fiction should be understood as a dialectical third term, a "negation of a negation" that conserves aspects of both the "thesis," romance, and the "antithesis," the novel, particularly in the latter's expression, dominant in the late nineteenth century, of naturalism. For two different views of the relationship between utopia, the novel, and science fiction, see Darko Suvin, "Science Fiction and Utopian Fiction: Degrees of Kinship," in *Positions and Presuppositions in Science Fiction* (Kent, OH: Kent State University Press, 1988), 33–43; and Carl Freedman, *Critical Theory and Science Fiction* (Hanover, NH: Wesleyan University Press, 2000), 62–86.

38. For an important, more general discussion of the circularity of many traditional models of literary evaluation, see Barbara Herrnstein Smith, *Contingencies of Value: Alternative Perspectives for Critical Theory* (Cambridge: Harvard University Press, 1988).

39. Jameson, *Political Unconscious*, 112.

40. For an important study of the role of the novel in producing the modern self and individual psychology, see Nancy Armstrong, *Desire and Domestic Fiction: A Political History of the Novel* (New York: Oxford University Press, 1987).

41. Dreyfus, *Being-in-the-World*, 134.

42. Jameson, *Political Unconscious*, 112.

43. Henri Lefebvre, *La production de l'espace,* 3ème Édition (Paris: Éditiones Anthropos, 1986), 35–36; *The Production of Space,* trans. Donald Nicholson-Smith (Oxford: Blackwell, 1991), 26–27.

44. For Lefebvre's discussion of his deployment of Marx's "regressive-progressive" approach and the status of the "concrete abstraction," see *Production of Space,* 65–67 and 99–105. Michael McKeon addresses similar issues in his introduction to *The Origins of the English Novel, 1600–1740* (Baltimore: Johns Hopkins University Press, 1987), 15–22.

45. Lefebvre, *Production of Space,* 33–46, especially 38–39; *La production de l'espace,* 43–57, especially 42–43. For clarity's sake, I have modified Nicholson-Smith's translation of Lefebvre's "*les espaces de représentation,*" which he renders as "representational space." For another rich deployment of this three-part schema, see Soja, *Thirdspace.* Soja's efforts to transform sociology and geography by making them more attentive to issues of "lived" space parallel my attempts to make a literary and cultural studies already sensitive to the lived more attuned to questions of "perceived" and, especially, "conceived" spaces (the latter, conversely, already at the center of Soja's discipline). In both cases, our common goal is one of disciplinary "de-reification."

46. See for example, Lefebvre, *The Survival of Capitalism: Reproduction of the Relations of Production,* trans. Frank Bryant (New York: St. Martin's Press, 1973), 59–68. For some reconsiderations of the status of science in Marxism, see Darko Suvin, "'Utopian' and 'Scientific': Two Attributes for Socialism from Engels," *Minnesota Review* 6 (1976): 59–70; Fredric Jameson, "Science Versus Ideology," *Humanities in Society* 6, no. 2 (1983): 283–302; and Stephen A. Resnick and Richard D. Wolff, *Knowledge and Class: A Marxian Critique of Political Economy* (Chicago: University of Chicago Press, 1987).

47. Lefebvre, *Production of Space,* 38. In a reading of the space produced by the home of architect Frank Gehry, a discussion which very much seems to draw implicitly upon and set into play in extremely productive ways Lefebvre's original abstract formulations, Jameson writes, "At any rate, the very concept of space here demonstrates its supremely mediatory function, in the way in which its aesthetic formulation begins at once to entail cognitive consequences on the one hand and sociopolitical consequences on the other;" and later, "The problem, then, which the Gehry house tries to think is the relationship between that abstract knowledge and conviction or belief about the superstate and the existential daily life of people in their traditional rooms and tract houses"; see *Postmodernism,* 104 and 128.

48. Harvey, *Condition of Postmodernity,* 218–21. For Harvey's earlier treatment of Lefebvre's schema, see his *The Urban Experience* (Baltimore: Johns Hopkins University Press, 1989), 261–62.

49. Jacques Lacan, "The Mirror Stage as Formative of the Function of the I," in *Ecrits: A Selection,* trans. Alan Sheridan (New York: W. W. Norton, 1977), 1–7; and Lefebvre, "Spatial Architectonics," in *Production of Space,* chap. 3, 169–228. However, in order to avoid too hastily assimilating the work of one to the other, see Lefebvre's own deployment of the figure of the mirror in the constitution of space (181–88). Jameson too suggests the link between the Lacanian Imaginary and the concerns of phenomenology in his "Imaginary and Symbolic in Lacan," in *Ideologies of Theory,* 1: 101.

50. Louis Althusser, "Ideology and Ideological State Apparatuses (Notes toward an Investigation)," in *Lenin and Philosophy and Other Essays,* trans. Ben Brewster (New York: Monthly Review Press, 1971), 162.

51. Jameson, "Imaginary and Symbolic in Lacan," 104. For a powerful deployment of the Lacanian concept of the Real in cultural criticism, see the work of Žižek, beginning with *Looking Awry.*

52. Lefebvre, *Production of Space,* 3.

53. Jameson, *Postmodernism,* 51. Jameson himself makes the link between his notion of cognitive mapping and the Lacanian Symbolic a few pages later (53–54). This too enables us more fully to grasp Jameson's later claim, "This is surely the most crucial terrain of ideological struggle today, which has migrated from concepts to representations" (321). I explore the relationship between Jameson's and Lefebvre's work in "Horizons, Figures, and Machines: The Dialectic of Utopia in the Work of Fredric Jameson," *Utopian Studies* 9, no. 2 (1998): 58–73.

54. This is contrary to Harvey, who locates utopias under spaces of representation; see *Condition of Postmodernity,* 221. However, now also see David Harvey, *Spaces of Hope* (Berkeley: University of California Press, 2000).

55. Lefebvre, *Production of Space,* 39.

56. Roland Barthes, *Sade, Fourier, Loyola,* trans. Richard Miller (New York: Hill and Wang, 1976), 37.

57. Carter, *Road to Botany Bay,* xxii.

58. Ibid. For another useful discussion contrasting the representational strategies of the map and the itinerary, see Michel de Certeau, *The Practice of Everyday Life,* trans. Steven Randall (Berkeley: University of California Press,

1984), 118–22. For a discussion of the crucial differences between "totality" and the praxis of "totalization," see Jameson, *Postmodernism*, 331–33.

59. Suvin, "Science Fiction and Utopian Fiction," 39.

60. Tom Moylan, *Demand the Impossible: Science Fiction and the Utopian Imagination* (New York: Methuen, 1986), 37.

61. Fredric Jameson, *The Seeds of Time* (New York: Columbia University Press, 1994), 56–59. Williams similarly points out that in the utopian mode of "willed social transformation," and especially in its particular subset of "technological transformation," "technology need not be only a marvelous new energy source, or some industrial resource of that kind, but can be also a new set of laws, new abstract property relations, indeed precisely new *social machinery*"; see Williams, "Utopia and Science Fiction," in *Problems in Materialism and Culture*, 202–3.

62. Marc Angenot, "The Absent Paradigm: An Introduction to the Semiotics of Science Fiction," *Science Fiction Studies* 6 (1979): 9–19. For the relationship of utopia and science fiction, also see note 37 above. One of the fundamental points Dreyfus makes in his discussion of Heidegger's *Being and Time* is that such paradigms, or worlds, are always largely "absent" to *Dasein* in its everyday activities. It is the goal, as I will suggest momentarily, of estranging forms like narrative utopias, science fiction, and literary modernism to make us aware of precisely this fact.

63. Barthes, *Sade, Fourier, Loyola*, 105.

64. Louis Marin, *Utopics: The Semiological Play of Textual Spaces*, trans. Robert A. Vollrath (Atlantic Highlands, NJ: Humanities Press International, 1984).

65. Suvin, "Science Fiction and Utopian Fiction," 35. Additionally, see his discussion in *Metamorphoses of Science Fiction: On the Poetics and History of a Literary Genre* (New Haven, CT: Yale University Press, 1979), 37–62. This estrangement effect is also what E. P. Thompson means in his description of utopia's role as "the education of desire"; see *William Morris: Romantic to Revolutionary*, rev. ed. (New York: Pantheon Books, 1977), 791.

66. Paul Ricoeur, *Lectures on Ideology and Utopia*, ed. George H. Taylor (New York: Columbia University Press, 1986), 16.

67. Ibid., 16–17.

68. For some English-language introductions to Bloch's work, see Fredric Jameson, *Marxism and Form* (Princeton, NJ: Princeton University Press, 1971), 116–59; Ruth Levitas, *The Concept of Utopia* (Syracuse, NY: Syracuse University Press, 1990), 83–105; Martin Jay, *Marxism and Totality: The Adventures of a Concept from Lukács to Habermas* (Berkeley: University of California Press, 1984), 174–95; Jack Zipes, introduction to *The Utopian Function of Art and Literature*, by Ernst Bloch (Cambridge: MIT Press, 1988), xi–xliii; the special section on Bloch in *Utopian Studies* 1, no. 2 (1990): 1–69; and the volume of essays edited by Jamie Owen Daniel and Tom Moylan, *Not Yet: Reconsidering Ernst Bloch* (New York: Verso, 1997).

69. Bloch, *Utopian Function of Art and Literature*, 38; italics in the original.

70. For Derrida's classic discussion of supplementarity, see *Of Grammatology*, trans. Gayatri Chakravorty Spivak (Baltimore: Johns Hopkins University

Press, 1976); and for the concept of the specter, especially as it relates to Benjamin's messianic history, see Derrida, *Specters of Marx.*

71. "Lukács's thought takes for granted a closed and integrated reality that does indeed exclude the subjectivity of idealism, but not the seamless 'totality' which has always thriven best in idealist systems, including those of classical German philosophy." See Ernst Bloch, "Discussing Expressionism," in *Aesthetics and Politics,* ed. Ronald Taylor (New York: Verso, 1980), 22. Also see Bloch's 1923 review, "Aktualität und Utopie zu Lukács' *Geschichte und Klassenbewusstsein,*" in *Philosophische Aufsätze zur Objektiven Phantasie* (Frankfurt am Main: Suhrkamp Verlag, 1969), 598–621.

72. Ernst Bloch, *The Principle of Hope,* trans. Neville Plaice, Stephen Plaice, and Paul Knight (Oxford: Basil Blackwell, 1986), 223.

73. See Ernst Bloch, "Nonsynchronism and the Obligations to Its Dialectics," *New German Critique* 11 (1977): 22–38. Also see Williams's related and influential concept of the emergent and residual, developed in *Marxism and Literature,* 121–27.

74. Jameson, *Marxism and Form,* 128.

75. Northrop Frye, "Varieties of Literary Utopias," in *Utopias and Utopian Thought,* ed. Frank E. Manuel (Boston: Houghton Mifflin, 1966), 38.

76. For a discussion of the productive role of memory in Marcuse's thought, see Jameson, *Marxism and Form,* 106–16; and Jay, *Marxism and Totality,* 220–40.

77. Ernst Bloch, *Natural Law and Human Dignity,* trans. Dennis J. Schmidt (Cambridge: MIT Press, 1987), 192. I take up this aspect of Bloch's work again in Chapter 5. Michel Foucault, late in his life, would similarly argue that "the problem is not to recover our 'lost' identity, to free our imprisoned nature, our deepest truth; but instead, the problem is to move towards something radically Other. The center, then, seems still to be found in Marx's phrase: man produces man. It's all in how you look at it. For me, what must be produced is not man identical to himself, exactly as nature would have designed him or according to his essence; on the contrary, we must produce something that doesn't yet exist and about which we cannot know how and what it will be"; see Foucault, *Remarks on Marx,* trans. R. James Goldstein and James Cascaito (New York: Semiotext(e), 1991), 121.

78. Bloch, *Principle of Hope,* 197. Again, see Derrida, *Specters of Marx.*

79. Bloch, *Principle of Hope,* 203.

80. Edward S. Casey, *The Fate of Place: A Philosophical History* (Berkeley: University of California Press, 1997), 255.

81. For a more elaborate discussion of the existential dilemmas raised by the film, see my "'A Nightmare on the Brain of the Living': Messianic Historicity, Alienations, and *Independence Day,*" *Rethinking Marxism* 12, no. 1 (2000): 65–86.

82. Moving from Heidegger's work, Dreyfus comes to a similar conclusion: "When we try to imagine another reality, as in science fiction, we can only imagine our world changed in certain details"; see *Being-in-the-World,* 91. A related issue is at work in Derrida's commentary on Foucault's *Madness and Civiliza-*

tion; see "Cogito and the History of Madness," in *Writing and Difference,* trans. Alan Bass (Chicago: University of Chicago Press, 1978), 31–63.

83. Jameson, *Marxism and Form,* 145–46. For two related discussions, see Kenneth Burke's analysis of what he calls the "bureaucratization of the imaginative," in *Attitudes toward History,* 3d ed. (Berkeley: University of California Press, 1984), 225–29; and, in a more specific vein, Arthur Lipow, *Authoritarian Socialism in America: Edward Bellamy and the Nationalist Movement* (Berkeley: University of California Press, 1982).

84. Bloch, *Principle of Hope,* 223. Lewis Mumford comes to much the same conclusions in his distinction between "utopias of escape" and "utopias of reconstruction." Mumford writes, "One of these functions is escape or compensation; it seeks an immediate release from the difficulties or frustrations of our lot. The other attempts to provide a condition for our release in the future. . . . The first leaves the external world the way it is; the second seeks to change it so that one may have intercourse with it on one's own terms. In one we build castles in the air; in the other we consult a surveyor and an architect and a mason and proceed to build a house which meets our essential needs. . . . The second type of utopia may likewise be colored by primitive desires and wishes; but these desires and wishes have come to reckon with the world in which they seek realization. . . . If the first utopia leads backward into the utopian's ego, the second leads outward—outward into the world." See Lewis Mumford, *The Story of Utopias* (New York: Viking, 1962), 15 and 21. And, finally, see Robert C. Elliott, *The Shape of Utopia: Studies in a Literary Genre* (Chicago: University of Chicago Press, 1970), especially 85.

85. Ruth Levitas, "Educated Hope: Ernst Bloch on Abstract and Concrete Utopia," *Utopian Studies* 1, no. 2 (1990): 15; reprinted in *Not Yet,* ed. Daniel and Moylan, 65–79. Levitas also argues for the centrality of this distinction in Bloch's work.

86. Although for an insightful discussion of Bloch's tendency at times to ignore his own lessons, and hypostatize concrete utopia in party orthodoxy, see Moylan, "Bloch against Bloch: The Theological Reception of *Das Prinzip Hoffnung* and the Liberation of the Utopian Function," *Utopian Studies* 1, no. 2 (1990): 27–51; reprinted in *Not Yet,* ed. Daniel and Moylan, 96–121.

87. Edward Bellamy, *Looking Backward, 2000–1887* (New York: New American Library, 1960), 121.

88. My reading of this passage draws upon Bloch's "A Philosophical View of the Novel of the Artist," in *Utopian Function of Art and Literature,* 265–77.

89. Fredric Jameson, "Progress versus Utopia; or Can We Imagine the Future?" in *Art after Modernism: Rethinking Representation,* ed. Brian Wallis (New York: New Museum of Contemporary Art, 1984), 247. For a further elaboration of this point, see Jameson, *Postmodernism,* 208–9.

90. Ricoeur, *Lectures,* 312–14.

91. Lefebvre, *Introduction to Modernity,* 105.

92. Anthony Giddens, *The Consequences of Modernity* (Stanford, CA: Stanford University Press, 1990), 37. Ricoeur offers his own discussion of the "modernness" of this sense of historical time in "Towards a Hermeneutics of Histor-

ical Consciousness," in *Time and Narrative,* vol. 3, trans. Kathleen Blamey and David Pellaver (Chicago: University of Chicago Press, 1988), 207–40.

93. Giddens, *Consequences of Modernity,* 38–39.

94. Karl Mannheim, *Ideology and Utopia: An Introduction to the Sociology of Knowledge,* trans. Louis Wirth and Edward Shils (New York: Harcourt Brace Jovanovich, 1936), 226. This event also produced its own utopian plan: Hans Hergot's *On the New Transformation of a Christian Life* (1527). For a brief discussion of this text, see Peter Blickle, *The Revolution of 1525,* trans. Thomas A. Brady and H. C. Erik Midelfort (Baltimore: Johns Hopkins University Press, 1981), 150–54.

95. Suvin, *Metamorphoses of Science Fiction,* 118. For a discussion of Mercier's work in the context of the broader emerging genre of narratives of the future, see Paul Alkon, *Origins of Futuristic Fiction* (Athens: University of Georgia Press, 1987).

96. Georg Lukács, *The Historical Novel,* trans. Hannah and Stanley Mitchell (Lincoln: University of Nebraska Press, 1983), 24. Interestingly, a few pages later, Lukács also notes that "in the works of the great Utopians [Fourier] the periodization of history already transcends the horizon of bourgeois society" (28).

97. Gilles Deleuze and Félix Guattari, *Anti-Oedipus: Capitalism and Schizophrenia,* trans. Robert Hurley, Mark Seem, and Helen R. Lane (Minneapolis: University of Minnesota Press, 1983), 34–35. They develop a related set of concepts in their description of "smooth" and "striated" spaces. See *A Thousand Plateaus: Capitalism and Schizophrenia,* trans. Brian Massumi (Minneapolis: University of Minnesota Press, 1987), 474–500. I briefly invoke this latter couple in Chapter 5. The phrase "norms and forms" is from Rabinow's *French Modern.*

2. *UTOPIA* AND THE BIRTH OF NATIONS

1. Nancy Armstrong and Leonard Tennenhouse, *The Imaginary Puritan: Literature, Intellectual Labor, and the Origins of Personal Life* (Berkeley: University of California Press, 1992).

2. For a critique of the implicit Platonism in much of narrative theory, see Barbara Herrnstein Smith, "Narrative Versions, Narrative Theories," in *On Narrative,* ed. W. J. T. Mitchell (Chicago: University of Chicago Press, 1981), 209–32.

3. Cited in Franco Moretti, *Modern Epic: The World System from Goethe to García Márquez* (New York: Verso, 1996), 188. In the discussion that follows, I draw extensively upon Moretti's theory of literary history developed here and in his earlier "On Literary Evolution," in *Signs Taken for Wonders,* rev. ed. (New York: Verso, 1988), 262–78.

4. Viktor Shklovsky, *Theory of Prose,* trans. Benjamin Sher (Elmwood Park, IL: Dalkey Archive Press, 1990), 20.

5. See for example, J. H. Hexter's introduction to *Utopia,* by Thomas More, ed. Edward Surtz and J. H. Hexter, vol. 4 of *The Yale Edition of the Complete Works of St. Thomas More.* ed. Louis L. Martz (New Haven, CT: Yale Univer-

sity Press, 1965), cliii–clxxix; and Marina Leslie, *Renaissance Utopias and the Problem of History* (Ithaca, NY: Cornell University Press, 1998), 2, where she also lists other genres at work in More's text. Leslie also suggestively expands Rosalie Colie's categories of "the *genera mixta,* or mixed genre" and "inclusionism" to include the Renaissance utopia. Colie develops these categories in *The Resources of Kind: Genre-Theory in the Renaissance,* ed. Barbara K. Lewalski (Berkeley: University of California Press, 1973).

6. Fredric Jameson, *The Political Unconscious: Narrative as a Socially Symbolic Act* (Ithaca, NY: Cornell University Press, 1981), 144. Interestingly, Jameson originally develops this concept in his work on science fiction. See his "Generic Discontinuities in SF: Brian Aldiss's *Starship,*" *Science Fiction Studies* 1, no. 2 (1973): 57–68.

7. Mikhail M. Bakhtin, "From the Prehistory of Novelistic Discourse," in *The Dialogic Imagination,* trans. Caryl Emerson and Michael Holquist (Austin: University of Texas Press, 1981), 41–83; Kenneth M. Roemer, "Contexts and Texts: The Influence of *Looking Backward,*" *The Centennial Review* 27 (1983): 205. Also see Roemer, "The Literary Domestication of Utopia: There's No *Looking Backward* without Uncle Tom and Uncle True," *American Transcendental Quarterly,* n.s., 3, no. 1 (1989): 101–22.

8. C. S. Lewis, *English Literature in the Sixteenth Century* (New York: Oxford University Press, 1954), 169. Cited in David Halpern, *The Poetics of Primitive Accumulation: English Renaissance Culture and the Genealogy of Capital* (Ithaca, NY: Cornell University Press, 1991), 140.

9. More, *Utopia,* vol. 4 of *The Yale Edition of the Complete Works,* 301. Hereafter cited in the text as More.

10. Frank E. Manuel and Fritzie P. Manuel, *Utopian Thought in the Western World* (Oxford: Basil Blackwell, 1979), 146. Also see Michael Holquist, "How to Play Utopia: Some Brief Notes on the Distinctiveness of Utopian Fiction," *Yale French Studies* 41 (1968): 106–23.

11. Stephen Greenblatt, *Renaissance Self-Fashioning from More to Shakespeare* (Chicago: University of Chicago Press, 1980), 24.

12. Ibid., 36. For a related discussion of the seriousness of utopian play, see Richard Helgerson, "Inventing Noplace, or the Power of Negative Thinking," in *The Power of Forms in the English Renaissance,* ed. Stephen Greenblatt (Norman, OK: Pilgrim Books, 1982), 101–21.

13. John M. Perlette, "Irresolution as Solution: Rhetoric and the Unresolved Debate in Book 1 of More's *Utopia,*" *Texas Studies in Literature and Language* 29 (1987): 47.

14. Ibid., 34.

15. Moretti, "On Literary Evolution," 266.

16. Michael McKeon, *The Origins of the English Novel, 1600–1740* (Baltimore: Johns Hopkins University Press, 1987), 20.

17. Gary Saul Morson, *The Boundaries of Genre: Dostoevsky's* Diary of a Writer *and the Traditions of Literary Utopia* (Austin: University of Texas Press, 1981), 75.

18. Slavoj Žižek, *The Sublime Object of Ideology* (New York: Verso, 1989), 61.

19. Darko Suvin, "Science Fiction and Utopian Fiction: Degrees of Kinship," in *Positions and Presuppositions in Science Fiction* (Kent, OH: Kent State University Press, 1988), 38.

20. Amy Boesky, *Founding Fictions: Utopias in Early Modern England* (Athens: University of Georgia Press, 1996). Boesky's astute analysis of the way that the genre of the narrative utopia contributes to the redefinition of national identity in early modern English culture, especially through its representation of the institutional structures through which such an identity is formed, usefully complements the discussion of More's work I offer later in this chapter.

21. The work which did the most to establish the now canonical status of this compositional history is J. H. Hexter's classic, *More's Utopia: The Biography of an Idea* (Princeton, NJ: Princeton University Press, 1952). Indeed, Hexter's work could be taken as a case-book example of what Stanley Fish describes as "an act of persuasion [that] has been so successful that it is no longer regarded as one, and instead has the status of a simple assertion about the world"; see *Doing What Comes Naturally: Change, Rhetoric, and the Practice of Theory in Literary and Legal Studies* (Durham, NC: Duke University Press, 1989), 194. Also see Hexter's influential introduction to the Yale edition of *Utopia,* xv–xxiii.

22. Helgerson offers an intriguing version of this position in terms of the composition of both *Utopia* and the masterpiece of François Rabelais: "In all combined editions, *Gargantua* precedes *Pantagruel.* Something similar happens with *Utopia.* The revolutionary depiction of the ideal anti-state, though written first, now follows an introductory dialogue replete with more moderate suggestions for piecemeal change" ("Inventing Noplace," 115). For another discussion of the relationship between these two texts, see Edwin M. Duval, *The Design of Rabelais's* Pantagruel (New Haven, CT: Yale University Press, 1991).

23. Hexter too views the first book as a kind of rereading of Book 2. See his introduction to *Utopia,* cxi–cxxiii.

24. Thomas More, *The Confutation of Tyndale's Answer,* ed. Louis A. Schuster et al., vol. 8 of *The Yale Edition of the Complete Works of St. Thomas More.* ed. Louis L. Martz (New Haven, CT: Yale University Press, 1973), 179. For other views of More's changing attitudes toward *Utopia,* see Greenblatt, *Renaissance Self-Fashioning,* 58–64; and Leslie, *Renaissance Utopias,* 80.

25. The use of the text by Thomas Müntzer and the other rebel leaders is cited in Manuel and Manuel, *Utopian Thought,* 136.

26. See for example the discussions of Marin's work in Greenblatt, *Renaissance Self-Fashioning,* 23–24; Halpern, *Poetics of Primitive Accumulation,* 137–40; and Christopher Kendrick, "More's Utopia and Uneven Development," *boundary 2* 13, no. 2–3 (1985): 237–40. For other useful overviews of Marin's project, see Fredric Jameson, "Of Islands and Trenches: Neutralization and the Production of Utopian Discourse," in *The Ideologies of Theory: Essays, 1971–1986,* vol. 2 (Minneapolis: University of Minnesota Press, 1988), 75–101; Eugene D. Hill, "The Place of the Future: Louis Marin and his *Utopiques,*" *Science Fiction Studies* 9 (1982): 167–79; and Peter Ruppert, *Reader in a Strange Land: The Activity of Reading Literary Utopias* (Athens: University of Georgia Press, 1986), 81–89.

27. Louis Marin, *Utopiques: Jeux d'espaces* (Paris: Les Éditions de Minuit, 1973), 9; *Utopics: The Semiological Play of Textual Spaces,* trans. Robert A. Vollrath (Atlantic Highlands, NJ: Humanities Press International, 1984), xiii. All subsequent citations will be in the text; where I modify the translation, I indicate so by also providing page numbers from the original.

28. Louis Marin, "Frontiers of Utopia: Past and Present," *Critical Inquiry* 19, no. 3 (Spring, 1993): 404. For a discussion of the importance of Greimas's work to Marin's critical project, see Jameson, "Of Islands and Trenches," 74–75.

29. Classic representatives of each of these still-influential readings are as follows: R. W. Chambers, *Thomas More* (London: Jonathan Cape, 1953) for the medieval monastic *Utopia;* and Karl Kautsky, *Thomas More and His* Utopia (New York: International Publishers, 1927) for the communist. Arthur E. Morgan in his *Nowhere Was Somewhere* (Chapel Hill: University of North Carolina Press, 1946), claims that More's Utopia was not fictitious, but rather based on a description of the Incan Empire relayed to him by a real-world Raphael Hythlodaeus. More recently, Victor N. Baptiste suggests that More in writing *Utopia* drew on Bartolome de las Casas's description of the island of Cuba; see *Bartolome de las Casas and Thomas More's* Utopia: *Connections and Similarities* (Culver City, CA: Labyrinthos, 1990). Lorainne Stobbart traces the parallels between More's portrayal of Utopia and early descriptions of Mayan civilization in *Utopia Fact or Fiction? The Evidence from the Americas* (Wolfboro Falls, NH: Alan Sutton Publishing, 1992).

30. See, respectively, *Utopics,* 42–48; 99–110; and 115–16.

31. Jameson, "Of Islands and Trenches," 82–84. Also see the interesting, related discussion of the role of negativity in *Utopia,* and especially the way it distinguishes the new genre from older fictions of the Golden Age, in Helgerson, "Inventing Noplace."

32. Claude Lévi-Strauss, *Structural Anthropology,* trans. Claire Jacobson and Brooke Grundfest Schoepf (New York: Basic Books, 1963), 229.

33. For an illuminating discussion of the "discovery" of history by the Renaissance humanists, see Thomas Greene, *The Light in Troy: Imitation and Discovery in Renaissance Poetry* (New Haven, CT: Yale University Press, 1982). And for a subtle, recent discussion of the exploration of history within early Modern English narrative utopias, see Leslie, *Renaissance Utopias.*

34. For a related discussion, see Marc Angenot, "The Absent Paradigm: An Introduction to the Semiotics of Science Fiction," *Science Fiction Studies* 6 (1979): 9–19.

35. For another brilliant discussion of figuration, primarily as a medieval Christian practice, see Erich Auerbach, "Figura," in *Scenes from the Drama of European Literature: Six Essays,* trans. Ralph Mannheim (New York: Meridian Books, 1959), 11–76; and especially his distinction between the "concrete" historical and pedagogical dimensions of figural interpretations and the more abstract spiritual qualities of allegorical readings on 54–56 and 73–74.

36. It may be useful for the reader to see the homologies between some of the theoretical discourses we have touched on thus far:

Lefebvre:	spatial practice	representations of space	spaces of representation
Lefebvre:	perceived	conceived	lived
Lacan:	Real	Symbolic	Imaginary
Althusser:	Science		Ideology
Jameson:	Theory	Cognitive Mapping	Ideology
Barthes:	Critique	Semiosis	Mimesis (Mythology)
Carter:	Imperial History	Spatial/Symbolic History	Imitative History
Marin:	Theory	Utopic Figure	Ideology/Myth

37. Louis Marin, "Disneyland: A Degenerate Utopia," *Glyph,* no. 1 (1977): 52. This essay also contains a shortened version of *Utopiques,* chap. 12.

38. Similarly, Marin later writes, "Utopia is the infinite *potentia* of historical figures: it is this infinite, this 'work,' this *potentia* that the Greek negation *ou* allows to be understood as a prefix to the name *topos.* Utopia is the plural figure of the infinite work of the limit or frontier or difference in history" ("Frontiers of Utopia," 413).

39. In an important related discussion, Terry Eagleton has suggested that when we "horizontalize" the conventionally vertical base-superstructure metaphor, "The 'base' might then emerge as the future: that is to say, that which is *still to be done* in any process of revolutionary political change"; see "Base and Superstructure in Raymond Williams," in *Raymond Williams: Critical Perspectives,* ed. Eagleton (Boston: Northeastern University Press, 1989), 175.

40. Also see Henri Lefebvre's instructive comments on the concept of "mode of production" in *The Survival of Capitalism: Reproduction of the Relations of Production,* trans. Frank Bryant (New York: St. Martin's Press, 1973).

41. Lefebvre too had already come to similar conclusions in his call for socialist politics to be involved in the process of transforming "everyday life" in all its dimensions. See his classic, *Critique of Everyday Life,* vol. 1, trans. John Moore (New York: Verso, 1991).

42. Also see Halpern's brilliant extension of Marin's reading of this section of *Utopia* in *Poetics of Primitive Accumulation,* 152–60. Building upon Marin's work, Halpern demonstrates precisely how the critical decoding of the ethico-political and juridical structures of late feudal Europe then enables the figuration of both the mechanisms and ideology of capitalist political economy.

43. Karl Marx, *Capital: A Critique of Political Economy,* vol. 1, trans. Ben Fowkes (New York: Vintage Books, 1977), 873–930. Marx cites *Utopia* on 880 and 893.

44. See the Commentary to *Utopia,* 295.

45. Halpern, *Poetics of Primitive Accumulation,* 155.

46. See Northrop Frye, "Varieties of Literary Utopias," in *Utopias and Utopian Thought,* ed. Frank E. Manuel (Boston: Houghton Mifflin Company, 1966), 25–49.

47. Raymond Williams, "Base and Superstructure in Marxist Cultural Theory," in *Problems in Materialism and Culture* (New York: Verso, 1980), 38.

Also see his *Marxism and Literature* (Oxford: Oxford University Press, 1977), 101–7.

48. See Georg Lukács, *History and Class Consciousness: Studies in Marxist Dialectics*, trans. Rodney Livingstone (Cambridge: MIT Press, 1986); and Theodor Adorno, *Negative Dialectics*, trans. E. B. Ashton (New York: Continuum, 1973).

49. See Henri Lefebvre, *The Production of Space*, trans. Donald Nicholson-Smith (Oxford: Blackwell, 1991); and David Harvey, *The Condition of Postmodernity* (Oxford: Basil Blackwell, 1989). For a useful discussion of Lefebvre's concept of abstract space, see Edward Dimendberg, "Henri Lefebvre on Abstract Space," in *Philosophy and Geography II: The Production of Public Space,* ed. Andrew Light and Jonathan M. Smith (Lanham, MD: Rowman & Littlefield, 1998), 17–47. This volume also contains another essay on Lefebvre by Neil Smith, and a reply to both by Edward S. Casey. Kendrick, in his rich and detailed placing of More's work in relationship to its historical situation, also notes that the "utopian project produces space" ("More's Utopia and Uneven Development," 241).

50. Slavoj Žižek, *Looking Awry: An Introduction to Jacques Lacan through Popular Culture* (Cambridge: MIT Press, 1991), 165.

51. Žižek, *Sublime Object of Ideology,* 21–22.

52. Slavoj Žižek, *Tarrying with the Negative: Kant, Hegel, and the Critique of Ideology* (Durham, NC: Duke University Press, 1993), 209.

53. Etienne Balibar and Immanuel Wallerstein, *Race, Nation, Class: Ambiguous Identities,* trans. Chris Turner (New York: Verso, 1992), 7.

54. Similarly, Gilles Deleuze and Félix Guattari argue, "The immense relative deterritorialization of world capitalism needs to be reterritorialized on the modern national State, which finds an outcome in democracy, the new society of 'brothers,' the capitalist version of the society of friends. As Braudel shows, capitalism started out from city-towns, but these pushed deterritorialization so far that immanent modern States had to temper their madness, to recapture and invest them so as to carry out necessary reterritorializations in the form of new internal limits." See *What Is Philosophy?* trans. Hugh Tomlinson and Graham Burchell (New York: Columbia University Press, 1994), 98.

55. Žižek, *Sublime Object of Ideology,* 162.

56. Anthony Giddens, *The Nation-State and Violence* (Berkeley: University of California Press, 1987), 49–50.

57. See the discussion of the effects of this suspension of the theological in Halpern, *Poetics of Primitive Accumulation,* 297, n. 38. Kendrick offers another detailed reading of the mediatory role of the figuration of Utopian religious practice in "More's Utopia and Uneven Development."

58. I use "imagine" here in the sense given by Benedict Anderson in his ground-breaking work, *Imagined Communities: Reflections on the Origin and Spread of Nationalism,* rev. ed. (New York: Verso, 1991), 5–7. One need not point out that to describe such a bond as "imagined" is also to maintain that it is "real" in the sense that it has concrete and material consequences: indeed, Anderson uses the concept of the imagined here in a manner not unlike Lacan's

Imaginary—or Lefebvre's "spaces of representation"—to refer to the way these relationships are concretely "lived" by a particular embodied subject.

59. For a discussion of the changing definition of the term, see Liah Greenfeld, *Nationalism: Five Roads to Modernity* (Cambridge: Harvard University Press, 1992), 35.

60. See Marin, *Utopics*, chap. 6

61. Halpern, *Poetics of Primitive Accumulation*, 145–46.

62. Žižek, *Looking Awry*, 162.

63. Giddens, *Nation-State and Violence*, 94. Also see Perry Anderson, *Lineages of the Absolutist State* (London: New Left Books, 1974), 113–42; McKeon, *Origins of the English Novel*, 178–82; Ernst H. Kantorowicz, *The King's Two Bodies: A Study in Medieval Political Theology* (Princeton, NJ: Princeton University Press, 1957); and Louis Marin, *Portrait of the King*, trans. Martha M. Houle (Minneapolis: University of Minnesota Press, 1988).

64. Cited in the *Oxford English Dictionary*, vol. 11 (Oxford: Oxford University Press, 1933), 485.

65. Fredric Jameson develops the concept of the "vanishing mediator" in "The Vanishing Mediator; or, Max Weber as Storyteller," in *Ideologies of Theory*, 2: 3–34; also see Žižek's use of the concept in *Tarrying with the Negative*, 226–31.

66. Halpern, *Poetics of Primitive Accumulation*, 173.

67. Fredric Jameson, *The Seeds of Time* (New York: Columbia University Press, 1994), 56–57.

68. Žižek, *Tarrying with the Negative*, 201.

69. For further analysis of the way in which More's work figures a Foucauldian-style disciplinary apparatus, see Greenblatt, *Renaissance Self-Fashioning*, and Boesky, *Founding Fictions*.

70. See the Commentary to *Utopia*, 387, 392, and 393.

71. Jeffrey Knapp, *An Empire Nowhere: England, America, and Literature from* Utopia *to* The Tempest (Berkeley: University of California Press, 1992), 31, 34. Knapp's discussion of the trope of English insularity in Renaissance literature helped clarify my own thoughts on the relationship between the emergence of the discourse of nationalism and the genre of the narrative utopia. And for the role of the "fictional Nobody" in the later consolidation of the novel, see Catherine Gallagher, *Nobody's Story: The Vanishing Acts of Women Writers in the Marketplace, 1670–1820* (Berkeley: University of California Press, 1994).

72. Greenfeld, *Nationalism*, 23. Greenfeld shows that the development of English nationalism, and hence of the very concept of the nation-state, begins in the early sixteenth century, not two centuries later, as often has been maintained.

73. Also see Anderson, *Lineages of the Absolutist State*, 130–37. For an important discussion of how the English national self later becomes transformed into a "British" one, see Linda Colley, *Britons: Forging the Nation, 1707–1783* (New Haven, CT: Yale University Press, 1992).

74. I use the term "world system" here in the sense given by Immanuel Wallerstein, *The Modern World System*, 3 vols. (New York: Academic Press, 1974–1989); *The Capitalist World Economy* (Cambridge: Cambridge University Press, 1979); and *Historical Capitalism* (New York: Verso, 1983). Also see

Giovanni Arrighi, *The Long Twentieth Century: Money, Power, and the Origins of Our Times* (New York: Verso, 1994).

75. Anderson, *Imagined Communities*, 41–49. Leslie discusses the role of the Utopian alphabet in more detail in *Renaissance Utopias*, chap. 3. For an influential discussion of the role played by changes in literacy and the monopoly on education in the formation of modern national communities, see Ernest Gellner, *Nations and Nationalism* (Ithaca, NY: Cornell University Press, 1983). Boesky reads *Utopia* as a figure of the new educational institutions projected onto a national stage, an issue I take up again in Chapter 3. I will return to the issue of national language again in Chapter 4 in my discussion of Alexander Bogdanov's *Red Star.*

76. Greenfeld, *Nationalism*, 30.

77. For three quite different discussions of the role of Christian humanism in *Utopia*, see Hexter's introduction to *Utopia*, lxiv–lxxxi; Kendrick, "More's Utopia and Uneven Development;" and Colin Starnes, *The New Republic: A Commentary on Book I of More's* Utopia *Showing Its Relation to Plato's* Republic (Waterloo, Ontario: Wilfred Laurier University Press, 1990), 91–106.

78. Greenblatt, *Renaissance Self-Fashioning*, 42.

79. Starnes, *New Republic*, 96.

80. Jameson, "Vanishing Mediator," 24. For a further elaboration of the mediatory role of Protestantism in English history, see McKeon, *Origins of the English Novel*, 189–205; and for a fascinating account of the role of Reformation, and particularly Calvinist, confessionalism in establishing the preconditions for the emergence of the modern nation-state, see Philip S. Gorski, "Calvinism and State-Formation in Early Modern Europe," in *State/Culture: State-Formation after the Cultural Turn*, ed. George Steinmetz (Ithaca, NY: Cornell University Press, 1999), 147–81. Gorski points out that the historical originality of the nation-state lies in its fusion of the "extensive" territorial power of tribute-taking empires *and* the "intensive" mobilization and regulation of populations found in the older city states (156–57).

81. For valuable discussions of the rich tradition of English utopian fiction in the seventeenth century, especially in the years surrounding the Civil War and the Interregnum, see Boesky, *Founding Fictions*, and J. C. Davis, *Utopia and the Ideal Society: A Study of English Utopian Writing 1516–1700* (Cambridge: Cambridge University Press, 1981).

82. For a discussion of the relationship between the rise of experimental science and English nationalism, see Greenfeld, *Nationalism*, 78–87; and for a reading of Bacon's texts along these lines, see Boesky, *Founding Fictions*, chap. 3, and Leslie, *Renaissance Utopias*, chap. 4.

83. For the relationship between the sense of "status inconsistency" in the emerging bourgeoisie and the development of the ideologies of nationalism, see Greenfeld, *Nationalism*, 44–51.

84. For a discussion of *Gulliver's Travels* along these lines, see McKeon, *Origins of the English Novel*, 338–56.

85. Armstrong and Tennenhouse contend that the form of the individuated subjectivity instantiated in the modern novel, their case being Samuel Richardson's *Pamela*, first emerges in the genre of the captivity narrative. The captivity

narrative defines such a subject by way of national identity. That is, it is the interior consciousness of her "Englishness" that enables the captive to feel superior to the undifferentiated mass of the Native American: "She is self-reflective and thus a whole world unto herself" (*Imaginary Puritan,* 207). However, this kind of "insularity" also defines the modern nation-state itself, a definition which achieves one of its first formulations, as I have shown above, in the narrative utopia. Also see Franco Moretti, "The Novel, the Nation-State," in *Atlas of the European Novel, 1800–1900* (New York: Verso, 1998), 11–73.

86. For this reason, the operations of utopian neutralization and figuration can also be seen at work in ostensibly non-utopian texts. For example, in my essay, " 'Life as He Would Have It:' The Invention of India in Kipling's *Kim,*" *Cultural Critique* no. 26 (1994): 129–59, I show how Rudyard Kipling neutralizes the threat represented by the rising tide of Indian nationalism, and thereby produces an "otherworldly" figure of the imperial space.

3. WRITING THE NEW AMERICAN (RE)PUBLIC

1. Homi K. Bhabha, "DissemiNation," in *Nation and Narration,* ed. Homi K. Bhabha (New York: Routledge, 1990), 311. Epigraph from 310. Benedict Anderson discusses the complex dialectic of remembering and forgetting in the nineteenth-century historiography of national identity in "Memory and Forgetting," in *Imagined Communities,* rev. ed. (New York: Verso, 1991), 187–206.

2. Ernest Renan, "What Is a Nation?" trans. Martin Thom, in *Nation and Narration,* ed. Bhabha, 19.

3. Edward Bellamy, *Looking Backward, 2000–1887* (New York: New American Library, 1960), xxii. Hereafter cited in the text as *LB.*

4. Discussions of the book's publication history can be found in Sylvia E. Bowman, *The Year 2000: A Critical Biography of Edward Bellamy* (New York: Bookman, 1958), 121; John L. Thomas, *Alternative America* (Cambridge: Belknap, 1983), 262; and James D. Hart, *The Popular Book: A History of America's Literary Taste* (New York: Oxford University Press, 1950), 170–71.

5. Kenneth M. Roemer's still indispensable *The Obsolete Necessity: America in Utopian Writings, 1888–1900* (Kent, OH: Kent State University Press, 1976), along with Jean Pfaelzer, *The Utopian Novel In America, 1886–1896: The Politics of Form* (Pittsburgh, PA: University of Pittsburgh Press, 1984), do the crucial work of excavating the rich tradition of utopian narratives published in the decade following *Looking Backward.*

6. Some discussions of the political program and influences of the Nationalist movement are to be found in John Hope Franklin, "Edward Bellamy and the Nationalist Movement," *New England Quarterly* 11 (December, 1938): 739–72; Thomas, *Alternative America,* especially 266–77 and 310–17; Krishan Kumar, *Utopia and Anti-Utopia in Modern Times* (Oxford: Basil Blackwell, 1987), 132–40; Francis Robert Shor, *Utopianism and Radicalism in a Reforming America, 1888–1918* (Westport, CN: Greenwood Press, 1997), 9–17; and, from a more critical perspective, Arthur Lipow, *Authoritarian Socialism in America: Edward Bellamy and the Nationalist Movement* (Berkeley: University of California Press, 1982).

7. Elizabeth Sadler, "One Book's Influence: Edward Bellamy's *Looking Backward*," *New England Quarterly* 17 (1944): 553.

8. Irving Howe, "The Fiction of Antiutopia," in *Decline of the New* (New York: Harcourt, Brace & World, 1963), 67. In Chapters 5 and 6, I explore the significant differences between these three often-linked narrative utopias.

9. A wonderful overview of postwar science fiction utopias, negative and positive, is available in Lyman Tower Sargent's bibliographical essay, "Eutopias and Dystopias in Science Fiction: 1950–75," in *America as Utopia*, ed. Kenneth Roemer (New York: Burt Franklin, 1981), 347–66.

10. See Kenneth M. Roemer, "Contexts and Texts: The Influence of *Looking Backward*," *The Centennial Review* 27 (1983): 204–23. Another contemporary portrayal of middle-class anxieties about striking workers can be found in William Dean Howells's *A Hazard of New Fortunes* (1890).

11. Jay Martin, *Harvests of Change: American Literature, 1865–1914* (Englewood Cliffs, NJ: Prentice-Hall, 1967), 225.

12. For a discussion of the parable as narrative form located between the sentence-long metaphor and the longer narrative text, and the unique ways it elaborates estranging "possible worlds," see Darko Suvin, *Positions and Presuppositions in Science Fiction* (Kent, OH: Kent State University Press, 1988), 197–204.

13. Another example of this popular late-nineteenth-century image can be found in Henry Adams's *Democracy*, where Madeline Lee realizes, "She had barely escaped being dragged under the wheels of the machine, and so coming to an untimely end"; see *Democracy: An American Novel* (New York: Harmony, 1982), 224–25.

14. Lipow discusses the unstable situation of the contemporary middle class in *Authoritarian Socialism*, chap. 3.

15. Alan Trachtenberg, *The Incorporation of America: Culture and Society in the Gilded Age* (New York: Hill & Wang, 1982), 80.

16. A brief discussion of the Haymarket incident can be found in Thomas, *Alternative America*, 203–7; for a more extended analysis, see Paul Avrich, *The Haymarket Tragedy* (Princeton, NJ: Princeton University Press, 1984), and Dave Roediger and Franklin Rosemont, *The Haymarket Scrapbook* (Chicago: C.H. Kerr, 1986).

17. Bellamy's attitude toward worker's rights would change dramatically over the course of his career. In a *Springfield Union* editorial written a little more than a decade before *Looking Backward*, Bellamy viciously attacked the striking railroad workers of 1877, and argued for the severe punishment of those who destroyed private property. However, with the string of events following the publication of *Looking Backward*—the eventual collapse of the Nationalist movement, William Morris's stinging critique of Bellamy's passive evolutionism, and, the final blow, the bitterly disappointing elections of 1896, in which the conservative McKinley Republicans soundly defeated the coalition of Agrarian Populists, Greenback democrats, and Progressives like Bellamy—he would dramatically revise his earlier position. Thus, in *Equality*, Bellamy compares the heroism of the strikers to that of the founding fathers, and describes the strike itself as "the cry . . . of men made desperate by oppression, to whom existence

through suffering had become of no value. It was the same cry that in varied
form but in one sense has been the watchword of every revolution that has
marked an advance of the race—'Give us liberty, or give us death!' and never
did it ring out with a cause so adequate, or wake the world to an issue so mighty,
as in the mouths of these first rebels against the folly and the tyranny of private
capital"; see *Equality* (New York: D. Appleton and Company, 1897), 210.
Lipow reads this later text as more divided between the "authoritarian utopian
soul of *Looking Backward* and the new, democratic spirit of the emergent socialist movement of the 1890s" (*Authoritarian Socialism,* 288).

18. June 17, 1888. For the full text of the letter, see Joseph Schiffman, "Mutual Indebtedness: Unpublished Letters of Edward Bellamy to William Dean
Howells," *Harvard Library Bulletin* 12, no. 3 (1958): 370–71.

19. Quoted in F. O. Matthiessen, *The James Family* (New York: Alfred A.
Knopf, 1947), 622; and see Frank Lentricchia, "Philosophers of Modernism at
Harvard, circa 1900," in *Modernist Quartet* (Cambridge: Cambridge University
Press, 1994), 25.

20. However, this is not to denigrate the important role played by the immigrant communities in the development of U.S. socialist thought in the later
part of the nineteenth century. See Paul Buhle, *Marxism in the United States,* rev.
ed. (New York: Verso, 1987), 19–57.

21. Robert M. Fogelson, *America's Armories: Architecture, Society, and
Public Order* (Cambridge: Harvard University Press, 1989), 35–37.

22. Richard Slotkin, *The Fatal Environment: The Myth of the Frontier in the
Age of Industrialization, 1800–1890* (New York: Atheneum, 1985), especially
chap. 19.

23. Edward Bellamy, *Edward Bellamy Speaks Again!* (Kansas City: Peerage
Press, 1937), 203.

24. For a detailed analysis of both the progressive intentions and devastating effects of the Dawes Act, see Ronald Takaki, *Iron Cages: Race and Culture
in Nineteenth-Century America* (New York: Oxford University Press, 1990),
188–93; and Francis Paul Prucha, *The Great Father: The United States Government and the American Indians,* abridged ed. (Lincoln: University of Nebraska Press, 1986), 224–28.

25. Northrop Frye, "Varieties of Literary Utopias," in *Utopias and Utopian
Thought,* ed. Frank E. Manuel (Boston: Houghton Mifflin, 1966), 25–49; and
Leo Marx, *The Machine in the Garden* (New York: Oxford University Press,
1964).

26. R. Jackson Wilson, "Experience and Utopia: The Making of Edward
Bellamy's *Looking Backward,*" *Journal of American Studies* 2, no. 7 (1977): 45.

27. See Robert Fishman, *Urban Utopias in the Twentieth Century* (Cambridge: MIT Press, 1982), 32–36.

28. Milton Cantor, "The Backward Look of Bellamy's Socialism," in *Looking Backward, 1988–1888: Essays on Edward Bellamy,* ed. Daphne Patai (Amherst: The University of Massachusetts Press, 1988), 24.

29. See Bellamy, *Equality,* 54.

30. See T. J. Jackson Lears, *No Place of Grace: Antimodernism and the
Transformation of American Culture* (New York: Pantheon, 1981).

31. William Morris, "Looking Backward," in *Political Writings of William Morris*, ed. A. L. Morton (London: Lawrence and Wishart, 1984), 249; and Ernst Bloch, *The Principle of Hope*, trans. Neville Plaice, Stephen Plaice, and Paul Knight (Oxford: Basil Blackwell, 1986), 613.

32. Darko Suvin, *Metamorphoses of Science Fiction* (New Haven: Yale University Press, 1979), 182 and 184.

33. See John Goode, "Gissing, Morris, and English Socialism," *Victorian Studies* 12 (1968): 201–26; E. P. Thompson, *William Morris: Romantic to Revolutionary*, rev. ed. (New York: Pantheon Books, 1977); and Fredric Jameson, *The Political Unconscious: Narrative as a Socially Symbolic Act* (Ithaca, NY: Cornell University Press, 1981), 193. I return to this question again in Chapter 6.

34. Quoted in A. L. Morton, "Utopia Yesterday and Today," in *History and Imagination: Selected Writings of A. L. Morton,* ed. Margot Heinemann and Willie Thompson (London: Lawrence and Wishart, 1990), 82.

35. Lears, *No Place of Grace,* 63.

36. Wilson, in a footnote, writes, "In some ways, it might make sense to call Bellamy's social fantasy 'post-industrial' rather than 'pre-' or 'non-industrial.' . . . But given the explanation of Bellamy's mentality that I am proposing here, the term 'pre-industrial' seems the more useful" ("Experience and Utopia," 49).

37. Ernst Bloch, "Nonsynchronism and the Obligations to Its Dialectics," *New German Critique* 11 (1977): 22–38; and Herbert G. Gutman, *Work, Culture, and Society in Industrializing America: Essays in American Working-Class and Social History* (New York: Alfred A. Knopf, 1976), 13.

38. Trachtenberg, *Incorporation of America,* 130 and 133. Also see William Leach, *Land of Desire: Merchants, Power, and the Rise of a New American Culture* (New York: Vintage Books, 1994). And for a provocative recent reading that shows the relationship between Bellamy's vision of consumerism and the twentieth-century form of globalization known as Americanization, see Thomas Peyser, *Utopia and Cosmopolis: Globalization in the Era of American Literary Realism* (Durham, NC: Duke University Press, 1998), especially chap. 1. Peyser's discussion of Bellamy's "assaults on the local" resonate in some productive ways with my discussion of identity and memory later in this chapter.

39. For a similar reading of these passages, see John F. Kasson, *Civilizing the Machine: Technology and Republican Values in America, 1776–1900* (New York: Penguin, 1977), 198–201.

40. Bellamy's figural transformation of society into a marketplace would become literalized in a little-known utopian narrative written by the Horatio Algeresque Bradford Peck, founder of a large department store in Lewiston, Maine. His narrative was entitled, appropriately enough, *The World a Department Store* (1900). See Wallace Evan Davies, "A Collectivist Experiment Down East: Bradford Peck and the Coöperative Association of America," *New England Quarterly* 20, no. 4 (1947): 471–91; and Roemer, *Obsolete Necessity,* 90–91.

41. Wilson, "Experience and Utopia," 59.

42. Michel Aglietta, in *A Theory of Capitalist Regulation: The U.S. Experience,* trans. David Fernbach (New York: Verso, 1979), shows that even by the

middle of the 1920s nearly 50 percent of the nation's households had still not been integrated into a Fordist consumerism. For a related discussion, see Mike Davis, "'Fordism' in Crisis, a Review of Michel Aglietta's *Regulation et crises: L'experience des Etats-Unis*," *Review* 2, no. 2 (1978): 207–69.

43. Kumar, *Utopia and Anti-Utopia*, 149.

44. Lipow, *Authoritarian Socialism*, 85.

45. In *Equality*, Bellamy lessens the severity of this sentence, without in any way modifying its binary, inside-outside logic. Dr. Leete, echoing the reasoning of the Dawes Act discussed above, now observes, "If an adult, being neither criminal nor insane, should deliberately and fixedly refuse to render his quota of service in any way, either in a chosen occupation or, on failure to choose, in an assigned one, he would be furnished with such a collection of seeds and tools as he might choose and turned loose on a reservation expressly prepared for such persons, corresponding a little perhaps with the reservations set apart for such Indians in your day as were unwilling to accept civilization. There he would be left to work out a better solution of the problem of existence than our society offers, if he could do so" (41). The Controller Mustapha Mond, in Aldous Huxley's *Brave New World*, offers a strikingly similar "escape" to the Savage.

46. Marie Louise Berneri, *Journey through Utopia* (London: Routledge & Kegan Paul, 1950), 243. Lipow offers a provocative left twist on this old critique—in response to those who find in Bellamy's Nationalism an "American version of Marxism," Lipow claims that Bellamy's "authoritarian socialism" in fact "foreshadowed tendencies in modern American statist liberalism." See *Authoritarian Socialism*, especially 96–118. For a sophisticated rereading of the text's bureaucratic vision and its relationship to emerging ideologies of nationalism, see Jonathan Auerbach, "'The Nation Organized': Utopian Impotence in Edward Bellamy's *Looking Backward*," *American Literary History* 6, no. 1 (spring, 1994): 24–47. I return to Auerbach's work below.

47. Walter Benn Michaels, "An American Tragedy, or the Promise of American Life," *Representations* no. 25 (1989): 81. Richard A. Spurgeon Hall also challenges, albeit moving from a very different set of interests, the commonplace assumption that Bellamy's utopia squashes individualism; see "The Religious Ethics of Edward Bellamy and Jonathan Edwards," *Utopian Studies* 8, no. 2 (1997): 13–31.

48. For a useful discussion of the issue of gender in the text, see Sylvia Strauss, "Gender, Class, and Race in Utopia," *Looking Backward, 1988–1888*, ed. Patai, 68–90. Roemer explores some of Bellamy's revisions in *Equality* of these representations in "Getting Nowhere," 141–42; as does Shor in *Utopianism and Radicalism*, 28–32. Also see Nancy Armstrong, *Desire and Domestic Fiction: A Political History of the Novel* (Oxford: Oxford University Press, 1987) for a very different view of eighteenth- and nineteenth-century, middle-class women's power within the apparently subordinate domestic space.

49. Robert H. Wiebe, *The Search for Order, 1877–1920* (New York: Hill and Wang, 1967), 114.

50. See Barbara Ehrenreich and Deirdre English, *For Her Own Good: 150 Years of Experts' Advice to Women* (Garden City, NY: Anchor Books, 1979).

51. Lipow, *Authoritarian Socialism*, 142–43.

52. Raymond Williams, "The Bloomsbury Fraction," in *Problems in Materialism and Culture* (New York: Verso, 1980), 153. This essay provides an important reconsideration of the relationship between groups and classes in the study of culture.

53. For the debate concerning the status of the "professional-managerial class," see Pat Walker, ed., *Between Labor and Capital* (Montreal: Black Rose Books, 1978). And for a powerful discussion of the way literary texts continue this operation of figuring the changing world of the U.S. middle class in the first half of the twentieth century, see Robert Seguin, *Around Quitting Time: Work and Middle-Class Fantasy in American Fiction* (Durham, NC: Duke University Press, 2001).

54. See Robert Fishman, "The Classic Suburb: The Railroad Suburbs of Philadelphia," in *Bourgeois Utopias: The Rise and Fall of Suburbia* (New York: Basic Books, 1987), 134–54.

55. Kenneth M. Roemer traces out Bellamy's deployment of many of the conventions of sentimental fiction in his "The Literary Domestication of Utopia: There's No *Looking Backward* without Uncle Tom and Uncle True," *American Transcendental Quarterly* n.s., 1, 3 (1989): 101–22. Some of the most significant general discussions of these issues are to be found in Ann Douglas, *The Feminization of American Culture* (New York: Alfred A. Knopf, 1977); Jane Tompkins, *Sensational Designs: The Cultural Work of American Fiction, 1790–1860* (New York: Oxford University Press, 1985); and T. J. Jackson Lears, "From Salvation to Self-Realization: Advertising and the Therapeutic Roots of the Consumer Culture, 1880–1930," in *The Culture of Consumption*, ed. Richard Wightman Fox and Lears (New York: Pantheon Books, 1983), 1–38. For an important discussion of the contemporary transformation of the gendering of consumption, see Evan Watkins, *Throwaways: Work Culture and Consumer Education* (Stanford, CA: Stanford University Press, 1993).

56. See Arthur Dudley Vinton, *Looking Further Backward* (Albany, NY: Albany Book Company, 1890), 180, 29, and 183. Hereafter cited in the text as *FB*.

57. For a discussion of Vinton's narrative as a dystopia, see Pfaelzer, *Utopian Novel in America*, 86–92.

58. Peter Fitting, "Utopias Beyond Our Ideals: The Dilemma of Right-Wing Utopias," *Utopian Studies* 2, nos. 1, 2 (1991): 95–109. This doubleness of the text—right-wing, libertarian utopia and dystopian critique—also make Vinton's text an example of the "conservative utopia" that I discuss in more detail in Chapter 6.

59. Herbert Spencer, *Principles of Sociology* (Hamden, CT: Archon Books, 1969), especially 7–31. For a discussion of the impact of Herbert Spencer's work on nineteenth-century American social theory, see Richard Hoffstadter, *Social Darwinism in American Thought* (Boston: Beacon Press, 1975), 31–50.

60. For a now-classic analysis of the epidemic of "nervous illnesses" in the late nineteenth century, see Lears, "A Psychic Crisis: Neurasthenia and the Emergence of a Therapeutic World View," in *No Place of Grace*, 47–58.

61. Gilles Deleuze, and Félix Guattari, *Anti-Oedipus: Capitalism and Schizophrenia*, trans. Robert Hurley, Mark Seem, and Helen R. Lane (Minneapolis: University of Minnesota Press, 1983).

62. For the classic psychoanalytic discussion of the figure of the double, see Sigmund Freud, "The Uncanny," in *The Standard Edition of the Complete Psychological Works,* vol. 17. trans. and ed. James Strachey (London: Hogarth Press, 1964), 219–56.

63. Edward Bellamy, "The Religion of Solidarity," in *Selected Writings on Religion and Society,* ed. Joseph Schiffman (New York: Liberal Arts Press, 1955), 26. Auerbach details Bellamy's specific reworkings of Emerson's original theories in " 'Nation Organized,' " 38–39.

64. Hall, "Religious Ethics," 17. Hall goes on to show how operating from the same set of principles, Edwards and Bellamy come to very different conclusions about the self's moral responsibility for past actions (19).

65. Bellamy, "Religion of Solidarity," 18.

66. Edward Bellamy, *Six to One: A Nantucket Idyll* (New York: G. P. Putnam's Sons, 1878), 81.

67. Schiffman, "Mutual Indebtedness," 368. Also see W. D. Howells's "Biographical Sketch" in *The Blindman's World and Other Stories,* by Edward Bellamy (Boston: Houghton, Mifflin, 1898), v–xiii. For further discussion, see Louis J. Budd, "W. D. Howells' Defense of the Romance," *PMLA* 47 (1952): 32–42.

68. Edward Bellamy, *Dr. Heidenhoff's Process* (New York: D. Appleton and Company, 1880), 6–7. Hereafter cited in the text as *HP.*

69. Edward Bellamy, "The Blindman's World," in *Future Perfect: American Science Fiction of the Nineteenth Century,* ed. H. Bruce Franklin (New York: Oxford University Press, 1978), 304. Also reprinted in Bellamy, *Apparitions of Things to Come: Tales of Mystery and Imagination,* ed. Franklin Rosemont (Chicago: Charles H. Kerr, 1990), 29–45.

70. Ibid., 309; 311.

71. Roemer points out that with the concluding images of the narrative, "West had been purged by trials and tears. He is now purified. He is also powerless. He cannot help to change the past: he is dead to that era" ("Literary Domestication of Utopia," 106). Auerbach also notes, "Much more than a cheap gimmick, this ending is Bellamy's masterstroke: the repressed realism that has uncannily returned with such a vengeance turns out to be fiction, while utopian romance is restored as the truth. History is a nightmare from which you *can* escape; the escape route depends simply on recognizing your impotence" (" 'Nation Organized,' " 41). I suggest in the next chapter that a similar conclusion is reached in Alexander Bogdanov's *Red Star.*

72. Friedrich Nietzsche, "On the Uses and Disadvantages of History for Life," in *Untimely Meditations,* trans. R. J. Hollingdale (New York: Cambridge University Press, 1983), 61 and 62.

73. Paul de Man, "Literary History and Literary Modernity," in *Blindness and Insight: Essays in the Rhetoric of Contemporary Criticism* (Minneapolis: University of Minnesota Press, 1983), 147–48.

74. I use the notion of "specters" here in the sense given by Jacques Derrida in his *Specters of Marx: The State of the Debt, the Work of Mourning, and the New International,* trans. Peggy Kamuf (New York: Routledge, 1994).

75. Auerbach, " 'Nation Organized,' " 33–34.

76. I deploy the combinatory schema of the "semiotic rectangle," developed by French semiotician A. J. Greimas and refined by Jameson, more directly in Chapters 5 and 6.

77. In his discussion of the modern nation-state, Ernest Gellner argues, "The monopoly of legitimate education is now more important, more central than is the monopoly of legitimate violence"; see *Nations and Nationalism* (Ithaca, NY: Cornell University Press, 1983), 34. Louis Althusser similarly maintains in his classic essay, "Ideology and Ideological State Apparatuses (Notes towards an Investigation)," that the central modern ISA is that of the school; see *Lenin and Philosophy and Other Essays*, trans. Ben Brewster (New York: Monthly Review Press, 1971), 155–57. Finally, for a brilliant examination of the contemporary displacement of this schooling apparatus by a new machinery of hegemonic education, see Watkins, "What Are You Doing Here?" in *Throwaways*, 164–216.

78. Slavoj Žižek, *Tarrying with the Negative: Kant, Hegel, and the Critique of Ideology* (Durham, NC: Duke University Press, 1994), 203; emphasis added.

79. Bellamy continues the argument for "universal" education in *Equality*, 245–52.

80. There is an additional consequence of Bellamy's narrative equation of memory and guilt. Benedict Anderson has recently noted that "shame," or guilt, is a necessary part of any healthy national subjectivity, for in its absence, the genocides and other catastrophes that have scarred the preceding century become possible; see "Indonesian Nationalism Today and in the Future," *New Left Review* 235 (1999): 3–17. In this sense too, Bellamy's vision of forgetting helps establish the preconditions for the emergence of the twentieth century's imperial United States. Indeed, perhaps it is no coincidence that the "new dawn" of the conservative decades that ended the century also required one more act of forgetting—a willed forgetting of our collective shame for the nation's actions in Vietnam.

4. THE OCCLUDED FUTURE

1. Tom Moylan, *Demand the Impossible: Science Fiction and the Utopian Imagination* (New York: Methuen, 1986), 10–11. In his latest work, Moylan extends these insights to encompass contemporary "critical dystopias." See *Scraps of the Untainted Sky: Science Fiction, Utopia, Dystopia* (Boulder, CO: Westview Press, 2001).

2. Keith M. Jensen, "*Red Star*: Bogdanov Builds a Utopia," *Studies in Soviet Thought* 23, no. 1 (1982): 3.

3. Malcolm Cowley, "American Books Abroad," in *Literary History of the United States*, ed. Robert E. Spiller et al., 3d rev. ed. (New York: Macmillan, 1963), 1385–86.

4. Patrick L. McGuire, *Red Stars: Political Aspects of Soviet Science Fiction* (Ann Arbor, MI: UMI Research Press, 1985), 9.

5. Cited, for example, in Joan London, *Jack London and His Times: An Unconventional Biography* (New York: The Book League of America, 1939), 378–79.

6. Roland Barthes, *Mythologies,* trans. Annette Lavers (New York: Hill & Wang, 1972), 146.

7. Ibid., 146–47.

8. Darko Suvin, *Metamorphoses of Science Fiction* (New Haven, CT: Yale University Press, 1979), 252; and Richard Stites, *Revolutionary Dreams: Utopian Vision and Experimental Life in the Russian Revolution* (Oxford: Oxford University Press, 1989).

9. See Richard Stites, "Fantasy and Revolution: Alexander Bogdanov and the Origins of Bolshevik Science Fiction," printed as an Introduction to *Red Star: The First Bolshevik Utopia,* by Alexander Bogdanov (Bloomington: Indiana University Press, 1984), 1–16.

10. Alexander Bogdanov, *Krasnaya Zvezda: Roman-Utopiya* (Hamburg: Helmut Buske Verlag), 180; Alexander Bogdanov, *Red Star: The First Bolshevik Utopia,* ed. Loren R. Graham and Richard Stites, trans. Charles Rougle (Bloomington: Indiana University Press, 1984), 131: IV, 3. The Rougle translation is hereafter cited in the text as *RS,* with the page number followed by the part and chapter designations for the convenience of those using any of the other available editions or translations of the text.

11. There is some speculation that Bogdanov's death may have been a suicide. For two different views, see Loren R. Graham, "Bogdanov's Inner Message," printed as an afterword to *Red Star,* 251–52; and Jensen, "*Red Star:* Bogdanov Builds a Utopia," 32.

12. For further discussion of Bogdanov's attitudes toward Taylorism, see Kendall E. Bailes, "Alexei Gastev and the Soviet Controversy over Taylorism, 1918–24," *Soviet Studies* 29, no. 3 (1977): 373–94. In the next chapter, I look further at the cultural responses to Taylorism in postrevolutionary Soviet society.

13. Jensen, "*Red Star:* Bogdanov Builds a Utopia," 22.

14. One of the most significant of the utopian narratives of the latter half of the twentieth century, Le Guin's *The Dispossessed,* similarly explores the relationship between scarcity and utopia. I deal further with this text in the next chapter. For an examination of the role of the concept of scarcity in the history of Western modernization, see Nicholas Xenos, *Scarcity and Modernity* (New York: Routledge, 1989).

15. For further discussion of the Leninist critique of Machism, see Louis Althusser, "Lenin and Philosophy," in *Lenin and Philosophy and Other Essays,* trans. Ben Brewster (New York: Monthly Review Press, 1971), 23–70. For the intellectual divergences between the two, see Zenovia A. Sochor, *Revolution and Culture: The Bogdanov-Lenin Controversy* (Ithaca, NY: Cornell University Press, 1988).

16. An English translation of Bogdanov's philosophical work is available in *Essays in Tektology: The General Science of Organization,* 2d ed., trans. George Gorelik (Seaside, CA: Intersystems Publications, 1984). For an insightful discussion of Bogdanov's thought and its relationship to the later development of official Soviet ideology, see Dominique Lecourt, "Bogdanov, Mirror of the Soviet Intelligentsia," in *Proletarian Science? The Case of Lysenko,* trans. Ben Brewster (London: New Left Books, 1977), 137–62. For a more celebratory

introduction to Bogdanov's philosophy, see Jensen, *Beyond Marx and Mach: Aleksandr Bogdanov's Philosophy of Living Experience* (Boston: D. Reidel, 1978).

17. Lecourt, "Bogdanov, Mirror of the Soviet Intelligentsia," 153.

18. The fluidity between narratives of space and time travel leads Mark Rose to conclude "that fictions of time are drawn by the force of a kind of inner linguistic gravity until they collapse into fiction of space. This tendency may be understood as the reciprocal of that through which spatially conceived narratives such as *Journey to the Centre of the Earth* and *The War of the Worlds* expand toward a concern with time"; see *Alien Encounters: Anatomy of Science Fiction* (Cambridge: Harvard University Press, 1981), 127. For a related discussion, see Fredric Jameson, "Science Fiction as a Spatial Genre: Generic Discontinuities and the Problem of Figuration in Vonda McIntyre's *The Exile Waiting,*" *Science Fiction Studies* 14 (1987): 44–59.

19. Edward Bellamy, *Looking Backward, 2000–1887* (New York: New American Library, 1960), 121–22. I discuss this passage in Chapter 1.

20. Jensen, *"Red Star: Bogdanov Builds a Utopia,"* 33.

21. A similar attitude toward patriotism is expressed in Charlotte Perkins Gilman's feminist utopia, *Herland* (1915): "Patriotism, red hot, is compatible with the existence of a neglect of national interests, a dishonesty, a cold indifference to the suffering of millions. Patriotism is largely pride, and very largely combativeness. Patriotism generally has a chip on its shoulder"; see *Herland* (New York: Pantheon Books, 1979), 94. However, there are crucial differences between these two narrative utopias. First, Gilman rejects Bogdanov's (and London's) view of the inevitability of revolutionary violence, and maintains instead that peaceful collective action on the part of women could found a more equitable social order for all. Secondly, while Gilman's work also reinforces, on the eve of the first World War, nativist and isolationist ideologies—attitudes even more explicitly elaborated in the sequel to *Herland, with Her in Ourland* (1916), "Ourland" being the United States—her crucial separation of "patriotism" and "national interests" suggests directions only recently explored in the institution of the narrative utopia. For a discussion of the isolationism of *Herland* as a response to an incipient globalization, see Thomas Peyser, *Utopia and Cosmopolis: Globalization in the Era of American Literary Realism* (Durham, NC: Duke University Press, 1998), chap. 2.

22. Slavoj Žižek, *Tarrying with the Negative: Kant, Hegel, and the Critique of Ideology* (Durham, NC: Duke University Press 1994), 201.

23. H. G. Wells, *A Modern Utopia* (Lincoln: University of Nebraska Press, 1967), 11–12.

24. For further discussion of *A Modern Utopia,* see W. Warren Wagar, *H. G. Wells and the World State* (New Haven, CT: Yale University Press, 1961); and Krishan Kumar, *Utopia and Anti-Utopia in Modern Times* (Oxford: Basil Blackwell, 1987), chap. 6.

25. H. G. Wells, *H. G. Wells's Literary Criticism,* ed. Patrick Parrinder and Robert M. Philmus (Sussex: Harvester Press, 1980), 238 and 240. For the central importance of Wells's work, especially *The Time Machine* (1895), in the development of science fiction, see Suvin, *Metamorphoses,* 208–42; the collection

of essays in Suvin and Philmus, ed., *H. G. Wells and Modern Science Fiction* (Lewisburg, PA: Bucknell University Press, 1977); and Brian W. Aldiss, *Trillion Year Spree* (New York: Avon Books, 1986), 117–33. For some discussions of the relationship between science fiction and narrative utopias, see Suvin, *Metamorphoses,* 37–63; Suvin, *Positions and Presuppositions in Science Fiction* (Kent, OH: Kent State University Press, 1988), 33–43; Carl Freedman, *Critical Theory and Science Fiction* (Hanover, NH: Wesleyan University Press, 2000), 62–86; and Moylan, *Scraps of the Untainted Sky;* also see Chapter 1, n. 37. For the relationship between Wells's work and twentieth-century traditions of utopian fiction, see Mark R. Hilegas, *The Future as Nightmare: H. G. Wells and the Anti-Utopians* (New York: Oxford University Press, 1967); and John Huntington, *The Logic of Fantasy: H. G. Wells and Science Fiction* (New York: Columbia University Press, 1982).

26. H. G. Wells, "The Star," in *Science Fiction: A Historical Anthology,* ed. Eric S. Rabkin (Oxford: Oxford University Press, 1983), 232–33.

27. H. G. Wells, *A Critical Edition of The War of the Worlds: H. G. Wells's Scientific Romance,* intro. and notes by David Y. Hughes and Harry M. Geduld (Bloomington: Indiana University Press, 1993), 192.

28. Kumar offers a useful schematic outline of the four-stage historical process in Wells's later work by which utopia is achieved, in *Utopia and Anti-Utopia,* 221–22.

29. For a further discussion of the role of this device in *Independence Day,* as well as its political pedagogical consequences, see my "'A Nightmare on the Brain of the Living': Messianic Historicity, Alienations, and *Independence Day,*" *Rethinking Marxism* 12, no. 1 (2000): 65–86

30. Benedict Anderson, *Imagined Communities: Reflections on the Origin and Spread of Nationalism,* rev. ed. (New York: Verso, 1991), especially chaps. 2 and 3.

31. Perry Anderson, *Considerations on Western Marxism* (New York: Verso, 1979), 14. Also see the insightful discussion of this "trauma" in Žižek, *Tarrying with the Negative,* 207–8.

32. Marshall Berman, *All That Is Solid Melts into Air: The Experience of Modernity* (New York: Penguin, 1988), 175–76. This same opposition, as we shall see in the next chapter, also play a key role in Zamyatin's *We.*

33. See Lecourt, "Bogdanov, Mirror of the Soviet Intelligentsia," 140–41 and 153–54. Lecourt notes of Bogdanov's contribution to a theory of ideology: "If ideology is an expression of the forms of organization of labour, and if the workers of modern industry therefore express in their ideology the 'collectivist' essence of mechanized production, anticipations of the organization of the whole society and its ideology, then the ideology of the classes in alliance with them, notably the peasantry, which is profoundly individualistic, has to be destroyed. These theses simultaneously justify an economistic practice of ideological struggle which waits for the technical transformation of agricultural units to change peasant ideology (Bukharin's position, and, to a certain extent, Stalin's) and coercive methods against the peasants, especially in religious matters" (154, n. 32).

34. A similar dilemma appears in the last paragraphs of *Looking Backward.*

After his return from his brief, nightmarish visit to the nineteenth century, Julian West states, "'Better for you, better for you,' a voice within me rang, 'had this evil dream been the reality, and this fair reality the dream; better your part pleading for crucified humanity with a scoffing generation, than here, drinking of wells you digged not, and eating of trees whose husbandmen you stoned.' And my spirit answered, 'Better, truly'" (*Looking Backward*, 218). Needless to say, such a mourned-for lost opportunity for political action contradicts the determinism of the rest of the work. Also see the discussion of political agency in Bellamy's work in Jonathan Auerbach, "'The Nation Organized': Utopian Impotence in Edward Bellamy's *Looking Backward*," *American Literary History* 6, no. 1 (spring, 1994): 24–47; and for a fascinating reflection on the dilemma of "determinism and voluntarism" within Marxism, see Fredric Jameson, *Postmodernism, or the Cultural Logic of Late Capitalism* (Durham, NC: Duke University Press, 1990), 326–39. I take up this question again in the next chapter.

35. Jack London, *The Iron Heel* included in *Novels and Social Writings* (New York: Library of America, 1982), 319–22. Hereafter cited in the text as *IH*.

36. For a discussion of London's response to the events of 1905, see Joan London, *Jack London and His Times*, chaps. 21 and 22. Of all the biographies of London now available, I still find Joan London's among the most useful and provocative. Originally published during the 1930s and informed by the author's Trotskyite philosophy, the work offers a balanced critical assessment of London's political attitudes and beliefs, especially in the years leading up to the publication of *The Iron Heel*, in relation to both events in his personal history and the wider social context. Not surprisingly, many of the later biographies move in the opposite direction and give short shrift to the author's socialism (although also see the great labor historian Philip S. Foner's *Jack London: American Rebel* [New York: Citadel Press, 1964]). Lois Rather, in *Jack London, 1905* (Oakland, CA: Rather Press, 1974) offers a month-by-month look at London's life in that monumental year.

37. For a brief survey of the contemporary response, see Joan London, *Jack London and His Times*, 309–15; Susan Ward, "Ideology for the Masses: Jack London's *The Iron Heel*," in *Critical Essays on Jack London*, ed. Jacqueline Tavernier-Courbin (Boston: G. K. Hall, 1983), 178–79, n. 30; and Francis Robert Shor, *Utopianism and Radicalism in a Reforming America, 1888–1918* (Westport, CT: Greenwood Press, 1997), 86–90. For a sampling of some of these reviews, see Susan M. Nuernberg, ed., *The Critical Response to Jack London* (Westport, CT: Greenwood Press, 1995), 129–36.

38. Anatole France, "Preface to *The Iron Heel*," in *Critical Essays on Jack London*, ed. Tavernier-Courbin, 35–37; the text of Trotsky's 1937 review can be found in Joan London, *Jack London and His Times*, 313–15, and in Nuernberg, ed., *The Critical Response*, 137–38. This trend is continued by an early 1980s Lawrence Hill edition of *The Iron Heel* whose cover suggests that London's book foreshadows the brutal 1973 military overthrow of Chile's democratically elected socialist government.

39. See Charles N. Watson Jr., *The Novels of Jack London: A Reappraisal* (Madison: University of Wisconsin Press, 1983), 268, n. 38.

40. Although variations on the frame-story have a long tradition in the history of utopian fiction—extending back to More's founding narrative and including both the texts by Bellamy and Bogdanov that we examined earlier—London's use of it here, as well as in much of his other fiction, probably has its more direct source in the work of Joseph Conrad, whom London acknowledged to have been an important influence in his early development as writer.

41. In a 1902 letter to his editor at Macmillan, George P. Brett, London noted that he desired to write a political novel that would "bid for popularity such as Bellamy received." Quoted in Watson, *Novels of Jack London,* 99. For a broad comparison of the "bourgeois" and "Marxist" socialism of the two texts, see Gorman Beauchamp, "*The Iron Heel* and *Looking Backward*: Two Paths to Utopia," *American Literary Realism* 9 (1976): 307–14.

42. For an excellent reading of naturalist literature in the light of the Sartrean concept of *Totalité detotalisée,* see L. S. Dembo, *Detotalized Totalities: Synthesis and Disintegration in Naturalist, Existential, and Socialist Fiction* (Madison: The University of Wisconsin Press, 1989). I take up this issue again in Chapter 6.

43. The macho *nom parlant* of this character was, fantastically enough, not London's own invention, but rather borrowed from a cousin in Michigan whom the author had met during the tramping journeys that he records in *The Road.* Watson, *Novels of Jack London,* 102. "Revolution" is reprinted in London, *Novels and Social Writings,* 1147–65.

44. Joan London, *Jack London and His Times,* 307. Jonathan Auerbach, in his *Male Call: Becoming Jack London* (Durham, NC: Duke University Press, 1996), offers a persuasive reading of the way London's self-conscious construction of his self as a writer, through a negotiation of the then emergent institutions of publication, unifies these disparate personae. Moreover, Auerbach extends back London's grappling with the question of his career to his earliest published work; see especially, his marvelous reading in chap. 3 of the figure of Buck in *Call of the Wild* as another stand-in for London himself.

45. Auerbach also notes the importance of the claims to "experience" as opening up new fields for writing throughout London's career; see *Male Call.*

46. Nadia Khouri, for example, contends that the first ten chapters of Avis's manuscript comprise "a theoretical education in historical materialism"; see "Utopia and Epic: Ideological Confrontation in Jack London's *The Iron Heel,*" *Science Fiction Studies* 3, no. 2 (1976): 174–81.

47. Alessandro Portelli, "Jack London's Missing Revolution: Notes on *The Iron Heel,*" *Science Fiction Studies* 9 (1982): 188.

48. In his 1901 review of Norris's *The Octopus,* London writes, "One needs must feel a sympathy for these men, workers and fighters, and for all of their weakness, a respect. And, after all, as Norris has well shown, their weakness is not inherent. It is the weakness of unorganization, the weakness of the force which they represent and of which they are a part, the agricultural force as opposed to the capitalistic force, the farmers against the financier, the tiller of the soil against the captain of industry"; see *No Mentor But Myself: Jack London on Writing and Writers,* 2d rev. ed., ed. Dale L. Walker and Jeanne Campbell Reesman (Stanford, CA: Stanford University Press), 34.

49. Watson examines the influence of *Caesar's Column* on the composition of *The Iron Heel*, and notes that London's personal library contained two copies of Donnelly's book; see *Novels of Jack London*, 109–12 and 267, n. 29.

50. Ignatius Donnelly, *Caesar's Column: A Story of the Twentieth Century,* ed. Walter B. Rideout (Cambridge: Belknap Press, 1960), 62–63.

51. Anxieties about racial identity are at play throughout Donnelly's narrative. Earlier, we learn that the capitalist aristocracy "is now almost altogether of Hebrew origin," while of the multitudes in the ghettos, Weltstein observes, "the slant eyes of many, and their imperfect, Tartar-like features, reminded me that the laws made by the Republic, in the elder and better days, against the invasion of the Mongolian hordes, had long since become a dead letter" (ibid., 32 and 38).

52. Ibid., chaps. 12 and 40.

53. Harriet Beecher Stowe, *Uncle Tom's Cabin* (New York: Bantam Books, 1981), chap. 43. For a discussion of the transvalued America-Africa opposition in the novel, see Rachel Bowlby, "Breakfast in America—*Uncle Tom's* Cultural Histories," in *Nation and Narration,* ed. Homi K. Bhabha (New York: Routledge, 1990), 197–212.

54. Moreover, by portraying power as an ontological rather than an historical condition, London runs the risk of undermining the ethical basis of his imaginary revolution. Later, in the text, Everhard asserts that both the revolutionaries and the oligarches share the high-minded belief that "they are doing right" (*IH,* 519). But when both are similarly shown to be doing no more than acting out a will-to-power—and Everhard admits that for the revolution, too, "Power will be the arbiter, *as it always has been* the arbiter" (*IH,* 385; emphasis added)—the determination of which side is in fact "right" becomes increasingly difficult, if not impossible. As we shall see in Chapter 6, a similar ontologization of power is introduced in George Orwell's *Nineteen Eighty-Four.* However, Orwell is far less averse to facing the terrible conclusions to which such a notion invariably leads.

55. Portelli, "Jack London's Missing Revolution," 184.

56. Ibid., 187.

57. For two discussions of the development and later influence of Haeckel's thought, see David H. Degrood, *Haeckel's Theory of the Unity of Nature* (Amsterdam: B. R. Grüner, 1982); and David Gasman, *The Scientific Origins of National Socialism: Social Darwinism in Ernst Haeckel and the German Monist League* (New York: American Elsevier, 1971).

58. Quoted in Degrood, *Haeckel's Theory,* 24.

59. Frederick Engels, "Ludwig Feuerbach and the Outcome of Classical German Philosophy," in *Karl Marx Selected Works,* vol. 1, ed. V. Adoratsky (New York: International Publishers, 1933), 435–36.

60. Ernst Haeckel, *The Riddle of the Universe at the Close of the Nineteenth Century,* trans. Joseph McCabe (New York: Harper and Brothers, 1900), 20–21. Hereafter cited in the text as *RU.*

61. For a discussion of this problem, see Jacques Derrida, "White Mythology: Metaphor in the Text of Philosophy," in *Margins of Philosophy,* trans. Alan Bass (Chicago: University of Chicago Press, 1982), 207–71. Also see Althusser, "Lenin and Philosophy," 54–60.

62. See, for example, Ronald E. Martin, *American Literature and the Universe of Force* (Durham, NC: Duke University Press, 1981); June Howard, *Form and History in American Literary Naturalism* (Chapel Hill: University of North Carolina Press, 1985); and Mark Seltzer, *Bodies and Machines* (New York: Routledge, 1992), especially 28–32.

63. In his preface to the manuscript, Meredith writes, "Following upon Capitalism, it was held, even by such intellectual and antagonistic giants as Herbert Spencer, that Socialism would come. Out of the decay of self-seeking capitalism, it was held, would arise that flower of the ages, the Brotherhood of Man" (*IH*, 321).

64. Suvin suggests that Mary Shelley's original, reanimated monster in *Frankenstein; or The Modern Prometheus* (1818) was itself a figure for the broad popular masses of the earlier French Revolution; see Suvin, *Metamorphoses*, 127–36.

65. Walter Benn Michaels, *The Gold Standard and the Logic of Naturalism* (Berkeley: University of California Press, 1987), 206. Also see the discussion of Michaels's book in Jameson, *Postmodernism*, especially 214–17.

66. American Social History Project, *Who Built America? Working People and the Nation's Economy, Politics, Culture, and Society*, vol. 2, *From the Gilded Age to the Present* (New York: Pantheon Books, 1992), 169.

67. Bellamy, *Looking Backward*, 116.

68. Karl Marx, "Manifesto of the Communist Party," in *The Marx-Engels Reader*, ed. Robert C. Tucker (New York: W. W. Norton, 1978), 474.

69. This connection has also been pointed out by Paul N. Siegel, *Revolution and the Twentieth-Century Novel* (New York: Monad Press, 1979), 42.

70. For further discussion, see Jameson's reading of the philanthropic project in the naturalist fiction of George Gissing in *The Political Unconscious: Narrative as a Socially Symbolic Act* (Ithaca, NY: Cornell University Press, 1981), especially 191–96.

71. Marx, "Manifesto," 492.

72. See Earle Labor, *Jack London* (New York: Twayne Publishers, Inc., 1974), 154, n. 8.

73. London, *Jack London: No Mentor but Myself*, 71.

74. Ibid., 66.

75. Marx, "Manifesto," 492–93.

76. "The lower middle class, the small manufacturer, the shopkeeper, the artisan, the peasant, all these fight against the bourgeoisie, to save from extinction their existence as fractions of the middle class. They are therefore not revolutionary, but conservative. Nay more, they are reactionary, for they try to roll back the wheel of history" (ibid., 482).

77. Again fulfilling a "prophecy" of the "Manifesto." Of the "lower middle class," Marx further writes, "If by chance they are revolutionary, they are so only in view of their impending transfer into the proletariat, they thus defend not their present, but their future interests, they desert their own standpoint to place themselves at that of the proletariat" (ibid., 482).

78. See American Social History Project, *Who Built America*, 144–52; Lawrence Goodwyn, *The Populist Moment: A Short History of the Agrarian Re-*

volt in America (New York: Oxford University Press, 1978); and Michael Kazin, *The Populist Persuasion: An American History* (New York: Basic Books, 1995), chap. 2.

79. For three different, although generally critical, assessments of the role of Avis in the narrative, see Watson, *Novels of Jack London*, 113–17; Joan D. Hedrick, *Solitary Comrade: Jack London and His Work* (Chapel Hill: University of North Carolina Press, 1982), 188–99; and Labor, *Jack London*, 103–4. Labor's view that Avis's overly sentimental voice is the major flaw of the narrative—"It is *1984* as it might have been penned by Elizabeth Barret Browning"—seems to be shared by many London scholars. Ward points out the roots of this character in the popular nineteenth-century sentimental novel, in "Ideology for the Masses," 169 and 177, nn. 20 and 21.

80. Portelli, "Jack London's Missing Revolution," 185. Portelli goes on to suggest that this might account for the tremendous popularity of the book among European communist parties in the 1940s and 50s.

81. See Melvin Dubofsky, *We Shall Be All: A History of the Industrial Workers of the World*, 2d ed. (Urbana: University of Illinois Press, 1988); Paul Buhle, *Marxism in the United States*, rev. ed. (New York: Verso, 1991), chap. 3; and Philip S. Foner, *History of the Labor Movement in the United States*, vol. 4 (New York: International Publishers, 1964). For an outstanding study of labor politics in the San Francisco Bay area during London's lifetime, see Michael Kazin, *Barons of Labor: The San Francisco Building Trades and Union Power in the Progressive Era* (Urbana: University of Illinois Press, 1987).

82. Many readings of the text have taken this position. See, for example, Joan London, *Jack London and his Times*, 290–95 and 305; and more recently, Shor, *Utopianism and Radicalism*, 77.

83. Kazin, *Barons of Labor*, 53–56, 289.

84. London also provides us with a clue here to at least one of his more local polemical targets. Everhard first learns of the defection of great unions from "O'Connor, the president of the Association of Machinists" (*IH*, 464). Then president of the real-world International Association of Machinists (IAM), James O'Connell did issue a call for a national strike: not for socialism, as London might have liked, but for the establishment of the nine-hour work day. For a discussion of the IAM in this period, see David Montgomery, *Workers' Control in America: Studies in the History of Work, Technology, and Labor Struggles* (Cambridge: Cambridge University Press, 1979), chap. 3.

85. London drew on a number of sources for the catastrophic descriptions that fill these chapters: his own experience of the 1906 San Francisco earthquake, described in the May 5, 1906 issue of *Collier's* magazine, and later the basis for his apocalyptical fantasy *The Scarlet Plague*; W. Pembroke Fetridge's *The Rise and Fall of the Paris Commune in 1871*; and again, Donnelly's *Caesar's Column*. See Joan London, *Jack London and His Times*, 307–8; and Watson, *Novels of Jack London*, 99–112; 264, n. 3; and 267, n. 29.

86. London here also may have drawn upon Marx's observation on the revolutionary potential of the quite different bloc of the European lumpenproletariat: "The 'dangerous class,' the social scum, that passively rotting mass thrown off by the lowest layers of old society, may, here and there, be swept into

the movement by a proletariat revolution; its conditions of life, however, prepare it far more for the part of a bribed tool of reactionary intrigue" ("Manifesto," 482).

87. It has become something of a commonplace to point out London's debt in *The Iron Heel* to W. J. Ghent's *Our Benevolent Feudalism.* (Meredith cites the work on *IH,* 464.) However, London's review of Ghent's book couples it with John Graham Brooks's quite different *The Social Unrest.* The final sentences of this review suggest the equal importance of London's reading of both works in the formulation of his narrative's vision: "Mr. Ghent beholds the capitalistic class rising to dominate the state and the working class; Mr. Brooks beholds the working class rising to dominate the state and the capitalistic class. One fears the paternalism of a class; the other, the tyranny of the mass"; see London, *War of the Classes* (New York: Macmillan, 1905), 214.

88. Joan London, *Jack London and His Times,* 284. London's anti-Japanese racism would be celebrated in a World War II propaganda film, a "biography" of the author, *The Adventures of Jack London* (1943).

89. The classic study of nativist prejudice in the United States in this period is John Higham, *Strangers in the Land: Patterns of American Nativism, 1860–1925,* 2d ed. (New Brunswick, NJ: Rutgers University Press, 1988). For a discussion of nativism in the San Francisco organized labor movement, see Kazin, *Barons of Labor,* chap. 6. For a discussion of similar sentiments concerning immigrants in Gilman's contemporary "A Woman's Utopia" (1907), see Shor, *Utopianism and Radicalism,* 35–37.

90. Kazin, *Barons of Labor,* 23–24.

91. Jameson, *Political Unconscious,* 189.

92. Paralleling the growth of his racism (see for example the short story "The Red One"), London's populist leanings become more explicit later in his life. In his autobiographical narrative concerning his bout with alcoholism, *John Barleycorn* (1913), London writes the only thing that saved him from a "long sickness of pessimism" and suicidal despair was his "one remaining illusion— the PEOPLE. . . . By the PEOPLE I was handcuffed to life" (*Novels and Social Writings,* 1065–66).

93. Marx, "Manifesto," 498.

94. Auerbach, *Male Call,* 27.

95. For two of the classic analyses of Taylorism, see Antonio Gramsci, *Selections from the Prison Notebooks,* ed. and trans. Quintin Hoare and Geoffrey Nowell Smith (New York: International Publishers, 1971), 277–318; and Harry Braverman, *Labor and Monopoly Capital: The Degradation of Work in the Twentieth Century* (New York: Monthly Review Press, 1974). For further discussion, see Seltzer, *Bodies and Machines,* and Frank Lentricchia, *Ariel and the Police: Michel Foucault, William James, Wallace Stevens* (Madison: University of Wisconsin Press, 1988), chap. 1.

96. London, *Novels and Social Writings,* 690–91.

97. See the superb discussion of the way these fears play out in *The People of the Abyss* in Auerbach, *Male Call,* chap. 4. London's anxieties about his "lower-class origins" are similarly explored in Hedrick, *Solitary Comrade.*

98. I thus take London at his word when he argues that *Martin Eden* was "an attack on Nietzschean philosophy, which even the socialists missed the point of"; quoted in George M. Spangler, "Divided Self and World in *Martin Eden*," in *Critical Essays*, ed. Tavernier-Courbin, 155.

99. London, *Novels and Social Writings*, 1120.

100. Ibid., 1119. All but the last line are italicized in the original. Also see Auerbach's discussion of this essay in *Male Call*, 100–101.

101. Jack London, "The Apostate," in *Short Stories of Jack London* (New York: Collier Books, 1991), 247.

102. Seltzer, *Bodies and Machines*, 13.

103. T. J. Jackson Lears, *No Place of Grace: Antimodernism and the Transformation of American Culture* (New York: Pantheon Books, 1981), 47–58. Also see my discussion of Julian West's middle-class "nervousness" in Chapter 3.

104. Peter Dobkin Hall, *The Organization of American Culture, 1700–1900: Private Institutions, Elites, and the Origins of American Nationality* (New York: New York University Press, 1984), 250.

105. For further discussion of the relationship between the formation of the modern corporation and the growth of a bureaucratic middle class strata, see Alfred D. Chandler, Jr., *The Visible Hand: The Managerial Revolution in American Business* (Cambridge: Belknap Press, 1977); and Oliver Zunz, *Making America Corporate, 1870–1920* (Chicago: University of Chicago Press, 1990).

106. See Hall, *Organization of American Culture*, 249–70.

107. Max Weber, "Bureaucracy," in *From Max Weber: Essays in Sociology*, ed. and trans. H. H. Gerth and C. Wright Mills (New York: Oxford University Press, 1946), 230.

5. A MAP OF UTOPIA'S "POSSIBLE WORLDS"

1. Fredric Jameson, *The Political Unconscious: Narrative as a Socially Symbolic Act* (Ithaca, NY: Cornell University Press, 1981), 9.

2. Stanley Fish, *Doing What Comes Naturally: Change, Rhetoric, and the Practice of Theory in Literary and Legal Studies* (Durham, NC: Duke University Press, 1989), 194.

3. Isaac Deutscher was among the first to observe the connection between the two narratives in his 1954 critique of Orwell's novel, "1984—The Mysticism of Cruelty"; reprinted in *George Orwell: A Collection of Critical Essays*, ed. Raymond Williams (Englewood Cliffs, NJ: Prentice-Hall, 1974), 119–32. Other discussions of *We* as a prototype of the negative utopia include E. J. Brown, "*Brave New World, 1984* and *We*: An Essay on Anti-Utopia," in *Zamyatin's We: A Collection of Critical Essays*, ed. Gary Kern (Ann Arbor, MI: Ardis, 1988), 209–27 (but also see Brown's classic, *Russian Literature Since the Revolution*, rev. ed. [Cambridge: Harvard University Press, 1982], 55–60); Mark Hillegas, *The Future as Nightmare: H. G. Wells and the Anti-utopians* (New York: Oxford University Press, 1967), 99–109; and Krishan Kumar, *Utopia and Anti-Utopia in Modern Times* (Oxford: Basil Blackwell, 1987). How-

ever, significant challenges to this critical view can be found in Mark Rose, *Alien Encounters: Anatomy of Science Fiction* (Cambridge: Harvard University Press, 1981), 167–75; Peter Ruppert, *Reader in a Strange Land: The Activity of Reading Literary Utopias* (Athens: University of Georgia Press, 1986), 105–18, which, while beginning from different suppositions, comes to conclusions about the open-ended dialectical nature of Zamyatin's narrative similar to my own; and Darko Suvin, *Metamorphoses of Science Fiction* (New Haven, CT: Yale University Press, 1979), 255–59. As is often the case, I benefited immensely from this last discussion.

4. Richard Stites, *Revolutionary Dreams: Utopian Vision and Experimental Life in the Russian Revolution* (Oxford: Oxford University Press, 1989), 188.

5. Irving Howe, "The Fiction of Antiutopia," in *Decline of the New* (New York: Harcourt, Brace & World, 1963), 67.

6. Suvin, *Metamorphoses,* 256.

7. Alex M. Shane, *The Life and Works of Evgenij Zamjatin* (Berkeley: University of California Press, 1968), 19.

8. Yevgeny Zamyatin, *The Dragon: Fifteen Stories,* trans. Mirra Ginsburg (New York: Random House, 1967), xvii.

9. Mikhail Bakhtin, *Problems of Dostoevsky's Poetics,* trans. Caryl Emerson (Minneapolis: University of Minnesota Press, 1984), 43.

10. For only a few of the discussions of the influences of Dostoevsky's work on *We,* see Robert L. Jackson, *Dostoevsky's Underground Man in Russian Literature* (The Hague: Mouton, 1958), 150–57; Shane, *Life and Works of Evgenij Zamjatin,* 138–44; Richard A. Gregg, "Two Adams and Eve in the Crystal Palace: Dostoevsky, the Bible, and *We,*" in *A Collection of Critical Essays,* ed. Kern, 61–69; T. R. N. Edwards, *Three Russian Writers and the Irrational: Zamyatin, Pil'nyak, and Bulgakov* (Cambridge: Cambridge University Press, 1982), especially 52–55; Gary Saul Morson, *The Boundaries of Genre: Dostoevsky's Diary of a Writer and the Traditions of Literary Utopia* (Austin: University of Texas Press, 1981), including his provocative "Anti-Utopia as a Parodic Genre," 115–42; and John Hoyles, *The Literary Underground: Writers and the Totalitarian Experience, 1900–1950* (New York: St. Martin's Press, 1991).

11. Bakhtin, *Problems of Dostoevsky's Poetics,* 6.

12. Ibid., 28. There is also a connection here to Bakhtin's later concept of the Chronotope developed in "Forms of Time and the Chronotope in the Novel," in *The Dialogic Imagination: Four Essays,* trans. Caryl Emerson and Michael Holquist (Austin: University of Texas Press, 1981), 84–258.

13. Darko Suvin, "Locus, Horizon, and Orientation: The Concept of Possible Worlds as a Key to Utopian Studies," *Utopian Studies* 1, no. 2 (1990): 69–83. Originally published in a slightly different version in *Utopia e Modernita: Teorie e prassi utopiche nell'eta moderna e postmoderna,* ed. Giuseppa Saccaro Del Buffa and Arthur O. Lewis (Rome: Gangemi editore, 1989), 47–65; and also reprinted in *Not Yet: Reconsidering Ernst Bloch,* ed. Jamie Owen Daniel and Tom Moylan (New York: Verso, 1997), 122–37.

14. For the place of *We* in the history of Russian utopian and science fiction literature, see Suvin, "Russian SF and Its Tradition," in *Metamorphoses,* 243–69; Patrick L. McGuire, *Red Stars: Political Aspects of Soviet Science Fiction*

(Ann Arbor, MI: UMI Research Press, 1985); and Richard Stites "Fantasy and Revolution: Alexander Bogdanov and the Origins of Bolshevik Science Fiction," Introduction to *Red Star: The First Bolshevik Utopia,* by Alexander Bogdanov (Bloomington: Indiana University Press, 1984), as well as Stites's rich and wide-ranging survey of the artistic, social, and cultural experiments of the revolutionary era, *Revolutionary Dreams.*

15. Zamyatin, *My* (London: Bristol Classical Press, 1994), 12; Zamyatin, *We,* trans. Mirra Ginsburg (New York: Avon Books, 1987), 21; 5. The Ginsburg translation is hereafter cited in the text, with the page number followed by the chapter number for the convenience of those using any of the other editions and translations of the text now available.

16. One of these intellectuals, of course, was none other than Zamyatin's most significant Russian predecessor working in the utopian genre: Alexander Bogdanov. Of Bogdanov's earlier *Red Star,* Zamyatin wrote simply that it "has more journalistic than literary value." See his "H. G. Wells," in *A Soviet Heretic: The Essays of Yevgeny Zamyatin,* trans. Mirra Ginsburg (Chicago: University of Chicago Press, 1970), 290. Kathleen Lewis and Harry Weber suggest a connection between the two utopian narratives that runs deeper than Zamyatin's perfunctory statement would indicate; see their detailed discussion of the parallels between the two works in "Zamyatin's *We,* the Proletarian Poets, and Bogdanov's *Red Star,*" in *A Collection of Critical Essays,* ed. Kern, 196–205. I only want to point out what appears to be a another level of critique of Bogdanov's thought at work in *We.* Dominique Lecourt has convincingly shown that Bogdanov's teleological systems philosophy, the Tectology, already implicitly contains the ideological justifications that would later be employed in the violent repression of the peasantry—exactly what D-503 suggests occurred in the Two Hundred Years' War, which I-330 later confirms (*We,* 164; 28). See Lecourt, "Bogdanov, Mirror of the Soviet Intelligentsia," in *Proletarian Science? The Case of Lysenko,* trans. Ben Brewster (London: New Left Books, 1977), 137–62.

17. Raymond Williams, *The Country and the City* (New York: Oxford University Press, 1973).

18. Edwards, *Three Russian Writers,* 85.

19. See Stites, *Revolutionary Dream,* 35 and 184–87, although I disagree with his monological assessment of *We* as an "antiurban dystopia."

20. Marshall Berman, *All That Is Solid Melts into Air: The Experience of Modernity* (New York: Penguin, 1988), 175.

21. Ibid., 247–48. I would like to thank Michael Speaks for first pointing out to me Berman's discussion of these issues.

22. Lewis Mumford even claims that "the first utopia was the city itself." See his "Utopia, the City, and the Machine," in *Utopias and Utopian Thought,* ed. Frank E. Manuel (Boston: Houghton Mifflin, 1966), 3–24.

23. One of the most useful typological distinctions between *dystopia* and *anti-utopia,* two terms too often used interchangeably, is that offered by Lyman Tower Sargent. Sargent defines the "Dystopia or negative utopia" as "a nonexistent society described in considerable detail and normally located in time and space that the author intended a contemporaneous reader to view as con-

siderably worse than the society in which the reader lived," and the "Anti-utopia" as "a non-existent society described in considerable detail and normally located in time and space that the author intended a contemporaneous reader to view as a criticism of utopianism or of some particular eutopia"; see "The Three Faces of Utopianism Revisited," *Utopian Studies* 5, no. 1 (1994), 9. Also see Sargent, "Utopia—The Problem of Definition," *Extrapolation* 16, no. 2 (1975): 137–48. Tom Moylan traces out the considerable critical confusion between the two terms, and further develops Sargent's distinctions in *Scraps of the Untainted Sky: Science Fiction, Utopia, Dystopia* (Boulder, CO: Westview Press, 2001). For two additional attempts to distinguish between these two narrative forms, see Morson, *The Boundaries of Genre*, 115–16; and Ruppert, *Reader in a Strange Land,* chap. 5 passim, and 174–75, n. 5. Suvin also reminded me in conversation that the "anti-utopia" is more often than not "anti-socialist," a point Jameson bears out as well: "anti-Utopianism constitutes a far more easily decodable and unambiguous political position: . . . Utopia is a transparent synonym for socialism itself, and the enemies of Utopia sooner or later turn out to be the enemies of socialism"; see Fredric Jameson, "Of Islands and Trenches: Neutralization and the Production of Utopian Discourse," in *The Ideologies of Theory, Essays, 1971–1986,* vol. 2 (Minneapolis: University of Minnesota Press, 1988), 76–77. This formulation is crucial for thinking about the differences between Zamyatin's and Orwell's narratives.

24. In the original 1924 edition of *We*, Gregory Zilboorg translates the name of the society in narrative as the "United State," thereby suggesting that Zamyatin's critique may also be applied to the birthplace of Taylorism. Zilboorg further bears this out in his foreword: "The problem of the creative individual versus the mob is not merely a Russian problem. It is as apparent in a Ford factory as under a Bolshevik dictatorship" (*We,* by Eugene Zamiatin [New York: E. P. Dutton, 1959], xv). For a more detailed discussion of the play of Taylorism in the narrative, see Gorman Beauchamp, "Man as Robot: The Taylor System in *We,*" in *Clockwork Worlds: Mechanized Environments in SF,* ed. Richard D. Erlich and Thomas P. Dunn (Westport, CT: Greenwood Press, 1983), 85–93. And for some general discussions of Taylorism, see Antonio Gramsci, *Selections from the Prison Notebooks,* ed. and trans. Quintin Hoare and Geoffrey Nowell Smith (New York: International Publishers, 1971), 277–318; and Harry Braverman, *Labor and Monopoly Capital: The Degradation of Work in the Twentieth Century* (New York: Monthly Review Press, 1974).

25. For a useful survey of the contemporary cultural responses to Taylorist modernization, see Peter Wollen, "Modern Times: Cinema/Americanism/The Robot," in *Raiding the Icebox: Reflections on Twentieth-Century Culture* (Bloomington: Indiana University Press, 1993), 35–71.

26. Here Zamyatin's social and aesthetic critiques interestingly converge. One of the leading proponents of Taylorism in the early Soviet Union was Alexei Gastev, who also happened to be one of the founders of the Proletarian Poetry movement. Zamyatin elsewhere icily observed that the practitioners of this "new" art combined "the most revolutionary content and the most reactionary form," and thus appear like "aviators astride a locomotive. The locomotive huffs and puffs sincerely and assiduously, but it does not look as if it can rise

aloft" (*Soviet Heretic,* 56). For an analysis of Zamyatin's use of the Proletarian Poets, see Lewis and Weber, "Zamyatin's *We,* the Proletarian Poets, and Bogdanov's *Red Star,*" 186–96; and the informative discussions of Gastev in Stites, *Revolutionary Dreams,* 149–55; as well as Kendall E. Bailes, "Alexei Gastev and the Soviet Controversy over Taylorism, 1918–24," *Soviet Studies* 29, no. 3 (1977): 373–94.

27. For Zamyatin's own espousal of modernist technical experimentation, see his manifesto "On Literature, Revolution, and Entropy," in *Soviet Heretic,* 173–79. For some useful introductions to the matter of literary style and form in *We,* see the essays by Carl R. Proffer, Ray Parrott, Kern, Milton Ehre, and Susan Layton in *A Collection of Critical Essays,* ed. Kern, 118–48.

28. In Zamyatin's satire on the modern English bourgeoisie, *The Islanders* (1918), we already find many of the themes that will be developed in *We.* On the first page, the character Vicar Dooley declares, "life must become an harmonious machine and with mechanical inevitability lead us to the desired goal." And at the narrative's conclusion, after the disorder that was introduced into his world has been corrected, Dooley offers this reflection, "If the state would forcefully lead the weak souls along the one path—it would not be necessary to resort to such sad though just measures. . . . Salvation would come with mathematical inevitability, understand—mathematical?" (*The Islanders,* trans. T. S. Berczynski [Ann Arbor, MI: Trilogy Publishers, 1978], 2 and 44).

29. Louis Althusser, "Ideology and Ideological State Apparatuses (Notes towards an Investigation)," in *Lenin and Philosophy and Other Essays,* trans. Ben Brewster (New York: Monthly Review Press, 1971), 170–82.

30. Ernesto Laclau and Chantal Mouffe, *Hegemony and Socialist Strategy: Towards a Radical Democratic Politics* (New York: Verso, 1985), 129.

31. For a discussion that emphasizes the role of the irrational antithesis in Zamyatin's work, see Edwards, *Three Russian Writers;* and for a reading of D-503's mathematical errors, see Leighton Brett Cooke, "Ancient and Modern Mathematics in Zamyatin's *We,*" in *A Collection of Critical Essays,* ed. Kern, 149–67.

32. Ernst Bloch, *Natural Law and Human Dignity,* trans. Dennis J. Schmidt (Cambridge: MIT Press, 1987), 205.

33. Ibid., 208.

34. For examinations of the influence of Mayer on Zamyatin's thought, see Shane, *Life and Works of Evgenij Zamjatin,* 45–48; and Olga Muller Cooke, "Bely's Moscow Novels and Zamyatin's Robert Mayer: A Literary Response to Thermodynamics," *Slavonic and East European Review* 63, no. 2 (1985): 194–209.

35. See H. G. Wells, *The Time Machine* (New York: Ballantine Books, 1983), chap. 11. Zamyatin was quite familiar with Wells's work and served as the editor of a five-volume edition of Wells's works for the World Literature publishing house. See his essay "H. G. Wells," in *Soviet Heretic,* 259–90; and for further discussion, see Hillegas, *Future as Nightmare;* and John Huntington, "Utopian and Anti-Utopian Logic: H. G. Wells and his Successors," *Science Fiction Studies,* 9 (1982): 122–46.

36. See Bogdanov, *Red Star,* 225–28.

37. Theodor W. Adorno and Max Horkheimer, *Dialectic of Enlightenment,* trans. John Cumming (New York: Continuum, 1987).

38. Michel de Certeau, *The Practice of Everyday Life,* trans. Steven Rendall (Berkeley: University of California Press, 1984), 94.

39. Again, in Zamyatin's *The Islanders,* Vicar Dooley declares, "If the individual—always criminal and disorderly—is replaced by the will of The Great Machine of the State, then with mechanical inevitability—understand that?—mechanical . . ." (8).

40. de Certeau, *Practice of Everyday Life,* 94.

41. Alexandra Aldridge, "Myths of Origin and Destiny in Utopian Literature: Zamiatin's *We,*" *Extrapolation* 19 (1977): 74. However, also see Aldridge's, "Origins of Dystopia: *When the Sleeper Awakes* and *We,*" in *Clockwork Worlds,* ed. Erlich and Dunn, 63–84; as well as her *The Scientific World View in Dystopia* (Ann Arbor, MI: UMI Research Press, 1984), 33–44.

42. Gorman Beauchamp, "Zamiatin's *We,*" in *No Place Else: Explorations in Utopian and Dystopian Fiction,* ed. Eric S. Rabkin, Martin H. Greenberg, and Joseph D. Olander (Carbondale: Southern Illinois University Press, 1983), 70. Nor are these two critics alone in this conclusion. Hoyles writes, "If there is a theocratic utopia at the absent centre of Dostoevsky's discourse, then there is a romantic primitivist one in Zamyatin, however modernistically garbed" (*Literary Underground,* 108). Edwards's rich, detailed discussion of the text in *Three Russian Writers* also arrives at a similar conclusion.

43. Sargent, "Three Faces," 10–11. Also see Robert C. Elliot's classic discussion of the prehistoric roots of the form in *The Shape of Utopia* (Chicago: University of Chicago Press, 1970), especially chap. 1.

44. Richard Helgerson, "Inventing Noplace, or the Power of Negative Thinking," in *The Power of Forms in the English Renaissance,* ed. Stephen Greenblatt (Norman: Pilgrim Books, 1982), 101–21. For the classic discussion of the sensual, bodily dimension of Rabelais's work, see Mikhail Bakhtin, *Rabelais and His World,* trans. Hélène Iswolsky (Bloomington: Indiana University Press, 1984), and *The Dialogic Imagination.* For a more recent discussion of Rabelais's earlier and more explicit engagement with More's work, see Edwin M. Duval, *The Design of Rabelais's* Pantagruel (New Haven, CT: Yale University Press, 1991), especially chap. 5.

45. Raymond Williams, *George Orwell* (New York: Columbia University Press, 1971), 79–80.

46. For another example of the occasionally vicious anti-utopianism in Huxley's writing (although also see note 54 below), see his nasty little essay on the early-twentieth-century California socialist community of Llano del Rio, "Ozymandias, the Utopia That Failed," in *Tomorrow and Tomorrow and Tomorrow* (New York: Signet, 1964), 68–81. For counterreadings of Llano's history—whose founder, the one-time Los Angeles socialist mayoral candidate Job Harriman, began his political career as a member of a Bellamite Nationalist Club—see Mike Davis, *City of Quartz: Excavating the Future in Los Angeles* (New York: Verso, 1991), 3–14; and Paul Greenstein, Nigley Lennon, and Lionel Rolfe, *Bread and Hyacinths: The Rise and Fall of Utopian Los Angeles* (Los Angeles: California Classics Books, 1992).

47. Algirdas Julien Greimas, *On Meaning: Selected Writings in Semiotic Theory*, trans. Paul J. Perron and Frank H. Collins (Minneapolis: University of Minnesota Press, 1987). For further discussions and applications of this device, see Fredric Jameson, *The Prison-House of Language: A Critical Account of Structuralism and Russian Formalism* (Princeton, NJ: Princeton University Press, 1972), 162–68, "Character Systems in *Dr. Bloodmoney*," *Science Fiction Studies* 2 (1975): 31–42, and *Political Unconscious*, especially 46–49 and 82–83.

48. For a discussion of the relationship between the contract myth and utopia, see Northrop Frye, "Varieties of Literary Utopias," in *Utopias and Utopian Thought*, ed. Manuel, 25–49.

49. Christopher Collins in his essay "Zamyatin's *We* as Myth," reads the text as an archetype of the struggle between the ego and the Jungian anima. Reprinted in *A Collection of Critical Essays*, ed. Kern, 70–79.

50. Istvan Csicsery-Ronay Jr., "Zamyatin and the Strugatskys: The Representation of Freedom in *We* and *The Snail on the Slope*," in *A Collection of Critical Essays*, ed. Kern, 242–44. Huntington, in his insightful analysis, also argues that the relentless "anti-utopian" irony of *We* undercuts the production of any positive stable utopian world in the text. "Utopian and Anti-Utopian Logic," 128–34.

51. Fredric Jameson, *Marxism and Form* (Princeton, NJ: Princeton University Press, 1971), 135. Also see Ernst Bloch, *The Principle of Hope*, trans. Neville Plaice, Stephen Plaice, and Paul Knight (Oxford: Basil Blackwell, 1986), 1103–82.

52. As will become clear in the next chapter, I-330 and Julia in *Nineteen Eighty-Four* serve quite different functions in their respective narratives. While the differences between these two characters reveal a good deal about the specific concerns of Zamyatin and Orwell, they also point toward a more general divergence in the treatment of gender in Russian and Anglo-American utopian fiction. Morson points out that the representations of women in earlier Anglo-American utopias rarely challenge conventional patriarchal attitudes. We need only think of Bellamy's presentation of Edith and Mrs. Leete, or London's of Avis to confirm this. In the quite different tradition of Russian utopian fiction, on the other hand—and here, we should keep in mind Vera Pavlovna in Chernyshevsky's *What Is to Be Done?* Netti in Bogdanov's *Red Star*, and I-330—the problem of the reconstruction of gender roles forms a central component of the utopian vision; see Morson, *Boundaries of Genre*, 79–81. This may explain why in Russia and the early Soviet Union we do not see the same explosive growth that occurs, especially in the United States, of feminist utopias. For some significant discussions of the latter form and its relationship to the broader generic institution, see Marleen Barr, ed., *Future Females: A Critical Anthology* (Bowling Green, KY: Bowling Green State University Popular Press, 1981); Jean Pfaelzer, *The Utopian Novel In America, 1886–1896: The Politics of Form* (Pittsburgh, PA: University of Pittsburgh Press, 1984), chap. 7; Tom Moylan, *Demand the Impossible: Science Fiction and the Utopian Imagination* (New York: Methuen, 1986), especially chaps. 4 and 6; Frances Bartkowski, *Feminist Utopias* (Lincoln: University of Nebraska Press, 1989); Robin Roberts, *A New*

Species: Gender and Science Fiction (Urbana: University of Illinois Press, 1993), chap. 3; Marleen S. Barr, *Lost in Space: Probing Feminist Science Fiction and Beyond* (Chapel Hill: University of North Carolina Press, 1993); and Jennifer Burwell, *Notes on Nowhere: Feminism, Utopian Logic, and Social Transformation* (Minneapolis: University of Minnesota Press, 1997).

53. In the 1919 essay "Tomorrow," Zamyatin suggests his affinity for a dialectical understanding of historical process: "He who has found his ideal today is, like Lot's wife, already turned into a pillar of salt, has already sunk into the earth and does not move ahead. . . . Today denies yesterday, but is a denial of denial tomorrow. This is the constant dialectic path which in a grandiose parabola sweeps the world into infinity. Yesterday, the thesis; today, the antithesis; and tomorrow, the synthesis" (*Soviet Heretic,* 51). Also see Shane, *Life and Works of Evgenij Zamjatin,* 22–23.

54. Huxley too seems to have later come to rethink his text, however vaguely, along similar lines. In the 1946 preface he writes, "If I were now to rewrite the book, I would offer the Savage a third alternative. Between the utopia and the primitive horns of his dilemma would lie the possibility of sanity—a possibility already actualized, to some extent in the community of exiles and refugees from the Brave New World, living within the borders of the Reservation. . . . Brought up among the primitives, the Savage (in this hypothetical new version of the book) would not be transported to Utopia until he had an opportunity of learning something at first hand about the nature of a society composed of freely co-operating individuals devoted to the pursuit of sanity" (*Brave New World* [New York: Harper and Row, 1969], viii–ix). Any treatment of his late narrative utopia *Island* (1962) needs to take this statement into consideration; for one reading that does so, see Ruppert, *Reader in a Strange Land,* 131–33.

Interestingly, a similar tripartite schema of "worlds" is to be found in one of the founding texts of modern anthropology—and a work which influenced Marx's own late thinking—Lewis Henry Morgan's *Ancient Society* (1877). Jameson points out that for Morgan, the ideal world is that of "barbarism," a dialectical other to both "civilization" and "savagery," the latter two terms "evaluated negatively" in Morgan's schema; see "The Space of Science Fiction: Narrative in Van Vogt," *Polygraph* 2/3 (1989): 63–64. In a celebrated passage, also cited at the conclusion of Engels's *The Origin of the Family, Private Property and the State* (1884), Morgan claims, "the next higher plane of society to which experience, intelligence and knowledge are steadily tending . . . will be a revival, in a higher form, of the liberty, equality and fraternity of the ancient gentes." See Engels, *The Origin of the Family, Private Property and the State* (Moscow: Progress Publishers, 1948), 175. For a fascinating reconsideration of Marx's reading of Morgan's text, see Raya Dunayevskaya, *Rosa Luxemburg, Women's Liberation, and Marx's Philosophy of Revolution,* 2d ed. (Urbana: University of Illinois Press, 1991), 175–97; and for the intimations of a more general "third stage" in Marx's thought, see Kristin Ross, *The Emergence of Social Space: Rimbaud and the Paris Commune* (Minneapolis: University of Minnesota Press, 1988), 21–25; and Etienne Balibar, *The Philosophy of Marx,* trans. Chris Turner (New York: Verso, 1995), 100–112. That such a process of narrative figuration continues in later anthropological discourse is also made evident by Susan Hegeman, who, in an original reading of Ruth Benedict's *Patterns of Culture* (1934), traces out a four-fold schema of "Possible Worlds" bearing a striking similarity to that I have uncovered in Zamyatin's text. See Hegeman, *Patterns for America: Modernism and the Concept of Culture* (Princeton, NJ: Princeton University Press, 1999), 96–103.

55. Bloch, *Principle of Hope,* 203. Also see Chapter 1 for further discussion of this dimension of Bloch's work.

56. I would argue that a similar problematic is explored in the work of Zamyatin's brilliant successors, the brothers Arkady and Boris Strugatsky. Csicsery-Ronay offers another reading of this relationship in "Zamyatin and the Strugatskys," 236–59.

57. There may be one more level of irony operating here: according to theoretical models of an oscillating universe, if spatial expansion is finite, then absolute entropy would not occur. From this point of view, the universe would be infinite—although, importantly, the same could *not* be said for our familiar time-space configuration.

58. A related and prophetic Marxist critique of the eventual fate of the economism of the Soviet experiment can be found in Henri Lefebvre, *Critique of Everyday Life,* vol. 1, trans. John Moore (New York: Verso, 1991), 44–49.

59. Also see Dunayevskaya's notes on Marx's own concept of the "revolution in permanence" in *Rosa Luxemburg,* 158–73. Eugene Holland offers a Greimasian mapping of the "three social forms"—savagery, despotism, and capitalism—outlined in Gilles Deleuze and Félix Guattari's *Anti-Oedipus: Capitalism and Schizophrenia* (1972). To this he adds a fourth category, "permanent revolution," to produce a schema that bears an uncanny resemblance to that I have outlined in Zamyatin's text—and which, as will become evident in the next section of this chapter, is also at work in the fiction of Deleuze and Guattari's contemporary, Ursula K. Le Guin. See Eugene Holland, "Schizoanalysis: The Postmodern Contextualization of Psychoanalysis," in *Marxism and the Interpretation of Culture,* ed. Cary Nelson and Lawrence Grossberg (Urbana: University of Illinois Press, 1988), 405–16.

60. For some of the most significant and insightful selections of the still growing literature on this work, see the various studies listed in note 52 above, as well as Peter Fitting, "The Modern Anglo-American SF Novel: Utopian Longing and Capitalist Cooptation," *Science Fiction Studies* 6, no. 1 (1979): 59–76, and "The Turn from Utopia in Recent Feminist Fiction," in *Feminism, Utopia, and Narrative,* ed. Libby Falk Jones and Sarah Webster Goodwin (Knoxville: University of Tennessee Press, 1990), 130–40; Ruppert, *Reader in a Strange Land,* chap. 6; Bülent Somay, "Toward an Open-Ended Utopia," *Science Fiction Studies* 11(1984): 25–38; Hoda M. Zaki, *Phoenix Renewed: The Survival and Mutation of Utopian Thought in North American Science Fiction, 1965–1982* (New York: Stormount House, 1988); Carl Freedman, *Critical Theory and Science Fiction* (Hanover, NH: Wesleyan University Press, 2000); and Moylan, *Scraps of the Untainted Sky.*

61. Ursula K. Le Guin, "The Stalin in the Soul," in *The Language of the Night: Essays on Fantasy and Science Fiction* (New York: HarperCollins, 1992), 213–14.

62. Frederic Jameson, "World Reduction in Le Guin: The Emergence of Utopian Narrative," *Science Fiction Studies* 2, no. 3 (1975): 228.

63. For further discussion of the relationship between these two texts, see Moylan, *Demand the Impossible,* chap. 7, and Somay, "Toward an Open-Ended Utopia."

64. Ursula K. Le Guin, *The Dispossessed: An Ambiguous Utopia* (New York: HarperPrism, 1994), 207. Hereafter cited in the text as *TD.*

65. Darko Suvin, "Parables of De-Alienation: Le Guin's Widdershins Dance," in *Positions and Presuppositions in Science Fiction* (Kent, OH: Kent State University Press, 1988), 138. For a bibliographic overview of the scholarship on Le Guin's work, see Donna R. White, *Dancing with Dragons: Ursula K. Le Guin and the Critics* (Columbia, SC: Camden House, 1999).

66. See *TD,* 128, 140–41, and 216–17 for evidence of A-Io's aristocratic heritage; and *TD,* 82 for its practices of "ecological control and the husbanding of natural resources." This dislocation thus hints at another way to read the text: as an allegory of the history of the United States, poised between the promise of the West, the new world of the frontier (Anarres), and the burden of history in the East, the old world of Europe (A-Io). Bolstering this reading, Suvin suggestively points out that Le Guin's more general "political position can be thought of as a radical critic and ally of socialism defending its duty to inherit the heretic democratic, civic traditions, for example Jefferson's or indeed Tom Paine's" (*Positions and Presuppositions,* 147). The fact that the followers of Odo had originally fled to Anarres in order to escape persecution for their "beliefs" offers further evidence for such a reading of the text. Freedman points out a possible link here as well between Odo and Etienne Cabet, who fled to the New World to establish his utopian community Icarie. *Critical Theory and Science Fiction,* 124. Also, see the discussion of Marx's letter to Cabet in Louis Marin, *Utopics: The Semiological Play of Textual Spaces,* trans. Robert A. Vollrath (Atlantic Highlands, NJ: Humanities Press International, 1984), chap. 14.

67. The narrative's placement in this geopolitical context is also usefully discussed by Robert Philmus, "Ursula Le Guin and Time's Dispossession," in *Science Fiction Roots and Branches: Contemporary Critical Approaches,* ed. Rhys Garnett and R. J. Ellis (New York: St. Martin's Press, 1990), 147–48.

68. Freedman, *Critical Theory and Science Fiction,* 115–16. For another discussion of the text's anarchism, see Victor Urbanowicz, "Personal and Political in *The Dispossessed,*" in *Ursula K. Le Guin: Modern Critical Views,* ed. Harold Bloom (New York: Chelsea House Publishers, 1986),145–54.

69. For the placement of this narrative within Le Guin's larger Ekumenical cycle, as well as in her fictional *oeuvre* as a whole, see Susan Wood, "Discovering Worlds: The Fiction of Ursula K. Le Guin," in *Ursula K. Le Guin: Modern Critical Views,* ed. Bloom, 183–209; and Suzanne Elizabeth Reid, *Presenting Ursula K. Le Guin* (New York: Twayne Publishers, 1997).

70. Freedman interestingly links this image to Trotsky's warning of the dangers inherent in attempting to establish socialism in a situation of technological underdevelopment and scarcity; see *Critical Theory and Science Fiction,* 122–24.

71. Ecological disaster also plays a crucial mediating role in the founding of

Le Guin's next utopian society, that of the Kesh in *Always Coming Home* (New York: Harper and Row, 1985).

72. Although Le Guin has suggested that Odo and the people of Anarres are the "ones who walk away" in her often-anthologized short story, "The Ones Who Walk Away From Omelas," I would argue that, in fact, we see a similar fourfold schema structuring the text: the walkers are equivalent to the utopian horizon of the Hainish; the citizens of Omelas, the people of Anarres; our own implied "estranged" readerly presence, Urras; and the tortured child, Terra. Also see the lively exchange concerning this story in *Utopian Studies* 2, nos. 1 and 2 (1991): 1–62.

73. Philmus, "Ursula Le Guin and Time's *Dispossession*," 145.

74. This is even more the case in Le Guin's next utopian text, the short story, "The New Atlantis." Of the "new and better creation" seen arising in this text, Suvin writes, "We cannot tell exactly who they are and what they will be like: we can only tell that they are being raised up by tides stronger than even the ultimate class society of the corporate State, by the slow and inexorable geological tides of history so to speak" (*Positions and Presuppositions*, 143). The imagery of natural "geological" processes here hints at a central dilemma I will address momentarily.

75. Somay, "Toward an Open-Ended Utopia," 34. Somay's opposition of "locus" and "horizon" is similar to Raymond Williams's "systematic" and "heuristic" modes of utopian fiction. See Williams, "Utopia and Science Fiction," in *Problems in Materialism and Culture* (New York: Verso, 1980), 202–3.

76. Le Guin does offer an interesting anthropological portrait of cultural pluralism on the Hainish home world in her more recent *Four Ways to Forgiveness* (New York: HarperPrism, 1995).

77. Somay, "Toward an Open-Ended Utopia," 35.

78. E. P. Thompson, *William Morris: Romantic to Revolutionary*, rev. ed. (New York: Pantheon Books, 1977), 791. For a related discussion, see the beautiful essay by Lefebvre, from which the epigraph for this chapter was taken, "On Irony, Maieutic, and History," in *Introduction to Modernity: Twelve Preludes, September 1959–May 1961*, trans. John Moore (New York: Verso, 1995), 7–48; epigraph from 42.

79. Gilles Deleuze and Félix Guattari, *A Thousand Plateaus: Capitalism and Schizophrenia*, trans. Brian Massumi (Minneapolis: University of Minnesota Press, 1987), 474. There is an interesting link to be teased out between their conceptual opposition of the "striated" and "smooth" and Paul Carter's "imperial" and "spatial" histories. Carter too draws a connection between imperial history and state power, as well as between spatial history and nomads, in this particular case, the Aboriginal peoples of Australia; see *The Road to Botany Bay: An Essay in Spatial History* (London: Faber and Faber, 1987), especially the introduction and final chapter.

80. Deleuze and Guattari, *A Thousand Plateaus*, 486.

81. Ibid., 500.

82. Henri Lefebvre, *The Production of Space*, trans. Donald Nicholson-Smith (Oxford: Blackwell, 1991), 168. However, both Edward Dimendberg and

Neil Smith point out Lefebvre's unwillingness to delineate concretely what he calls "differential space." See their respective essays in *Philosophy and Geography II: The Production of Public Space,* ed. Andrew Light and Jonathan M. Smith (Lanham, MD: Rowman & Littlefield, 1998), 37 and 52.

83. Slavoj Žižek, *Looking Awry: An Introduction to Jacques Lacan through Popular Culture* (Cambridge: MIT Press, 1991), 165. I develop a related discussion in "'A Nightmare on the Brain of the Living': Messianic Historicity, Alienations, and *Independence Day,*" *Rethinking Marxism* 12, no. 1 (2000): 65–86.

84. Gramsci, *Selections from the Prison Notebooks,* 241.

85. Ibid., 336.

86. Ibid., 337.

6. MODERNITY, NOSTALGIA, AND THE ENDS OF
NATIONS IN ORWELL'S *NINETEEN EIGHTY-FOUR*

1. See Jean Baudrillard, *Jean Baudrillard: Selected Writings,* ed. Mark Poster (Stanford, CA: Stanford University Press, 1988); and Francis Fukuyama, *The End of History and the Last Man* (New York: The Free Press, 1992). For two useful commentaries on these types of narratives, see Meaghan Morris, "Banality in Cultural Studies," *Block* 14 (1988): 15–26 (a modified version is reprinted in *Logics of Television: Essays in Cultural Criticism,* ed. Patricia Mellencamp [Bloomington: Indiana University Press, 1990], 14–43); and Jacques Derrida, *Specters of Marx: The State of the Debt, the Work of Mourning, and the New International,* trans. Peggy Kamuf (New York: Routledge, 1994). I also discuss these issues in "'A Nightmare on the Brain of the Living': Messianic Historicity, Alienations, and *Independence Day,*" *Rethinking Marxism* 12, no. 1 (2000): 65–86.

2. For example, Eric Hobsbawm argues for the difference between the classical nation-state and neo-tribalisms in *Nations and Nationalism Since 1780: Programme, Myth, Reality,* 2d ed. (Cambridge: Cambridge University Press, 1992). For an effective critique of this view, see Tom Nairn, "Demonising Nationality," in *Faces of Nationalism: Janus Revisited* (New York: Verso, 1997), 57–67.

3. Derrida, *Specters of Marx,* 14.

4. Irving Howe, *Politics and the Novel* (Greenwich, CT: Fawcett, 1967), 255; and Harold Bloom, introduction to *Modern Critical Views: George Orwell,* ed. Harold Bloom (New York: Chelsea House, 1987), 5. For an exhaustive discussion of the uses over four decades of Orwell and his fiction by a diverse range of groups, see John Rodden, *The Politics of Literary Reputation: The Making and Claiming of "St. George" Orwell* (New York: Oxford University Press, 1989). This immensely useful study is accompanied by a few hagiographies of its own, and is not without the occasional ax to grind (see especially the representation of Raymond Williams's lifelong dialogue with Orwell's work.)

5. There has been an explosion of new literature on the topic of globalization. For a few especially useful discussions, see Giovanni Arrighi, *The Long Twentieth Century: Money, Power, and the Origins of Our Times* (New York: Verso, 1994); Arjun Appadurai, *Modernity at Large: Cultural Dimensions of*

Globalization (Minneapolis: University of Minnesota Press, 1996); Paul Smith, *Millennial Dreams: Contemporary Culture and Capital in the North* (New York: Verso, 1997); Saskia Sassen, *Globalization and Its Discontents: Essays on the New Mobility of People and Money* (New York: New Press, 1998); Fredric Jameson and Masao Miyoshi, ed., *The Cultures of Globalization* (Durham, NC: Duke University Press, 1998); Pierre Bourdieu, *Acts of Resistance: Against the Tyranny of the Market,* trans. Richard Nice (New York: The New Press, 1998); David Held, Anthony McGrew, David Goldblatt, and Jonathan Perraton, *Global Transformations: Politics, Economics and Culture* (Stanford, CA: Stanford University Press, 1999); Bruce Robbins, *Feeling Global: Internationalism in Distress* (New York: New York University Press, 1999); and David Harvey, *Spaces of Hope* (Berkeley: University of California Press, 2000).

6. Jürgen Habermas, *The Inclusion of the Other: Studies in Political Theory,* ed. Ciaran Cronin and Pablo De Greiff (Cambridge: MIT Press, 1998), 124.

7. See William Steinhoff, *George Orwell and the Origins of* 1984 (Ann Arbor: University of Michigan Press, 1975), 216–22.

8. See John Goode, "Gissing, Morris, and English Socialism," *Victorian Studies* 12, no. 2 (1968): 201–26. For a fine recent discussion of the debilitating contradictions inherent in Orwell's vision of socialism, see Robert Paul Resch, "Utopia, Dystopia, and the Middle Class in George Orwell's *Nineteen Eighty-Four,*" *boundary* 2 24, no. 1 (1997): 137–76. Resch's excellent reading of Orwell's "absent middle-class hero" also resonates in interesting ways with my analysis of the text's vision of intellectual labor (see below).

9. George Orwell, "Wells, Hitler, and the World State," in *The Collected Essays, Journalism and Letters of George Orwell,* vol. 2, ed. Sonia Orwell and Ian Angus (New York: Harcourt, Brace, and World, 1968), 142.

10. Ibid., 143.

11. Ibid., 143, 144, and 145. Wells comes to some interestingly similar conclusions (though with notable differences too) in his final book, *Mind at the End of Its Tether.* H. G. Wells, *The Last Books of H G. Wells:* The Happy Turning *and* Mind at the End of Its Tether, ed. G. P. Wells (London: H. G. Wells Society, 1968).

12. George Orwell, *Nineteen Eighty-Four* (New York: Harcourt Brace Jovanovich, 1949), 155–56. Hereafter cited in the text as *NEF.*

13. For two opposed views of the extent of Orwell's reliance on *We* in writing *Nineteen Eighty-Four,* see Isaac Deutscher, "*1984*—The Mysticism of Cruelty," in *George Orwell: A Collection of Critical Essays,* ed. Raymond Williams (Englewood Cliffs, NJ: Prentice-Hall, 1974), 120–26; and Steinhoff, *George Orwell and the Origins of* 1984, 23–29.

14. He had learned of *We* from Gleb Struve's *Twenty-Five Years of Soviet Russian Literature.* See the letter to Struve dated February 17, 1944, reprinted in *The Collected Essays,* vol. 3, 95–96. Michael Shelden states that Orwell began composing *Nineteen Eighty-Four* in October, 1946, long after he had read Zamyatin's novel; see *Orwell: The Authorized Biography* (New York: Harper Collins, 1991), 416.

15. An acknowledgment of a reliance on *We* in formulating elements of the plot and themes of *Nineteen Eighty-Four* seems also to have made its way into

Orwell's 1946 review of the French translation of Zamyatin's book. There, Orwell projects his own use of *We* onto Aldous Huxley, early in his review speculating that "*Brave New World* must be partly derived from it" (a charge Huxley himself vehemently denied); see *Collected Essays*, vol. 4, 72.

16. L. S. Dembo, *Detotalized Totalities: Synthesis and Disintegration in Naturalist, Existential, and Socialist Fiction* (Madison: University of Wisconsin Press, 1989), 163–64.

17. The importance of the Appendix to Orwell's project is borne out by the fact that the author refused to allow the publication of a Book-of-the-Month Club edition with the Appendix (as well as the excerpts from Goldstein's book) removed—even though it meant the potential loss of £40,000 in revenue (Shelden, *Orwell: The Authorized Biography*, 430). Larry W. Caldwell suggests that the Newspeak Appendix functions, like the more explicit "Historical Notes" pages of Margaret Atwood's *The Handmaid's Tale*, as "a kind of ironic anticlosure" to the narrative. According to Caldwell, in Orwell's Appendix, "The temporal ambivalence of the verbs and of the adverbial locutions expressly confounds the Party's 'forever' and destabilizes its closed narrative"; see "Wells, Orwell, and Atwood: (EPI)Logic and Eu/Utopia," *Extrapolation* 33, no. 4 (1992): 338 and 339. Also see Richard K. Sanderson, "The Two Narrators and the 'Happy Ending' of *Nineteen Eighty-Four*," *Modern Fiction Studies* 34 (1988): 587–95. Resch provocatively suggests that we view *Nineteen Eighty-Four* as a fictional "historical novel." (It would be interesting to read *Nineteen Eighty-Four* against the description of the genre of the historical novel offered by Georg Lukács in *The Historical Novel*.) However, Resch also rightly points out that the "world" of the appendix's author is truly a " 'no-place' that *cannot* exist given the sociological reality of Oceania. . . . No theory of transition can be imagined from within the limits of Orwell's political ideology" ("Utopia, Dystopia, and the Middle Class," 158–59).

18. Shelden, *Orwell: The Authorized Biography*, 359. For a more detailed treatment of Orwell's connection to Gissing, see Mark Connelly, *Orwell and Gissing* (New York: Peter Lang Publishing, 1998).

19. Orwell, *Collected Essays*, vol. 4, 430.

20. Frank Lentricchia, *The Gaiety of Language: An Essay on the Radical Poetics of W. B. Yeats and Wallace Stevens* (Berkeley: University of California Press, 1968), 20–25. W. Warren Wagar has likewise described Orwell's critical role as that of the "Political Secretary of the Zeitgeist." See his essay of the same name printed in *The Future of* Nineteen Eighty-Four, ed. Ejner J. Jensen (Ann Arbor: University of Michigan Press, 1984), 177–99.

21. Orwell acknowledged the difficulties of fusing a naturalist prose style to the form of the narrative utopia. In a May, 1947 letter to F. J. Warburg, the original English publisher of *Nineteen Eighty-Four*, he writes, "I will tell you now that this is a novel about the future—that is, it is in a sense a fantasy, but in the form of a naturalistic novel. That is what makes it a difficult job—of course as a book of anticipations it would be comparatively simple to write" (*Collected Essays*, vol. 4, 329–30).

22. György Dalos, *1985: A Historical Report (Hongkong 2036) from the*

Hungarian of ***, trans. Stuart Hood and Estella Schmid (New York: Pantheon, 1983); epigraph from 47.

23. The link between the narrative strategies of Gissing's naturalism and Morris's "reinvention" of the narrative utopia is made by Fredric Jameson, *The Political Unconscious: Narrative as a Socially Symbolic Act* (Ithaca, NY: Cornell University Press, 1981), 193.

24. George Orwell, *A Collection of Essays* (Garden City, NY: Doubleday, 1954), 318. For a recent discussion of the uses of the concept of totalitarianism that resonates in some interesting ways with my reading of Orwell, see Slavoj Žižek, *Did Somebody Say Totalitarianism? Five Interventions in the (Mis)use of a Notion* (New York: Verso, 2001).

25. For a discussion of Orwell's relationship to contemporary socialist and communist theory and practice, see Alex Zwerdling, *Orwell and the Left* (New Haven, CT: Yale University Press, 1974), chap. 1. Zwerdling maintains that while Orwell saw himself as a student of Marxism, he was highly critical of "what he took to be its anachronisms and untenable assumptions: its theories of class and revolution, its historicist tactics, its materialist basis and consequent neglect of psychology, and its refusal to think seriously about the nature of a socialist state" (*Orwell and the Left*, 21). Exactly what remains "Marxist" in Orwell's thought after such a thoroughgoing revisionism is unclear. More important, Zwerdling's statements suggest Orwell's total ignorance of the developments in continental Western Marxist theory—although this makes him no different from many socialists then active in Great Britain. On this latter issue, see Perry Anderson, "Components of the National Culture," *New Left Review*, no. 50 (1968): 3–57, reprinted, with follow-up discussions, in *English Questions* (New York: Verso, 1992); and *Arguments within English Marxism* (London: Verso, 1980).

26. George Orwell, *The Road to Wigan Pier* (New York: Harcourt Brace Jovanovich, 1958), 176.

27. Ibid., 161–62.

28. Karl Mannheim, *Ideology and Utopia: An Introduction to the Sociology of Knowledge*, trans. Louis Wirth and Edward Shils (New York: Harcourt Brace Jovanovich, 1936), 192–263. Hereafter cited in the text as *IU*.

29. Theodor Adorno writes, "The answer to Mannheim's reverence for the intelligentsia as 'free-floating' is to be found not in the reactionary postulate of its 'rootedness in Being' but rather in the reminder that the very intelligentsia that pretends to float freely is fundamentally rooted in the very being that must be changed and which it merely pretends to criticize" (*Prisms*, trans. Samuel and Shierry Weber [Cambridge: MIT Press, 1983], 48). For a more recent discussion of the ideological status of Mannheim's sociology of knowledge, see Terry Eagleton, *Ideology: An Introduction* (New York: Verso, 1991), 107–10.

30. Walter Benjamin, "Theses on the Philosophy of History," in *Illuminations: Essays and Reflections*, trans. Harry Zohn (New York: Schocken, 1969), 261. Also see Paul Ricoeur, *Lectures on Ideology and Utopia*, ed. George H. Taylor (New York: Columbia University Press, 1986), 276–80.

31. Ricoeur, *Lectures*, 278.

32. Hayden White, *Metahistory: The Historical Imagination in Nineteenth-Century Europe* (Baltimore: Johns Hopkins University Press, 1975), 25.

33. Ibid., 23, n. 12.

34. Ibid., 23.

35. Ibid., 22.

36. The last pages of Orwell's allegory of the history of the Soviet Union—wherein the once ceremonially revered skull of the founder of the revolution is finally buried, as the animals renounce their former goals of transforming the conditions of existence for all animals and assert their new desire to enter into "normal business relations" with men—take on new resonances in the light of the events of the last decade of the twentieth century; see *Animal Farm* (New York: Harcourt Brace Jovanovich, 1946), 127.

37. Orwell, *Collected Essays*, vol. 4, 18.

38. For a discussion of the various romantic, primitive, and millenarian anarchist groups that flourished in the context of the immediate postrevolutionary Soviet Union, see Richard Stites, *Revolutionary Dreams: Utopian Vision and Experimental Life in the Russian Revolution* (Oxford: Oxford University Press, 1989). Mannheim too argues that following Marx's decisive victory over Bakunin, anarchism had already begun to fade as a viable option in the Western political imagination (*IU*, 243–44). However, Ricoeur points out that all this changes once again in the 1960s (*Lectures on Ideology and Utopia*, 281), something Le Guin's work bears out.

39. For a different use of the concept of "conservative utopias," see Jean Pfaelzer, *The Utopian Novel in America, 1886–1896: The Politics of Form* (Pittsburgh, PA: University of Pittsburgh Press, 1984), chap. 5. And for an important related discussion, see Peter Fitting, "Utopias Beyond Our Ideals: The Dilemma of the Right-Wing Utopia," *Utopian Studies* 2, nos. 1 and 2 (1991): 95–109.

40. Orwell, *Collected Essays*, vol. 4, 75.

41. Ibid., 24–25. Also see Orwell's contrast of Wells's and London's visions in "Wells, Hitler and the World State," 144; and "Prophecies of Fascism," in *Collected Essays*, vol. 2, 30–33.

42. I also have in mind here Derrida's critique of Michel Foucault's *Madness and Civilization*. Derrida shows how the figure of "madness" as it appears in Foucault's book is finally unable to break absolutely with "reason," to become the kind of utopian Other that Foucault wishes it to be; instead, the two figures, madness and reason, should be understood to be always already situated in an irreducible economy of relationships; see "Cogito and the History of Madness," in *Writing and Difference*, trans. Alan Bass (Chicago: University of Chicago Press, 1978), 31–63. Also see Foucault's response, "My Body, This Paper, This Fire" reprinted in *Aesthetics, Method, and Epistemology: Essential Works of Foucault, 1954–1984*, ed. James D. Faubion (New York: The New Press, 1998), 393–417.

43. Yevgeny Zamyatin, *A Soviet Heretic: The Essays of Yevgeny Zamyatin*, ed. and trans. Mirra Ginsburg (Chicago: University of Chicago Press, 1970), 51. For the distinction between instrumental and dialectical reason (*Verstand* and *Vernunft*) as developed in the work of Horkheimer and Adorno, see Fredric

Jameson, *Late Marxism: Adorno, or, The Persistence of the Dialectic* (New York: Verso, 1990).

44. Louis Marin, *Utopics: The Semiological Play of Textual Spaces,* trans. Robert A. Vollrath (Atlantic Highlands, NJ: Humanities Press International, 1984), 14.

45. See especially Orwell's remarks in the essays "Notes on Nationalism," and "The Prevention of Literature," in *Collected Essays,* vol. 3, 365–66, and vol. 4, 61. For a discussion of Orwell's animosity toward Roman Catholicism and his reception by British Catholic intellectuals, see Rodden, *Politics of Literary Reputation,* 362–82.

46. Orwell, *Road to Wigan Pier,* 177.

47. Habermas, "Modernity—An Incomplete Project," in *The Anti-Aesthetic: Essays on Postmodern Culture,* ed. Hal Foster (Port Townsend, WA: Bay Press, 1983), 9. For a more extended discussion, also see Habermas, *The Philosophical Discourse of Modernity: Twelve Lectures,* trans. Frederick Lawrence (Cambridge: MIT Press, 1987).

48. The various sources of this figure are usefully discussed in Steinhoff, *George Orwell and the Origins of 1984,* 170–75.

49. Lionel Trilling, "Orwell on the Future," *The New Yorker,* 18 June 1949: 82.

50. Richard Rorty, *Contingency, Irony, and Solidarity* (Cambridge: Cambridge University Press, 1989), 179.

51. Antonio Gramsci, *Selections from the Prison Notebooks,* ed. and trans. Quintin Hoare and Geoffrey Nowell Smith (New York: International Publishers, 1971), 12. Also see Gramsci's insightful remarks concerning "common sense" in the same volume, especially 323–33 and 348–50.

52. Quoted in Steinhoff, *George Orwell and the Origins of 1984,* 49. Steinhoff offers one of the most complete discussions of the centrality of Burnham's ideas in the genesis of *Nineteen Eighty-Four.* Also see Dembo, *Detotalized Totalities,* 164–165; and Paul N. Siegel, *Revolution and the Twentieth-Century Novel* (New York: Monad Press, 1979), 149–70.

53. Jack London, *The Iron Heel* in *Novels and Social Writings* (New York: Library of America, 1982), 518–19.

54. In his 1946 essay "James Burnham and the Managerial Revolution," Orwell writes, "It would be grossly unfair to suggest that power worship is the only motive for russophile feeling, but it is one motive, and among intellectuals it is probably the strongest one" (*Collected Essays,* vol. 4, 174). Also see Orwell's earlier well-known essay "Raffles and Miss Blandish," in *Collected Essays,* vol. 3, 212–24; and for further discussion, see Zwerdling, *Orwell and the Left,* 99–102. For one of the best discussions of the ideologeme of *ressentiment* in European literature, see Jameson, *Political Unconscious,* especially chaps. 4 and 5.

55. My reading of *Nineteen Eighty-Four* here, and in what follows, draws freely on the remarkable discussion of Adorno and Horkheimer's *Dialectic of Enlightenment* found in Jameson's *Late Marxism,* 99–110 and 123–54. I would further maintain that while the differences are significant, there exists a marked and largely unexplored convergence between the mappings of the social present provided in *Nineteen Eighty-Four* and *Dialectic of Enlightenment.* For one ad-

ditional striking example of this similarity, compare their views of the fate of tragedy in the present: "Today tragedy has melted away into the nothingness of that false identity of society and individual, whose terror still shows for a moment in the empty semblance of the tragic. . . . This liquidation of tragedy confirms the abolition of the individual" (*Dialectic of Enlightenment,* trans. John Cumming [New York: Continuum, 1987], 154); "Tragedy, he perceived, belonged to the ancient time, to a time when there was still privacy, love, and friendship" (*NEF,* 28). Finally, for a reading that would allow us similarly to situate Wallace Steven's later poetry within this same "late modernist" cultural complex, see Frank Lentricchia, *Ariel and the Police: Michel Foucault, William James, Wallace Stevens* (Madison: University of Wisconsin Press, 1988), especially the second part of chap. 3.

56. Rorty offers a useful reading of this aspect of the narrative in light of Elaine Scarry's *The Body in Pain: The Making and Unmaking of the World* (Oxford: Oxford University Press, 1985) in his *Contingency, Irony, and Solidarity,* 176–80. Also see Zwerdling, "Orwell's Psychopolitics," in *The Future of Nineteen Eighty-Four,* ed. Jensen, 87–110.

57. For another discussion of the aesthetic dimensions of Charrington's wares, one that suggests another kind of link between Orwell's work and that of the Frankfurt School, see R. K. Meiner, "Dialectics at a Standstill: Orwell, Benjamin, and the Difficulties of Poetry," *boundary* 2 20, no. 2 (1993): 116–39.

58. See Herbert Marcuse, *Eros and Civilization: A Philosophical Inquiry into Freud* (New York: Vintage Books, 1955). For a reading of these images closer to that of Marcuse—viewing the room, the paperweight, and the Golden Country as figures for the psychic unity of the child in the womb—see Kathryn M. Grossman, "'Through a Glass Darkly': Utopian Imagery in *Nineteen Eighty-Four,*" *Utopian Studies* 1 (1987): 52–59.

59. Slavoj Žižek, *Tarrying with the Negative: Kant, Hegel, and the Critique of Ideology* (Durham, NC: Duke University Press, 1993), 203.

60. In *The Lion and the Unicorn,* Orwell justified his preference for the use of the term "England" over "Britain:" "It is quite true that the so-called races of Britain feel themselves to be very different from one another. . . . You can see the hesitation we feel on this point by the fact that we call our islands by no less than six different names, England, Britain, Great Britain, the British Isles, the United Kingdom and, in very exalted moments, Albion. Even the differences between north and south England loom large in our own eyes. But somehow these differences fade away the moment that any two Britons are confronted by a European. It is very rare to meet a foreigner, other than an American, who can distinguish between English and Scots or even English and Irish" (*Collected Essays,* vol. 2, 64).

61. Orwell, *Coming Up for Air* (New York: Harcourt Brace Jovanovich, 1950), 87.

62. Orwell, *Collection of Essays,* 223.

63. Dick Hebdige makes this point in his now classic, *Subculture: The Meaning of Style* (London: Routledge, 1979), 8.

64. For a general discussion of Orwell's writings on popular culture and his

efforts to distinguish between a good popular and bad mass culture, see Rodden, *Politics of Literary Reputation*, 226–39.

65. For the connection between the vision of the Ministry of Truth and Orwell's experiences as a wartime radio propagandist at the BBC, see Martin Esslin, "Television and Telescreen," in *On* Nineteen Eighty-Four, ed. Peter Stansky (San Francisco: W. H. Freeman, 1983), 126–38.

66. Orwell, *Collected Essays*, vol. 4, 69.

67. A similar image of cultural absorption is present in *Coming Up for Air.* When the middle-aged George Bowling finally accomplishes his return to his boyhood home of Lower Binfield, another figure for English autonomy, he discovers that it has disappeared: "I don't mean that it had been demolished. It had merely been swallowed" (*Coming Up for Air*, 211).

68. In the 1943 essay "Poetry and the Microphone," Orwell asserts, "Broadcasting is what it is, not because there is something inherently vulgar, silly and dishonest about the whole apparatus of microphone and transmitter, but because all the broadcasting that now happens all over the world is under the control of governments or great monopoly companies which are actively interested in maintaining the *status quo* and therefore in preventing the common man from becoming too intelligent. Something of the same kind has happened to the cinema, which, like the radio, made its appearance during the monopoly stage of capitalism and is fantastically expensive to operate. In all the arts the tendency is similar" (*Collected Essays*, vol. 2, 334–35).

69. Thus, I disagree with Hans Magnus Enzensberger's famous argument concerning the untenability of Orwell's view of the mass media as a mechanism for social control. See his *The Consciousness Industry*, trans. Stuart Hood (New York: The Seabury Press, 1974), 101.

70. Orwell, *Collected Essays*, vol. 4, 80. In a critique of Enzensberger's celebration of the liberatory potential of media technologies, Baudrillard comes far nearer to Orwell's position expressed here: "It is useless to fantasize about state projection of police control through TV (as Enzensberger has remarked of Orwell's *1984*): TV, by virtue of its mere presence, is a social control in itself. There is no need to imagine it as a state periscope spying on everyone's private life— the situation as it stands is more efficient than that: it is the *certainty that people are no longer speaking to each other,* that they are definitively isolated in the face of a speech without response." *For a Critique of the Political Economy of the Sign*, trans. Charles Levin (St. Louis: Telos Press, 1981), 172. Also see Baudrillard's later reflections, "The Masses: The Implosion of the Social in the Media," in *Jean Baudrillard: Selected Writings*, 207–19.

71. Howe, *Politics and the Novel*, 246.

72. Orwell, *Coming Up for Air*, 26 and 27–28.

73. Walter J. Ong, *Orality and Literacy: The Technologizing of the Word* (New York: Methuen, 1982), 46.

74. Ibid., 136.

75. For the discussion of serial group formation, see Jean-Paul Sartre, *Critique of Dialectical Reason I: Theory of Practical Ensembles*, trans. Alan Sheridan-Smith (London: New Left Books, 1976), especially 256–76. Also see

Fredric Jameson's discussion of this concept in *Marxism and Form: Twentieth-Century Dialectical Theories of Literature* (Princeton, NJ: Princeton University Press, 1971), 247–50. For the specific relationship between seriality and television, see Richard Dienst, *Still Life In Real Time: Theory after Television* (Durham, NC: Duke University Press, 1994), 8–11; and, for another discussion of seriality and mass media in postwar culture, see Robert Seguin, *Around Quitting Time: Work and Middle-Class Fantasy in American Fiction* (Durham, NC: Duke University Press, 2001).

76. Benedict Anderson, *Imagined Communities: Reflections on the Origin and Spread of Nationalism,* rev. ed. (New York: Verso, 1991), 41–49.

77. For some discussions of Orwell's attitudes toward women, a number of which also trace out the same link with his views of the proles, see Daphne Patai, *The Orwell Mystique: A Study in Male Ideology* (Amherst: University of Massachusetts Press, 1984); Leslie Tentler, " 'I'm Not Literary, Dear': George Orwell on Women and the Family," in *The Future of* Nineteen Eighty-Four, ed. Jensen, 47–63; Anne Mellor, " 'You're Only a Rebel from the Waist Downwards': Orwell's View of Women," in *On* Nineteen Eighty-Four, ed. Stansky, 115–25; and Beatrix Campbell, "Orwell—Paterfamilias or Big Brother?" in *New Casebooks: George Orwell,* ed. Graham Holderness, et al. (New York: St Martin's Press, 1998): 64–75.

78. Raymond Williams, *George Orwell* (New York: Columbia University Press, 1971), 79. Williams's book influenced all of my thinking on Orwell's work.

79. That Julia was intended by Orwell to serve as a kind of analogue to the proles is further borne out by the description of her job in the Ministry of Truth: unlike the other Outer Party intellectual laborers that we encounter, "she had some mechanical job on one of the novel-writing machines" (*NEF,* 12).

80. Shelden, *Orwell: The Authorized Biography,* 350.

81. For a reading of Orwell's work in terms of his own social class position, see Williams, *George Orwell;* Resch, "Utopia, Dystopia, and the Middle Class"; and Eagleton, "Orwell and the Lower-Middle-Class Novel," in *Exiles and Emigrés* (New York: Schocken, 1970), 78–108. Also see Williams's brilliant essay, "The Bloomsbury Fraction," in *Problems in Materialism and Culture* (New York: Verso, 1980), 148–69, and its reworked version in *The Sociology of Culture* (Chicago: University of Chicago Press, 1995), 79–83.

82. For the best discussion of the historical development of the Fordist regime—a regime that has been reconfigured over the course of the last two decades—see the work of the Regulationist school of economics, especially Michel Aglietta, *A Theory of Capitalist Regulation: The U.S. Experience,* trans. David Fernbach (New York: Verso, 1979); and Robert Boyer, *The Regulation School: A Critical Introduction,* trans. Craig Charney (New York: Columbia University Press, 1990). Also see David Harvey, *The Condition of Postmodernity: An Enquiry into the Origins of Cultural Change* (Oxford: Basil Blackwell, 1989), especially chap. 8; and Arrighi, *Long Twentieth Century.*

83. Orwell, *Collected Essays,* vol. 2, 77–78.

84. See, for example, his deeply ambivalent essays on Sean O'Casey and Mohandas Karamchand Gandhi (*Collected Essays,* vol. 4, 13–15 and 463–70).

85. Orwell, *Collected Essays*, vol. 2, 91. He outlines his plan for Indian "independence" on 98–100.

86. Even as early as the mid-thirties, Orwell marks out the dilemmas involved in ending empire: "For, apart from any other consideration, the high standard of life we enjoy in England depends upon our keeping a tight hold on the Empire, particularly the tropical portions of it such as India and Africa. . . . The alternative is to throw the Empire overboard and reduce England to a cold and unimportant little island where we should all have to work very hard and live mainly on herrings and potatoes" (*Road to Wigan Pier,* 159–60). The latter sounds very much like the England envisioned in *Nineteen Eighty-Four.*

87. Although Williams points out that this is already true even in Orwell's earlier socialist writings—only in this way could Orwell have even suggested in *The Road to Wigan Pier* that socialism might come about in England simply through a "complete abandonment of the upper-class and middle-class *attitude* to life" (161–62; see *George Orwell,* 22).

88. Orwell, *Collection of Essays,* 247 and 255.

89. Ibid., 245–46. Similarly in the 1948 essay "Writers and Leviathan," Orwell writes, "When a writer engages in politics he should do so as a citizen, as a human being, but not *as a writer*" (*Collected Essays,* vol. 4, 412).

90. Resch, on the other hand, characterizes figures like Syme as "gullible flunkies" and "unwitting dupes, as much the victims as the conscious agents of the evil system they serve" ("Utopia, Dystopia, and the Middle Class," 156).

91. Orwell, *Collection of Essays,* 318.

92. See Trilling, "George Orwell and the Politics of Truth," in *George Orwell: A Collection of Critical Essays,* ed. Williams, 62–79; also reprinted as the introduction to George Orwell, *Homage to Catalonia* (New York: Harcourt Brace Jovanovich, 1952), v–xxiii.

93. That Orwell saw himself as playing a similar role is borne out in a brief note on his place in the BBC: "But for heaven's sake don't think I don't see how they are using me. A subsidiary point is that one can't effectively remain outside the war & by working inside an institution like the BBC one can perhaps deoderise it to some small extent" (*Collected Essays,* vol. 2, 268).

94. Dembo distinguishes between the concepts of rebellion and revolution in this way: "*Rebellion* is, simply put, an instrument of detotalization, nothing more, nothing less. *Revolution* is a retotalizing force; it destroys to recreate" (*Detotalized Totalities,* 210). For Gianni Vattimo's distinction between "strong" and "weak" philosophical thought, see his collection of essays, *The End of Modernity: Nihilism and Hermeneutics in Postmodern Culture,* ed. and trans. Jon R. Snyder (Cambridge, U.K.: Polity Press, 1988). For some quite different readings of the relationship between the writer and political commitment contemporaneous with *Nineteen Eighty-Four,* see Jean-Paul Sartre, *"What Is Literature?" and Other Essays* (Cambridge: Harvard University Press, 1988), from which one of the epigraphs of this chapter is taken (252); and Theodor Adorno, "Commitment," in *Aesthetics and Politics,* ed. Ronald Taylor (New York: Verso, 1980), 177–95.

95. Also see the astute discussion of the relationship between Winston and O'Brien in Resch, "Utopia, Dystopia, and the Middle Class," 167–73. Resch

more damningly concludes, "Winston's quest for individual freedom has been not a moral quest for universal human freedom but an egoistic search for his own personal freedom" (172).

96. Dembo offers a fine reading of the consistency of this theme of failure throughout Orwell's fiction in his chapter "Orwell's Unrevolutionary Rebels," in *Detotalized Totalities,* 147–68. Williams points out that *Animal Farm* too is consistent with this pattern, only in this work the figure of the "isolated man who breaks from conformity but is then defeated and reabsorbed . . . is, rather, projected into a collective action: this is what happens to the animals who free themselves and then, through violence and fraud, are again enslaved" (*George Orwell,* 74). Jameson similarly notes that in the case of Orwell's naturalist predecessor, "Gissing faces a situation in which the universal commodification of desire stamps any achieved desire or wish as inauthentic, while an authenticity at best pathetic clings to images of failure" (*Political Unconscious,* 204). Also see Fredric Jameson, "Literary Innovation and Modes of Production: A Commentary," *Modern Chinese Literature* 1, no. 1 (1984): 69–70.

97. For discussions of the effects of Orwell's narrative on the efficacy of left political activism in England, see Conor Cruise O'Brien, "Orwell Looks at the World," in *George Orwell: A Collection of Critical Essays,* ed. Williams, 157–58; and Alan Sinfield, *Literature, Politics, and Culture in Postwar Britain* (Oxford: Basil Blackwell, 1989).

98. Thomas Hill Schaub, *American Fiction in the Cold War* (Madison: University of Wisconsin Press, 1991).

99. Orwell, *Collected Essays,* vol. 2, 75.

100. For some of the outstanding recent accounts of the ideologies involved in the creation of the postwar U.S. intellectual establishment, see Serge Guillbaut, *How New York Stole the Idea of Modern Art,* trans. Arthur Goldhammer (Chicago: University of Chicago Press, 1983); Andrew Ross, *No Respect: Intellectuals and Popular Culture* (New York: Routledge, 1989); Schaub, *American Fiction in the Cold War;* Lary May, ed., *Recasting America: Culture and Politics in the Age of Cold War* (Chicago: University of Chicago Press, 1989); Noam Chomsky et al., *The Cold War and the University: Toward an Intellectual History,* ed. André Schiffrin (New York: The New Press, 1997); Stephen J. Whitfield, *The Culture of the Cold War,* 2d ed. (Baltimore: Johns Hopkins University Press, 1996); and Susan Hegeman, *Patterns for America: Modernism and the Concept of Culture* (Princeton, NJ: Princeton University Press, 1999).

101. Wells, *A Modern Utopia* (Lincoln: University of Nebraska Press, 1967), 11–12.

102. Also see Williams's important discussion of Orwell's fiction of the "eternal" England in *George Orwell,* 11–24.

103. See Arrighi, *Long Twentieth Century,* especially chap. 4.

Index

Compositor: G & S Typesetters, Inc.
Text: Sabon
Display: Sabon